The Art of Followership

Warren Bennis

A WARREN BENNIS BOOK

This collection of books is devoted exclusively to new and exemplary contributions to management thought and practice. The books in this series are addressed to thoughtful leaders, executives, and managers of all organizations who are struggling with and committed to responsible change. My hope and goal is to spark new intellectual capital by sharing ideas positioned at an angle to conventional thought—in short, to publish books that disturb the present in the service of a better future.

BOOKS IN THE WARREN BENNIS SIGNATURE SERIES

The Art of Followership

HOW GREAT FOLLOWERS CREATE GREAT LEADERS AND ORGANIZATIONS

Editors
Ronald E. Riggio
Ira Chaleff
Jean Lipman-
Blumen

Foreword by
James MacGregor Burns

JOSSEY-BASS
A Wiley Imprint
www.josseybass.com

Published by Jossey-Bass
A Wiley Imprint
989 Market Street, San Francisco, CA 94103-1741—www.josseybass.com

Jossey-Bass books and products are available through most bookstores. To contact Jossey-Bass directly call our Customer Care Department within the U.S. at 800-956-7739, outside the U.S. at 317-572-3986, or fax 317-572-4002.

Jossey-Bass also publishes its books in a variety of electronic formats. Some content that appears in print may not be available in electronic books.

Library of Congress Cataloging-in-Publication Data

The art of followership : how great followers create great leaders and organizations / Ronald E. Riggio, Ira Chaleff, Jean Lipman-Blumen, editors; foreword by James MacGregor Burns.
    p.   cm.—(The Warren Bennis signature series)
 Includes bibliographical references and index.
  ISBN 978-0-7879-9665-9 (cloth)
 1. Leadership. 2. Organizational behavior. I. Riggio, Ronald E. II. Chaleff, Ira. III. Lipman-Blumen, Jean.
 HD57.7.A78 2008
 658.4′092—dc22

2007035505

Printed in the United States of America
FIRST EDITION
HB Printing   10 9 8 7 6 5 4 3

CONTENTS

FOREWORD

James MacGregor Burns

We have been brought up as schoolchildren to think of leadership as only the realm of heroes and devils—as in the lives of Caesar, Napoleon, Churchill, the three Roosevelts, Hitler, Stalin, Mao, and the like. The people—the voters, the masses—provided only a vague background. But if you define leadership as the mobilization of followers who then become leaders of the original leaders, and if you measure these mobilizations by the harsh tests of moral and ethical values, you begin to understand the complex processes of leadership. You can see Franklin Roosevelt, for example, as a president who entered office without a comprehensive program, then mobilized a desperate people who demanded action, people who in turn forced the administration to fashion the "Second New Deal of 1935," which embodied FDR's lasting leadership.

Sometimes, when I contemplate the endless complexities and mysteries of leadership, I try to simplify its essence by imagining the following: a candidate for local office spots a possible supporter across the street. She crosses over to ask for his vote. He asks her about an environmental issue, she responds, and he promises his support. A reporter happening on the scene might dismiss this as a quick-fix deal. But a student of leadership should see this episode as reflecting a far more complex set of phenomena: their backgrounds and attitudes, the social and political context, and the other factors ranging from the immediate and practical to the psychological and ideological. But the student should note too that *the candidate* crossed the street, initiating the engagement.

Thirty years ago, I wrote that "one of the most serious failures in the study of leadership has been the bifurcation between the literature on leadership and the literature on followership." Surely, I added, it was "time that the two literatures" be brought together, "that the study of leadership be lifted out of the anecdotal and eulogistic and placed squarely in the structure and processes of human development and political action." Making this linkage has proved exceptionally difficult. Dealing with the complexities—the multiple roles of leaders and followers in diverse polities, the intersecting as well as the clashing of leadership cultures, the traps inevitable in "toxic" or "bad" leadership, the potential of leadership created or undermined by benign or hostile forces, and above all the moral and ethical values that penetrate (or should penetrate) leaders' decision making—this type of challenging question faces students and practitioners of leadership. I know of no work that faces this challenge so well as *The Art of Followership*. I expect it to be a landmark work in the complexities of the leader-follower dynamic.

ACKNOWLEDGMENTS

First and foremost, we want to thank our chapter authors for their excellent contributions to the book and to the Kravis–de Roulet Leadership Conference. We thank Adrienne Boardman and Ross Boomer for their roles at both the conference and in book development, as well as Sandy Counts, who helped produce the final manuscript. Thank you also to the terrific KLI professional staff and faculty, Kevin Arnold, Barbara Ascher, Rebecca Reichard, Susan Murphy, and Jay Conger, who helped make the conference a success.

THE KRAVIS–DE ROULET LEADERSHIP CONFERENCE

The Kravis–de Roulet Leadership Conference, which began in 1990, is an annual leadership conference funded jointly by an endowment from Henry R. Kravis and the de Roulet family. This perpetual funding, along with additional support from the Kravis Leadership Institute, the Institute for Advanced Studies in Leadership at Claremont Graduate University, the Peter F. Drucker and Masatoshi Ito Graduate School of Management, and Claremont McKenna College, enables us to attract the finest leadership scholars and practitioners as conference presenters and participants. The sixteenth annual Kravis–de Roulet conference, Rethinking Followership, was held in Claremont February 24–25, 2006.

THE KRAVIS LEADERSHIP INSTITUTE

The Kravis Leadership Institute plays an active role in the development of young leaders through educational programs, research and scholarship, and the development of technologies for enhancing leadership potential.

http://kli.claremontmckenna.edu/

THE INSTITUTE FOR ADVANCED STUDIES IN LEADERSHIP

The Institute for Advanced Studies in Leadership has crafted a twofold mission: (1) to develop leaders whose contributions will enrich the meaning and quality of the lives they touch, and (2) to generate and share knowledge of leadership for the betterment of society.

www.cgu.edu/pages/303.asp

ABOUT THE CONTRIBUTORS

Ronald E. Riggio is the Henry R. Kravis Professor of Leadership and Organizational Psychology at Claremont McKenna College and director of the Kravis Leadership Institute. He has published more than a dozen books and over one hundred articles on leadership, management, and psychology. His latest book, edited with Jay Conger, is *The Practice of Leadership: Developing the Next Generation of Leaders* (Jossey-Bass, 2007).

Ira Chaleff is the author of *The Courageous Follower: Standing Up to and for Our Leaders* (Berrett-Koehler), first published in 1995 and updated in a second edition in 2003. This influential book has been translated into several languages and made into an award-winning training video, *Courageous Followers, Courageous Leaders: New Relationships for Changing Times*. Chaleff is a prominent speaker and trainer on courageous followership. Chaleff is president of Executive Coaching & Consulting Associates (www.exe-coach.com) and chairman of the Congressional Management Foundation (www.cmfweb.org), both located in Washington, D.C. In these roles, he works with a wide range of for-profit, non-profit, public sector, and international organizations. He is adjunct faculty at Georgetown University.

Jean Lipman-Blumen holds the Thornton F. Bradshaw Chair in Public Policy and also serves as professor of organizational behavior at the Peter F. Drucker and Masatoshi Ito Graduate School of Management, Claremont Graduate University, Claremont, California. She is director of the Institute for Advanced Studies in Leadership at the Drucker-Ito School. Lipman-Blumen's most recent book, *The Allure of Toxic Leaders: Why We Follow Destructive Bosses and Corrupt*

Politicians—and How We Can Survive Them (Oxford University Press), was cited by *FastCompany* magazine as one of the ten top business books of 2004. *The Connective Edge: Leading in an Interdependent World* (Jossey-Bass, 1996) was nominated for a Pulitzer Prize.

Rodger Adair has focused on organization development and training in the Arizona market. Adair has a BS in adult/workforce education from Southern Illinois University Carbondale, a master's in organizational management, and an MBA from the University of Phoenix, and is working toward a PhD in organizational psychology. He teaches several classes in the University of Phoenix undergraduate program as well as at Apollo Corporate University.

C. Fred Alford is professor of government and Distinguished Scholar-Teacher at the University of Maryland, College Park. He is the author of over a dozen books in moral psychology, including *Whistleblowers: Broken Lives and Organizational Power* (Cornell University Press, 2001). Alford is executive director of the Association for Psychoanalysis, Culture, and Society, and coeditor of the Psychoanalysis and Society Series published by Cornell University Press.

Bruce J. Avolio is the Clifton Chair in Leadership at the College of Business Administration at the University of Nebraska-Lincoln (UNL). Avolio is also director of the Gallup Leadership Institute, codirector of the UNL and Gallup MBA/MA program in executive leadership, and director of the PhD program with a specialization in leadership at the College of Business Administration at UNL. Avolio has published six books and more than one hundred articles. His most recent books are *Leadership Development in Balance* (Erlbaum, 2005), *The High Impact Leader: Moments Matter in Accelerating Leadership Development* (McGraw-Hill, 2006) with Fred Luthans, and *Authentic Leadership Theory and Practice* (Elsevier, 2006) with William Gardner and Fred Walumbwa.

Warren Bennis is Distinguished Professor of Business Administration and founding chairman of the Leadership Institute at the University of Southern California. He has also been chairman of the organization studies department at MIT, taught at Harvard and Boston Universities, and served as provost and executive vice president of the State University of New York-Buffalo and president of the University of Cincinnati. He has been awarded numerous honorary degrees including the Distinguished Service Award of the American Board of Professional Psychologists and the Perry L. Rohrer Consulting Practice Award of the American Psychological Association.

Thomas Blass is a professor in the Department of Psychology at the University of Maryland Baltimore County. Although he has had a research interest in a number of topics in social psychology, for several years now his primary focus has been on a multicomponent program of research on the social psychology of Stanley Milgram, comprising a new experimental paradigm, literature reviews and analyses, and historical and biographical research. Among his dozens of publications is the first and only biography of Milgram, *The Man Who Shocked the World: The Life and Legacy of Stanley Milgram* (Basic Books, 2004), which *Discover* magazine named one of the best books of the year.

Michelle C. Bligh is an assistant professor in the School of Behavioral and Organizational Sciences at Claremont Graduate University. Her research interests include charismatic leadership, organizational culture, interpersonal trust, and political and executive leadership. Her recent work has appeared in *Journal of Applied Psychology*, the *Leadership Quarterly*, and *Journal of Managerial Psychology*. Bligh serves on the editorial review board of the *Leadership Quarterly*, and coedited a recent book titled *Follower-Centered Perspectives on Leadership: A Tribute to the Memory of James R. Meindl* (Information Age, 2007) as part of the Leadership Horizons series.

Lorna S. Blumen is an educational consultant with Parent Education Network and CCI Design in Toronto, Canada. Blumen leads training workshops on bullying prevention and conflict resolution skills for adults who work with children—teachers, parents, mental health professionals, camp counselors, and school councils. She also works with children in grades 1–8, in classrooms, after-school programs, camps, and private groups.

James MacGregor Burns is professor emeritus of political science at Williams College. He teaches at the Academy of Leadership at the University of Maryland and has taught at the Jepson School of Leadership Studies at the University of Richmond, Virginia. He is the winner of the Pulitzer Prize and the National Book Award for his biography of Franklin Roosevelt. Author of the seminal book *Leadership* in 1978, and senior editor of the *Encyclopedia of Leadership* (Sage, 2004), he is a pioneer in the field of leadership studies. A political scientist and past president of the American Political Science Association and the International Society of Political Psychology, Burns received his education from Williams College, Harvard University, and the London School of Economics.

Melissa K. Carsten is a postdoctoral research associate in the Gallup Leadership Institute at the University of Nebraska-Lincoln. Her research extends follower-centered perspectives on leadership by examining follower roles in the leadership process, prototypes of followers, deference toward leaders, and how followers can display leadership behaviors in organizations. Carsten has also published several journal articles and book chapters on followership.

David Collinson is professor of leadership and organization at Lancaster University Management School. Formerly at the Universities of Warwick, Manchester, St. Andrews, and South Florida, Collinson is the founding coeditor of *Leadership* (www.sagepub.com/journal.aspx?pid=10325). He is the author of six books and more than one hundred articles on power, identity, management, gender, masculinity, safety, resistance, and humor. His recent work has been published in *Leadership Quarterly, Human Relations, Organization,* and *Journal of Management Studies* and includes "Questions of Leadership Distance," "Dialectics of Leadership," "The Power of Time: Leadership, Management and Gender," "Humour and Leadership," and "The Leadership of Elizabeth I."

Patricia G. Devlin is a curriculum designer, creativity trainer, and keynote speaker at Play, a creativity and innovation consultancy located in Richmond, Virginia. In her role as What's Next (Play doesn't have conventional titles), Devlin brings a multitude of talents to the business table. Her consulting experience spans the topics of leadership, culture, product development, marketplace insights and trends, marketing, growth strategy, and internal communication and branding. From London to Dubai, she has led a variety of engagements for a client list that spans the financial services, consumer packaged goods, and media industries. Her passion for followership is fueled by her bachelor's degree from the Jepson School of Leadership Studies.

Gene Dixon is a faculty member in the Engineering Department at Eastern Carolina University in engineering, holding a PhD in engineering management from the University of Alabama in Huntsville, an MBA from Nova Southeastern University, and a BS in engineering from the Auburn University. He has over twenty-years of industrial experience. Noted for a quick wit, Dixon can bring a smile while explaining complex theories of management and engineering. His research interests include leading and following in organizations, decision processes, engineering economics and teamwork.

Michael A. Hogg is professor of social psychology at Claremont Graduate University. His research is most closely associated with the development and application of social identity theory, and he has over 240 scholarly publications in this and related areas. He is coeditor of the journal *Group Processes and Intergroup*

Relations, an associate editor of the *Journal of Experimental Social Psychology,* and senior consultant editor for the Sage Social Psychology Program.

Linda Hopper has thirty years of experience in organization and human resource development, consulting, training, and executive management. She is currently the director of the Office of Training and Organizational Development for Georgetown University, where she directs the university's leadership and management programs and consults with schools and departments to resolve organizational problems. Hopper has been part-time faculty in organizational communication at George Mason University, the University of Pittsburgh, and the University of Memphis.

Jon P. Howell is professor emeritus at New Mexico State University. He has published a leadership textbook titled *Understanding Behaviors for Effective Leadership* (Prentice Hall, 2006), as well as book chapters and articles in various management journals. He has received several awards for his research and is a member of the Global Leadership and Organizational Behavior Effectiveness project. His primary research interests are leadership and followership, leadership across cultures, and substitutes for leadership.

Kimberly S. Jaussi is a teaching award–winning professor of organizational behavior and leadership in the School of Management at Binghamton University and a Faculty Fellow of the Center for Leadership Studies. She has a PhD from the University of Southern California. Her work has been published in the *Academy of Management Journal* and the *Leadership Quarterly,* and she is also a coauthor of *Dream Weavers: Strategy Focused Leadership in Technology Driven Organizations* (Information Age, 2004). Jaussi's research interests include unconventional leader behavior, creativity in organizations, followership, strategic leadership, organizational commitment, and identity issues in diverse groups.

Robert E. Kelley pioneered the concept of followership in his best-selling book *The Power of Followership* and his *Harvard Business Review* article "In Praise of Followers" (a top twenty-five best-selling reprint for *HBR*). His work is credited with moving the field away from its leadership-centric view of follower-leader dynamics and making followership a topic of inquiry in its own right. He works with organizations around the globe to better understand the link between star followers and organizational success. He currently teaches at the Tepper School of Business at Carnegie Mellon University and is president of Consultants to Executives and Organizations, Ltd.

Krista Kleiner is a senior at Fullerton Union High School. She has authored or coauthored four additional articles that have been either published or accepted for publication in the following refereed journals: *Journal of Business, Industry and Economics; Business Quest; Global Education Journal;* and *Ethics and Critical Thinking Journal*

Robert G. Lord earned his BA in economics from the University of Michigan and his PhD in industrial/organizational psychology from Carnegie Mellon University. He is a Distinguished Professor at the University of Akron. His research has focused on implicit leadership theories, leadership categorization theory, the role of follower identities in the leadership process, and the development of leadership skills. He has published widely in the leadership field and has coauthored the books *Leadership and Information Processing* (Unwin Hyman, 1990) with Karen J. Maher and *Leadership Processes and Follower Self-Identity* (Erlbaum, 2004) with Douglas J. Brown.

Michael Maccoby is a psychoanalyst and anthropologist. He is president of the Maccoby Group, consultants to leaders in companies, government, unions, and universities. He has taught at Harvard, University of Chicago, Oxford, University of California, Science Po, Brookings Institution, and Washington School of Psychiatry. He is author or coauthor of thirteen books, including *Social Character in a Mexican Village* (Prentice Hall, 1970), *The Gamesman* (Simon & Schuster, 1977), *Agents of Change* (Oxford University Press, 2003), *Narcissistic Leaders* (Broadway Books, 2003; Harvard University Press, 2007), and *The Leaders We Need* (Harvard Business School Press, 2007).

James Maroosis is a recipient of the Innovations Award in American Government from the JFK School of Government at Harvard University. He has a PhD in philosophy from the University of Toronto and teaches leadership seminars at Fordham's Graduate School of Business Administration. He is currently writing *Management Is the Liberal Arts* for the ISI Books Culture of Enterprise Initiative, sponsored by the John Templeton Foundation.

María J. Méndez is a doctoral candidate in organizational behavior at New Mexico State University. She holds a graduate degree in industrial engineering from the Universidade de Vigo, Spain. Her current research interests include shared or distributed leadership and followership roles in self-managed teams. She has published in the areas of CEO compensation and cross-cultural leadership. Méndez is currently teaching leadership at New Mexico State University.

Rebecca J. Reichard earned her doctorate in business from the Gallup Leadership Institute, University of Nebraska-Lincoln. In addition to studying followership, Reichard is conducting ongoing research on evaluating the impact of leadership and undergraduate leadership education, understanding the motivational aspects driving leader self-development, and building the development of a global mind-set. Reichard currently serves as the Postdoctoral Research Fellow in Leadership at the Kravis Leadership Institute, Claremont McKenna College.

Joseph Rost began his professional career as a high school teacher, principal, and school district superintendent. His doctoral dissertation focused on the leadership involved in the passage of the law merging the University of Wisconsin and Wisconsin State University systems into one university system. In 1976 he became a professor of leadership studies at the University of San Diego (USD), where he inaugurated a multidisciplinary doctoral program in leadership. He now serves as professor emeritus of leadership studies at USD. He is the author of *Leadership for the Twenty-First Century* (Praeger, 1991, 1993) and numerous articles and publications on leadership and policymaking.

Ernest L. "Ernie" Stech is an adjunct professor in the Department of Communication Studies at Arizona State University and principal in Chief Mountain Consulting. He is author of *Leadership Communication* (Nelson-Hall, 1983) and *The Transformed Leader* (Trafford, 2004). Stech is the contributor of a chapter on the psychodynamic approach in Northouse's *Leadership Theory and Practice,* 4th ed. In addition, he has published numerous articles on leadership and organizational communication. He received his PhD in organizational and small group communication from the University of Denver. Stech is the former president and CEO of Frost Engineering Development Corporation in the Denver area, a prime contractor to the U.S. Air Force and U.S. Army and a subcontractor to the Boeing Commercial Aircraft Company.

Andy Stefanovich is In Charge of What's Next and the founder of Play. A Fellow of the Center for Leadership Studies at the School of Management, Binghamton University, he is one of the most disruptive and effective consultants in business. He cofounded Play, the creativity and innovation consultancy headquartered in Richmond, Virginia, in 1990. He has served as a visiting professor for University of Virginia's Darden Business School, University of Michigan's Ross School of Business, the University of Richmond's Robins School of Business, and Dartmouth's Tuck School of Business. An award-winning businessperson, he has committed his life to making business a lot more interesting and vastly more creative.

Brent Uken, CFA ASA, is a principal in Ernst & Young's Transaction Advisory Services practice, specializing in providing valuation and business modeling services to the firm's clients. During his seventeen-year tenure with the firm, he has served in several leadership roles, including those focused on learning, performance management, and knowledge management. He currently lives in Atlanta, Georgia.

Gail S. Williams began her thirty-two-year career in the federal government at NASA Goddard Space Flight Center in 1974 and was loaned for fourteen months to the Executive Office of the President in the mid-1990s. As the special assistant to the Goddard CFO, Williams is program manager for the award-winning Leadership Alchemy Program and coordinator of the Exploring Leadership Colloquia series. She is a member of 13L, a leadership collective of midcareer employees who promote effective leadership throughout the federal government. Williams earned a BA in psychology from the University of Connecticut and an MPA at the Maxwell School of Syracuse University.

INTRODUCTION

Warren Bennis

Who is not fascinated by the dance between leaders and followers, who depend on each other as surely as animals and air? But until recently, followers have been largely neglected in the study of leadership, an omission famously addressed by contributor Robert Kelley in his 1988 *Harvard Business Review* article "In Praise of Followers." Now, almost twenty years later, we have this welcome book, a long overdue exploration of leadership's underappreciated complement in all its complexity, as role, relationship, and process. It is no surprise that books on leadership, promising to reveal the secrets of countless football coaches and historical figures as disparate as Moses and Attila the Hun, outnumber those on followership several thousand to one. After all, leadership is the prize that ambitious men and women have struggled and even died for at least since Alexander the Great. Whether their field is politics, business, science, or the arts, leaders are at the center of the action, the envied if not enviable stars whose lives seem to burn a little brighter than our own. We aspire to their power and its perquisites even as we take unseemly pleasure when one of them stumbles and falls. Indeed, the moment when each of us realizes he or she is mostly a follower, not a leader, is a genuine developmental milestone; who forgets that painful leap over the line of demarcation between the boundless fantasies of childhood and the sober reality of an adulthood in which we will never quite become the god we hoped to be?

Reading the diverse essays that make up this valuable book, I was reminded how hollow the label of leadership sometimes is and how heroic followership can be. As coeditor Jean Lipman-Blumen and other contributors point out, followers play an especially vital role in the presence of "toxic leaders," those malignant wielders of power who have made the last century the bloodiest in all of humanity's decidedly sanguinary history. When evil leaders emerge, followers have no moral choice but to try to wrest power from them. Such behavior is usually termed resistance, but it is in fact a heroic form of action. Moreover, this honorable rebellion reflects an underlying truth. Yes, leaders have enormous power, but so do those who follow them. Without their followers, tyrants can accomplish little. Even toxic leaders sleep and are subject to other human constraints, so they depend on others to wield the gas, the guns, and the machetes. For better or for ill, followers do the heavy lifting of any successful enterprise. No matter who is memorialized as founder, no nation or organization is built without the collective effort of a group of able, energetic, unsung followers. Moreover, the led bear the brunt of the horrors conceived by toxic leaders. While their nations reeled, many of the most notorious despots of modern times spent their last days in luxurious exile, sleeping on Frette sheets.

In organizational life, the consequences of toxic leadership are less obvious but no less dire. In recent years, we have seen more and more examples of courageous followership, as nameless, faceless shareholders rebelled against arrogant, underperforming executives when their corporate boards failed to do so. The last couple of decades have served as a corrective to the once widespread view of the CEO as demigod. Our recent disillusionment with much corporate leadership is the cumulative effect of too many insider stock trades, too much executive venality, too many $6,000 shower curtains. As executive compensation packages began to approach the size of the budgets of some countries, observers began to wonder if they had not given too much of their own power over to those at the top. The cult of the celebrity CEO gave way to a renewed appreciation of the leader as steward of the collective treasure of his or her followers.

A gathering of research such as this not only reminds us of the importance of followers but also emphasizes how blurred the line is between leaders and those they lead. When followers check the power of their leaders, they clearly function as leaders themselves, albeit less well paid ones. And whether by augmenting the actions of their leaders or conscientiously challenging them, followers both advance the collective enterprise and polish their own leadership skills, a fact neatly reflected in the title of Rodger Adair's chapter, "Developing Great Leaders, One Follower at a Time."

One of the most important—and potentially perilous—arenas for follower action is within the organization. We tend to value the leader who acts decisively, whether right or wrong, but followers are expected to behave with more restraint. Too often a follower who dares to poke holes in a leader's plan is seen as a maverick at best, a troublemaker, even a lunatic. But such internal critics are invaluable, the people most likely to save the organization from wasting time and resources on a doomed product or project. Historians tell us that George Washington routinely solicited the advice of subordinates before going into battle, unlike his tradition-bound British counterparts. And in order to elicit candid feedback from his men, Washington did not tell them that a particular plan under consideration was his own. Washington had an intuitive understanding of what good followers bring to the table. Sadly such understanding is rare. Most of us can tick off the attributes of a great leader, but the nature and functions of a great follower are little understood and almost never articulated. Too often, followers are expected to be agreeable and acquiescent and are rewarded for being so, when in fact followers who practice knee-jerk obedience are of little value and are often dangerous.

If I had to reduce the responsibilities of a good follower to a single rule, it would be to speak truth to power. We know that toxic followers can put even good leaders on a disastrous path—Shakespeare's Iago comes immediately to mind. But heroic followers can also save leaders from their worst follies, especially leaders so isolated that the only voice they hear is their own. When the leader cannot be persuaded, the follower is sometimes forced to break the collective rules and become a whistleblower, a kind of rogue leader, driven by conscience, who borrows the power of the media and often pays a terrible personal price for doing so. But the most effective followers are those who possess or acquire the skills that allow them to make their case and effect change without damaging the organization. One important function of a book like this is to get more people thinking about how to create and become great followers, especially in light of the fact that we spend much of our lives in that capacity, whatever exalted titles we may hold. The tools of great followership are not so different from those of leadership, including the ability to persuade. In fact, given that followers usually lack the power to order and insist, they are wise to acquire a quiver of diplomatic tools, including an expansive knowledge of the psychology of human behavior and mastery of such neglected persuasive arts as rhetoric and acting.

In many ways, great followership is harder than leadership. It has more dangers and fewer rewards, and it must routinely be exercised with much more subtlety. But great followership has never been more important, if only because of the seriousness of the global problems we face and the fact that they must be solved collaboratively, not by leaders alone but by leaders working in tandem with able and dedicated followers. No single leader, however brilliant, however charismatic, can solve the problem of climate change. It can be addressed only by millions of creative, passionate individuals who know they must act now, no matter what their leaders tell them.

In fact, I will go out on a limb and predict that a decade from now, the terms *leader* and *follower* will seem as dated as bell bottoms and Nehru jackets. The world is changing with dizzying speed, and among those changes is an erosion of traditional notions of leadership. What does leadership mean in a world in which anonymous bloggers can choose presidents and bring down regimes? When John F. Kennedy ran against Nixon, his biggest challenge was mastering the relatively new medium of television in order to win the presidency. But the days are gone when a leader's rise to power is linear and relatively orderly. Today, power is being democratized by new media that spread ideas virally and can topple the established order without violence or manifesto. Today a teenager with a camera phone may be more powerful than a politician who spends decades acquiring his or her position. Not traditional leaders, but people whose fingers are on the send key rule this brave new world. Agendas are being set, sometimes with murderous seriousness, sometimes whimsically, by global networks of people who effect change without meeting anywhere except in cyberspace. Recently, a virtual journalist interviewed a virtual U.S. congressman on a computer-generated set in Second Life, the electronic playground where real fortunes are being made and alternative futures explored. Whatever else transpires in the next ten years, it is safe to say that we will have very different notions of leadership and followership, if only because each of us will be able to peek into and expose any corner of an increasingly wired world, upending any current notion of what constitutes the status quo.

Let me make one more prediction. One of the pleasures of this book is its references to the discoveries about how humans influence each other (the beating heart of leadership), made by such pioneering social scientists as Solomon Asch, Stanley Milgram, and others. Each age has its paradigmatic science, and none is more important today than neuroscience. I am sure that generously supported researchers are even now using functional magnetic resonance imaging to explore how leaders and followers think. The best of that work will be a worthy addition to the insights offered by this volume.

The Art of Followership

PART ONE

Defining and Redefining Followership

Since Plato's articulation of the philosopher king, scholars and researchers from many disciplines have explored the Great Plains of leadership while hardly noticing followers. In addition, they have scaled the peaks and examined the endless crannies of leadership, following a treasure map whose destination was the Holy Grail of leadership. Seldom on that map did a "Followers" signpost appear.

Some leadership researchers have excavated ancient cultures to determine how leaders lived and ruled in times and worlds past. Others navigated the turbulent waters of history, in search of lost ideas and ideals of leadership. Still others have sifted the sands of individual leaders' lives, seeking biographical shards that might offer clues to this elusive phenomenon. During all these arduous, centuries-long searches for leaders, followers appeared only infrequently.

Oddly enough, despite a significant literature on social movements directly concerned with followers' behavior, linkages to the field of leadership are sparse. Even the social psychological experiments on conformity played a minor role in leadership theory.

It took sociologist Max Weber to nudge the exploration of leadership toward a consideration of followers and their perceptions.[1] His discussion of charismatic leadership that "compelled" the awe of followers would lay some early groundwork on which leadership theorists could build. In fact, James MacGregor Burns's seminal distinction between transactional and transformational leaders did exactly that, highlighting the difference in followers' behavior with the two kinds of leaders.[2]

Yet, a full decade later, Robert E. Kelley's *Harvard Business Review* article constituted a sharp rap on the knuckles of the field of leadership for neglecting followers.[3] With some notable exceptions, most subsequent scholars continued to focus on what James Meindl and colleagues labeled the "romance of leadership," attributing most group and contextual effects—both good and bad—to larger-than-life leaders.[4]

Despite the widespread consensus that one must have followers to warrant the label of leader, the spotlight has remained tightly centered on leaders. This distorting and overly positive bias toward leaders predisposed the field to concentrate on what these impressive figures did to followers, not vice versa. Followers were simply noted in passing, those objects on whom leaders foisted their decisions and actions.

Even those scholars who escaped the adorational chains of most leadership research emphasized primarily the leaders'—not the followers'—negative qualities and actions. Kelley's plea notwithstanding, only infrequently did leadership researchers recognize followers as active, thinking, and perceiving individuals. Aside from Burns and later Bass, and an occasional less well-known study, few scholars emphasized the *interaction* between leaders and followers.[5] Moreover, most failed to explore the *inaction* of followers in the face of destructive leaders. Even those who considered leadership as a process or relationship treated followers mostly by implication.

But the winds of change are gradually rising. Followers, by their actions, are calling attention to themselves—in massive political uprisings in diverse societies, and in incidents of individual whistle-blowing within organizations of all descriptions. Given the increasingly compelling actions of real-life followers vis-à-vis their leaders, perhaps it was inevitable that the leadership spotlight would broaden to include them.

Here and there within the field of leadership, scholars and practitioners are starting to acknowledge the significance of followers. Followers with moral courage[6] sometimes in the guise of whistle-blowers,[7] sometimes in less dramatic dress, have entered center stage. A few scholars have begun to raise questions about the impact of bad leaders on their followers[8] and to explore why followers only rarely resist toxic leaders.[9] Gradually, a more follower-centric leadership model, inspired by Meindl and his colleagues' insight, is emerging.

With the empirical world's intrusion upon leadership studies, it was probably not coincidental that a practitioner—not a leadership researcher—was the one who originally sought collaborators to convene a group of scholars and practitioners to rethink the meaning of followership. At the urging of Ira Chaleff, a consultant based in Washington, D.C., the Kravis Leadership Institute at Claremont McKenna College and the Institute for Advanced Studies in Leadership at the Peter F. Drucker and Masatoshi Ito Graduate School of Management, Claremont Graduate University, cosponsored a groundbreaking conference in February 2006, titled Rethinking Followership.

For two days, the air bristled with the excitement of healthy contradictions, constructive controversies, alternative concepts, and potential strategies for drawing a new treasure map, this one with "Followership" clearly marked as "ground zero." Researchers, scholars, and practitioners from diverse disciplines and fields created a heady conversation. From those unprecedented days, it became evident that a new subfield was emerging, one that should be shared with a much larger audience than that inaugural followership conference could possibly accommodate.

This volume is an effort to do just that. It not only includes chapters first presented at the Rethinking Followership Conference but also introduces the thinking of key researchers and practitioners who could not be present on those two innovative days. We believe that this collection marks the dawn of a new day, a new journey of inquiry. We invite you to join in this exhilarating adventure of scholarship and practice.

Rethinking Followership

Robert E. Kelley

When I began my work on followership twenty-five years ago, I was not particularly aware of what I was doing in the bigger scheme of things. My only goal was to bring attention to the study of followers. I was simply thinking about followers and followership roles, and I wanted to explore the subject.

At the time, leadership was the primary focus for just about all scholars in the field. Very little research or theorizing considered followers, and if it did, its purpose was to better understand leadership.[1] I felt like the odd person out. Executives, academics, and even people sitting next to me on airplanes questioned why I would bother with followership when leadership spurred the media attention, research funding, and high-paying corporate training gigs. Most people held a very negative view of followership and discounted anything positive that could come from the role. No one talked about followership; it was never part of the conversation, unless it was tagged on as an afterthought. At some point, I finally decided to put a stake in the ground and say to the world, "We need to pay attention to followers. Followership is worthy of its own discrete research and training. Plus, conversations about leadership need to include followership because leaders neither exist nor act in a vacuum without followers."

The road I went down was not easy at first. I made a major step with my 1988 *Harvard Business Review* article, "In Praise of Followers."[2] In it, I explained that we view the world as a map with leadership in the center and everything else on the periphery. I remember a perspective-altering trip to Japan, where I was shown a world map with Japan in the center and the United States tucked over in the corner. This is what I wanted to do for followership: to put it in the middle of the map and to let everything else be on the periphery.

"In Praise of Followers" turned out to be fairly controversial. Some people just flat out didn't like it, comparing followers to sled dogs whose destiny is always to look at the rear end of the dog in front of them, but never to see the wider horizon or make the decisions of the lead dog. Other readers could not thank me enough for articulating what they secretly held in their heart. These folks believed that being a strong #2 often allowed for greater contributions than being in the #1 spot and that making the assist was just as important as making the score. Many had no desire to be leaders.

Controversy, I learned, can be good for spreading the word. So many people read, discussed, argued, and tried to apply the ideas in the article that it became one of *HBR*'s best-selling reprints and earned the article the "HBR Classic" designation. My 1992 book, *The Power of Followership*, and Ira Chaleff's 1995 book, *The Courageous Follower*, propelled the concept even further.[3] In the years since then, followership has made increasing headway into the mainstream, and the amount of interest in the topic seems to be escalating. For example, the word itself is now part of the organizational vocabulary. It is rare for someone to talk about leadership without also discussing the corresponding role of followership. Most leadership courses now have a section devoted to followership, and followership is increasingly taught as a stand-alone course in universities and corporations, such as Barbara Kellerman's followership course at Harvard's Kennedy School. Several master's theses and doctoral dissertations have studied followership in nursing, education, business, and sports. A 2007 Google search turned up over 187,000 hits for the term *follower* and over 92,000 hits for *followership research*. Ron Riggio, Jean Lipman-Blumen, and Ira Chaleff organized at Claremont McKenna College in 2006 the first national followership conference. On a personal level, more and more people contact me now wanting to know about followership. Most important, more people admit to me that they not only play the followership role but also prefer it. The landscape for followership has changed considerably in the last twenty-five years.

FOLLOWERSHIP STYLES

My previous work, which served as a launching point for the field, involved basic preliminary research on the styles of followership. Two dimensions seemed to define the way that people follow:

1. Do they think for themselves? Are they independent critical thinkers? Or do they look to the leader to do the thinking for them?

2. Are they actively engaged in creating positive energy for the organization? Or is there negative energy or passive involvement?

Based on these two dimensions, there are five basic styles of followership:

The sheep. Sheep are passive and look to the leader to do the thinking for them and to motivate them. If you are the boss and in your car on the way to work, and you're thinking about what you're going to get your workers to do and how you're going to do that, then you're dealing with sheep.

The yes-people. Yes-people are positive, always on the leader's side, but still looking to the leader for the thinking, the direction, the vision. If the leader asks them to do something, they've got the energy, and they'll go forward with it. When they finish that task, they'll come back to the leader, asking, "What do you want me to do next?" However, yes-people don't see themselves this way. One of the things I've learned is that the different styles of followers will almost always put a positive spin on their style. Yes-people will say, "I'm a doer; that's my job. The boss gets paid to think, and I'm the one who does the work." But the rest of us would say there's more to being a good follower than simply doing.

The alienated. Alienated followers think for themselves, but have a lot of negative energy. Every time the leader or organization tries to move forward, these are the ones who have ten reasons why the leader or organization shouldn't. They are not coming up with the next solution, but are skeptical, cynical about the current plan of action. They have energy, they can think for themselves, they can be smart. But they are not moving in a positive direction. However, they see themselves as the mavericks, the only people in the organization who have the guts to stand up to the boss.

The pragmatics. Pragmatics sit on the fence and see which way the wind blows. Once they see where things are headed, they'll get on board. They'll never be the first on board, but they will never let the leader or organization leave without them. They see themselves as preservers of the status quo. Their internal dialogue goes something like this: "If I got all excited every time there was a new leader or a change of direction, my wheels would be spinning constantly. Leaders come and go. New visions come and go. If I just sit here and wait it out, I won't have to do all that work." So they do what they must to survive, but wait it out until the storms of change blow over.

The star followers. Star followers think for themselves, are very active, and have very positive energy. They do not accept the leader's decision without their own independent evaluation of its soundness. If they agree with the leader, they give full support. If they disagree, they challenge the leader, offering constructive alternatives that will help the leader and organization get where they want to go. Some people view these people as really "leaders in disguise," but this is basically because those people have a hard time accepting that followers can display such independence and positive behavior. Star followers are often referred to as "my right-hand person" or my "go-to person."

So this was the basic model I used to understand followership styles. It offered me and a number of organizations a way to think about the type of behavior that led to all the negative stereotypes, as well as to conceive of the positive followership that rarely got mentioned. In my work, I try not to ignore reality or feedback. Rather than pretend that the negative stereotypes did not exist and come up with some idealized follower that the world should embrace, I wanted to explore the full reality of how people follow. Are people stuck in followership styles? Is a person's style static or dynamic? Once you are a pragmatic, are you always a pragmatic? Or do people's styles change depending on the leader they have or the job they find themselves in? Can a person be a star follower in one situation and an alienated follower in another situation? Why do people adopt a particular style? Why would someone end up as a pragmatic follower? What conditions might lead to that? Are there ways to help people move toward a chosen style?

This model, in my experience, tends to be very powerful for people, having a lot of face validity as well as some statistical validity. For example, when my colleagues and I teach a weeklong leadership program at Carnegie Mellon University,

I am no longer surprised that the overwhelming response from the participants about what opened their eyes the most, the thing that got them the most excited, is the followership model. So I continue to use it.

RETHINKING FOLLOWERSHIP

As I look forward for the field of followership, my thoughts swirl around the following seven topics:

1. World events

2. Culture

3. Leader(ship)

4. Follower qualities

5. Role of the follower

6. Language of followership

7. Courageous conscience

In some of these areas, I think followership should be playing a more important role than it is. In other areas, I see research opportunities for all the scholars involved in the field.

World Events

One of the things I'm concerned about is that we scholars have gotten too "micro" and too "parochial" when discussing followership. We overly examine the follower-leader interaction on the small stage of college student life or coach-player dramas. Can followership help us unravel the big issues happening in the world, issues that affect many people's lives—suicide bombers; the rise of religious fundamentalism and its corresponding lack of tolerance; democratically elected dictators and corrupt government officials of any kind who harm their followers and the larger society; or corporate abuses of power that cheat employees, customers, suppliers, investors, and in some cases the larger society?[4]

For example, the increase in suicide bombings and in the types of suicide bombers (for example, more women, more middle-class people, more professionals) has much of society searching for an explanation. If we take a psychological approach, we might look for answers in the bombers' needs for power, revenge, or the promise of heaven. We might also see it from an economic vantage point in that the bombers are guaranteed the economic well-being of their families in return for their acts. Or we could search for sociological root causes, such as poverty, unemployment, or societal disenfranchisement. Each of these inquiries might yield some valuable insights.

My question is, Why are we not making a followership inquiry into the issue of suicide bombers? Surely followership plays a role and might offer more powerful insights into the phenomenon. What kind of followers are suicide bombers? Are they sheep, pragmatics, or star followers? What motivates their followership? Are they disciples, dreamers, or something else? What human needs are at work? Can the world "afford" this type of followership? Would more "enlightened" followership reduce the occurrence of and damage done by this behavior (or any of the others that I mentioned earlier)? How can any of the scholarly work on followership help us answer these questions? How do we unlock the practical applications of our knowledge about followership? It seems to me that followership could help us address these world events equally as well as leadership can.

Culture

Culture affects people's belief systems and behaviors. So do we need to consider the cultural aspects of followership? If you were raised in Japan, are you going to think about followership and carry out the role differently than if you were raised in the United States or Kenya? In terms of religion, if you were brought up in the Judaic tradition, you arrive at truth by questioning. That is a very different approach than that of evangelical fundamentalists, who are supposed to accept on faith. These perspectives will likely produce different approaches to followership, and it would help if we understood these differences. In our suicide bomber example, how does culture affect followership? Which factors (for example, country of origin, ethnic identity, or religious background) affect culture the most, and how do these factors play a role in a suicide bomber's followership behavior?

Followership is also influenced at the subcultural level. Consider how followership varies between civilian employees versus those in the military, members of tribes versus urban residents, or prison inmates versus members of middle-class society. This is just a starter list that can energize our inquiries.

Do some cultures produce more yes-people or star followers? If so, then why? Do cultures characterize followership differently, thus producing different followership styles and behaviors that are not generalizable across cultures? Or are there universal followership styles, motivations, and role performance?

We can take this a step further and look at followership during cultural clashes. When a culture that advocates free speech and a free press produces a political cartoon that is viewed as insulting by another culture, how does followership play out? What drives followers in the offended group to start rioting and harming members of the free speech culture? What makes the followers in the free speech culture surprised by this retaliation, but not retaliate in return?

Leader(ship)

Traditionally, we have viewed the world from a leadership-centric vantage point. We have assumed that all other factors, including followership, are secondary to leadership. When followers have been surveyed, it was to determine their views of the leaders. But what if we turned all this around? What if we put followership center stage and asked all the same questions, but only in reference to the followers instead of leaders? For example, when we talk about leader-follower distance, we always talk about the follower's distance from the leader, but we should also talk about the leader's distance from the follower. Likewise, what are the interactions between leaders and followers from the follower's point of view? We tend to think of leaders as the proactive "cause" and followership as the reactive "effect." But what if the opposite were true? Are leadership attitudes, behavior, and performance more a result of followership than the other way around? For example, do sheep produce a particular style of leadership, regardless of the leader's personality or predisposition? Is it this turn of events that leads to a particular outcome?

I'm reminded of the psychology cartoon depicting two dogs in a park talking to each other. One says to the other, "Humans are hard to train, but once you break them in, they are pretty predictable. I've finally taught mine so that when I bark, he drops whatever he's doing and prepares my meal. When I feel like getting some exercise, I scratch the floor to signal him to get on his jacket and to walk alongside of me to keep me company. And when I need a massage, I just sit down next to him and he starts rubbing me. He's learned these things so well that I don't even have to say anything anymore." We tend to believe that the leaders are in charge, directing and shaping followership behavior. Yet maybe leaders are malleable products of cumulative followership actions.

We might also reframe the interaction effects between followers and leaders. For example, when we talk about charismatic leadership, we can ask, What style of follower would a charismatic leader attract? However, we should also ask, What style of leader would a yes-person attract? What is the psychological and emotional dynamic between them? These possible interactions between different followership and leadership styles, and the complexity therein, would be fertile areas for research, complementing Kellerman's and Lipman-Blumen's work on bad leaders.[5] This topic also ties in to the aforementioned world events and culture areas.

Follower Qualities

The question that still sticks in my head after twenty-plus years is, In our society, why does anyone want to be a follower, when all the perks and all the attention go to leaders? Although I identified seven paths to followership in my book *The Power of Followership*, we still have a long way to go to understand it more fully. For example, college applications ask for examples of leadership, but not of followership. It would be an unusual kid who would take the risk to extol followership qualities and the even more unusual admissions officer who would reward it.

So from where do followership attitudes, styles, and aspirations come? What's the role of parenting, early childhood experience, school, religion, sports participation, the media, or important role models on followership development? Consider peer pressure in middle school, for example. Most of the serious social issues students may face—alcohol and drug experimentation, gangs, sex, fear of social ostracism—are peer-pressure driven. Schools treat peer pressure as a leadership issue when actually it's a followership issue. They believe that if they teach leadership skills, they will alleviate the negative effects of peer pressure. A better approach may be to teach better followership skills. Kids need to learn how to protect themselves from leaders who encourage them to engage in either self-destructive or socially destructive behavior, as well as learn how to support positive leaders.

But peer pressure and toxic leaders are not just a middle school problem. Many of the world events mentioned earlier involve peer pressure and toxic leaders. We need to learn what life events produce followers who can think for themselves; exercise their own independent, critical judgment; and act in the best interests of the organization or the society, even if doing so means going against the leader or the group.

Role of the Follower

One of the questions that I ask executives is, "If you could have an ideal mix of the five followership styles in your organization, what percentage of each style would you prefer?" I'm surprised at how many say they would like all yes-people. Their reasons are that (1) yes-people are "doers" who are willing to do the grunt work and who get the job done with little fuss; (2) yes-people have limited aspirations and will neither pressure the leader for promotions nor quit for better jobs elsewhere; and (3) yes-people are loyal and dependable.

Other executives say they would prefer the following mix. Start with a sprinkling of alienated because they keep the leader honest. Add a small group of star followers who would lead the charge, but avoid adding too many because they can get demanding, and they think for themselves too much. Then split the remaining majority among pragmatics who serve as an institutionalized, status quo base and yes-people who will get the job done.

It is the rare executive who wants all star followers. Most executives fear that they can neither keep star followers challenged by the job nor satisfied with their role in the organization. They believe that star followers will grow bored and disillusioned, seeking greener pastures and leading to high turnover. My own experience is that organizations with more star followers perform better because the star followers need not depend on the leader for direction or motivation. This reduces the transaction costs that hinder organizational success.

Pondering the roles of followers results in intriguing research questions. What assumptions do leaders make about the various followership styles? Are those assumptions accurate, or are they dysfunctional stereotypes? Is the common leader preference for loyal doers justified or problematic? Is there an ideal mix of followership styles, or is the search for such a mix a quixotic quest? Is the ideal mix dependent on the context or situation? Do certain mixes attract certain types of leaders? Do certain leaders reshape the mix to suit their own preference? If we prefer a certain mix, say all star followers, can people move from one followership style to another, such as from yes-person to star follower? If so, how does that happen? Rethinking the role of followers can help the field move forward.

Language of Followership

If I had a dollar for every time someone said to me, "You need to come up with a word other than 'follower' because it's socially unacceptable," I would be much wealthier today. "If you had a sexier, easier term," they say, "then you'd be able to sell this concept much more easily." My response is always "I would be glad to do that as soon as we get rid of the word 'leader.' Once you're ready to do that, then we can talk."

My rigid stance actually stems from the point that these people are making—that language does make a difference. Language has an effect. If we stop using "follower" (as some businesses, such as Wal-Mart, have done, using words like "associate" in its place), can we really continue to use the word "leader"? Does "leader-associate" have the same dialectical relationship as "leader-follower"? I think not. Instead, it masks the underlying beliefs that the leaders have about their "associates" with a more democratic sheen.

Language is important not only in terms of the words we use but also in terms of the script that they suggest. The words "leader" and "follower" bring to mind a common script in which the leader is in charge, saying, "You do this, and you do that." Meanwhile, followers are imagined as inferior beings in need of the leader's direction, motivation, and protection. We need to rethink this outdated script. What societal purpose does it serve? Is it still functional in today's world? What personal purpose does it serve for the people who promulgate it or for the people who actually follow it? We need to ask ourselves whether we need a new script. Can we start to reframe the entire conversation in a new way? If so, what does the new script sound like? What words and imagery do we use to suggest either a more accurate or a more desirable relationship between followers and leaders?

Courageous Conscience

Related to the issue of peer pressure discussed earlier is the responsibility that followers have to keep leaders and peers ethically and legally in check. Instead of viewing followers as the "good soldiers" who carry out commands dutifully, we need to view followers as the primary defenders against toxic leaders or dysfunctional organizations. The buck stops more with followers than leaders. In fact, they are often in a better position to see the day-to-day events or leader decisions that lead to disastrous consequences. However, our current script of followership does not include this responsibility in the role description. For the most part, society neither prepares nor expects followers to exercise what I label as the "courageous conscience."

The ability to make ethical and legal judgments, to take proactive steps to promote ethical and legal activities, and then to stand up against unethical and illegal decisions and actions, is a crucial aspect of followership. Followers cannot abdicate their courageous conscience by outsourcing it to the leader. Rather, followers need to learn how to blow the whistle effectively, how to combat groupthink, how to avoid the dispersion of responsibility so often found in groups, and how to advance institutional integrity.

How do we make this happen? How do we help people be successful when they have to stand up? The answer has at least three parts: (1) teaching people that the followership role includes the courageous conscience, thus not only legitimating this responsibility but also mandating it; (2) helping followers find the personal courage to stand up, and providing the societal supports that encourage people to exercise their courageous conscience; and (3) preparing followers so that when they do stand up, they are successful.

If all followers actively used their courageous conscience, we would likely have fewer toxic leaders who steer the organization down the path of organizational corruption or societal damage. This could go a long way in limiting the fallout of the world events I discussed earlier. To this end, I would like someone to develop an entire curriculum that brings the ethical, legal, and social science tools together to equip every person with a strong, active courageous conscience.

CONCLUSION

The field of followership is still in its infancy. It is rare that people get a chance to build and shape a new area of inquiry. This twenty-five-year journey has been a wonderful experience for me: when I started, I only wanted to put my stake in the ground, and now many people have joined the journey, taking it in new directions. I am confident that fellow travelers will generate their own ways to rethink the followership field and create novel research agendas. Collectively, we can grow the followership field so that it makes powerful contributions to society and to the individuals who make up society.

Leadership: A Partnership in Reciprocal Following

James Maroosis

> *There is a conception of leadership gaining ground to-day very different from our old notion. . . . It is a conception very far removed from the leader-follower relation. With that conception you had to be either a leader or a leaner. To-day our thinking is tending less and less to be confined within the boundaries of those two alternatives. There is the idea of a reciprocal leadership. There is also the idea of a partnership of following, of following the invisible leader—the common purpose. The relation of the rest of the group to the leader is not a passive one.*
>
> Mary Parker Follett[1]

Leadership, in the words of Mary Parker Follett, is a partnership in reciprocal following. This partnership follows what she calls the invisible leader, the common purpose, the law of the situation. Thus leadership as responding to a call is a type of following, and following because it needs to hear the call is a type of leading.

Followership, like leadership, requires discrimination. Both need to be able to pick who and what to follow. Followership and leadership are two necessary components of what it means to be either a good leader or a good follower. In other words, there are no leaders who are not followers, nor followers who are not leaders; both need to learn what and how to follow—that is, to lead themselves and others to heed, recognize, and respond in a humane manner to what is being called for in a given situation.

It is the situation that calls for action, by dictating the need for leadership, and it is a partnership of reciprocal following that enacts a response.

This notion of leading and following as responding to a calling, centers the whole notion of leadership and followership around something outside the leaders and followers themselves. It requires that they turn their attention "outward." They need to use all their senses to scrutinize and pick up what and how something needs to be done.

Hence followership, like leadership, is a discipline of competencies and "response-abilities." The difference between response-able and responsible is the difference between something you can do and something you should do. Response-ability is readiness. Responsibility is abstract duty or job description. Leadership and followership are competencies that work in tandem as a shared discipline of reciprocal response-abilities.

The words *discipline* and *disciple* have the same root. A disciple is someone who learns by following. Disciplined disciples take nothing for granted. They learn to express their ignorance, whenever and however it appears. This is always a sign of a good follower. They are so interested in learning how to do things that they are willing to express their every doubt, misgiving, confusion, apprehension, or fear.

Followership and feedback go hand in hand.

What followership needs is leadership. There is something the follower does not know, that the follower cannot or will not see, that leadership brings to the relationship. The disciple-follower *needs* what the leader reveals, manifests, points outs, or sets as a course. In this regard the leader is like a teacher leading students to draw their own conclusions by training their sensibilities and allowing them to learn what they need in order to accomplish their tasks.

In this sense, followership is essentially a learning function. The leader teaches what followers need to learn and understand. The leader speaks the law of the situation in a way that the followers can hear what is being said. The leader helps the followers see or achieve their shared goals.

Neither leader nor follower is a sycophant; neither is on an ego trip (on the contrary, this an anti–ego trip relationship). Both are learning how to follow what is being called for in a given situation. Both are defined by their ability to make responsible decisions and take actions in a responsible manner.

So described, this selfless or ego-less approach to leadership and followership points to a medieval model of learning as a discovery process in which the teacher leads students to learn for themselves, not by themselves. Thomas Aquinas, for example, describes teaching as a discovery process in which the teacher leads students to make their own discoveries. For Aquinas, the teacher-leader expresses learning in such a way that students learn how to learn by learning things for themselves:

> For the teacher leads the pupils to knowledge of things they do not know in the same way that someone directs himself through the process of discovering something they do not know. . . . One person is said to teach another inasmuch as . . . he manifests to that other the reasoning process which he himself goes through by his own natural reason. . . . Therefore, just as the doctor is said to heal a patient through the activity of nature, so a man is said to cause the knowledge in another through the activity of the learners own natural reason, and this is teaching.[2]

Please note that in this notion of teaching, the leader lets learning happen in the classroom by sharing with his or her followers (the students) how the leader arrived at his or her own conclusions.

This is what makes leadership so much more difficult than followership. The leader is forging the trail and laying it out for others to follow.

Martin Heidegger reiterates this theme by taking us right to the heart of leadership or learning as being a partnership of reciprocal following. Here again, one need only substitute "follower" for "student" and "leader" for "teacher" to see the way this process works.

> True teaching is even more difficult than learning. We know that; but we rarely think about it. And why is teaching more difficult than

learning? Not because the teacher must have a larger store of information, and have it always ready. Teaching is more difficult than learning because what teaching calls for is this: to let learning. The real teacher, in fact, lets nothing else be learned than—learning. His conduct, therefore, often produces the impression that we properly learn nothing from him, if by "learning" we now suddenly understand merely the procurement of useful information. The teacher is ahead of his apprentices in this alone, that he still has far more to learn than they—he has to learn to let them learn. The teacher must be capable of being more teachable than the apprentices. The teacher is far less assured of his ground than those who learn are of theirs. If the relation between the teacher and the taught is genuine, therefore, there is never a place in it for the authority of the know it all or the authoritative sway of the official.[3]

Here we see that leadership is a learning process that is not only centered in what needs to be said but also in learning how to say it in ways that others can understand and follow. Both leader and follower (teacher and student) are learning to follow what is called for; what needs to be said, learned, taught as dictated by the situation; the one pointing out to the other where the learning or teaching needs to go. This is a dynamic, educational relationship of give and take.

The follower's job is to let the leader *know* what he or she needs to learn—what the follower does and does not see—and this is done by both of them acting honestly, working together with mutual respect, honoring their respective roles and responsibilities as leader and follower.

This relationship of mutual response-abilities is the leader-follower relation. Both create it so that both can do the right things, thus creating new situations that dictate anew what is most needed. This is an ongoing process in which leaders and followers may change their roles, but leadership and followership always function the same way.

THE ETHICS OF FOLLOWERSHIP: FOLLOWERSHIP IS MORE THAN AN ART

This learning process is neither abstract nor academic in nature. What is being learned is how to comport oneself in the world. Followership is about saying and doing the right things. Followership is acting properly and well in a given situation. It is doing and saying what the situation dictates. This is what the ancients called eloquence and decorum, saying and doing the right things. What we might call walking the talk. As such, followership is an ethical and moral discipline and must be taught and learned as such.

The point is that what is most needed in any *human* situation is a *humane response*, what Peter Drucker calls "doing first things first." And first things, in the context of leadership, are always the moral things—that is, the right things to do. The reason for this is that a first thing always requires a sense of purpose or end, so that first things and last things always go hand in hand.

This means that to live in a world of first things is simultaneously to live in a world of last things. What makes something a first thing is the reason why you are doing it. It is your goal or purpose that tells you what to do first. The next right thing to do is the thing that will most effectively lead you to achieve your goal.

The "first thing" is always a function of the final product or effect one has in mind. Not to think from effect to cause is not to think effectively. Here is where Stephen Covey's and Peter Drucker's distinction between doing the right things (effectiveness) and doing things right (efficiency) is so helpful.

Leadership and followership are about doing the right things. They are about saying the right words and hearing them in the right ways.

The difference between the right word and the almost-right word can be immense. Mark Twain once described this difference as being the difference between lightning and the lightning bug. Or as Isocrates put it over twenty-five hundred years ago, "The right word is a sure sign of right thinking."

Leadership and followership are all about walking the talk, saying the right things, and doing them in the right way. Response-able action means having a sense of purpose and acting with propriety. This is an ancient meaning of decorum—not as maintaining the status quo but renewing identity through change. Response-able followership is transformative precisely in the way it responds to changing situations. Followership is a habit of responsive effectiveness. What needs to be internalized and learned as a habit is externalized and brought into existence through our day-to-day actions.

Habits are actualized through doing, and doing develops the type of "right" habits that get things done. This is pure Aristotle. It embodies and animates the ancient tradition of virtue ethics that once was taught and understood as a commonplace.

A quick snapshot of the four cardinal virtues will show how habits need to be ethical if they are to be effective. Doing the right thing *(prudence)*, for the right reasons *(justice)*, often requires *courage*, and always requires not acting out *(temperance, soundness of mind)*.

These virtues are not a product of wishful thinking. On the contrary, they have been studied and applied throughout the ages because, and only because, of their "rightness," their efficacy and their track record as best practices.

The virtues integrate doing things right with doing the right things. The virtues let us do the right things right, which means doing things the right way for the right reasons. In short, the virtues constitute best practices for living a highly effective human life.

A life of virtue is a life that distinguishes itself as human in its personhood, its freedom, its creativity, its truthfulness, its beauty, its integrity, its happiness, and its ability to manifest "response-able" competencies of leadership and followership on a fairly regular basis.

As disciplines of response-ability, leadership and followership depend on these virtues to stay in reality. To be virtuous, powerful, and competent consists in large part in knowing what and who to follow and how to lead and comport oneself response-ably in a given situation.

Again, the virtues are not ideas. They are practices that must be learned. As practices they can be developed only through practicing them. The virtues constitute the basis for rock-solid practical thinking that is driven by a desire to achieve bottom-line practical results.

The practicality of the virtues manifests itself everywhere on earth; wherever they are put to use, they have been shown to work. It is in no way restricted to the West. One need only look at the great tales, myths, and teachings of the great cultures, traditions that have survived and flourished with dignity all over the planet.

Learning to practice followership through the virtues is fundamental to our safety and sanity as human beings.

To follow is to do the next right thing. This often requires distinguishing doing what is called for (doing the right things) from doing what you are told (doing things right).

The virtue of followership always requires learning to "do first things first and second things not at all," the point being that to do second things first is to lose sight of the goal. To do second things first is the essence of what it means to be misled. It is for followership to degenerate into followership, that is, to diminish itself and languish in a type of living that simply leads elsewhere.

Hence following, like leading, is a free act of surrendering and acting in accord with what is being called for in a given situation. This requires insight, forethought, physical and mental discipline, and the ability to put that understanding into action.

Thus, followership tends to be a mentoring or mimetic situation in which the followers learn to *think* like the leader—who does not think for them but lets their thinking and learning manifest itself in and through the way they respond to situations. Followers manifest leadership the way the dancers manifest the dance.

Hence, the leadership-followership relation is a partnership of reciprocal following. It is like a conversation where leader and follower both are learning about the law of the situation. And like any conversation, leadership and followership can move from person to person as the dialogue twists and turns.

Followership, like leadership, needs to stay fresh, and open to the newness of things. It needs to dwell in and manifest the novelty of a situation as a moral imperative. It does this through its responses. This is a world brought forth through response-able action of doing first things first and second things not at all.

In this sense, followership, like leadership, points us to the essence of what it means to be human. It points out our need to follow things by taking responsible-able attitudes toward them. Depending on the situation, and what is being called for, a response-able attitude could be one of prayer, speculation, wonder, sympathy, planning, implementing, laughing, sharing, and so on.

The difference between followers and leaders is that followers need leaders to help them follow what leaders themselves are following. This relationship takes the form of a shared response-ability to a shared calling. Both find each other in a true fellowship *to create the world responsibly.*

Followership, like leadership, is a vocation. Leadership teaches the way by sharing and co-creating a path for both to follow.

All of this implies that the human situation is more than a cipher. On the contrary, the world calls us to response-able action. It calls us to develop highly creative deeply moral solutions to our most pressing needs.

The authority to do this comes from the situations in which we find ourselves. The author is the leader who co-authors our response with followership. At the core of all of this is a prerequisite of sanity, soundness of mind—what the ancients called Sophrosyne or Temperance.

The heart of followership is the call for a sane, imaginative, normal, and humane response to "do first things first and second things not at all." True followership enacts a form of practical wisdom; false followership and the leadership it engenders act out bias, ignorance, and error, to the detriment of all.

Followership is a basic mode of human existence. It is a moral practice

- Requiring discipline and discrimination
- Using the same thinking as leadership
- Needing guidance to develop a response-able attitude to things

It is an ongoing process of learning to do first things first by

- Questioning leadership
- Giving leadership a sense of traction and tools for discovery
- Keeping leaders on purpose by sharing their ignorance with them
- Continually training in the virtues to avoid devolving into fallowness

Fallowness leads to a form of intemperate, toxic leadership that disempowers our ability to act and think in a humane manner. It is everything followership is not.

Followership is a reciprocal partnership of ethical response-abilities. This partnership is as ancient as it is new. Examples of it abound in the great literatures and wisdom traditions of China and India, and the aboriginal myths of Africa, Australia and the Native Peoples of North and South America.

As it is written in the *I Ching*, "To lead others, a person must first know what it is to follow and then seek willing agreement rather than coercion or trickery. The cause must be just, both when we lead and when we follow others, if the outcome is to be successful."

Three Perspectives on Followership

Jon P. Howell
María J. Méndez

S everal important forces are operating in organizations today that cause people to assume a followership role. These forces can be viewed as responses to an implied exchange with the leader (for example, exchanging loyalty for security or performance for rewards) or to a lack of willingness or capability to assume a leadership role.[1] In this chapter, we hope to contribute to the understanding of this important role by offering three perspectives on followership. Each perspective reflects a somewhat different role orientation on the part of the follower. We believe that the three perspectives offer value to researchers and organizational practitioners in several ways. First, they may help organize the gradually expanding research literature on followership by clarifying the different roles followers play in organizations. Followers may work closely or at a distance from their leaders, with varying amounts of interaction and independence in determining their own actions. The perspectives described here reflect different leader-follower relationships found in the literature and in organizations. Second, the three perspectives described here may clarify why some followers have trouble adjusting to new leaders and may help followers prepare for their roles vis-à-vis specific leaders. A leader's expectations for a follower may not match the follower's initial perceptions of his or her role, creating dissonance and possible conflict. A shared understanding of different perspectives of followership may provide grounds for early discussions to help address these potential problems. Third, the different perspectives are the basis for research questions and issues that can be subjected to empirical research to add to our knowledge of followership in organizations. The issues of person-job and person-organization fit, change in organizations, career mobility, and individual and group effectiveness are all affected by the different followership perspectives described here and are important for organizations and employees today.

Individuals' *role orientations* refer to how they conceptualize their duties and responsibilities in their organizational positions. This role orientation is influenced by communications and expectations from others and by the individual's self-expectations. Most adults in developed societies have experienced an extended period of training and socialization in assuming organizational roles, resulting in specific perceptions and cognitions regarding their position.[2] Studies of employees in a variety of occupations show that how people define their role importantly affects how they spend their time and effort as well as the form of their interactions with others.[3] Most of the literature on followership rejects a subservient role for followers as inappropriate for organizations today, although it is likely that some leaders still tacitly reward this behavior in followers.[4] Most experts view followership as an active role that complements the leader's role in achieving results. The role orientations described here address this active role in different ways, and each has the potential to produce effective or ineffective leader-follower interactions and successful or unsuccessful performance.

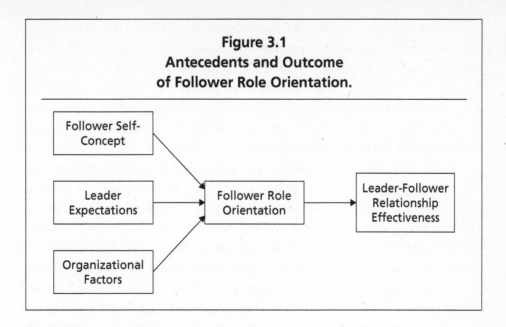

**Figure 3.1
Antecedents and Outcome
of Follower Role Orientation.**

Follower Self-Concept

Leader Expectations

Organizational Factors

Follower Role Orientation

Leader-Follower Relationship Effectiveness

In this chapter, we first describe each type of follower role orientation and how it can contribute to effectiveness or ineffectiveness in the leader-follower relationship. We then describe antecedents of each role orientation, including the follower's self-concept or identity (how the follower views himself or herself), the leader's expectations (which significantly shape the follower's role behavior), and the organizational context (including structural and interpersonal factors that encourage or constrain the follower's behavior). Our general model is shown in Figure 3.1. The chapter concludes with a discussion of several research questions and organizational issues for future research on followership.

FOLLOWERSHIP AS AN INTERACTIVE ROLE

The first role orientation views followership as an interactive role that may complement and support the leadership role. In its most effective form, this role orientation is equivalent to leadership in importance for achieving group and organizational goals. We know that leaders cannot exist without followers and that most of the work in organizations is done by followers.[5] Effective followers often forgo rewards like money, status, and fame that accrue to leaders and instead find meaning in working with their leader to achieve worthwhile goals. Howell and Shamir recently noted that followers often fulfill an "active role in constructing the leadership relationship, empowering the leader and influencing his or her behavior, and ultimately determining the consequences of the leadership relationship."[6] This type of interaction between leaders and followers is based on cooperation and mutual influence rather than obedience.[7] Both parties have responsibilities to exercise their power for the benefit of their relationship and their group's or organization's performance.

The following are effective followership behaviors that fit this role orientation: (1) demonstrating job knowledge and competence at work tasks; (2) building collaborative and supportive relationships with coworkers and the leader; (3) defending and supporting the leader in front of others; (4) exerting influence on the leader in a confident and unemotional manner to help the leader avoid costly mistakes; (5) demonstrating proper comportment for the organization (including proper speech, dress, etiquette); (6) showing a concern for performance as well as a supportive friendly atmosphere; and (7) showing a willingness to participate in necessary organizational changes.[8] These behaviors describe followers who are engaged with their leaders to actively cooperate in achieving organizational goals and are represented in much of the existing literature on followership.[9]

Other forms of followership as an interactive role are often less effective. Kelley described one type of ineffective follower who interacts frequently with his leader. He labeled these followers "sheep" or "yes-people" who rely on the leader to do their thinking. They attach themselves to their leader and go along with whatever the leader decides. Their motivation is often calculative, to secure desired rewards from the leader or to satisfy their need for safety or security in a threatening environment. They yield to the leader's judgment and "know their place." They tend to say what the leader wants to hear and withhold important information that the leader may dislike. In some cultures and organizations, this style of followership is encouraged and rewarded, although it can have dire consequences when important risks, obstacles, and alternatives are overlooked by the leader.[10]

Another type of interactive follower who is ineffective is the political gamesman, who spends his time and effort interacting with leaders to monitor organizational trends and adjusting his behavior and communication to fit in with the dominant flow of events. These individuals carry out orders exactly, even if they are aware of improvements that could be made, and maintain a paper trail to protect themselves if things go wrong. They judiciously avoid disagreeing with powerful individuals and constantly try to manipulate the system for their own benefit.[11] Collinson described a similar type of interactive follower as the "upwardly mobile knowledge worker" who treats every interaction as a means to further his or her own career.[12] These followers offer little to the leader-follower relationship, and they often consume organizational resources in their political maneuvering and ingratiating behaviors toward powerful persons.

Shamir described a third type of interactive follower who may be ineffective. This individual lacks a sense of personal identity and seeks to establish an identity in a close relationship with another person (often a leader) or a group, organization, or social movement. Much as children identify with their parents or sports fans identify with a star athlete, individuals build a sense of esteem and power through interactions with powerful individuals or groups.[13] These individuals may follow a leader who represents a group they identify with, as is true of the followers of Osama bin Laden. The leader and the group provide order and meaning for followers, who often actively defend the leader because he or she represents their image of an ideal person. This type of followership can become ineffective when followers overlook unethical behavior by the leader or the organization to preserve their self-image. In an extreme form, these individuals may become fanatics and completely suspend their own judgment. In this case, followers may carry out horrible acts to preserve their relationship with the leader and group, as occurred with the followers of Charles Manson or Jim Jones.

Antecedents of an Interactive Role Orientation

Many factors can be important antecedents of an interactive role orientation by followers. One follower characteristic that likely encourages an interactive supportive role orientation is what Brewer and Gardner refer to as a *relational self-concept* by followers.[14] A relational self-concept implies that followers see themselves primarily as acting out roles in relation to significant others. Their self-worth is often heavily dependent on their behavior in these roles and is directly related to appraisals of them by the other person in the relationship.[15] In the most effective form of this interactive role orientation, followers are motivated to enhance their relationship partner's well-being and both parties derive mutual benefits from the relationship.[16] We expect that followers with a healthy relational self-concept will tend to view their followership role as strongly interactive and supportive of the leader, and they will be especially effective at these interactive followership roles.

However, followers who seek personal benefits or safety or who lack a strong personal identity may adopt an interactive role orientation with the leader with other motives in mind. If followers view the interactive relationship as solely instrumental for obtaining personal benefits, then their interaction with the leader is designed to exploit the organization and its constituents. We do not view this type of relationship as truly reflective of a relational self-concept, even though these individuals may actively support and defend the leader. Their underlying self-concept is probably highly individualized (described in the following section), and their support for the leader will likely last only until another relationship promises higher personal rewards. If followers view the interactive relationship as providing safety, security, or personal identity, then they likely do have a true relational self-concept. However, these motives may result in highly dependent followers who become unquestioning disciples of the leader or even fanatics who will do anything the leader asks of them. Tragic consequences can result when followers suspend their own ethical judgment.

Research by Eden and his colleagues clearly shows the importance of *leader expectations* for follower role performance and behavior.[17] Leaders who have a relational self-concept will likely expect and appreciate followers who share the same identity. Shared relational identities will facilitate frequent interaction as well as shared understandings and sense making. Leaders with relational self-concepts tend to be supportive and participative with followers, and expect the same from the follower.[18] Leaders who have an interactive supportive role orientation with their own superiors will model these behaviors for their followers to emulate.[19] Each of these leadership factors will tend to shape the followers' role orientation toward an interactive and supportive perspective with the leader. Some leaders may view their relationship with followers and others as a source for personal benefit, and they will likely model and encourage a relational orientation in their followers. They may interact with followers to conspire and maximize their joint personal gains, as occurred with Enron. These relationships can clearly damage people and organizations.

Contextual factors such as task requirements that necessitate a high degree of leader-follower interaction will likely elicit an interactive role orientation in both leaders and followers. Reward systems that encourage cooperative efforts between leaders and individual followers will also facilitate an interactive role.

Mentoring programs are also likely to encourage mutually supportive behaviors between leaders and followers. These contextual factors encourage interactive and supportive follower role orientations to ensure the accomplishment of tasks, the receipt of adequate rewards, and the continued development of followers. However, if reward systems encourage adventuring for personal gain with little or no concern for others outside the leader-follower relationship, an interactive role orientation may be detrimental to the organization. Both leader and follower motives and reward systems must be consistent with legitimate organizational goals for an interactive role orientation between leaders and followers to benefit the organization and its people.

FOLLOWERSHIP AS AN INDEPENDENT ROLE

A second role orientation reflects a trend for followers to act more independently of their leaders than in the past. This trend probably results from increases in the education and training of the workforce, employees' desire to be more self-determining in their work, and leaner organizations with fewer middle managers. These factors can create constructive and nonconstructive situations for organizations. A constructive result has been the creation of follower substitutes for leadership that actually take the place of specific behaviors previously carried out by hierarchical leaders.[20] When leadership substitutes exist, leaders can focus on other tasks that often go unattended, such as follower development, advocacy, and obtaining resources. Several follower-based substitutes for leadership are described here.

One example of a follower substitute for leadership is a high degree of follower ability, experience, training, and job knowledge. When employees have extensive training and experience, they can provide their own self-direction and solve work problems on their own without reliance on their formal leader. This is evident in employees in high-stress occupations, such as pilots who land jet fighters on nuclear aircraft carriers, and air traffic controllers at international airports. Researchers found that directive leadership was relatively unimportant compared to the extensive experience and continuous training required in these occupations. They noted that "in the white heat of danger, when the whole system threatens to collapse," it is the individual's competence and cooperation among colleagues that is essential.[21] These individuals are trained extensively and daily to redirect operations or bring them to an abrupt halt. This may involve ignoring directions from managers who are not on the front line of action. Followers gain relevant ability and job knowledge from formal training and informal experiences, and these follower characteristics can substitute for a leader's directive leadership.[22]

Another example, which is becoming increasingly common in developed countries, occurs with employees who have extensive professional education. These employees can often perform their work assignments without relying on technical guidance from their hierarchical superiors. Their education often includes a strong socialization component, instilling in them a desire for autonomous, self-controlling behavior and the tendency to look to their professional colleagues for support and recognition. This often occurs with university professors who are highly educated and tenured. These individuals often view their university as a place to practice their teaching and research skills with little interference by administrators. They work with and obtain feedback from colleagues, they read academic journals for up-to-date information on their field, and they derive intrinsic satisfaction from their publications and recognition at academic conferences. Similar tendencies exist in firms that provide consulting and accounting services. In these instances, professional education and socialization can replace or substitute for a leader's direction and supportive behavior.[23]

Employee self-management programs may also develop follower substitutes for leadership. These programs encourage followers to set challenging but realistic work goals on their own, to control their work environment, and to self-evaluate and reinforce their own performance. They may also include developing collegial and mentoring relationships that can increase their potential to be self-regulating for high performance and create supportive relationships that help followers through rough times. Follower self-management may therefore substitute for hierarchical leaders' directive and supportive behaviors.[24]

A final example of a follower substitute occurred in a study of engineering personnel and the number of years the followers had worked for their leader. A large number of years with the leader allowed followers to share the same mental maps as their leader and resulted in their taking the same decisions and actions that the leader would have taken. Years with the supervisor may simply be a useful way of measuring a follower's ability, confidence, or simply "job savvy," which substituted for the leader's directive leadership.[25]

A nonconstructive form of the independent role orientation can occur when follower-based neutralizers of leadership develop in organizations. Neutralizers interfere with a leader's attempts to influence followers. Unlike substitutes, however, neutralizers do not provide an alternate source of guidance or good feelings to replace the leader's influence. Followers may possess certain characteristics or create situations that essentially neutralize a leader's influence, resulting in an "influence vacuum" that may have serious negative consequences for the organization. This can occur when followers' personalities reflect a high need for independence, and they believe (erroneously) that they are more capable than the leader to make job-related decisions. This situation may also occur if the follower has become alienated from the leader or the organization due to unfair treatment in the follower's eyes. Followers may belong to unions or work under civil service policies that remove the leader's control over important organizational rewards such as salary level or promotions. Several of these situations can be exacerbated when followers work at a physical distance from the leader, such as telecommuters or service workers. In these situations, leaders' attempts to influence followers are easily frustrated, and if followers do not possess the needed abilities to work effectively on their own, the organization and its clients suffer.

Antecedents of an Independent Role Orientation

Follower-based substitutes for leadership imply a predominantly individualized orientation in the follower's self-concept.[26] An *individualized self-concept* emphasizes personal characteristics that distinguish the individual from other individuals. Follower-based substitutes, such as a high level of ability, experience, training and knowledge, extensive professional education, skills at self-management, or years with the leader, imply personal attributes and learning by followers that may significantly differentiate them from other followers or the leader. These personal factors also are likely to make followers more effective at working on their own. Comparisons with others and with possible future selves (what one hopes to become or fears to become) represent important internal motivators for a person with an individualized self-concept. We expect that followers who have predominantly individualized self-concepts will tend to adopt a relatively independent role orientation in dealing with their leader. If they also possess the skills and abilities described earlier, they will likely enact leadership substitutes that contribute to effective organizational performance. However, many followers do not possess these skills and abilities, but they may view themselves as independent operators or even as rebels who are alienated from the organization. For these followers, an independent role orientation may result in leadership neutralizers that can have deleterious consequences for the organization.

Leader expectations that followers will act independently and competently without regular guidance from the leader are common among professionals and highly trained service workers. Further, the increasing importance of leaders' boundary spanning duties means they are less available to supervise and guide follower behavior on a regular basis.[27] Leaders in these situations likely have an independent role orientation themselves and expect their followers to have the same. Conversely, if a leader does not enact an independent role orientation with his or her own leader, then that individual is unlikely to expect it from his or her followers. Here followers are more likely to fulfill an interactive and perhaps dependent role with the leader.

Organizational programs for self-management, job enrichment, emergency training, and computer-based guidance and feedback are all *contextual factors* that encourage followers to act independently and competently without regular supervision by the leader. Organizational strategies that include reducing the number of middle managers result in wide spans of control that necessitate more independent action by followers. These contextual factors promote an independent role orientation by followers to guide their own behavior and to seek advice and support from colleagues and coworkers rather than the hierarchical leader. These programs thus enact substitutes for leadership in organizations.[28] However, if the organizational context includes simple jobs, close control by hierarchical superiors, and operating information that is available only to management, it will not encourage an independent role orientation by followers. This may result in either a highly subservient interactive role orientation, or resentment and a possible independent rebellious orientation that can have major negative consequences.

FOLLOWERSHIP AS A SHIFTING ROLE

A third followership role orientation reflects the need to alternate between the leadership and followership roles that many individuals face in current organizations. Virtually all individuals spend some time as followers. Indeed, leaders in hierarchical organizations need to report to someone. However, shifting roles is especially common and challenging in current flexible organizations that rely on team-based work structures.[29] Members within these teams usually have complementary knowledge and professional experience. Through the integration of these diverse capacities, teams can often achieve higher performance.[30] Leadership in this type of organization is explained by Rost as a complex influence process in which all team members interact toward the attainment of a common goal.[31] Leadership tends to be distributed among the team members and is more flexible and dynamic. Individuals are expected to adapt themselves to the team leadership structure by leading or following, and their role is often temporal and dependent on the requirements of a particular project or task.[32] Burke, Fiore, and Salas described this as a situation in which people enact "fluid leadership roles."[33] Not only are team members challenged to enact followership and leadership roles effectively, but they also must be able to switch between the roles. In such an environment, team members with a high tolerance for ambiguity are well fit to accept leadership from different people and enact this fluid role effectively.

Close coordination among team members is extremely challenging and important in these dynamic organizations. Clearly defined roles and extensive communication are essential to this coordination within the fluid leadership structure. A curious example is that of the Orpheus Chamber Orchestra, in which musicians hold the leadership roles, as there is no permanent conductor. They rotate through leadership and followership roles at different points as required by the musical piece. A clear division of the tasks ensures that all musicians understand their own and others' responsibilities for a particular performance, resulting in overall coordination.[34]

Different followership behaviors that are consistent with this role include (1) monitoring and interpreting the environment to identify needed changes in the team; (2) actively participating in the group's decision making while taking responsibility for achieving its goals; (3) challenging the team when necessary and maintaining a critical perspective on the group's decisions; (4) role-modeling the team member prototype by observing and adhering to the norms of the group; and (5) maintaining an empathic relationship with rich communication among teammates.[35]

The shifting follower role orientation may be ineffective when the follower fails to challenge the group. Often highly cohesive groups exert high pressure toward conformity in individuals who challenge the collective norms or decisions.

This pressure leads to self-censorship, thus decreasing critical thinking. When group members yield to this pressure, they may jeopardize the common objectives. This group dynamic, termed *groupthink,* has been responsible for major failures both in the corporate world and in government.[36] Such was the case in the tragedies of *Columbia* and *Challenger,* both NASA space shuttles that ended in disaster. A main factor for failure in both of these cases resulted from the self-censorship of both managers and engineers involved in the project. Fear of separation and a generalized illusion of invulnerability led to interpreting signals of danger as "acceptable risks."[37] Constructive conflict through team members' mutual challenge is an element essential to performing a richer analysis of the different alternatives and making more effective decisions. However, these natural disagreements may easily turn into interpersonal conflict leading to dysfunctional team dynamics. Handling conflict effectively requires active effort from all team members to communicate, to listen with empathy, and to clearly allocate tasks and accountability among team members.[38]

In their analysis of collaboration in teamwork, LaFasto and Larson describe another ineffective form of the shifting role orientation.[39] It occurs with people who engage in teamwork because they seek in the relationship a personal benefit, but do not have a real interest in collaborating with other team members to attain common goals. This is also the case of social loafers, who obtain their proportion of benefits from the team without contributing their proportional share of the work.[40] These individuals prioritize their personal interests over the interests of the team and therefore decrease the effectiveness of the team.

Antecedents of a Shifting Role Orientation

A shifting followership role orientation corresponds to individuals who prioritize the goals of the group over their own interests and accept the leadership or followership role the group needs them to play. Individuals who internalize the achievements of their team and derive their self-worth from these achievements are motivated to take actions that benefit the team, and to accept an evolving team leadership model. This role orientation corresponds to an individual's social identity or *collective self-concept.* This social identity reflects an individual's self-perception that involves identifying with the group member prototype. We believe that these individuals will value a dynamic and flexible leadership structure as long as it increases the effectiveness of the team. They will tend to perceive their role in the team as dynamic and flexible—a shifting role. However, a capable individual with a strong collective orientation may refrain from playing a leadership role if there are countervailing external norms (for example, if external norms discourage attracting attention to oneself).[41] In this situation, the individual's reticence may jeopardize the group's effectiveness.

Team expectations are reflected in the team's norms and objectives. When team norms include a shifting role orientation for members, team members tend to adopt this orientation as a part of their collective identity. The team's assignation of leadership roles is usually influenced by the team's transactive memory, which involves a shared notion of who in the team is an expert on what area.[42] A team with inaccurate transactive memory may expect a member to perform a particular leadership role when another member is more capable. In this case, team expectations may damage the team's performance. A hierarchical *leader's expectations* are shown in the leader's training activities for team members and use of social reinforcement when different team members effectively shift roles. Administering team-based rewards for effective performance also reinforces the team's leadership-followership role structure.

A rapid and constantly changing environment and a high reliance on teamwork are *contextual factors* that we believe will influence the tendency of the followers to adopt a shifting role orientation. For instance, current fast-paced markets that depend on frequent decision making tend to require flexible organizational structures and teamwork that are adapted to the situation. In this type of environment, professionals are expected to adapt to new leadership structures frequently and to effectively shift projects and roles. In addition, tasks that are highly interdependent and complex and that require high levels of creativity will benefit from the use of teamwork with shared and distributed leadership structures that require followers to shift roles as needed.[43]

CONCLUSION AND ISSUES FOR FURTHER RESEARCH

The different follower role orientations described in this chapter imply different patterns of behavior by leaders and followers. These behavior patterns define the leader-follower relationship and suggest an association between followers' self-concepts, role orientations, and effective followership behavior. Viewing followership from an interactive role orientation that supports the leader is currently a major research perspective. We have suggested that under certain conditions, this type of role orientation may be counterproductive, depending on the organizational rewards and motives of the leaders and followers involved. Viewing followership from an independent role orientation that can substitute for (or neutralize) leadership has received little attention in the literature. This is in spite of numerous organizational trends, which indicate that followers are expected to enact various types of substitutes on the job. In addition, every practicing manager is aware of some followers who have resisted leader efforts to influence them, which can at least partially neutralize their leadership effectiveness. Enacting follower-based leadership substitutes and addressing neutralizers warrant attention by followership scholars, as recent researchers have concluded that they are important for effective organizational functioning.[44] Viewing followership from a shifting role orientation has also received little attention by followership researchers, in spite of the increased popularity of self-managed and empowered teams in organizations. The definitions of leader and follower are especially blurred in these team situations, and effective rotation between leader and follower roles deserves more efforts by leadership and followership scholars. We believe that mutually agreeable and effective working relationships require role orientations that fit leaders' expectations, followers' identities, and the situational context.

Regarding the self-concepts or identities of leaders and followers, we expect that when these identities are aligned (that is, both are predominantly relational, individualized, or collective), they should facilitate better communication, tacit understanding, and shared expectations. Although Lord and Brown imply that leaders can change or influence followers' self-concepts, Collinson argues that because self-concepts are "socially constructed, multiple, and shifting" in character, the impact of leaders is highly uncertain.[45] Because self-concepts of leaders and followers are important determinants of follower role orientations, an important question for future research is how alignment between leaders' and followers' self-concepts can be facilitated.

A related issue is whether followers can adapt their self-concepts to elicit a proper role orientation that fits the situation. Can a follower with an individualized orientation shift to a collective orientation when assigned to a self-managed team? Can a follower with a relational orientation shift to an individualized orientation and enact an individualized substitute for leadership (such as self-management) when needed? Another question is whether the "best fitting" role orientation is necessarily the most effective role orientation.

A leader's expectations and behaviors are one set of factors affecting followers' role orientation, but the followers' self-concepts and motives and the organizational context are also likely to influence how followers view their role. Followership researchers must address themselves to increasing our understanding of these role orientations, the factors that affect them, the behaviors they imply, and how they interact with organizational situations to produce effective leader and follower performance.

chapter FOUR

A New Leadership-Followership Paradigm

Ernest L. Stech

The usual ways of looking at leaders and followers are no longer useful. In a world of instant communication, rapid technological advance, and globalization, the traditional view of the leader as commander, chief, director, or boss simply does not permit organizations, nations, communities, or associations to adapt to their ever-changing environments. The time has come to embrace a different and more effective way of dealing with leadership and followership. Two paradigms have dominated the ways in which practitioners, scholars, writers, and trainers have looked at leaders and leadership. They were appropriate to a world in which communication was via surface mail or telephone, the pace of innovation was slower, and organizations operated on a national scale. A new paradigm is available.

A paradigm is a way of thinking and operating. It is a system of concepts, assumptions, values, and methods or techniques and is the way in which members of the community who share the paradigm view reality. Persons operating within the paradigm may be and usually are unaware of the concepts, assumptions, values, and methods as they engage in their work. Unless made explicit, the nature of the paradigm is rarely understood or acknowledged. It is simply accepted as the only way to operate.[1]

A leadership-followership paradigm ought, first, to address both leadership and followership at the same time and, second, to be applicable to a wide range of leadership and followership contexts, not just in hierarchical bureaucratic organizations. Followership is inherent in any leadership scheme but is rarely if ever made explicit. Contexts beyond the traditional organization include voluntary associations, elected bodies, neighborhoods and communities, social movements, and occupations and professions.[2] In those contexts leadership occurs among peers in flat nonhierarchical entities.

I propose a paradigm shift in which leadership and followership are considered together in ways that address the contemporary challenge of operating within a rapidly changing and even chaotic world. The two traditional paradigms described below focused primarily on leaders and leadership, with rare and scant consideration of followers or followership. However, every perspective, model, or theory of leadership is part of an overarching leadership paradigm and has in it an implicit conception of followership. The proposed paradigm directly addresses both leadership and followership.

The next sections present and discuss the concepts, assumptions, values, and methods involved in each paradigm and briefly describe limitations. The *leader-follower paradigm* focuses on the individual leader and follower. The *organizational position paradigm* looks at the location of individuals in a hierarchy and can also be considered a superior-subordinate or manager-employee paradigm. The proposed third option, the *leadership-followership state paradigm*, represents a new and different way of looking at leadership and followership.

THE LEADER-FOLLOWER PARADIGM

The leader-follower paradigm ranges historically from Homer's *Iliad* to such contemporary works as the autobiographical description and prescription on leadership from Rudolph Giuliani, the former mayor of New York City.[3] This is a pervasive paradigm in "commonsense" thinking about leadership. It focuses on the leader as an individual exemplar or hero.

Concepts

The fundamental concepts in this paradigm are the leader and follower, with the addition of the idea of traits. A person is identified as the leader in a given situation, and other persons are followers. The prototypes are well known from literature and the popular media. They are, in fact, representatives of an archetype: the strong, quiet, and effective person who takes control of events and other people. This archetype is close to that of the "warrior" in Carol Pearson's typology.[4] The warrior is characterized as having goals of strength and effectiveness; as learning through competition, achievement, and motivation; and as dealing with relationships by molding others to please himself or herself. Emotionally the warrior is controlled and represses feelings in order to achieve and prevail. The archetypal warrior's relationships with others involve shaping followers to satisfy the leader's personal needs and values. The follower is someone who can be formed and sculpted.

Assumptions

An underlying assumption in this paradigm is that there are some people who are destined to be leaders. They emerge from the crowd and are able to command respect. They are knowledgeable, competent, and strong. These leaders are "born to command." They rise through the ranks by sheer will to become leaders. This is the "Great Person" model of leadership and is represented by the hundreds if not thousands of biographies of kings, generals, admirals, presidents, and prime ministers. A second assumption is that there are traits that identify leaders and potential leaders. Northouse summarized his review of trait approach studies with five characteristics: intelligence, self-confidence, determination, integrity, and sociability.[5] In the earliest studies, it was assumed that individuals were born with these important traits. Kirkpatrick and Locke believed that important traits may be inborn or developed through early life or education.[6]

Values

In this paradigm, a leader is expected to exhibit strength. In earlier times, particularly in the industrial, railroad, and construction worlds, physical strength was needed so that the leader could dominate followers. Today it implies a psychic and mental strength, the ability to withstand difficulties and crises and to be able to bring to bear knowledge and expertise. Associated with strength is the value of discipline. The effective natural leader remains focused on a specific mission or goal, working tirelessly toward it. Distractions are brushed aside. The leader remains true to her or his values and beliefs.

Conversely, the "natural follower" values loyalty and conformity. An insight into the characteristics of the follower in the leader-follower paradigm can be gleaned from the synonyms for *follower* found in thesauri: *assistant, attendant, henchman, minion, lackey, toady, servant, page, squire, sidekick, hanger-on, supporter, believer, companion,* and *escort.* There exists a larger pool of synonyms for the verb *to follow: be inferior, subordinate, subservient, dependent, acquiescent, second rank, supporting role, conforming, pliant, obedient, passive, submissive, loyal, devoted, serve, pay homage, willing, go behind, go after, come behind, come after, tread on the heels of, disciplined,* and *in service.*[7] There is a clear connotation in these lists of persons who are lesser beings.

Techniques

In the leader-follower paradigm, the leader is strong and powerful, the follower malleable and passive. Therefore, leadership is to command, direct, and control. These are the methods traditionally used in military and quasi-military organizations and in industrial situations. There is no or little need for training and development of leaders because the strong will emerge in the heat of competition. The less strong will fall by the wayside. An individual's right to lead will be dictated by his or her aggressiveness and ability.

Limitations

According to this paradigm, being a leader is inherent in certain people, whether through genetics or learning in early life. They will be leaders in any context or situation. In a more restricted version, they will be leaders in the appropriate context or situation. They cannot be denied. Similarly, being a follower is a personal trait. People who are followers are doomed to that status forever. They cannot escape being in a subordinate position. For these reasons, leaders cannot be trained or developed. They can be selected, either through the course of events while engaged in their work or through formal assessment methods.

THE LEADERSHIP-FOLLOWERSHIP ORGANIZATIONAL POSITION PARADIGM

Much of the research and application in the field of leadership has been devoted to individuals working in hierarchical organizations.[8] This has led to the ongoing debate over leadership versus management. Rost noted that a "school" of leadership had emerged from the 1930s on. In what Rost termed the industrial culture, "the scholars and practitioners in that culture could do no less than give the coveted and new concept of leadership a definition that equated it not with just management but with good management."[9] In this paradigm, a leader is anyone with a position of authority within a formal organization.

Concepts

Fundamental to the leader-follower position paradigm is the concept of the formal, hierarchical, and bureaucratic organization that has division of labor, multiple levels of management, and written policies and procedures. The hierarchy is represented in the classic organization chart, and the bureaucracy can be seen in written documents, such as manuals and handbooks. Within the hierarchy, every manager has the authority to operate within his or her own unit but must report to someone in the next level above.

The result is a series of superior-subordinate relationships. However, it is common practice to refer to the superior as a leader and the subordinate as a follower. Much of the literature on leadership is based on this leader-follower relationship that is actually about superiors-subordinates.

Assumptions

A basic assumption underlying the organizational position paradigm is that some people are better suited to leadership than others. That superiority may result from more experience, better education, higher skill levels, greater seniority, or other criteria. However, individuals accede to positions of authority also as a result of assertiveness and aggressiveness combined with superior social and, sometimes, political skills. A leader, therefore, is someone who has achieved a position of authority through a combination of job and social skills.

The equivalent assumption with regard to followers or subordinates is that they somehow lack the experience, education, skills, seniority, or training to act effectively on their own initiative. Followers must be led; that is, they must be directed, supervised, controlled, and motivated in order to get them to accomplish their tasks. This assumption is rarely if ever stated, but it nevertheless represents the prevalent view of followers (subordinates) in organizations.

Values

Along with the basic concepts and underlying assumptions just described, the organizational position paradigm includes a set of values based on the requirements of a hierarchical and bureaucratic organization. For an organization to continue to function, it is necessary to ensure continuity. It is the role of the leader or superior to make sure that there is continuity. The leader should therefore exhibit loyalty to the organization and its mission and goals—if not to the organization as a whole, then at least to her or his part of the organization. In turn, the leader requires loyalty from followers. They should be dedicated and trustworthy.

Techniques

Persons operating in the organizational position paradigm use methods taught in business schools or university departments of educational leadership, public administration, health care administration, and similar programs. They consist of accounting and finance, marketing, human resources, quality control, planning and budgeting, and many others.

In addition, methods have been developed to deal specifically with the relationship of a superior to subordinates. These include Blake and Mouton's managerial grid, Fiedler's contingency model, Blanchard's situational approach, and Kouzes and Posner's leadership practices.[10]

Limitations

There are several difficulties inherent in the organizational position paradigm. One is that anyone operating from a position of authority in a hierarchy is also a subordinate and therefore subject to the authority of someone at a higher level. Every leader is also a follower. All the thousands of middle managers are indeed in the middle, leading subordinates but subject to the direction and whims of those above. Little attention has been paid in the literature to the necessity for a manager-leader to assume the role of subordinate-follower in relationship to people in higher echelons.

A major difficulty with the organizational position paradigm is that in many cases subordinates have expertise and knowledge beyond that available to the leader, who must rely on the competence of those followers. The traditional hierarchical organization was based on the assumption that the leader has all the knowledge and expertise needed to solve problems and deal with issues.

Furthermore, real organizations involve informal networks overlaid on the formal organization chart. Subordinates may be able to communicate with persons in other groups or departments, and in many cases they are required to do so as a function of their responsibilities.

There is an alternative to both the leader-follower and the organizational position paradigms, an alternative that is better suited to a world of rapid change and a world in which the values of teamwork and equality are primary. Both the leader-follower and leadership-followership organizational position paradigms have long histories and represent, as noted, versions and visions of leadership and followership that are ingrained in the minds of journalists, readers, practitioners, trainers, and scholars. A paradigm shift is needed, and it is the subject of the leadership-followership state paradigm described in the next section. That paradigm shift is heralded in the work of three prophets in the field of leadership: Joseph Rost, Margaret Wheatley, and Abraham Maslow.[11]

THE LEADERSHIP-FOLLOWERSHIP STATE PARADIGM

The basic premise behind the leadership-followership state paradigm is that both leadership and followership are states or conditions that can be occupied at various times by persons in working groups, teams, or organizations. The suffix *ship* has five dictionary definitions: (1) a state or condition (friendship); (2) an office, dignity, or profession (clerkship); (3) an art or skill (horsemanship); (4) something showing, exhibiting, or embodying a quality or state (township); (5) one entitled to a rank, title, or appellation (judgeship).[12] Any of the five definitions could be applied to leaders and leading, although the fifth would be a stretch. It seems unlikely that we will get to the point where someone will be designated "Her Leadership." The second definition has possibilities in that leadership may be or could become a profession, perhaps independent of management or administration, but such academic degrees or organizational positions do not currently exist. However, leadership could represent an art or skill, a meaning that has been used in the past as in the third definition, but to this point there seems to be little agreement on the exact nature of that art or skill aside from that of traditional "scientific" management.

Two somewhat related meanings, the first and fourth, are proposed for use here. Leadership could (1) connote a state or condition in which a person would find herself or himself or (2) imply that someone showed or exhibited leadership to others. The two meanings distinguish between an internal state or condition and an external appearance. In this chapter, leadership will be taken to mean a state or condition within an individual and, at the same time, the exhibition or embodiment of the quality or state of leadership in action. Similarly, followership is a state or condition or, again, the exhibition or embodiment of the quality or state of followership.

Concepts

If we say that leadership denotes a state or condition or the embodiment of a quality, it follows that an individual may or may not be in that state or condition or may or may not embody the quality at any given time. Rost noted this possibility in his definition of leadership: "(1) anyone can be a leader and/or follower; (2) followers persuade leaders and other followers, as do leaders; (3) leaders and followers may change places . . . in the relationship."[13] He specifically used the phrase "change places" rather than "change roles." From the present discussion, we can substitute "states" for "places." This gets away from the notion that a person either is or is not a leader. It also frees the subordinate or follower from being pinned in an inferior place for all time.

Leadership, in this sense, also distinguishes a state or condition or embodiment of a quality from a position or role in an organization or from a role. A manager may or may not be in a leadership state or condition at any point in his or her workday or career. Similarly, a manager may or may not embody the quality of leadership at any time.

Leadership, as defined by Rost,[14] is influence directed at one or more other persons without coercion and toward a common purpose. Followership, therefore, is the acceptance of influence from another person or persons without feeling coerced and toward what is perceived to be a common purpose. Coercion is used here in the sense of power, force, intimidation, or strong persuasion. It can be quite subtle. The feeling of being coerced may arise from the potential of being criticized or chastised or from the possibility of having certain rewards withheld, such a raises, better assignments, or preferred working times and places in a formal organization. At its worst, coercion occurs as bullying and harassment.

According to our definitions of leadership and followership—that is, as states, conditions, or embodiments—it is possible for someone who is not in a position of authority, not a manager or administrator, to lead others by influencing them. It is also possible for a person in a position of authority to lead, but that requires exerting the influence without the coercion that could exist as a result of having authority. Finally, it is possible to exert influence and to have someone accept it where both acts are the result of coercion, whether subtle or direct. The latter case is not leadership, but rather controlling, managing, administrating, or directing.

Assumptions

A basic assumption in the leadership-followership state paradigm is that expertise is diverse and distributed among the members of an organization, workgroup, or team. No one person possesses all the knowledge or skills needed to address an issue or problem. Thus the manager, administrator, or director cannot single-handedly work through to an outcome. Those persons, in positions of authority, must be willing to accept influence from subordinates. They must be willing to assume the condition of followership while a subordinate operates in the state of leadership. The subordinate leads the superior in such a case. Furthermore, the proposed paradigm allows for an individual in a position of authority also to be a subordinate and follower to others at a higher echelon in an organization, as well as at times to lead them. To complicate matters further, the required expertise shifts depending on the particular issue or problem being addressed and the stage of the process in which it is being addressed. For this reason almost any member of the organization, workgroup, or team has the potential for being in a leadership state at some point in the process of working through a program or project.

An additional assumption is that an organization, workgroup, or team is a social organization. This implies that individuals develop roles in addition to those assigned through job descriptions and organization charts. Furthermore, complex networks of relationships exist that are created by such factors as proximity and homophily.[15]

Finally, the leadership-followership state paradigm assumes that individuals are capable of self-motivation and self-direction.[16] Once given an overall purpose, people can understand their part in the process and will accept the responsibility for doing the work they need to do so that the overall effort can move forward. This is the assumption that people can and will operate as professionals if they are given the opportunity and freedom to do so.

Values

It follows from the assumptions that certain values obtain in the leadership-followership state paradigm. One of those values is that influence should be based on expertise, knowledge, and skill. The person who has the information, the methodology, or the insight is the person who should be believed and "followed." Similarly, an individual who has needed contacts with persons who are stakeholders or constituents may occupy that state of leadership at times. Conversely, there is little value attached to being in a position of authority and using that authority to influence through coercion, either subtle or explicit.

A related value has to do with the ability of individuals to self-assess their expertise, knowledge, and level of skill. This involves a belief in the maturity of individuals and their willingness to accept responsibility. Rather than having a superior decide whether or not someone is capable of making suggestions or carrying out a task, each person is expected to take on those kinds of responsibilities and be individually accountable. Further, each individual can request and expect to be "led" in a way that fits his or her self-defined needs.

Another major value is teamwork. To move forward in a project or program or for an entire organization, individuals need to work together toward a common purpose. Some individuals may have more influence through their expertise and knowledge regarding highly technical or core issues, but others are needed to lend their expertise and knowledge with regard to what might be considered mundane tasks. Teamwork also implies that the team members will regulate one another, so that if someone is delaying the work of the group, the people in the group will confront and, if necessary, help that person.

Techniques

Methods and practices in the leadership-followership state paradigm are more fluid and open ended than in the organizational position paradigm. In place of procedures, there are processes. A process may follow a general path but permits shifts and changes along the way. In place of specific goals or objectives, there are purposes and intents. Purposes and intents provide general guidance while allowing innovation along the way.

The key to an effective operation in the leadership-followership state paradigm is communication. Instead of communication down and occasionally up in a hierarchy, messages flow in every direction. This kind of communication is needed if the talents and expertise of individuals are to be applied to the problem or issue at hand. Suggestions, proposals, and answers can originate anywhere and must be capable of being put forward toward all the persons involved. In that way, improvements to the suggestions, proposals, and answers can be generated.

An important method in the leadership-followership state paradigm is ongoing training, education, and development for everyone in an organization, workgroup, or team. Changes occur rapidly in almost all aspects of modern society. Team members need to keep abreast of innovations. Attendance at workshops, seminars, and conferences is mandatory. Insights and knowledge obtained from such events must be communicated within the team or workgroup.

As opposed to practices in the leadership-followership paradigm, the techniques used by a superior, the individual invested with authority, in a formal organization have been those that direct, supervise, and coach subordinates, again with the assumption that people in lesser positions have lesser capabilities. Wheatley noted that metaphors for leaders in modern terms include gardeners, midwives, stewards, servants, missionaries, facilitators, and convenors.[17] These terms suggest that a manager-leader will keep everyone informed on key issues and criteria and use education and encouragement. Such labels are more consistent with the idea that leadership is a state that is occupied at times by a person in a position of authority but that others in the organization, workgroup, association, or other entity are capable of thinking, creating, innovating, planning, organizing, and executing, often with only minimal involvement by a superior.

The leadership-followership state paradigm can be visualized as follows: each person in a workgroup or team is represented by two small lights on a board: one blue, the other green. Whenever someone is in the leadership state, the blue light representing that person lights up. For someone in a followership state, the green light illuminates. Over time, there will be shifting of the lights from blue to green and back to blue depending on the activity of each individual. The result, if recorded, would be evidence of the process of state-shifting among the members of a workgroup or team.

Limitations

The major issue faced by the leadership-followership state paradigm is that it is at odds with the traditional leader-follower and leadership-followership organizational position paradigms. In the popular press and even in academic circles, leadership is associated with persons in positions of authority, and followership with people in subordinate positions. Whether they are writers, consultants, scholars, leadership development specialists, or persons currently in positions of authority, individuals operate within these two paradigms. These paradigms are part of the culture of the United States, Europe, and developing countries.

Within an entity such as an organization or association, the leadership-followership state paradigm faces difficulties because it appears to require individuals in positions of authority, the superiors and "bosses," to give up some of their authority and power.

A further issue is that the leadership-followership state paradigm results in a radically new and different way of looking at what is traditionally considered to be leader or leadership development. Those efforts are usually devoted to persons who are already in positions of authority or individuals who have been designated as potentially capable of assuming such positions. The leadership-followership state paradigm suggests that everyone in an organization, workgroup, or team ought to be exposed to "leadership" training. Such training would consist of ways to generate and present useful information or suggestions to other people in an organization, workgroup, or team.

Chaleff has proposed the development of "courageous followers."[18] In essence, Chaleff proposed educating and training subordinates or followers to act as leaders—that is, to occupy the leadership state, in certain situations and circumstances. Eventually, if the leadership-followership state paradigm takes hold in organizations and elsewhere, then there should be no need for some in a subordinate position to be "courageous," because her or his inputs will be not only solicited but expected.

Followership: An Outmoded Concept

Joseph Rost

The theme of this chapter is that followership as a concept and practice is out of tune with the twenty-first-century paradigmatic revolution evolving as we witness the world changing dramatically. Followership is discordant with the dominant melody being played in our culture and the culture of many (not all) nations throughout the world.

Conceptually, this is the easiest part of the follower problem to solve in leadership studies. But practically, it remains a difficult language problem for leadership scholars and practitioners, as it fits with the traditional and dominant leadership model. Followership is the issue discussed in the first part of this chapter.

The tougher issue is the concept of followers. The second section of this chapter addresses the problematic use of the word *followers*. The concept of followers is at the root of the problem, however one might want to frame the issues. Followers, as a concept, present modern scholars and practitioners of leadership with difficulties that are not easily resolved. In an attempt to be helpful, I present some ideas that will, I hope, contribute to several resolutions of this issue.

FOLLOWERSHIP

I have stated my views on followership in my book *Leadership for the Twenty-First Century* quite clearly.[1] I have read or seen little that would make me want to change my thinking since the book was published. As a result, the argument in this first section is much the same as that in my book, but with some updated approaches.

Words in the English language that end with the suffix *ship* usually define some kind of process that is going on. Examples are apprenticeship, workmanship, musicianship, dictatorship, relationship, partnership, artisanship, internship, citizenship, sponsorship, kinship, stewardship, receivership, and so on. These examples show that the word is composed of a *name for a person in a context* with the suffix *ship* added to the name. The words *leadership* and *followership* adhere to that pattern.

There are other *ship* words that refer to a thing: battleship, township, and others. These do not adhere to the process pattern, so we should exclude those words from our consideration.

If the suffix has any meaning or purpose, it must set off the name word from the *ship* word. Thus, follower is not the same as followership, apprentice is not the same as apprenticeship, dictator is not the same as dictatorship. There is no reason to add the suffix *ship* to these words if the two words mean the same thing. If we are going to take the concept of followership seriously, we have to assume and explicitly state that followership means something different from follower. The same is true with leader and leadership.

Generally speaking, then, followership is the process people use to follow. Followership is what followers do when they follow. What or who is being followed cannot be part of the definition, as the possibilities widely vary. The degree also varies. Some people follow up close and with lots of conviction. Others follow from afar and are minimally committed.

Followers are the people who follow. Followers are persons who have blood flowing through their veins. Followers as a group or considered individually do not make the process of followership. Followers may be involved in the process, but they are not the process.

These definitions are not very helpful without a definition of the verb *to follow*. The appendix to this chapter has some relevant definitions.

If followership is the process people use to follow, the logical outcome is that followership is a process distinct from leadership. Conversely, leadership is a distinct process from followership. The problem is that these conclusions are not coherent with the view that leadership is a relationship, a view to which I adhere.

Followership as a process distinct from leadership is what I have called the industrial understanding of leadership, the notion that a leader practices leadership when the leader does good management. In the industrial view, leadership is what the leader does. There is no room for followers in the industrial definition of leadership. It is all about what the leader accomplishes through good management.

Thus, using the industrial view of leadership, it is logical to set up a separate process for followers. If leaders do leadership, followers do followership.

There are any number of problems that result from acting on the industrial model of leadership and followership. I will mention only a few.

First, never the twain shall meet. The model sets up two separate processes that run in parallel lines (under the best scenario) or in different, more or less opposite directions (under the worst scenario). In an industrialized world, the leader sets the direction, and the followers move in that direction. This is inherent in the Gospel parable about the Good Shepherd. The shepherd knows the best way to go, and the sheep know who their shepherd is and automatically follow their shepherd's direction. Although this view was not expressed as a model of leadership in the New Testament—it was, after all, a model of faith—people in the industrial world used it as a leadership model to encourage sheeplike followers to do followership while the elite did leadership.

In the real world of the twenty-first century, many of the followers do not follow the leader's direction at all; they pick and choose, or their views of the leader's direction are not the same as the leader's view. When the leaders do leadership by deciding the direction, the people who are supposed to be doing followership may go in different directions.

Second, setting up this dichotomy of leadership and followership means that followers can never participate in the leadership decision-making process authentically. They can go through the motions; they can advise, discuss, give opinions, state facts and suggest consequences, make comments, or silently observe the process; but they cannot make the decision. That is the leader's prerogative. This scenario is not consistent with modern views of leadership in a democracy.

Third, the two processes create and maintain dysfunctional organizations, as we have seen throughout the industrial era. They are dysfunctional because authoritarian empires where one person (or several people) on the top of the hierarchical organizational chart is not willing to invest in the common good, much less achieve equity for the various constituencies of the organization.

Fourth, the dichotomy allows leadership to be defined as a better form of management—good management. So it creates confusion as to what leadership is and its distinction from management. Managers do management, and leaders do good management. But both managers and leaders do management. How confusing can we get?

In the end, followership is a consequence of industrial assumptions and actions based on top-down management and the Great Person view of leadership. In short, if leaders do leadership, it follows, as night follows day, that followers do followership.

In the postindustrial economy, which I think is increasingly evident in the twenty-first century, leadership must be defined as a relationship wherein leaders and followers collaborate because they are mutually invested in a direction and because they are inherently interdependent in a common process.

Followership is an outmoded concept that is dysfunctional and even destructive in a postindustrial world. Followership, as a concept, is out of touch with the world we now live in. It can only become more out of touch with the world of the next generation.

The cultural imperatives of the new century have made the word *followership* less acceptable in political, business, and commonplace communications. One rarely hears it used by news commentators or reads it in popular magazines or hears it said in professional (or other) conversations, meetings, or even speeches. So now may be a good time for leadership scholars and practitioners to join those who have found the word rather demeaning and inappropriate in their language and writing by not using it in leadership studies.

FOLLOWER

If leadership is a relationship, leaders and followers both do leadership. The postindustrial definition of leadership developed and explicated in my 1993 book is "an influence relationship among leaders and followers who intend real changes that reflect their mutual interests."[2]

After the book was published, I gave presentations around the country, and I received a lot of feedback from people about the word *followers* in the definition.

The feedback was unanimous and very clear. It can be summarized in one sentence. The word *followers* is inconsistent with the postindustrial understanding of leadership. People said, "The word *followers* is a very industrial term connoting subordination, submissiveness, passivity, lacking responsible judgment, and willingness to allow others to control their lives and activities. You, on the other hand, are expecting followers to be active, intelligent, influential, responsible, and involved. The word *followers* will never work in the postindustrial view of leadership because it comes with too much baggage, most of which contradicts the idea of collaboration in any meaningful sense."

Mind you, this criticism came after I tried to transform the word *followers* in the book and in the presentations after the book was published. I used the word "followers" about two hundred times in the book and used the word in a very positive way. I ennobled followers by including them in the leadership dynamic.

I had seriously considered not using the word *followers* in the book except when the context of the material was the industrial view of leadership (basically the first four chapters of the book). But I made the decision that because I was calling for a new understanding of leadership, tackling the follower problem was a bit too much for readers to accept.

After the consistent feedback I received, however, I concluded that my critics were absolutely correct. Followers, as the concept is ordinarily understood, does not connect with the postindustrial understanding of leadership. So, around 1994, I began using other words for followers and ended up choosing the word *collaborators*. Eventually I dropped the "postindustrial" modifier and used the term *collaborative leadership* for the new paradigm. But the book is still out there, and most people probably do not know that I have rethought the use of the word *followers*.

My most recent definition is as follows: collaborative leadership is an influence relationship among leaders and collaborators who intend significant changes that reflect their mutual interests. This definition includes three changes from the original one: (1) a change of title from "postindustrial" to "collaborative," (2) a change from "followers" to "collaborators," and (3) a change from "real changes" to "significant changes." Some people have suggested that we use the word *people*, as in "an influence relationship among people who intend." That really takes leaders out of leadership, so I have not been willing to do that yet. If other people want to promote that wording, more power to them.

So far, I have argued that followership is outdated and that the notion of followers is inconsistent with collaborative leadership. The idea of collaborators sounds more inclusive, active, involved, influential, and responsible, and would be a better word to use. If leaders and collaborators do leadership, there is no need for the separate process of followership.

Many leadership authors and practitioners tend to isolate themselves from the popular cultures of Western civilization. Presumably leadership experts in non-Western cultures do the same, but I do not have enough data to support that assertion. There is, to some extent, an assumption that paying attention to the waves—movements and messages—that engage popular cultures is not intellectually courant. It seems to me, however, that cultural phenomena deserve considerable attention in our discussion of followers and followership. For instance, the transformation of full-figured (fat) blue-collar workers to chorus-line, bare-butt stars of a musical review in *The Full Monty* makes for interesting revisionist thinking regarding followers and followership.

The 2006 motion picture about John Lennon (*The U.S. vs. John Lennon*) shows how significant his impact was on President Nixon, the FBI and CIA, and U.S. policy on war as a strategy to contain communism, with songs such as "Power to the People" and "Give Peace a Chance."

Power to the people is not a concept that fits neatly into the follower and followership models of leadership experts who write leadership books and give leadership seminars to Fortune 500 companies. If you want a revolution, Lennon sings, get on your feet and in the streets singing power to the people. Can you imagine that going over well at a seminar sponsored by General Electric or Microsoft, or at a papal-bishops conference at the Vatican?

Returning to the musical theater, *Les Misérables*, a musical version of the famous book, was wildly applauded with standing ovations every night in numerous cities and nations throughout the world. Ethnicity, nationality, skin color, gender, physical condition, sexual orientation, religious beliefs, wealth, power, and authority—none of these mattered. The show's finale, sung by the chorus, helps explain this phenomenal reception and provides some insight into a modern-day view of followers and their role in transformation:

Do you hear the people sing?
Lost in the valley of the night!
It is the music of a people
Who are climbing to the light
For the wretched of the earth
There is a flame that never dies.
Even the darkest night will end
And the sun will rise.
They will live again in freedom
In the garden of the Lord.
They will walk behind the plough share
They will put away the sword
The chain will be broken
And all men will have their reward.
Will you join in our crusade?
Who will be strong and stand with me?
Somewhere beyond the barricade
Is there a world you long to be?
Do you hear the people sing?
Say, do you hear the distant drums?
It is the future that they bring
When tomorrow comes!
Will you join in our crusade?
Who will be strong and stand with me?
Somewhere beyond the barricade
Is there a world you long to see?
Do you hear the people sing?
Say, do you hear the distant drums?
It is the future that they bring
When tomorrow comes
Tomorrow comes!

There are many other songs from our popular culture that make the same point: that there are all these people out there, not just in the United States but all over the world, obtaining messages from cultural icons stating that followers don't count anymore and that the whole idea of following is passé. We have been taught in the last twenty-five years or more that we have to stop following and begin to take action and be responsible for what is happening in our lives and in the world.

The popular movements in the world for the last twenty-five years or more don't preach followership or encourage people to be followers. Feminism, civil rights, gay liberation, diversity, and environmentalism call for people to take up the gauntlet and rise up and demand respect, equality, and economic development. Even the Catholic Church in Vatican II called on the people of God to be the church, not the hierarchy. What is important here is that these movements did not call for only leaders to do these things; rather, they called for the people to do them. They did not state that leaders were unimportant or unnecessary, but they did state that leaders alone could not do this important work. This is what is important about their legacy. All these movements redefined what is needed to be successful in transforming organizations, governments, and cultures. None of them called for leaders to do the hard work of designing the future. Rather, they repeatedly called for collaborators who were active, responsible, assertive, influential, and change-making people. That never has been our understanding of who followers are.

To be fair, there is a conservative movement in the world today that is calling for people to be obedient, to be faithful to old values and traditions, and to sacrifice for the causes of leaders. There is a cultural environment that says, "Don't ask questions, just do as I say." This movement clearly wants to reinstate the value of followers as a necessary element in our religious, civil, and economic lives. We can see this very clearly in the Catholic Church's repudiation of Vatican II and other Christian denominations' emphasis on Old Testament values and principles. President Bush has been increasingly instrumental in reinstating a Great Person view of leadership and the traditional follower role for other people. We don't know the outcome of this backlash of conservatism, but the good news is that there are millions of people fighting against it, millions of people who are singing "Power to the people!"

Finally, let me say that I know that there are some authors, such as Ira Chaleff and Robert Kelley among others, who have tried to transform the concept of followers by attempting to change how we define or understand followers.[3] I also tried to do that in 1991, but you can see that I have backed off from that approach. I don't think that such a redefinition of followers is possible in the culture of the postindustrial era. If the world is flat, as Thomas Friedman[4] has argued very persuasively in his best-selling book, the flatness has not resulted from people being followers. It is because people have been involved in dynamic processes that have caused the death knell of hierarchy, authoritarianism, elitism, and power derived from wealth and corruption.

CONCLUSION

I have said thousands of times that not everything that happens in the world is leadership. In my book, one of my primary objectives was to encourage scholars and practitioners to put boundaries on what leadership is. That is why a definition of leadership is crucial—to distinguish between what is leadership and what are other ways of developing, managing, governing, and controlling people. In the postindustrial paradigm of leadership, the number of leadership activities in a typical day in any organization is minimal for the large majority of people. The reason for that is that the criteria for collaborative leadership are clear and strenuous. One of the four criteria is *intending significant change.* In a typical twenty-four-hour period, how many people in the numerous nations in the world are actually engaged in activities intending significant change? The answer, I believe, is few, and those that are so engaged pursue these activities for a small amount of time during the twenty-four hours.

Leadership scholars and practitioners have to learn that leadership is not vested in a person whom we call a leader. Rather, leadership is an episodic series of activities through which people develop a relationship to make significant changes. Episodic is the key concept here. We need to understand the episodic nature of the dynamic that is leadership.

Followers is a much more general term for people's behaviors in a variety of situations. Followers are not only followers in leadership relationships. Here are a few other follower situations:

- Followers exist in management relationships. We use a different word, *subordinates*, but they have the same pattern of behaviors: passivity and doing what one is told to do.

- Follower passivity is common among citizens in their relationships with governments and public officials. Many do not even vote, a minimal commitment to better democracy in civic affairs.

- Follower patterns of behavior and thought are often encouraged in religious organizations, as there is a belief system that religious people are told to uphold and obey.

- People follow signs, maps, oral directions, others they admire, guidebooks, assembly instructions, advice from doctors and other professional experts, and hunches, among many other examples.

- In their daily lives, people are active in some organizations and passive in others. People generally don't have the time, energy, attitude, emotional strength, or willpower to be active in all aspects of their lives. Furthermore, their commitment to various organizations varies; as a result, their activities vary.

- Personalities predispose some to be passive and others to be active. Note that I did not say "determine." This is a fact of human nature, and we ought not lose sight of human nature.

In this discussion, if we could limit our perspectives about followers to leadership relationships, we could engage in a much more intelligent discussion. Forget about all the other activities in the world that are not leadership; let's concentrate on those few activities that we are convinced are leadership.

Here are four questions about the people in leadership relationships that I think need to be discussed thoroughly:

First, if we analyze those leadership activities, how do we want nonleaders to act? Perhaps more accurately stated, what do we expect from those who are not leaders in a leadership relationship?

Second, can some of those who are not leaders become leaders during a series of activities that make up any one leadership relationship? Conversely, can some leaders become nonleaders in that series of activities?

Third, when an original leadership group proposes a significant change, is it possible for there to be other leadership relationships in that organization that intend changes that are quite different from those of the original leadership group? If so, do we have different expectations of those who are not leaders in the opposing group? In this regard, do we even have room in our models of leadership for two or more leadership relationships existing in the same organization, each of them promoting different proposals for significant change about the same issue? Does the existence of opposing leadership groups change our view of those who are not leaders?

Fourth, what do we call these nonleaders? If the word *followers* is odious to many people in the postindustrial, postmodern world, what word do we use? Many people have a more traditional mind-set and have no difficulty with the word, which certainly complicates our ambitions to change the word.

Maybe we can't answer these questions neatly or at all, but the discussions we have about these issues will help us come to some more intelligent and practical leadership conceptual frameworks than we have heretofore been able to develop.

My first conclusion is that we need to change our view of leadership in order to change our view of followers. Collaborative leadership demands more of nonleaders than followers generally contribute. The concept of followers is antithetical to the collaborative relationship that is leadership. We need to change the word *followers* to some other word that suggests more involvement in the decision-making process. I have suggested *collaborators*, but others may have a better word to propose.

Second, if we want to settle for some kind of shared leadership process wherein the leader leads and makes major decisions and the people who are not leaders involve themselves actively in giving advice and consent, we might want to change the word *followers* to something like *participants*, *contributors*, or something neutral, such as *members* or *associates*.

Third, if we don't change the word *followers*, the acceptance of the word can only continue to promote a view of leadership that is Great Person, good-management oriented. I believe very strongly that the word *followers* encourages people to think of leadership as something that only leaders do. Dividing the world into leaders and followers is not consistent with the flat world developing in the twenty-first century.

My final statement is that much of leadership studies as a field of academic learning and much of what is thought of as the practice of leadership in the world today are out of step with the tenor of the twenty-first century when viewed from a futures perspective that is even modestly progressive. The world is changing dramatically, and we seem to want to keep our paradigm of leadership the same as it was during the industrial era of the twentieth century. The same can be said of the concept of followers. We seem to want to keep the traditional notion of followers, perhaps modified a bit to allow for more participation. I don't think that is good enough. We need to seriously rethink the concept of followers and understand at the most basic, ontological level what the concept of followers means in any model of leadership proposed for the twenty-first century.

APPENDIX: DEFINITIONS OF THE VERB *TO FOLLOW*

There are as many as twenty definitions of the verb *to follow* in dictionaries. Most of them do not directly relate to leadership, but they are connected in a general sense or through connotation. Selected definitions from three dictionaries are listed below.

From the *Encarta World English Dictionary* (computer version, 2004):

To come after somebody or something in position, time, or sequence

To take the same course or go in the same direction as something else

To act in accordance with something, especially with instructions or directions given by somebody else

To be led, guided or influenced by somebody or something

To do the same as somebody or something, or take somebody or something as a model to be imitated

From *The American Heritage Dictionary* (3rd ed.):

To go in the direction of, be guided by

To act in agreement or compliance with, obey

To accept the guidance, command, or leadership of

To adhere to, practice

To take as a model, precedent, imitate

To come, move, or take place after another person or thing in order or time

From the *Merriam-Webster's Collegiate Dictionary* (11th ed.):

To go, proceed or come after

To be or act in accordance with

To accept as authority

To copy after, imitate

To go or come after a person or thing in place, time or sequence

PART TWO

Effective Followership

It is one thing to write about the need for more attention to followership. It is another to give it this attention in professional training programs and in corporate culture change efforts. In this part of the book we examine several efforts to do just this.

These examples are chosen not because of their proven record but because they represent early efforts to effectively introduce the subject of followership to individuals, groups, and organizations. The authors share their reasons for focusing on followership to support other core values and change efforts, and their experiences with creating new awareness and skills.

The effort to promote individual and group development in any field is greatly assisted by models that help those engaged in the effort understand existing styles and behavior, their consequences, and options for making different choices. In this section we introduce several additional models for describing follower behaviors and the intricate relationship of followership and leadership.

Our purpose in this section is to stimulate thinking about how to introduce the concepts of effective followership, regardless of the model or synthesis of models one chooses. What are strategies for building support for an empowered style of followership? What are pitfalls that must be avoided? What techniques can help followers and leaders perform these roles differently as they occupy and move between them? How can they build the needed skills for true partnership? What are the types of outcomes of these efforts?

We hear more from practitioners in this section than in others. What has their experience been in creating effective followership? Like all the chapters in this book, these are written by individuals with great depth of experience. But we chose to include an important perspective from someone at the beginning of her higher education. What are the consequences of a university admissions process that appears to value only leadership and doesn't encourage the effective followership that all leaders need? How can our institutions of higher learning select for and encourage exemplary followership as enthusiastically as they encourage exemplary leadership? Indeed, how can our culture?

Creating New Ways of Following

Ira Chaleff

At the Rethinking Followership Conference, Robert Kelley, the seminal writer in the field of followership, presented a schema for thinking about the various aspects of the subject. Each of the categories in his schema are compelling and deserve intense scrutiny by academics and practitioners. But the one that strikes closest to my core interest is the aspect Kelley refers to as "world events" and the question he asks: "Can followership help us unlock these?"

Those who have read my contribution to the field, *The Courageous Follower: Standing Up to and for Our Leaders*, know that it is this question that drove me to discover and present what I could learn about followership.[1] The defining event of my formative years was becoming aware of the World War II Holocaust. The awareness of the horror of that episode, in a history of mankind fraught with horror, left me with a moral imperative to seek answers. Why do human beings follow purveyors of hate and death and, in doing so, themselves become purveyors? And what, if anything, can be done to fundamentally change this scourge on civilization? These are questions that have also been taken up by other conference contributors, such as Jean Lipman-Blumen and Barbara Kellerman.

Earlier this year, I was invited to present the annual ethics lecture to the Graduate School of Public Accounting at the University of Wisconsin. At the end of the talk, one of the many very bright students asked a question that stopped me for a long moment. Having read of my motivation to have an impact on this deadly historic dynamic, he asked, How could I spend my energy teaching followership in business settings? What does one have to do with the other? A challenging question, indeed. Yet I think there is an answer, and the answer may lie in other categories in Kelley's schema—for example, his categories "follower qualities" (How are they shaped by parents, by teachers, by peer pressure, and so on?), "culture and followership," and "language and followership."

Let me, for a moment, take one of the most extreme examples of "dark" leadership and followership of our time. If you have not seen the documentary footage of Saddam Hussein assuming power in Iraq in 1979, I recommend that you do. It is harrowing. The footage is of a room of senior Iraqi army officers, perhaps several hundred, in auditorium seating. On the stage is Saddam, smoking a large cigar and jesting from time to time with a couple of aides. Armed guards ring the room, presumably the only ones in the room carrying weapons.

Saddam gives a tearful speech about how various officers in the room have betrayed him. One by one their names are called out. Each is immediately escorted out of the room to be shot. It is the classic act of a dictator consolidating power, much as Adolf Hitler consolidated his power in the "night of the long knives." Both acts were taken right out of Machiavelli's counsel in *The Prince*.

The rest of the officers in the room are frozen in their seats. Mature men at the peak of their careers, colonels and generals, frozen into inaction. You can feel the terror coursing through them and their shame and relief each time it is someone else's name that is called. Several dozen officers are singled out before the process is complete and the remaining officers reaffirm their undying fealty to Saddam.

It is not hard to put yourself in that auditorium and to imagine your own instinct to survive. To have stood up in protest when it was clear what was occurring would surely have resulted in immediate death. And not just to you, but in all probability to your entire family, as that was Saddam's vicious "insurance policy." So you had only two choices: acquiesce or effectively commit suicide and worse. The choice made was to acquiescence, and the consequence of this collective silence was Iraq's being subjected to two decades of terror by a ruthless brute and his sadistic sons, suffering tens of thousands of deaths by torture and millions by unprovoked war.

In the context of what we are trying to achieve in this volume, we must ask a question: What would be needed to create a third choice in the face of such brutal, perverted leadership? I believe the answer to that question takes us back to Kelley's other foci and suggests a response to my thoughtful interrogator at the University of Wisconsin.

Imagine if you lived in a culture that placed the highest value on human dignity and standing up firmly against oppression. Imagine that this value was as central to this culture as being a fearless warrior is in certain other cultures. In this culture that we are imagining, parents and teachers would be alert for instances of legitimate confrontation from children about their elders' arbitrary use of power (not to be confused with illegitimate manipulation by the children) and support this. In this culture, language would evolve to hold such meanings as "tolerating oppression equals cowardice," "leadership means stewardship of your followers' interests and dignity," "followership means partnering with leaders to achieve worthy ends." The culture would reinforce these values with rites of passage for appropriately exercising the power of followership. Awards and honors would be given at graduations not just for leadership, but also for constructive dissent. This culture would hold that to die opposing oppression was an ultimate act of heroism and to live by acquiescing to oppression was a mark of shame difficult for a family to erase.

In such a culture, what chance would Saddam have had that day had he tried to convert his administration into a terror machine? The first senior officer to stand in protest would be immediately supported by scores of his peers. As a unanimous group or an overwhelming majority, they would order the guards to refuse Saddam's orders. The guards, raised in the same culture, would immediately recognize their higher responsibility to support the officers. Saddam as a would-be tyrant would be nipped in the bud. If he had genuine leadership skills, he would have to apply these to decent ends through decent means or forfeit his right to lead.

But how is such a culture created? And how many generations does it take? No one has done it, so no one knows. But that should not stop us from holding a vision of its possibility and sowing as many seeds as we can to bring about that vision. Where and how should those seeds be sown?

To some degree, that is the function of this book, to ask and begin to answer these questions. As Robert Kelley has noted, we will have to dig deeply into the culture and address issues of language, child rearing, and values. My own work has centered around bringing new ways of following to those who work in hierarchical organizational structures, whether military, ecclesiastic, bureaucratic, educational, corporate, or the like. So this is the level of cultural impact I will focus on.

Large organizations, both commercial and public, are among the prime engines of contemporary culture. Every time we sow seeds among individuals and groups within these organizations, we are sowing the seeds for a culture in which people stand up for what is right. We are sowing seeds to support leaders who are trying to improve some aspect of the human condition. The fruit of these seeds will displace cynicism, which undermines leadership and is the bane of collaborative effort. We are also sowing seeds to constructively confront leaders whose actions are impeding the improvements the group seeks. By doing this we are reducing the personal and cultural weight of "authority" that has paralyzed us in the face of titles, uniforms, and the power to hire and fire. We are creating new norms of behavior based on mutual responsibility for the mission and respect for core human values.

Thus we walk down from the lofty goal to create a better world and address what can realistically be done now that will, over time, contribute to that world. We equip people with the mind-set and skills to energetically support positive leadership at all levels and to talk back constructively to these same leaders when necessary. If enough people are so equipped, one day we will reach a tipping point in which this becomes expected behavior.

But how do we equip people? How do we reach Joe Ordinary and Sally Everyday to inculcate these ideas for use in their workplace, with their families, in their civic groups, and in their houses of worship? How do we engage them as walking ambassadors for a new way of following so that one day it may become the given way?

In my book *The Courageous Follower*, I present a new model of followership and give many examples of how this role might be performed in different circumstances. What that book does not do is draw on my decade of experience in conducting training programs to help followers at frontline and middle levels of organizational activity reconceive the power and responsibility of their role. Therefore, I will use this chapter to share some of the lessons I have learned about helping group members reconceive the follower role and develop the skills that the enhanced concept of that role requires. It is my hope that those who read this will adapt these strategies and tools to the realities of their own groups and continue to sow the seeds.

I will mainly focus on approaches I have found useful in seminars and workshops, though these techniques can be adapted for use less formally in group discussions designed to foster change in the group dynamic and the follower-leader relationship.

THE NEED TO CREATE A NEW AWARENESS

In *The Courageous Follower*, I posit a model that states that followers do not serve leaders. This is a somewhat shocking statement, as it flies in the face of the traditional one-up, one-down concept of leader-follower relationships. Rather, I posit, both leaders and followers serve a common purpose, each from their own role. The simple graphic in Figure 6.1 illustrates this.

This characterization ennobles the role of the follower and creates a more equal and healthy psychological playing field with leaders. But this is hardly the concept of being a follower that participants bring into a workshop or seminar. And, I have learned, it is usually a good idea to start where people are before suggesting where they should be.

Therefore, I often begin with an icebreaker by asking a very simple question: "How many of you grew up wanting to be the best follower you could be?" At least in the United States, it is very rare for a single hand to go up. So we have

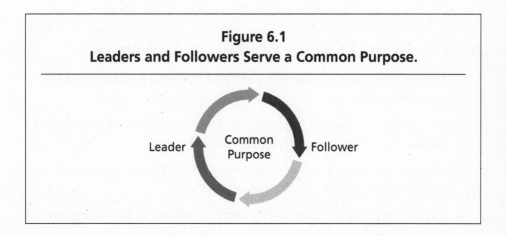

Figure 6.1
Leaders and Followers Serve a Common Purpose.

Leader   Common Purpose   Follower

immediately jumped into the heart of the cultural stereotype of followers. A titter goes around the room at the absurdity of the unexpected question, and we begin to examine the discomfort with the term.

Of course they didn't aspire to be a follower. Except in rare contexts, such as when speaking of religious persuasion, the term *follower* has carried a negative connotation. They often remember a parent chastising them for following others: "If everyone else jumped off a cliff, would you?"

The parents conveniently forget that the entire socialization system their children must master requires them to follow very clearly what others are doing, such as standing in a straight line or raising their hand to be called on before speaking or pledging allegiance to the flag.

I follow the laughter with a question. "What is the only thing a leader absolutely needs?" The answer, of course, is a follower. If no one is following, then no one is leading. You cannot have one without the other. Therefore, it makes no sense to honor leadership and disparage followership.

The light bulbs begin to turn on, often with some relief. "You mean it's okay for me to be a follower?" This is really the first step in reassessing the follower role. "Follower" is not a pejorative. It is a legitimate and necessary role. Sometimes we lead and sometimes we follow. Both roles are honorable *if they are performed with strength and accountability.*

THE MODEL

Once the idea is established that followership is as valid a subject to study as leadership, I introduce the Courageous Follower model of attitudes and behaviors. The model is fully described in *The Courageous Follower* and is referenced in other chapters in this book. Therefore I only enumerate its five dimensions:

1. The courage to support the leader and do everything possible to contribute to the leader's success

2. The courage to assume responsibility for the common purpose and act whether or not receiving direct orders from the leader

3. The courage to constructively challenge the leader or group's behaviors or policies if these threaten the common purpose

4. The courage to participate in any transformation needed to improve the leader-follower relationship and the organization's performance

5. The courage to take a moral stand when warranted to prevent ethical abuses or, at the very least, to refuse to participate in them

You will notice, of course, that courage is presumed necessary to actuate each of these behaviors. In my experience, the subject of courage must be addressed at some point in the development of effective followership. But before delving more deeply into the characteristics of effective followership, or the courage required, I have found it useful to further distill the model into its two most crucial behaviors and examine the styles of followership that their combinations produce.

STYLES OF FOLLOWERSHIP

When I began conducting training on courageous followership, I believed that the central focus would be on developing the willingness and ability of followers to stand up to leaders when their actions or behaviors were endangering the common purpose. Although this is true, to my surprise I found that it was a prerequisite, and just as critical, also to focus on raising the awareness of the need for followers to give leaders *the support* they require and to which they are entitled.

In any group I train, many participants enjoy and respect the formal leaders with whom they work. But, obviously, not all do. A segment no longer trust or respect their direct supervisor or manager.[2] If the training draws participants from different organizations, or different parts of a large organization, these participants will often be openly disparaging and cynical about their leaders. It is not possible to transform this relationship and potentially forge a partnership with a leader, unless the subordinate is willing to be a follower of that leader. This requires the willingness to give the leader genuine support, not just the minimal level of compliance required of a subordinate. Giving genuine support, in turn, requires a serious change in attitude and giving the leader "a second chance."

I sometimes tell the story of Carl to convey the spirit of what it really means to support a leader. Carl was a scientist at a prominent federal health agency. When his manager retired, he was offered the position but declined it. He preferred programmatic work to administrative duties. The manager who was recruited from outside the unit knew that Carl had first been offered the position and, out of her own insecurity, viewed Carl as a threat. Her style, in any case, tended toward micromanaging and, in Carl's case, oppressively so. Because of this, she soon lost the support of most of her unit of highly qualified professionals. Carl in particular found coming to work disturbingly stressful.

To influence the situation, Carl chose to focus on *the courage to support*. He went to see the manager every morning and asked, "What do you need from me today?" At first the manager was highly suspicious of his overtures. She suspected a trap of some sort, as she couldn't imagine someone she regarded as a potential rival being sincere in his offers to help. Nevertheless, Carl did his best to provide what she asked for each day. If he knew he would not be able to do so, he carefully explained what other priority he was working on and committed to work on what she requested as soon as that was taken care of. After several months, Carl reported a complete transformation in the relationship between him and his manager. Not only did she relax her management style with him, she did so with others as well. She eventually came to be treasured by her team. This may be an extreme application of the courage to support and an unusually rewarding result, but it demonstrates the power of this follower behavior that is fully in the control of the follower.

Even those who generally respect their leaders often underestimate the need to proactively support them if they are to earn the right to be viewed as partners. Leaders must experience followers as having their interests at heart before they will be open to the prospect of followers questioning or constructively challenging their behavior or policies.

The typology I use, therefore, is based on a matrix of these two characteristics of courageous followership: *the courage to support* the leader and *the courage to challenge* the leader's behavior or policies. As shown in Figure 6.2, this matrix comprises four styles.

Once again, these styles are well described in *The Courageous Follower* and are also referred to in other contributions to this volume. Therefore, I will only briefly enumerate them:

1. Resource = low support, low challenge. Will do enough to retain position but no more.

2. Individualist = low support, high challenge. Will speak up when others are silent, but voice is marginalized, as it is too chronically contrarian.

3. Implementer = high support, low challenge. Leader values this style but is at risk because follower will not caution against costly mistakes.

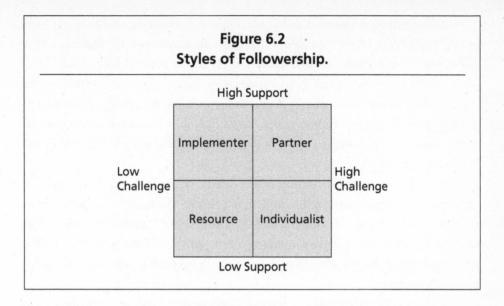

**Figure 6.2
Styles of Followership.**

High Support

| Implementer | Partner |
| Resource | Individualist |

Low Challenge   High Challenge

Low Support

4. Partner = high support, high challenge. Assumes full responsibility for own and leader's behavior and acts accordingly.

This typology bears resemblance to the one used by Robert Kelley in which "independent, critical thinking" forms one axis (roughly equivalent to the willingness to challenge) and "active/passive" (roughly equivalent to the willingness to support) forms the other axis.[3] There are other possible instruments one could use to form a picture of one's followership style, such as Gene Boccialetti's Authority Relations Inventory cited in his book *It Takes Two*[4] or Rodger Adair's model in this volume. The point is to use some method of helping participants generate a language of followership that will begin to suggest a developmental path for consciously increasing their agency in this role. Even without using an actual instrument, exposing participants to the model and letting them self-assign their style produce a starting point for self-reflection.[5]

As follower behaviors are relational to leader behaviors, there will be some variation in the participants' follower style depending on the leadership style of the hierarchy in which they currently work. But it is also true that there tends to be a core follower style that is relatively independent of the style of the leader. It is this core style that we want to identify so that participants can begin to understand the consequences of that style and make choices about reinforcing or changing it.

As the instrument I use is a self-reporting one, it is subject to the weaknesses of self-assessment. I have little doubt that the high number of participants whose scores place them in the Partner quadrant (typically around half) have somewhat idealized themselves in their responses to the questions. Nevertheless, the exercise has value: first, because it begins to form an internal image of what partnership (or courageous followership) looks like, and second, because participants' attention is drawn to the opportunities for further growth within the Partner quadrant.

The second highest distribution in the self-reporting process places most of the remaining participants in the Implementer style. The benefits of this style get validated in the ensuing discussion, and the growth path (becoming more willing to speak up when they believe something is not right) becomes very clear. For the two remaining styles, the growth path begins with becoming more willing to support their leaders.

Regardless of what instrument is used, I believe that there is a meta-benefit to offering a typology. The psychological strategies for dealing with authority have been developed by the individual at an early age; they are rarely examined and tend to be durable. As researchers such as Maccoby and Alford have observed, there are complex psychological processes that operate below the rational operational level between leaders and followers that can adversely affect the quality of their interactions.[6] It is beyond the mandate and capacity of training programs to explore these directly and individually. By presenting rational operational models for mature, healthy follower-leader relationships, participants can begin their own process of questioning the desirability of their current ways of relating to authority and begin testing ways that may prove more productive.

This is particularly important for individuals or groups who feel and act as victims of those in authority. As well described by Culbert and Ullmen, *hierarchical structures* are necessary to clarify who has what level of authority to commit the organization's resources. However, these structures often generate and are confused with *hierarchical relationships*, which are internalized rules of behavior toward authority that are counterproductive to self-responsible and mutually responsible action.[7] Followers who operate from unexamined and disempowering rule sets toward authority relinquish their natural adult sense of responsibility for productively dealing with situations that arise. They regress to ineffective complaining without acting to remedy the situation. This is unhealthy for their own sense of work-based satisfaction and unhealthy for the leader and organization that no longer benefit from followers' full commitment and capacity to pursue the organizational mission.

Offering positive models of followership styles, with descriptions of the typical behaviors deployed from those styles, can be combined with a review of the power that is available to and held by those in the follower role. Sources of power can include commitment to the organizational purpose, specialized technical knowledge, professional reputation, personal networks within the organization, and so on. The goal is to change followers' own internal estimations of their ability to influence leaders and generate an increased sense of agency and responsibility.

USING HYPOTHETICALS TO ENRICH APPRECIATION FOR STYLES OF FOLLOWERSHIP

Once people have a sense of the range of follower styles and of their own tendency, they need to connect these to situations they encounter in organizational settings. I have found it useful to first have them do so using hypothetical situations that are typical in their environment, rather than actual situations.

The hypothetical that I have found illustrates a range of real-world challenges that participants encounter involves an unworkable or problematic order to them or their group that originates from two organizational levels above them. In this scenario, it is not enough to be willing to speak up to one's immediate supervisor. That supervisor must also be willing to speak up to his or her manager.

This type of hypothetical is almost universally adaptable to specific organizational cultures. It quickly goes to the heart of the challenge that most participants face in organizations of any but the smallest size. In this case, to effectively deal with the situation, the individual not only has to be a courageous follower but also has to report to a supervisor who is also a courageous follower. If this is not the case, this person has to influence the immediate supervisor to perform acts of courageous followership, or he or she must work around the supervisor without damaging the relationship between them. A tall order.

This type of exercise helps participants come to grips with the elements of courageous followership and successful upward influencing. How do you exert lateral leadership to keep the group who receives the problematic order from becoming demoralized and cynical? How do you make good-faith efforts to successfully implement the order? How do you advise the supervisor when the order is not implementable or if its implementation will do more harm than good? Under what circumstances do you conclude that the problems with the order must be addressed directly at the level from which it originated? How do you involve your immediate supervisor in this dialogue? How do you deal with the supervisor's reluctance to push back to his or her manager? How do you frame your concerns so that the manager two or more levels above takes them seriously? What are your options if your concerns still are not addressed? Barring egregious incompetence or unethical behavior, the strategy of courageous followership involves working with, not around or against, one's leaders to correct organizational situations.

THE LIMITS OF HYPOTHETICAL SITUATIONS

Hypothetical exercises are wonderful vehicles for beginning to explore new follower behaviors. They can be comfortably used in mixed groups or with intact working groups without putting anyone on the defensive. They allow participants to grapple with new ways of seeing and thinking about situations, with no heavy emotional stakes involved. Participants can draw new mental maps of viable ways to respond to situations that they had not previously envisioned. Such exercises are good dry-run rehearsals before launching into choppy seas.

However, hypotheticals alone cannot fully prepare participants for the real-world sense of risk involved in standing up to authority, no matter how constructively done. I wish I could tell you that I have discovered how to effectively simulate in a workshop the real-world stress factors that come into play in important leader-follower interactions, but I cannot. What I can do is share with you approaches I have used for examining the subjects of risk, fear, and courage and suggest that other practitioners test the development of better learning strategies in this regard.

RISK AND COURAGE

When followers hesitate to tell leaders what they really believe, they are being self-protective. Most people only see the downside risk to disagreeing with leaders or raising sensitive issues. But there is upside potential as well.

To illustrate this, I tell a story of an individual I know named Steven, who dared to criticize some of the practices of the owner of the company for which he worked. Steven was an exemplary employee, but he felt that the owner's policies were unfair to the company's stakeholders, and let him know it. The owner had a legendary temper and let it loose when confronted by Steven. This didn't deter Steven from raising other issues with the owner at different points; these efforts initially were met with similar vociferous displeasure. Coworkers felt Steven's tenure at the company would be short.

But after a while, an interesting phenomenon occurred. When the owner had a business problem he was pondering, he would seek out Steven for his opinion. Why? Because the owner was confident that Steven would tell him the truth about what he thought. Even more dramatically, when the owner was ready to retire, he appointed Steven as his successor.

This is a very useful story, as most people don't give sufficient weight to the upside potential of standing up to authority when appropriate. *Worthy leaders* value honesty and courage, even if they may rail against these at the moment.

But this is not the only mileage I get from this story. There is still the question of why Steven had the courage to take a principled stand when his colleagues did not. This is an important question. Is it just that some people are naturally courageous and others are not? Or is there a structure to courage that we can use to help develop courage in others that will serve them both as followers and leaders?

I asked Steven about this. He explained that in his case what gave him the courage to take a stand, despite his family's financial dependence on him, was his religious upbringing. He had been taught that one should not stand by silently if one sees others being mistreated. So there was an identifiable source to his courage, in this case a core value transmitted through his family as a religious precept.

After sharing this story with workshop participants, we examine the range of possible sources of courage. Participants offer many, from the humorous ("a million dollars in the bank") to the professional ("having all my facts right") to the inspirational ("my grandma always taught me to do the right thing"). Then I invite participants to reflect on what sources they can draw on when a time comes that they need to do so.

FEAR

You cannot truly examine courage without examining fear. Contrary to some beliefs, being afraid is not the opposite of being courageous. It is the necessary condition for displaying courage. If there were nothing to fear, you would simply act and not need courage to do so.

But fear of what? And is the fear real or exaggerated? If you were in a one-company town with a labor surplus and a vengeful leader, you might be afraid of speaking up and getting fired when there are few other prospects for work and you have a family to feed. Your fear in that case is probably justified. More extreme, if you were serving in one of dozens of authoritarian regimes around the world, loss of your freedom or life if you speak truth to power could be a legitimate fear, as we acknowledged in the Saddam Hussein example at the beginning of this chapter.

But what about in the contemporary, highly diversified U.S. economy with relatively low unemployment? Is the fear of being dismissed inflated? Aren't there numerous other opportunities you could pursue for gainful, satisfying employment? Despite the trauma of being dismissed, the reality is that you would probably land on your feet before long, perhaps in an even better job. So what is the source of the fear?

This is where Abraham Maslow can help us. His famous Hierarchy of Needs, illustrated in Figure 6.3, contains a powerful clue.

In a diversified, middle-class culture, where individuals enjoy some choice over the situations in which they can work and make a living, the most powerful motivation for not speaking up against the leader or group consensus is not survival or safety, but the social need to belong and the fear of losing the group's acceptance. This observation is supported in a study conducted by Kathleen Ryan and Daniel Oestreich on the repercussions that people fear as a result of speaking up: Only 11 percent reported "loss of employment," while 49 percent reported "loss of credibility and reputation" or "rejection and damage to the relationship."[8] It is also supported by Janis's extensive work on groupthink and the powerful and detrimental "pressures toward uniformity" in a cohesive group.[9]

Fear is most inimical to action when it is unspecific or generalized. When participants are helped in clarifying and naming their fear, they can then examine it and make more realistic estimates of the risks. They can also devise strategies for minimizing the potential risks once these are appropriately understood.

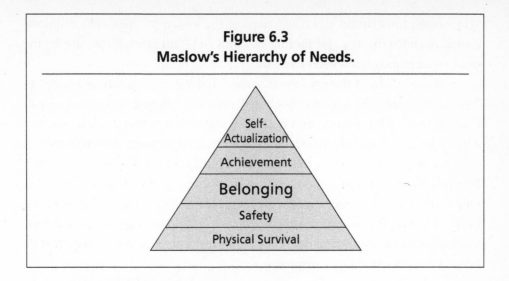

Figure 6.3
Maslow's Hierarchy of Needs.

Self-Actualization

Achievement

Belonging

Safety

Physical Survival

HIGH-PROFILE LEADERSHIP FAILURES AS CAUTIONARY TALES

Another method I use to relate the principles and behaviors of courageous followership to the world in which participants live is to stay alert for current relevant news stories. There are almost always stories of high-profile leaders whose flaws of character or judgment, regardless of their other considerable leadership skills, cause them to topple from lofty heights. In the really tragic cases, they bring their organizations down with them, affecting the lives of their many stakeholders. Some of these stories are of outright fraud, others of abrasive management style, pressure to ignore safety procedures, substance addictions, societally disapproved-of behaviors, and the general range of human fallibility.

The higher the level of participants in their organization, the more relevant this method becomes. It is the followers one or two levels below senior executives whose timely, courageous, and skillful interventions can potentially save their high-profile leaders from becoming headline material. Occasionally, the potential to do this exists at lower levels, where staff in accounting or elsewhere compile the reports on which the public reputation of the organization relies.

One article I used documented the fact that nearly thirty subordinates at Enron faced criminal charges for their role in Enron's accounting deceptions, and eighteen subordinates at HealthSouth were indicted for misstating company finances. There were similar occurrences at Adelphia Communications and at WorldCom.

Whereas the prosecution and convictions of the leaders of these once respected companies filled the news for months at a time in recent years, it was rare for the cases of the nameless followers to do so.

Yet the collusion of these followers squandered the opportunity to attempt to "nip in the bud" the leader's ill-advised impulses. They acquiesced to small requests to stretch the truth, and once they started down that road, it was very difficult to draw a line when the requests grew more significant. Although there is certainly no guarantee that a follower's principled stand will dissuade a leader's determination to commit fraud, neither should the potential to do so be dismissed. The successful interventions do not make headlines, nor are they reported by the follower. This is the paradox of courageous followership: its most crucial accomplishments are unheralded. Even if nothing else is accomplished, the follower doesn't become a co-conspirator.

Though the incidence of fraud is low in organizational life, the pressures to take actions that conflict with core values are not uncommon. Examining extreme situations that make headlines can be a jumping-off point for a healthy prophylactic dialogue with leaders. They can help prepare both followers and leaders to identify and respond to situations long before those situations assume proportions worthy of headlines.

SKILL

Although it is helpful to form a trusted relationship with leaders and necessary to have the courage to risk that relationship by taking a principled stand when needed, these two conditions by themselves are not sufficient for success at influencing upward. Tact and skill are also required, and, like any skill, these can be developed or improved with practice.

Skills can be broken down into their component steps and practiced in role plays that prepare followers to productively address sensitive issues with leaders. I use a scenario based on an actual situation I encountered when consulting to a firm that specialized in physician insurance. The leader in this case was beloved by his executive team and staff but had developed a blind spot when he hired a friend to fill a key position and the friend failed to perform. No one else on the team was able to get through to the underperforming friend, and the CEO was unwilling to hear criticism of his friend. A stalemate had developed that was sapping morale and customer goodwill. The CEO had to be confronted.

Of course, many scenarios can be developed to practice the needed skills, but it is not advised to use a situation that too closely resembles a highly charged existing situation in the group. First the skills must be honed.

The way I have used this scenario is to organize participants into triads in which they each take turns playing the leader, the follower, and a coach. The follower prepares how to approach the leader on this delicate subject. The leader is instructed to be somewhat resistant to feedback, but to be responsive when it is placed in the context of what the leader values. The coach is tasked with the responsibility to observe how well the follower manages each of the elements of successful upward feedback. These include how well the follower

- Opened the conversation
- Picked the appropriate time and place
- Conveyed respect
- Linked the issue to the leader's values
- Delivered the feedback
- Described the problem
- Stated the impact
- Offered potential solutions linked to the leader's values
- Responded to the leader's reactions
- Remained professional
- Expressed empathy
- Kept the focus on consequences
- Closed the conversation
- Restated the costs and benefits
- Asked for a commitment to act or give strong consideration
- Expressed appreciation

Of all these steps, the most critical is "*linking the issue to the leader's values*," which may be different from what the follower values. That is the only way to ensure that the follower will get the leader's attention and raise the prospects of favorable action.

In a nonclassroom setting, if a follower is planning a sensitive conversation with a leader and is concerned about getting thrown off by the leader's response, it is worth practicing the steps in this process. By doing a few dry runs, the follower will be better prepared for keeping the conversation on track.

APPLICATIONS

If you find yourself in a situation of being asked to or needing to coach a follower on dealing with a leader's actions, there are some questions that are useful to explore before rehearsing the follower's presentation to the leader.

- Does that which the follower wants of the leader seem reasonable?
- Does the follower need to build or repair trust by giving the leader more or better support?
- Is a better strategy needed for raising the issue with the leader?
- Is more research or documentation needed to present the case effectively?
- What options should be developed for the leader to consider?
- Does the follower need to change something about his own behavior if he wants the leader to transform her behavior?
- Does the follower need to do something to reinforce changes already agreed to in earlier conversations?
- Are there any other observations or suggestions?

The value of this exploration is obviously in doing a reality check on the follower's perceptions of a situation. Sometimes this type of questioning unearths unreasonable follower expectations or behaviors, which may benefit from candid peer feedback. In our effort to improve the willingness of followers to help leaders become aware of blind spots and correct counterproductive behaviors and policies, it is a mistake to assume that followers do not also have blind spots.

THE COURAGE TO TAKE MORAL ACTION

If followers exercise the other characteristics of courageous followership, theoretically at least it should be rare that they need to take moral action. But should they need to do so, this is arguably the most critical behavior to get right.

I often illustrate this topic with a stunning story a colleague of mine told me when coaching a vice president in an international energy holding company. His client was facing a dilemma of having received an order from the president of the company, who was under shareholder pressure to improve profits. The order was relayed to him by the senior vice president to whom he reported. It called for head-count reduction in a power plant that had already sustained two previous reductions in force. The VP considered further reductions a threat to plant safety.

His coach referred him to *The Courageous Follower*, which he read with great interest. At the next coaching session, he announced that he had realized what he needed to do and had taken the first steps. Although there are many gradations of moral action one can take, including simply querying the order or appealing it to a higher level, the VP had concluded that in this case the stakes were sufficiently high that he needed to escalate the action to one of the highest levels.

He approached his SVP and told him that he fully recognized that the SVP and the president were within their rights to order the further downsizing if they thought it was appropriate. However, he could not in good conscience implement the order. Therefore, if the order were to stand, he would offer to resign so that they could implement it directly.

The SVP was quite taken aback! The VP had earned an outstanding reputation for competence. The SVP requested that he and the VP quickly review the entire matter. After doing so, and examining all of the VP's well-researched and presented data, the SVP agreed with his assessment. He arranged for a meeting with the president. When the president heard their well-summarized data and how strongly they felt about the safety ramifications of further force reduction, he looked at them and said, "If the two of you feel this firmly that we shouldn't do this . . . then we won't."

We can easily imagine some situations in which the end of that sentence may have been "then I'll find others who *will* do it." I can relate stories that other clients have told me that ended in this threat. But the VP and SVP had clearly earned sufficient trust and respect that the leader wisely took their counsel in this case.

Did the VP have to take such a dramatic initial action? Possibly not. One can play the "offering to resign" card only extremely sparingly. But, as often happens, we are not privy to all the history that led the VP to take this moral position. It is very possible that any weaker stance may have been ineffectual. Could the strong stance have cost the VP his job? Clearly. But would that have been the worst possible consequence? Not when compared to what may have happened if a serious accident had resulted in major loss of life and property. This is why followership, like leadership, requires courage.

CONCLUDING ON A RIGHT NOTE

Ending a workshop on a discussion of the courage to take moral action may leave participants with a skewed perspective as they return to their workgroups. So may ending a chapter on this note. The capacity to take moral action when needed is critical. But we are decidedly not trying to create an atmosphere in which followers look at leaders through a prism of exaggerated alertness for morally questionable actions. We have been successful only if we help move readers and participants and colleagues closer to a stance of true partnership with leaders. Stating this clearly is helpful to counteract any impressions to the contrary.

In this spirit, I will share a quotation from a sermon delivered by the Reverend Paul Beedle, a Unitarian Universalist minister in Houston, Texas: "Followership is a discipline of supporting leaders and helping them to lead well. It is not submission, but the wise and good care of leaders, done out of a sense of gratitude for their willingness to take on the responsibilities of leadership, and a sense of hope and faith in their abilities and potential."

Clearly one cannot draw a connection from this spirit of followership to the situation with a Saddam Hussein described at the beginning of the chapter. Evil as a deeply ingrained way of being and endowed with the violent power of the State will not be deterred or transformed by caring followership. But we can postulate that a culture in which followers take their own responsibility seriously, in which they do not abdicate their moral choices and in which they are committed to caring for and supporting leaders who use their power for the common good, will reject budding tyrants, both minor and major, before they amass power. This culture would also nurture emerging servant leaders who will care for their followers fully as much as followers care for them.

At the adult level of development, this transformation begins by helping people become aware of their existing cultural and psychological programming in relation to authority. When they develop this awareness, we can give them new models for functioning in these relationships and provide them with the language, instruments, and skills for doing so. If we can also help them tap into the courage required, they take a decisive step from subordinate to partner. And we, too, take a step forward as a culture.

chapter SEVEN

Rethinking Leadership and Followership

A Student's Perspective

Krista Kleiner

"Colleges want leaders." Those three words have been drilled into my head by teachers, administrators, parents, and books that describe what colleges are looking for. Every time I receive a form I must fill out to apply for any type of position or to become a part of a group, I find myself feeling nauseated knowing that there will be at least five long blank lines headed "Leadership Positions Held."

On February 24, 2006, I arrived at Claremont McKenna College to attend what I understood to be a type of leadership conference titled Rethinking Followership. I had been furiously trying to think of what I could do to add more things to my college applications to show that I was a leader, as I had failed to obtain enough "titles" during my high school career. Given that I had been considering applying to Claremont McKenna, a renowned leadership school, I decided that attending that conference would be a great way to show them just how much of a leader I was.

To my dismay, the leadership conference I attended was one that focused not on leaders but on followers. I sat there for eight hours on the first day of the conference attentively trying to comprehend all that the distinguished speakers were conveying. In summary, all the professors and practitioners were telling me that our society underappreciated the value of being a good "follower" and that we should learn to embrace the follower in ourselves because society would not function if everyone was a leader all the time.

I truly believed that the adults speaking had a great point, and they certainly made me feel proud of all the contributions I've ever made. However, I realized that no matter how much I might want to apply this new attitude of simply doing things to promote teamwork and the success of my peers, this would put me at a disadvantage in life, given that all colleges seem to want is strong leaders.

It is true that the conference did something amazing for me. It made me feel appreciated for all the behind-the-scenes work I'd ever done and made me want to continue to do things because they benefited others, rather than because I had a title and the power to do so. However, I sat there frustrated, thinking that if I wanted to get into a good college and be successful in life, I *had* to be a leader. Everything seemed to contradict itself—I sat listening to presidents, professors, and chairmen (all people in leadership positions) telling me that it was crucial that we embrace the followers in ourselves.

Today's youth are bombarded with the supposed necessity of getting into a good college or otherwise being left behind for the rest of their lives. Due to the rising standards required for acceptance into noteworthy institutions of higher learning, a national obsession has erupted over "being what colleges want." As hopeful students panic to morph themselves into the ideal student, one quality seems to be continuously sought after—strong leadership. As quoted from the book *Guide to the Most Competitive Colleges*, the first paragraph concerning Claremont McKenna College states the following: "Claremont McKenna College sets itself apart from its counterparts by its focus on leadership. . . . Leadership is stressed everywhere, from the classroom to dorm life to athletics."

Unfortunately, the college admissions system has created a frenzy in which students feel obligated to find a way to stick out in order for their actions to receive any recognition. This is what I don't understand. Shouldn't students, along with working adults, be encouraged to make their best contributions in order to better a group? Shouldn't the goal be to work toward bettering a group as a *whole* and not have countless individuals trying to compete with each other over being the designated leader? In a world that holds billions of people, what would happen if every person decided that he or she wanted to be the designated leader of the group and no less? A great example of this is the often assigned task of choreographing a dance with a group of people for my dance team. Although we are all given equal responsibility for getting the job done, it is necessary for each individual to know when to be a leader and when to be a follower. Imagine a group of eight girls bickering over whether to do a kick, a leap, or a turn for every count of a three-minute dance! On a larger scale, imagine the chaos that would arise if an entire world of people were full of leaders arguing over much more important and crucial matters. It may be a great responsibility to lead other people, but it takes an immense amount of courage to trust in someone else to lead you in any aspect of your life.

The willingness to follow and collaborate, albeit actively and not passively, was one of the key points of the conference. Given this, a student's contribution to the learning experience in the numerous classroom groups in which he or she has participated in four years of high school is the critical reality for a university to assess. Practically speaking, these are the most important groups that students participate in during their high school experience and are what consumes the greatest amount of time and dedication. Outstanding learning is ultimately a collaborative experience between the formal leader (the teacher) and the informal leader-followers (the students). The degree to which students contribute to the workgroup through their effective participation is what directly enhances the learning experience.

A way of increasing student participation in the classroom would be to give students the criteria for how they will be assessed in the class participation portion of their grade. This could include such criteria as the following:

- Thorough preparation for the class discussions and exercises
- The courage to share your honest opinion and feelings, even when you suspect that these are not the same as those of your instructor or classmates
- Your willingness to ask questions on course-related issues that are important to you
- Your ability to draw out the quieter members in your class
- Your ability to contribute to the overall learning climate through your enthusiasm, vitality, good humor, help to fellow students inside and outside of class, and informal leadership when appropriate

To further promote students' helping other students become more involved, it should be made known that at the end of the semester, each person's class participation grade will be based on a class survey. This survey would include such questions as the following:

- During the semester, who displayed particularly helpful leadership in workgroups you participated in, and what did they do that was effective?

- During the semester, who displayed particularly helpful followership in groups you participated in, and what did they do that supported or balanced the leadership that emerged in the group or that was helpful to fellow group members?

The responses to the survey would bring to the teacher's attention the real contributions that students made in workgroups outside the classroom, which are often the most important contributions. The teacher would incorporate this information into the final grade, thus making it more fair; further, he or she would be better equipped to write references for college applications.

Although a student's contribution in the classroom has such high significance, the college admissions system has yet to find a way to recognize and reward students who have continuously made these contributions. Given that outstanding classroom contributions have been ignored, yet play such a vital role, it is the responsibility of the college admissions system to find a way to identify them. For example, by adding a required essay asking students to address the following question, colleges would have a more well-rounded selection process for identifying the "best of the best" in terms of the group work that their graduates will need to display when they enter the professional workforce:

- How have you contributed to the learning experience of your peers through your leadership-followership role in the classroom? How did you grow as both a constructive leader and a constructive follower through these experiences?

The pressure that the college admissions system produces has led me, and countless others, to calculate where we can describe our leadership with impressive sounding titles, rather than where we can make the biggest day-to-day contributions. If there were a process that allowed students to show their strength not only as leaders but also as followers and contributors, students would feel less compelled to obtain titles and would be more comfortable in making contributions regardless of the formal positions they hold.

In short, college admission officers need to place less emphasis on students' acquisition of leadership titles throughout high school and place more emphasis on understanding the domain that has been central to their lives—the classroom learning environment and their contributions to it. Both in significance and in hours invested, this area by far overshadows the extracurricular activities generally discussed when addressing "leadership" contributions in high school.

For this approach to have meaning, however, these same high schools need to help college admission officers by encouraging students to contribute to the classroom learning experience and finding ways to measure this, such as the one suggested earlier.

Leadership and followership are two sides of the same coin, each intimately connected with the other in a dynamic manner. This, of course, applies to the student-teacher relationship itself. How supportive is the student of the teacher's leadership? If the student is unhappy with something in the class, does the student find constructive ways to bring it to the teacher's attention? As I heard many times during the conference, this is part of healthy followership. And I believe that if teachers encouraged this, they would find ways of improving their classes and also contribute to their students' becoming both good leaders and followers. By helping their students do this, they are helping the future working generation of Americans develop skills critical not only to the workplace but to our society as a whole.

The Hero's Journey to Effective Followership and Leadership

A Practitioner's Focus

Gail S. Williams

This chapter focuses on how leadership and followership are compatible ways of being and describes the journey of developing powerful leadership and followership skills. It begins with a description of the current context of why skilled leadership and followership are critical to NASA's future, in general, and to Goddard Space Flight Center, specifically. It offers the findings of the Columbia Accident Investigation Board as context. I use these findings to reinforce the Leadership Alchemy program's belief that leaders and followers must cocreate a new culture by transforming themselves first—from the inside out—and then turning their attention to organizational transformation.

Next, using the metaphor of Joseph Campbell's Hero's Journey, I offer insights into how NASA Goddard Space Flight Center's Leadership Alchemy program cultivates a community of Ambassadors of Positive Change. I delineate the program's innovative whole-person learning approach, emphasizing several skills essential to being a powerful follower and leader. The chapter discusses the purposeful choices one is faced with, including the ability to design and hold powerful and fierce conversations, to clearly and influentially use language, to focus on the appreciative, and to consciously choose one's attitude and create a mood that is conducive to learning and the desired outcome. I describe several success stories emanating from the Leadership Alchemy community, all of which demonstrate another program principle: whatever one focuses on, expands.

SETTING THE CONTEXT

On February 1, 2003, the Space Shuttle *Columbia* and its seven-person crew were lost returning to Earth. The Columbia Accident Investigation Board, established within hours of the shuttle's loss, conducted an almost seven-month investigation, publishing their findings and recommendations in August 2003.[1] "The Board recognized early on that the accident was probably not an anomalous, random event, but rather likely rooted to some degree in NASA's history and the human space flight program's culture."[2] The investigation determined that the physical cause of the loss of *Columbia* and its crew was a breach in the thermal protection system on the leading edge of the left wing. The breach was caused by a piece of insulating foam separating from the external tank during launch and hitting the wing. The board also cited organizational practices, cultural traits, and leadership behaviors that were detrimental to safety. They found, for example, that organizational barriers prevented critical communication of safety information and stifled professional differences of opinion. The board's view was "that NASA's organizational culture had as much to do with this accident as the foam did. By examining safety history, organizational theory, best business practices, and current safety failures, the report notes that only significant structural changes to NASA's organizational culture will enable it to succeed. . . . The Board concludes that NASA's current organization does not provide effective checks and balances . . . and has not demonstrated the characteristics of a learning organization."[3]

"The loss of Shuttle *Columbia* and its crew was a single and tragic accident that has had far-reaching repercussions throughout NASA. The effects were immediately felt in the Shuttle program, but these were followed by the recognition of the relevance to other Human Space Flight programs and ultimately across the broad scope of the Agency's activities."[4] NASA recognized that returning to and sustaining safe flight required successfully addressing the engineering and organizational causes of the accident. The board challenged NASA to enhance the quality of its leadership, including leadership and management development, to effect the needed changes. After the accident, intense analysis and self-reflection occurred at the individual, team, departmental, and organizational levels throughout NASA. Because only a subset of NASA installations are integrally involved in human space flight, Sean O'Keefe, NASA administrator at that time, chartered an executive team to identify those elements of the board's report with agency-wide applicability and to develop measures to address each one. This team principally focused on the organizational causes described in the board's report, recognizing as did the board that leaders create culture. The following are a few of the agency-wide leadership themes that align with the Leadership Alchemy program:[5]

- Leaders must lead by example.

- Leaders should allow and encourage diversity of views, eliminate retribution toward those with differing opinions, and understand that "No" is an acceptable answer.

- Leaders should be grown throughout all levels of the organization, through succession planning and developmental experiences.

LEADERSHIP AND FOLLOWERSHIP ARE TWO SIDES OF THE SAME COIN

One of the Leadership Alchemy program's foundational beliefs is that everyone can and should be a leader as circumstances warrant, and that being a leader does not require a formal title or positional power. In fact, if we wait for either the title or power, then opportunities to influence outcomes and the future pass us by.

Strong and effective leadership require a clear vision, strong intention, and skill to choose when and how to make "leadership moves." In essence, effective leaders embody powerful leadership and readily access leadership skills and competencies to fit the circumstances. Powerful and effective leaders take data and transform them into knowledge and then into wisdom. Leadership is more than what one knows—it is how one shows up in the world.

Definitions of leadership are numerous, and they vary widely. One aspect they all seem to have in common is that in order to be a leader, one has followers. Very few of us have a job in which we consistently operate in a leadership mode, especially if we work in a hierarchical organization, such as NASA Goddard. Consequently, we can enhance our impact if we consciously and carefully choose when to lead and when to follow and if we possess the skill to seamlessly transition between these roles. The challenge lies in knowing when and how to transition, consistent with our personal core values and in service of both our personal vision and mission and those of the organization.

Stated simply, leadership and followership are two sides of the same coin. One's way of being—how one embodies leadership and followership wisdom—is paramount over what one knows. Collectively, NASA leaders and followers must cocreate a new culture that learns the lessons from the *Columbia* accident and enables us to attract and retain the best and the brightest employees.

LEADERSHIP AND FOLLOWERSHIP DEVELOPMENT AT NASA GODDARD SPACE FLIGHT CENTER

NASA Goddard Space Flight Center, located just outside Washington D.C., is one of nine NASA centers. Goddard is a scientific research center of over three thousand civil service employees and five thousand support contractors. Our mission is to expand knowledge of the Earth and its environment, the solar system, and the universe through observations from space. Although Goddard does not primarily focus on human space flight, many of the cultural and leadership concerns identified by the Columbia Accident Investigation Board apply at Goddard.

In 2001, Goddard initiated Leadership Alchemy, a state-of-the-art, whole-person leadership development program devoted to developing Ambassadors of Positive Change. Leadership Alchemy was designed in partnership with S. Kanu Kogod and Scott Coady.[6] The program's goal is to develop "forward thinking" leaders with the competency to proactively lead an organization whose mission and outcomes clearly benefit the American public.

Leadership Alchemy is an ontological leadership development program because it focuses on our "way of being," as distinct from our "way of doing." Think of our way of being as the external manifestation of our deeply held beliefs and perceptions and our conditioned behavioral tendencies. For example, each of us is unique in who we are, with our own set of distinctions that filter how we see the world. In Leadership Alchemy we call this the "observer we are." What kind of observer we are is often transparent to us, unless we consciously choose to reflect on the distinctions we possess, the filters we use, and our own thinking.

Participants in Leadership Alchemy embark on a life-changing nine-month hero's journey. Along this rigorous and challenging journey, program participants learn about leadership by practicing leadership in the context of real issues. This learning and practice occur in a supportive community where relationships are built on trust and respect for differences. The program intentionally creates what is, in essence, a safe space to grow at work. Along the way, participants gain personal insight and leadership mastery, enabling them to create their desired organizational future by transforming embodied knowledge and skill into wisdom and action.

THE LEADERSHIP ALCHEMY PROMISE

The Leadership Alchemy hero's journey changes the way people observe, experience, and show up in the world and how they impact the organization in which they work. So how does Leadership Alchemy keep these bold promises to transform program participants? Through an intensive and powerful whole-person learning experience in which people are challenged and supported to be bold, coupled with five key practices designed to change their way of being:

1. Action learning
2. Appreciative inquiry
3. Emotional intelligence and relationship building
4. Leadership presence
5. Reading and reflection

Participants build capacity and comfort with all five practices during the program, culminating in a capstone Action Learning Project designed to showcase their new leadership skills while tangibly "paying it forward" to the organization.

One of the reasons that Leadership Alchemy is unique is its whole-person emphasis and the importance it places on embodied leadership—what we call leadership presence. As applied in Leadership Alchemy, leadership presence is the awareness of one's "being" in any given moment. Some of the elements of presence are one's mood about the future, thoughts, body language, words, posture, energy level, and emotional state. The positive alignment and synergy of all these elements create leadership presence. This presence is of consequence to every leader and follower and to everyone with whom he or she interacts. As part of Leadership Alchemy, participants design their leadership presence by working in the realms of the body, language, and emotions. Leadership Alchemy offers in-depth experiences, in an experiential and interactive format, that enable individuals to embody profound and sustainable change. According to Scott Coady, "Embodied wisdom is the kind of wisdom that lives in your entire being, not just between your ears. It is constitutive with who you are and your authentic way of being. Embodied wisdom is acquired through experience, not by reading books."

The following is a list of the key learning that every participant will gain, on or before program completion, if he or she fully embraces the learning Leadership Alchemy offers. This is our program promise. Participants will

- Establish and articulate a powerful leadership vision for themselves that serves as their learning intention while also positively capturing the passion of others

- Notably enhance their presence, authority, and confidence, so that they can exceed the expectations of those they lead and follow

- Know their own capabilities, so that they can call on multiple inner resources and therefore also know when and how to call on the capabilities of others

- Set new leadership and followership standards for themselves, demonstrating progress in achieving those standards

- Powerfully design conversations for leadership and followership, including difficult and fierce conversations, making alliances, and putting vision into action

- Understand the importance of committing to wellness and actively create intentional balance in their lives

- Know how to influence others to create partnerships, alliances, and high-performing teams

- Possess the ability to build trusting relationships

- Shift the context and mood, so that others thrive, while maintaining awareness of their own and others' emotional and relationship needs
- Appreciate the richness of diversity and know how to utilize the full range of contributions of others
- Be capable of crafting stories as a way of influencing others and influencing change
- Possess the knowledge and skill to make effective choices from a wide array of possibilities for their and their organization's mutual benefit
- Understand the power of appreciative inquiry and be capable of analyzing and doing more of "what works"
- Possess competency to coordinate effective action by applying their learning and leadership skills to actual organizational challenges, employing action learning and reflection in many contexts

PROGRAM ATTENDEES AND THEIR FOLLOWERSHIP CHALLENGE

To date, almost one hundred NASA employees have graduated from Leadership Alchemy during its five-year history, equal to approximately 3 percent of Goddard's civil service workforce. Most were nonsupervisors, at or slightly above the journey level of their chosen career field in the science, engineering, or business disciplines. Using the federal government's nomenclature for grade structure, this translates into General Schedule levels 12–15. Fewer than 10 percent were supervisors or team leaders with formalized personnel and administrative responsibilities. The vast majority, regardless of grade, serve on project and other cross-functional teams, chairing these task teams an estimated 20 percent of the time.

In the context of Goddard's hierarchical structure, typically four or five layers of managers exist between the program graduates and the center director, with several additional layers at the agency/headquarter's level. Stated simply, the graduates spend the majority of their time in a followership role, intentionally choosing when and how to influence, regardless of whether they are in a leadership or followership position.

Given their level in the hierarchy, how do these Ambassadors of Positive Change influence up and out? One way the program endeavors to break down the barriers between those who benefited from Leadership Alchemy learning and others who might be more wedded to the status quo is by involving a subset of the 97 percent who are not enrolled in the program. Some are invited to serve as mentors. Others are interviewed or shadowed by the participants. Middle- and senior-level leaders and managers are also invited to informal conversations with program participants. These simple conversational exchanges, regardless of the context, can greatly enhance mutual understanding and create allies.

In Leadership Alchemy, we believe that the wisdom is in the room, and we seek ways for the participants to share their wisdom safely. Consequently, distinctions and tools are introduced in a mini-lecture format that lasts no more than twenty minutes. After that, the learners are asked to explore the concepts. By inviting the supervisors and mentors of those enrolled in the program to share learning opportunities with their employee-protégé, we strive to reach the organizational change "tipping point," to use a phrase recently popularized by Malcolm Gladwell.[7] Like the participants, mentors and supervisors are introduced to a wide range of topics and invited to share their insights and wisdom with the participants, and vice versa. While learning, they interact with current program participants. This interaction creates connections and reduces resistance to the knowledge and skills taught in the program. In particular, as the supervisors' comfort level increases with what their employee is learning, they are more willing to help the employee practice these skills "back in the office."

Despite program efforts to break down barriers, the vast majority of Goddard employees do not share common distinctions, tools, or mind-sets with the program graduates. Thus, graduates are often challenged as they navigate traditional Goddard culture from their new way of being.

The Leadership Alchemy graduates become part of a powerful and energetic community of leaders with a strong commitment to the future and to each other. Graduates are comfortable in seeking advice and collaboration from each other. Sometimes this takes the form of partnering in a new endeavor; other times they exchange information and insights. Sometimes they simply seek understanding and moral support. There are times when the graduates choose to reconnect in a social setting, paying currency into each other's emotional bank account, to use a phrase popularized by Stephen Covey.[8] Thus the trusting relationships developed during the program live on and manifest in many ways. One cannot readily objectively measure the benefit of a robust network, although graduates often remark on its utility and value. In fact, this community support, coupled with the new behaviors and skills learned during the program, enables Leadership Alchemy graduates to overcome the resistance to change mentioned above.

Although everyone's journey is unique, one benefit most participants derive is enhanced self-confidence. This self-confidence enables the graduates to make bold leadership moves previously unavailable to them. In other words, as their knowledge and skill increase, along with their self-confidence, the graduates are more willing to engage and challenge others at all organizational levels, exhibiting courageous followership.

During their initial leadership journey, the Leadership Alchemy participants rekindle their love of learning. Their desire to maintain contact with others in their learning community, coupled with a desire to expand their leadership and followership skills, led to the establishment of a formal continuous learning community, which we call a creative learning group (CLG). In a typical year, nine or ten CLG sessions are held. Recent CLG topics included leadership lessons from the Battle of Gettysburg, advanced concepts for building wellness and resilience, Systems Intelligence, Why Great Leaders Don't Take Yes for an Answer, and continuing to build the body and presence of a leader. Periodically, the Leadership Alchemy community invites participants from other Goddard leadership development programs, thus expanding their respective networks and spheres of influences. At the same time, allegiances are strengthened with others equally dedicated to Goddard's future.

In evaluating the followership-leadership challenge, especially postgraduation, we learned that it is essential to continue to cultivate and grow a robust community of support and practice. This community offers a safe place for like-minded leaders and followers to congregate, learn, and sometimes share their frustrations as Ambassadors of Positive Change. Maintaining a robust community requires continuous attention—by the graduates and for the graduates. Consequently, each class year elects a community coordinator for a two-year term; this coordinator organizes class-specific activities, contributes to planning the CLG calendar, and generally keeps his or her fingers on the pulse of classmates' accomplishments and challenges.

Designing and implementing Leadership Alchemy is a labor of love and partnership for the program facilitators. It is well known that our commitment to the success of each and every participant extends beyond his or her graduation date.

Consequently, the graduates know they can contact any of the program facilitators for advice, support, and even a coaching conversation. Hence, the program facilitators are integral members of the Leadership Alchemy community who remain committed to the success of the graduates long after the formal nine-month leadership program ends.

THE FUTURE WE DESIRE IS WHAT'S AT STAKE

NASA Goddard is a scientific research center, with approximately 50 percent of its civil servant employees in the engineering and science disciplines. Our workforce manages over forty programs and projects—more than any other NASA center. It is a passionate workforce, "hooked on" its mission, with high performance expectations. The Rogers Commission, investigating the shuttle *Challenger* accident, and the board investigating the *Columbia* accident both found that NASA has a can-do attitude that creates a culture of invincibility. Even though Goddard is not principally focused on human space flight, its culture also exhibits this attitude. Although I agree that it can have negative consequences, I also believe that kept in perspective, a can-do attitude is invaluable. Many of the skills learned in Leadership Alchemy offer the ability to achieve the necessary perspective.

In Leadership Alchemy, we believe that leaders, in partnership with able and committed followers, cocreate a new future. In fact, a leader in one context is often a follower in another. Leadership Alchemy envisions a shared values culture built on a foundation of trusting relationships and communal practices, with shared language and meaning and the joint use of tools. In that culture of the future, organizational silence and reluctance to speak (one of the cultural contributions identified by the board) is replaced by fierce and candid conversations in pursuit of a vision and mission in which all employees are passionately invested. How does this happen?

In Leadership Alchemy, participants learn to step back and reflect on how they view the world—what biases, filters, and conditioned tendencies they are using—and to decide whether these serve the future they wish to create for themselves and the organization. In doing so, they learn that life provides many choice points and that the intentional life yields greater rewards. This skill, which serves each individual incredibly well, is even more notable when outwardly focused on the organizational collective. Imagine sitting in a meeting with senior managers who are poised to make an important program decision. Next imagine a Leadership

Alchemy graduate sitting around the table (likely as a leader), or even in the back of the room (likely as a follower), asking a question designed to test the validity of strongly held assessments and beliefs. If asked with presence, with the right tone, and at the right time, whether one is in the leader or follower role, the question may shift the outcome. People begin to question what they previously considered the one and only truth and realize that their truth is not universally held by others. A different future is born out of a powerful question.

Another powerful question is "For the sake of what?" For the sake of what am I saying this? For the sake of what are you or we doing that? The enhanced self-confidence of the graduates enables them to ask "For the sake of what?" out of a mind-set of learning and curiosity and not of judgment,[9] increasing the likelihood that their question will be heard and reducing the likelihood of a defensive reaction by the listener. This "For the sake of what?" question is both simple and profound, usually causing the listener to pause and reflect. Out of this conversation, people question the status quo. Often they make different choices, enabling a new future.

Because leaders and their followers are in the business of creating the future, it is critical that they learn how to employ language powerfully and precisely and to design conversations for the outcome they desire. Program graduates, for example, understand what constitutes clear requests, offers, and promises. As they participate in meetings, the graduates seek to ensure a clear understanding between what we call "the customer" and what we call "the performer" (the provider of the product or service). Graduates strive first to understand the larger context and then seek to learn what is needed, by when, and for whom—establishing clear conditions of satisfaction. People sharing the same clarity of purpose and alignment to the desired outcome are much more productive and energized. At the same time, they establish and maintain trust. In Leadership Alchemy, people learn that in a healthy leadership-followership dynamic, creating and maintaining trust is the coin of the realm and that not keeping promises undermines trust.

Again referring to the *Columbia* accident, the board stated that it is the leader's responsibility to seek minority and diverse opinions. The board also noted that it is "difficult for minority and dissenting opinions to percolate up through the agency's hierarchy. Similarly, organizations committed to effective communications seek avenues through which unidentified concerns and dissenting insights can be raised, so that weak signals are not lost in background noise."[10] To address this and similar conversational roadblocks, Leadership Alchemy participants learn how to design an array of conversations, including fierce conversations. This skill of "naming the elephant in the room"[11] serves them and the organization well as they counteract the periodic tendency toward organizational silence. Stated differently, bringing background conversations to the foreground invites dialogue that is otherwise unlikely to occur.

The whole-person nature of the program challenges participants to shift their way of being and learn to consciously choose their attitude and create a mood that enables the outcome they seek. "Our emotions decide what is worth paying attention to."[12] Program participants learn how to harness the power of choosing, creating, and sustaining a mood conducive to their goals. Moods are contagious, and a negative mood is more contagious than a positive mood. Whether in the leader or the follower role, graduates can choose to model a mood and thereby influence others. Imagine a conversation with a group of engineers, scientists, and business personnel about current institutional budget constraints and how they are notably impacting all employees. This conversation can easily spiral into resentment and resignation, neither of which generates a positive future. Resigned or resentful individuals tend to see few possibilities for the future. Rather, they tend to envision a future equal to or worse than the past. Leadership Alchemy graduates possess the enhanced emotional intelligence to recognize their and others' moods and consciously choose the mood that aligns with their desired outcome. Graduates appreciate the power of intention and choice and the power that comes from being appreciative and future focused. This combination of attributes allows creative, future-focused ideas to emerge that otherwise would not.

"PAYING IT FORWARD": LEADERSHIP ALCHEMY SUCCESS STORIES

In the spirit of the program's appreciative future focus, about six months into the program the participants are officially anointed as Ambassadors of Positive Change. With a bit of pomp and circumstance, in ceremonial fashion, each is given personalized business cards with that title. Along with the title comes the responsibility to contribute to positive organizational change by "paying it forward" (to borrow a phrase from the film *Pay It Forward*).

As leaders and as followers, Ambassadors of Positive Change have many ways to pay it forward. The program requires that each Learning Team design and implement an action learning project that affords them the opportunity to apply the skills and tools they have learned to a real organizational issue. "Simply described, action learning is both a process and a powerful program that involves a small group of people solving real problems while at the same time focusing on what they are learning and how their learning can benefit each group member and the organization as a whole."[13] Over time the participants gain competency and build their action learning muscle, so to speak, in the context of work and their leadership journey. The project enables the participants to apply what they've learned and to share leadership tools with what is, in essence, their client. In doing so, each team member must set a learning stretch for himself or herself. Past action learning projects resulted in

1. Improved teamwork between a science division and its information technology support staff, as well as between NASA and the National Oceanic and Atmospheric Administration's National Environmental Satellite Data and Information Service

2. Enhanced collaboration and leveraging of resources between mentoring programs at two NASA installations

3. Improved synergy between Goddard's science and engineering disciplines

4. Enhancements to Goddard's individual development planning process

5. Visibly highlighting for all Goddard employees our "unsung heroes," enhancing everyone's connection with our mission

6. Streamlined the vetting process for foreign national visitors in order to facilitate conversations about partnering opportunities

After program completion, graduates frequently seek other ways of paying it forward at the center, from their roles as both follower and leader. Examples include participating in an initiative to enhance Goddard's awards and recognition approach, serving as mentors in one of several developmental programs, and attaining coaching credentials to build internal coaching capacity.

CONCLUSION

To date, approximately one hundred NASA Goddard employees have benefited from the unique and powerful Leadership Alchemy program experience.[14] By receiving "space to grow" and the support of a committed community, participants complete their nine-month hero's journey transformed. The graduates are more courageous followers and leaders, willing to challenge the status quo, scale the organizational silence barriers, and create a new behavioral norm. They've blurred the leadership-followership distinction in their belief that anyone can be a leader, regardless of his or her positional title and hierarchical placement. By believing that power is infinite, not finite,[15] they seek a win-win solution as they influence others at all levels of the organization. They've learned, as followers, that they can change the outcome and powerfully influence the future. As both leaders and followers, these Ambassadors of Positive Change vigilantly seek the right moment to choose to make powerful and intentional moves. They've learned that whatever one focuses on, expands, and they choose to focus on creating a brighter and more positive future for themselves and NASA Goddard Space Flight Center.

The program graduates were courageous enough to transform themselves and are now courageous enough to help transform their organization. They teach that each of us possesses the capability to be powerful and courageous leaders and followers if we dedicate ourselves to transforming our way of being from the inside out before turning our attention to changing our organization. They teach us that setting a bold intention and, as S. Kanu Kogod says, being ten times bolder" than they are otherwise inclined to be can have huge personal and organizational benefits. To illustrate, eleven of the sixteen graduates from the first year's program were promoted—a few several times over—for example, from the grade 12 nonsupervisory to grade 15 supervisory level. I predict bold and bright futures for all the Leadership Alchemy graduates.

The way of being of the Leadership Alchemy program graduates manifests what Margaret Wheatley describes in her book *Turning to One Another,* when she says, "I believe we can change the world if we start listening to one another again. Simple, honest, human conversation. Not mediation, negotiation, problem-solving, debate, or public meetings. Simple, truthful conversation where we each have a chance to speak, we each feel heard, and we each listen well."[16] This could also describe the ideal for mutually respectful and powerful leader-follower relations that break down hierarchical cultures, eradicate the conditions that contribute to catastrophic decisions, and enable accomplishments that move humanity toward its most daring dreams.

Courageous Followers, Servant-Leaders, and Organizational Transformations

Linda Hopper

I t was late in the fourth day of the supervisory training program for transit managers. The group had been very good—collaborative, cooperative, and interested. My colleague and I were pleased that the ideas had captured the imagination of the participants. We strongly believed in the program we had designed, and presented it with conviction. As we exhorted people to go back to the job and apply what they had learned, several people nodded and made notes. But one participant, a newly promoted facilities supervisor, said, "Okay. You want me to have faith that I can make all these changes. And I want to see things get better. But are *you* going to be there when they squash me like a bug for doing something different?"

This new supervisor wanted assurance that if she made a commitment I would be there to scrape her wounded ego off management's windshield. It was one of those Great Moments in Training, and I am grateful to her for putting me on the spot. Today her question might be phrased, "Will you walk *with* me on this journey?" I believe the question is relevant in today's workplace and that the answer greatly influences how successfully we do business.

Managers and supervisors often complain that not enough people care about doing a good job, that there is little accountability, and that efforts to define problems often result in finger pointing. Employees also gripe about management, complaining that people at the top are often unwilling to own decisions, especially unpopular ones. Employees complain that no one seems to be in charge.

In the last thirty or so years, we have all witnessed a parade of organization development techniques designed to address these complaints: management styles, personality types, wilderness jaunts, team-building exercises, total quality circles, transformational leadership, and so on. Although consultants report positive results from these trust-building change interventions, each year a new one hits the market and promises even more stunning results. The truth, however, is that quick-fix fads may improve *morale* for a very brief period of time, but produce few if any lasting results. Eventually e-mails announcing this year's staff retreat produce groans and eye rolling, because although the participants have one-minute-managed, moved cheese, and tossed fish, nothing changed once everyone returned to the office, because changing culture requires a thoughtful sustained effort to

- Create a greater understanding of how organizations establish environments of accountability and excellence
- Nurture and sustain this environment
- Develop leaders who foster employees' accountability and commitment to produce a high-quality service or product

Courageous followership provides a window through which we can see a new organization, one in which leaders and employees create and sustain a culture of accountability and commitment because the leaders know they cannot achieve these goals alone. The days of the Lone Ranger or Heroic Leader are over, although the myth still lives in popular management publications. Organizational success in today's market requires leaders to share power, strategic decision making, and authority. The idea that one person will lope into the twenty-first-century marketplace followed by a posse of IT folks to save the company is ludicrous, but every day some company hires and advertises the New Change Agent who will turn the company around. The troops in the cubicles roll their eyes once more, and prepare to keep their heads down until the latest and greatest new hire bites the dust. Instead of engaging the people who know what the problems are and how to resolve them, too many companies insist in finding "new blood" to infuse into tired and dysfunctional cultures. It does not work.

Margaret Wheatley compares change in organizations to self-renewing systems we see in nature and argues that

- Organizations that deal with change most effectively possess the ability to renew themselves in structure, process, and integrity.

- Networks of relationships that transform and reform are one of the keys to successful change. These "adaptive organizations" allow the task to determine the organizational form, instead of retrofitting innovations into a traditional structure.

- We need to embrace the void, confident that we will be able to create order out of chaos.[1]

Clearly, organizational culture, the elusive and slippery beast most frequently blamed for dysfunction, is not shaped, adapted, adjusted, changed, and sustained by leaders alone. Although the role of the leader in organizations is a topic that receives a great deal of attention, the action (or inaction) of followers, which actually determines the health and hardiness of an organization's culture and norms, has been addressed through the work of two authors, Robert E. Kelley *(The Power of Followership)* and Ira Chaleff *(The Courageous Follower)*. According to Chaleff (personal e-mail, Aug. 10, 2006), the underlying philosophy of courageous followership assumes that followers are not dependent on leaders' acts to live and behave as courageous followers. Their "motivation and power to do so stems from their commitment to common purpose and their own value system, not from the leader." Cultures that practice the principles of courageous followership have a greater chance of sustaining accountability and excellence because followers have the courage to assume responsibility, serve, challenge, participate in transformation, and take moral action. It is because courageous followers empower *themselves* to accept responsibility and accountability that the organization is more likely to develop a culture of critical thinking, deliberation, discernment, and judicious action. Courageous followers understand their own "agency" to work on behalf of the organization's mission and goals. Agency promotes commitment, responsibility, and service.

Sharing accountability is not always pretty, and it is not always fun. The impulse to "Let Mikey try it. He'll eat anything" (as portrayed in an old but popular cereal commercial) can be seductive. But if Wheatley is correct, letting Mikey eat it means that none of us ever develop our own taste buds—or abilities to conceive, develop, implement, and foster change efforts. Wheatley's advice to develop "networks of relationships to transform" cultures can be best achieved through developing a cadre of courageous followers, not an accommodating uncritical posse.

THE COURAGEOUS FOLLOWER AT GEORGETOWN UNIVERSITY

> *You're gonna have to serve somebody.*
>
> Bob Dylan

The Leadership Training Program at Georgetown University was established in 1996 when the offices of risk management, legal counsel, human resources, and affirmative action joined forces to decrease the university's liability that could result from ineffective management actions and decisions. The first director of the program, Sally Park, developed the program's architecture and created the Professional Manager Certificate (PMC). After about eighteen months, the lure of Colorado's mountains took Sally and her husband west, and I was hired to direct this new and exciting program.

Over the last ten years, the Leadership Training Program has grown at a rapid pace. What began with about thirty highly committed participants and twenty classes per year is now a program that fills over eighteen hundred seats annually in over 120 separate class sessions. We have awarded over 150 PMCs, logged in hundreds of hours of organizational and career development consultations, and provided targeted training sessions for each of our campuses (main, medical, and law).

To obtain the PMC, which is open to all staff and faculty, people must complete five required courses and earn sixty additional developmental units (six hours of class equal six units). We have open enrollment throughout the year so that people can begin attending classes as soon as they arrive at Georgetown. We open the program to all staff and faculty regardless of the job they currently hold, so that

- We model inclusiveness, a core value at Georgetown.

- People from different "worlds" at the university learn from each other.

- We can develop a culture of learning in which status and role are irrelevant.

Originally, there were only two required courses to earn the PMC: Fundamentals of Leadership and Practical and Legal Considerations in the Workplace. Ten years later, the requirements are Fundamentals of Leadership, Practical and Legal Considerations for Managers, Human Resources Policies and Procedures, Harassment Prevention, and the Courageous Follower.

We believe that Georgetown University is the only organization to require The Courageous Follower course in a similar training program. How and why we selected this course to become a requirement hearkens back to my predecessor, Sally Park, who had read and been impressed with Chaleff's *The Courageous Follower*. She suggested that its author might make an interesting keynote speaker and urged me to read the book as well.

After I finished the book later that week, I was similarly impressed that the topic of followership might make a significant contribution to our program, and invited Mr. Chaleff to teach a class. After several semesters of its receiving rave reviews from participants, we decided that the Courageous Follower course encompassed the values implicit in the PMC—phrased in stages of *courage* to assume responsibility, serve, challenge, participate in transformations, take moral action, and listen to followers—and therefore merited core curriculum status. More often than not, the evaluations from this course urged our office to require that every manager and senior leader at Georgetown attend this course. Since November 1998, over four hundred people have.

The Leadership Training Program serves as a laboratory for people to come together to learn about leadership and followership so that they can return to their schools, departments, and offices ready to influence our culture. We believe that real change is not driven from the top down, but, as argued by Margaret Wheatley, grows throughout the organization as seeds planted in a garden.

More important, we believe that The Courageous Follower class helps us focus on the special values inherent in Jesuit education. Loyola University identifies the essence of Jesuit education on its website in the following way:

> Jesuit education is a call to human excellence, to the fullest possible
> development of all human qualities. This implies a rigor and academic

excellence that challenges the student to develop all of his or her talents to the fullest. It is a call to critical thinking and disciplined studies, a call to develop the whole person, head and heart, intellect and feelings.

The Jesuit vision of education implies further that students learn how to be critical, examine attitudes, challenge assumptions, and analyze motives. All of this is important if they are to be able to make decisions in freedom, the freedom that allows one to make love-filled and faith-filled decisions.

The values of a Jesuit education are further expressed at Georgetown University by its vision and policies:

a place where issues of importance to the Church and society can be discussed in a spirit of dialogue and mutual respect. A sign of a healthy university community is the existence of an intellectual vitality in which a great range of ideas are expressed and considered. Our Speech and Expression Policy reflects our Catholic and Jesuit heritage in its inherent inclusive nature. This policy affords all of our students, faculty, and staff, both in and out of the Catholic community, the right to free thought and expression.

WHAT PMC OFFERS IN COMMON WITH "JESUIT EDUCATION": HOW WE PROMOTE "MEN AND WOMEN IN SERVICE TO EACH OTHER"

Creating leadership and management training programs in a Jesuit environment can be daunting as well as exciting. It is daunting to know that Ignatius set such high standards, and exciting because Jesuit universities are one of the few places in the world that provide such rich opportunity to live *cura personalis* (with attention to the whole person). Throughout the creation of our programs, we have striven to weave the following qualities into all our classes, which nurture both courageous leadership and followership:

Dedication to human dignity, a foundation of our program and taught by all instructors; a call to develop the whole person—head and heart, intellect and feelings

Critical thinking and disciplined studies, a transformational education that challenges people to develop the goals and values that will shape their lives; the opportunity to develop not only the intellect but also moral and spiritual character

Reverence for and an ongoing reflection on human experience

Creative companionship with colleagues

Spirit of dialogue and mutual respect

Courses that provide self-assessment, feedback, reflection, and creative collaboration

Classes in ethics, critical thinking, followership, ways to manage fairly and justly, diversity, and self-awareness

Before Georgetown University incorporated The Courageous Follower course into its requirements for the PMC program, we heard complaints about a lack of accountability and responsibility from leaders and staff. We have witnessed a decrease in those complaints over the last eight years, and attribute the increase in accountability and responsibility to our employees' understanding of what it means *to serve* in our complex environment. We have heard from leaders and staff that the principles of courageous followership have enabled them to work together to achieve ambitious goals, hear issues and problems more clearly, and face challenges openly and with new resolve.

Georgetown University is far from perfect, and although the participation in the PMC program has grown by leaps and bounds, we still have much work to accomplish; however, in those schools, departments, and offices where leaders and staff have completed The Courageous Follower course and other leadership classes, we have seen a decrease in unproductive conflict, complaints, and grievances. I will offer my analysis of why this is so in the following discussion of commitment.

COMMITMENT: THE FOUNDATION OF RESPONSIBILITY AND SERVICE

Shared commitment is the glue that reinforces the connections between leaders and followers. When the organization reels from internal or external threats, commitment and shared meaning act as binding agents to keep leaders and followers focused on critical goals, mission, and vision. Shared commitment in a healthy organization leads to mission- and vision-based decisions that enable it to adapt and transform itself. Organizations that lack shared commitment from both leaders and followers open the possibility that self-interest, silo management, and empire building will override the mission and vision, and result in serious deviation from companies' real meaning. Leaders and followers who understand the importance of commitment, I believe, are able to deal with change constructively and inclusively.

We make and keep commitments every day. In fact, established habits are often the result of commitments we made to initiate personal change or self-improvement. Sometimes the commitments were made to ourselves, but other times these commitments were made to family, friends, colleagues, or bosses. Many commitments are rooted in self-interest, but what motivates us to make and keep a commitment to others? And what actions from the other assist us in deciding to commit?

In his book *Influence,* Dr. Robert Cialdini argues that understanding the components of commitment, how we use—or don't use—them, is important to our ability to develop a workplace that practices accountability and excellence, which are intrinsic to exemplary leadership and followership. The following is a brief description of the components:

Liking/similarity. As a rule, people prefer doing things for people they like and people they perceive to be similar to themselves. Companies such as Amway, Tupperware, and Mary Kay have capitalized on the fact that we are more likely to buy products from friends than from strangers.[2] In large organizations, informal networks allow people to cut through bureaucracy and red tape. Frequent contact and familiarity with our colleagues makes team-oriented learning and cooperation more likely to occur.

Ability to view others as allies. One of the possible products of overarching and conjoint goals is the ability of groups to begin to see each other as allies, not enemies.[3] In large organizations, employees are not only divided according to title, department, division, and location but also separated by class, status, race, and gender. Frequently, the latter group of characteristics becomes the most divisive and the most difficult to address and overcome. Class, status, race, and gender create psychological distance that prevents identification and liking. Organizations are likely to increase commitment and accountability if they are able to overcome these barriers.

Conjoint efforts toward common goals. Being able to understand how individual efforts contribute to the overall success of the work unit, department, and organization provides a sense of belonging, increases self-esteem, encourages pride in work, and fosters cooperation.[4] Employees who believe that their individual goals coincide with those of the organization are more likely to go the extra mile for the good of the group. Moreover, when employees understand how their efforts are joined together with the efforts of other departments and work units, accountability for results increases; in addition, psychological distance is reduced, which permits dissimilar groups to see each other as allies and advocates.

Ability to "see" own success. No one wants to be associated with a loser. Professional sports teams fully understand how important it is for fans to hold up foam fingers that declare "We're Number One." If our team wins, we win. If they lose, well, we choose another team. This principle carries over into the workplace as well. Employees have no desire to work for an organization, department, or manager perceived to be a "loser." Cialdini states that we "purposefully manipulate the visibility of our connection with winners and losers in order to make ourselves look good to anyone who could view these connections."[5]

It follows that the more employees perceive their work unit, department, organization, or manager to be a loser, the more likely they are to separate from it and disown decisions, actions, and programs.[6] In order for employees to acknowledge the connection—and be accountable—they must be able to connect success to themselves.

Belief that individual actions make a difference. Employees who perceive that they are given responsibility but no authority are not likely to make a commitment to the decisions made by those who exercise power. However, employees who believe that they have the authority and the responsibility to effect organizational change are more likely to demonstrate commitment and accountability.[7]

THE BARRIERS TO COMMITMENT

No one gets up in the morning and muses over a cup of coffee, "Oh boy, I can't wait to go to work and screw things up again!" Employees want to believe that their work is meaningful, that their actions make a difference, and that they belong to a worthy group.

Many consultants have accepted assignments for projects with prestigious companies and expected to find highly motivated and committed employees, only to discover unhappy and cynical people. While those on the outside see a shining corporate reputation, those inside the cubicles often see a harsher reality. Worthiness does not lie in the P&L sheet, a spot on CNN, or momentarily happy stockholders. When we see disaffected, disgruntled, distrustful employees who appear reticent to make a commitment to and be accountable for work or decisions, then one or more of the following barriers exist:

- Lack of identification with the group, individuals, and goals
- Lack of involvement in decision making and problem solving
- Belief that individual actions do not really matter because external forces are in control
- Perceived status, authority, or class differences that are translated into we-they conflicts
- Social proof that actions don't matter, that the system will prevail despite an individual's actions

Through courageous followership, each of these barriers to commitment can be lowered. Leaders can help foster courageous followership though authenticity and integrity on their part as decision makers. Anything less will increase cynicism and distrust.

COURAGEOUS FOLLOWERSHIP AND COMMITMENT

Much has been written about the "breaking of the implied social contract" that existed between employers and employees prior to downsizing, right-sizing, and all those unfortunate euphemisms that preceded plant closings and layoffs. Outplacement consultants exhort companies to replace the old contract with a new one that lets employees know from the get-go that they are responsible for their own careers, and the organization need only provide opportunity to live up to its end of the deal. The result is often that CEOs and presidents complain that no one is accountable; no one cares anymore. It all comes down to this:

- If leaders do not care about the people who work for and with them, if they exhibit a lack of authenticity and genuineness, then employees feel no need to make a commitment or be accountable.

- If organizations do not establish authenticity, genuineness, and caring as primary values and back them up with real programs, then we will continue to hear that there's no accountability.

Why should we be surprised? Would you declare your devotion to someone who repeatedly lets you know that you are expendable or someone who can be ignored? The links between commitment, responsibility, and service must be in place. Courageous followers can and will confront leaders if these are missing. But if leaders are repeatedly unresponsive, the best employees will seek other opportunities where these links are valued.

Leaders who promote courageous followership invite their employees as partners to create and sustain the organization's culture. It is through this partnership in service that employees are able to create, nurture, and sustain their commitment to the goals of the organization and, more often than not, the leader.

"Will you walk *with* me on this perilous journey?" asked the employee afraid to go back to the workplace and implement what she had learned in the training program. The fear she felt was well founded because not all leaders are receptive to the courageous follower who points out how things can be better. In The Courageous Follower course at Georgetown, Ira Chaleff teaches that fear is the "necessary condition for displaying courage." By identifying that she was afraid that she would be "squashed like a bug," the fearful employee had taken the first step toward exhibiting courage. When she returned to the workplace, she worked with her manager and was successful in applying the supervisory concepts we had covered.

To be an effective follower, individuals must look beyond their personal experience to embrace practices that provide support to leaders in times of ambiguity and flux. Cialdini's influence schema provides important steps to achieve this goal.

First, effective followers seek ways to work for **conjoint efforts toward common goals** through methods such as "reframing" issues, analyzing the components of conflict for lapses in critical thinking, or simply recommitting to the mission of the organization. Courageous followers are more likely to look for connections to the goals than criticize the leader's approach. When leaders embrace commitment to conjoint goals, they successfully promote identification with the group, individuals, and goals. In addition, involvement in decision making and problem solving increases when leaders facilitate working together to achieve common goals.

Second, being a courageous follower requires an employee to **see others as allies** committed to the mission and goals of the organization. Courageous followership cannot involve personal power grabs and internal political games. To truly see others as allies, the courageous follower extends high levels of trust to colleagues and especially the leader. As a result, perceived status, authority, or class differences that are translated into we-they conflicts tend to disappear.

Third, courageous followers are able to **see their own success** as the goals of the organization become a reality. Success breeds even more motivation and success, and the commitment of the courageous redoubles.

Fourth, participating in successful change efforts further substantiates the **belief that efforts make a difference.** Apathy becomes the "bug squashed on the windshield" as employees see that collaborative processes can and do help transform the workplace.

In addition, courageous followership negates the employee's past social proof that actions don't matter because the system prevails despite an individual's actions.

Courageous followership ends parental roles too often seen in older organizational cultures by encouraging people to assume responsibility and accountability. Rather than wait or compete for the leader's attention or direction, courageous followers act on behalf of the leader to exercise their commitment to excellence.

THE CONNECTION OF ACCOUNTABILITY TO EXCELLENCE AND QUALITY

Without making a commitment to the organization, department, or work unit, employees cannot be accountable for what they do or don't do. In short, *what we do not own, we deflect and deny.*

In the absence of accountability, excellence and quality are only buzzwords that can become overused and eventually ignored. Employees aren't stupid. They know that when their managers deflect decisions to "the executive office," there is no real effort being made to achieve excellence. When the folks at the top refuse to own it, it's not likely that the folks at the bottom will step forward to claim the process, product, or decision.

If there are no systems to measure and evaluate excellence, if people are not rewarded for excellence, then people create social proof that it does not matter even though it is claimed as a "primary organizational value." We will create order out of chaos no matter what and will use social proof as our evidence. Even when organizations act in irrational and incomprehensible ways, employees will discover or create a way to "understand." To relinquish understanding is to accept ambiguity and chaos, something very difficult for even the most mature worker. Knowledge is power. Our ability to understand provides us the individual control we need to continue to structure reality. Unfortunately, in the absence of commitment and accountability, our view of reality can become cynical, which is the opposite of courageous followership.

THE ROLE OF THE LEADER'S PRACTICES

What do leaders need to demonstrate to create courageous followers? Chaleff advises leaders to model soliciting and accepting feedback, foster divergent points of view, encourage direct communication instead of complaints, and reward courage. In addition, Chaleff exhorts leaders to avoid defending their own points of view, be available, and follow up on conversations. However, leaders who want to create, nourish, and sustain effective courageous followership also need to heed the advice of Robert K. Greenleaf, who created the Servant-Leader model.

Greenleaf pointed out that the servant-leader manager honors five "unspoken" employee requests:

1. Hear me and understand me.

2. Even if you disagree with me, please don't make me wrong.

3. Acknowledge the greatness within me.

4. Remember to look for my loving intentions.

5. Tell me the truth with compassion.[8]

Leaders who practice awareness of these five "unspoken truths" rise above their peers because employees perceive that although the message might be difficult, the leader has fulfilled employees' need for dignity and respect. For leaders to engender the trust required to develop courageous followers, Greenleaf's five elegant steps are required. Employees who are not understood, who are told their ideas or concerns are wrong, who are made to feel socially inferior, whose intentions are always impugned, and who hear difficult messages in the harshest manner will not sign on as courageous followers.

THE PROBLEM WITH ERNIE

This is a true story, an event that changed the way I thought about management and supervision in radical ways. This event occurred over twenty years ago, but it still haunts me, and I still wonder if I could have changed what happened.

During the supervisory training program mentioned earlier in this chapter, a middle-aged man who had over twenty years of experience as a transit operator and supervisor was a participant. He was an affable, quiet man who smiled easily and genuinely seemed to enjoy attending the four-day program; however, when he arrived for the first of two follow-up sessions a few weeks later, he was anything but cheerful. As he sat at the table staring down at his handouts, his entire body appeared deflated.

I approached him and said, "Ernie, what's the problem? Is everything okay?" He replied in a monotone voice that he had recently received his performance review and that he had been totally bashed by his manager, who had a reputation as one of the harshest men in the organization. Subsequent participants in the training program also made similar complaints about this manager, and I decided that top management needed to know what was happening in this shop.

My meeting with the senior executive was well received. He thanked me for giving him the information and assured me that he would work with the manager so that his employees could receive focused and constructive feedback. I was relieved, and felt good about my meeting—that is, until I learned that the mid-level manager had been required to attend the *supervisory training* program, a directive that was sure to embarrass him with his peers and staff. After all, he had risen to the rank of *manager*. Being sent to the supervisory program (especially in 1985) was the same as receiving a demotion. He did attend, but was not participative: he was humiliated. Although I had begged senior management to change this decision, his attendance was required.

Ernie's second follow-up session occurred about a month after his manager had attended the supervisory program. When Ernie entered the room, I knew things had gotten worse in the shop. With visible anger, Ernie described what had happened. His manager had returned to the shop furious that he had been required to sit with the supervisors, and he had doubled down his hostility toward his men.

The day the clock fell off the wall in Ernie's office, things went from bad to worse. When the clock fell, Ernie gathered up all the pieces, placed them in a box, and proceeded to attempt a repair the clock—to save his office money. As he sat at his bench working on the clock, his manager entered and angrily demanded to know what happened. Ernie explained that the clock had fallen and that he was trying to repair it.

The manager raged that it was not Ernie's *job* to repair clocks, and that if he had been more careful, the clock would still be on the wall in working order. The manager gave Ernie a written reprimand and documented his "destruction of company property." Not only was Ernie furious, he also felt wrongly accused and persecuted. We talked about what he could do to change his manager's perception of him, but when he left that day, I was concerned about what would happen to this relationship.

A few weeks later, I left my position for a new and better job in the suburbs. One sunny afternoon after work, I picked up the evening paper on the stoop, and spotted an alarming headline: "Transit Manager's Daughter Injured by Mail Bomb."

My heart seemed to stop for a moment. Even before I read the story I knew whose daughter had been injured, and I suspected I knew who was responsible for this act of violence. A week later, another article appeared confirming that Ernie had mailed the package to his manager. Unfortunately, the manager's daughter had excitedly opened the mail, and her hands were badly damaged when the package exploded.

Certainly Ernie's manager never acknowledged Greenleaf's five unspoken requests. Had he bothered to look for Ernie's *loving intentions* or *acknowledge* Ernie's talents, he would not have charged him with destruction of property. Had he told Ernie the *truth with compassion*, perhaps Ernie would not have been so devastated after his performance review. It was clear that the manager might have *heard* Ernie, but surely never *understood* him. And the manager obviously needed to make Ernie *wrong*, which he demonstrated by officially reprimanding him for trying to repair a clock.

In addition to whatever serious psychological issues led Ernie to express his frustration violently, the "problem with Ernie" was in reality a much larger and more complex organizational problem. The culture of the organization was highly bureaucratic and often immobilized by issues of status and perceived power. That the manager felt humiliated by being in the room with supervisors, that status and class could be so important, spoke volumes about the culture. Had there been a culture of responsibility, service, transformation, moral action, and listening to followers, the situation between Ernie and his manager probably would have turned out differently.

The story of Ernie and his manager still haunts me, and the facts of the case inform all my work in organization development. I know from talking with him over a period of three years that Ernie had tried to be a courageous follower in a culture too structured, status oriented, and bureaucratic to accept his actions. Ernie was not a chronically disgruntled employee. His commitment to his company and his job was enormous. He cared about the agency's reputation, quality, and service. Like many of the supervisors, he had worked his way up through the ranks and had a close personal identification with the company. Ernie had been trying to improve things in his office, but unfortunately was viewed through a distorted managerial lens.

When I talk to senior executives about "open door policies" and "employee engagement," I ask probing questions to discover if the culture of the office or department merely provides lip service to buzzwords or has authentic practices to back them up. Ernie and his manager taught me more than I could ever have learned in a classroom. Although senior management wanted the transit authority trained in participative management, no one had sowed the seed for participative management to take root and grow. No one had imagined that sending the middle manager to a supervisory training program could have begun a series of events that ended with a young woman losing her fingers and a respected supervisor being sent to jail.

CONCLUSION

The development of *imagination* is a theme central to Jesuit education. Both Chaleff's *The Courageous Follower* and the work of Robert K. Greenleaf provide inroads to nurturing and sustaining *moral imagination,* the cornerstone of ethical organizational cultures. Through the study of courageous followership, the staff and faculty of Georgetown University gain insight into how they can join in the transformation of our culture.

Attention to the whole person in the workplace is not a New Age fad. Ignatius of Loyola lived from 1491 to 1556, and throughout his life, St. Ignatius worked to help individuals open up their imagination to the fullest possible development of all human qualities through meditation, prayer, and contemplation. Combining courageous followership with servant leadership creates a workplace dynamic to foster and sustain imaginative cultures of excellence and accountability while attending to the authentic need for dignity and respect so critical in today's workplace.

Followership, also an ancient practice, is the foundation of all partnerships. When Jesus of Galilee said, "Come, follow me," He did not seek blind obeisance, sycophants, or toadies. He knew that His path would be treacherous, and that making the decision to follow required personal discernment and commitment to God.

"Follow me." In two words we can extend an invitation to participate, collaborate, grow, and achieve. In two words, we can offer ourselves as servant-leaders worthy of support and commitment.

Edith Wharton wrote, "There are two ways of spreading light—to be the candle or the mirror that reflects it."[9] By being worthy servant-leaders and courageous followers, we bring light into our organizations.

Followership in a Professional Services Firm

Brent Uken

I t is a fundamental business tenet that corporations pursue activities that help them achieve competitive advantage and improve the underlying economics of their operations. Activities range from making strategic decisions that fuel growth to implementing programs focused on increasing the productivity and well-being of their employees.

Some practitioners argue that a strong, positive culture of empowerment and mutual respect is the most important component of sustainable competitive advantage, particularly in a professional services firm. Regardless of whether or not this claim is true, positive changes in the underlying culture of a corporation provide significant benefits, not the least of which are improvements in employee retention and creation of a differentiating factor in the market for corporate talent.

In my firm, I have experienced several organizational changes during my seventeen-year tenure, some driven by internal forces, such as our transition to global focus and alignment, and some required by current or anticipated future external forces, such as competitive challenges, the issuance of new accounting rules, and changes in securities industry regulations. In addition, given the size and structure

127

of our firm, we operate as a matrix organization, where individuals may have several solid- and dotted-line reporting relationships. This type of environment may be ambiguous and frustrating for team members, leaving some feeling disconnected and disenfranchised. Antidotes to these tendencies are important to our individual and collective success.

As proud as I am of my firm, and as much effort as it has made to support our people, I understand that it is not immune to flawed leadership. Consequently, I recognize the need—particularly in these changing times—to focus not just on our leadership but also on our followership. I am fortunate to work in a group that has seen minimal turnover in our leadership ranks, and we've built the trust required for courageous followership to come to the fore. I see the results of our efforts in higher employee engagement, better teaming, and a sense of shared responsibility—what we refer to as becoming good "stewards of our business."

INTRODUCING COURAGEOUS FOLLOWERSHIP IN MY FIRM

My first formal exposure to the concept of followership was in 2000, when I read Chaleff's *The Courageous Follower*. I was at the beginning of a three-year rotation as the managing partner of people and competency development for a practice that comprised several hundred U.S.-based professionals who provided corporate finance and related advisory services to middle-market and Fortune 500 firms. Because the key themes of his book resonated with me and were highly relevant for my firm, my learning team and I contacted Chaleff to discuss our plans for raising the awareness of the concept with our professionals. Ultimately, we purchased several hundred copies of the book for distribution within our practice, and we engaged Chaleff to lead his workshop at our annual orientation program for new managers.

My initial goal was to introduce the concept of courageous followership to the broadest audience to maximize our opportunity for acceptance and action. I had to be mindful, however, of the cost of implementation, given the number of competing initiatives already in place and in the pipeline.

My learning team and I focused on reaching two groups of professionals: (1) those new to the firm with no (or at least minimal) preconceptions about the culture of the practice; and (2) those newly promoted into a managerial role within the practice who would have the broadest day-to-day influence on team interaction and behavior. The first group was composed primarily of recent college graduates who ranged in age from twenty to twenty-five years old. The second group was made up of individuals with approximately four to six years of work experience; these individuals ranged in age from twenty-five to thirty years old. Given average retention rates, we realized that these groups of individuals would constitute the majority of our practice within a few years' time.

Our initial goal was to raise awareness in these groups and begin a dialogue about followership so that we could develop a baseline understanding of how receptive our team would be, how quickly we could implement, and how hard we could push. Over time the focus of our activities transitioned to a focus on individuals and small teams within our transaction advisory service practice and, more specifically, within the Valuation and Business Modeling group. We have been focused most recently on reconfirming and fine-tuning our values and on embedding the concepts of courageous followership implicitly in our training programs and other team-building activities.

BENEFITS OF FOSTERING A CULTURE OF COURAGEOUS FOLLOWERSHIP

Our experience has shown that there are several significant benefits that accrue to corporations that support and foster a culture of courageous followership, and to the individuals whose actions create and define this culture. Although the spectrum of benefits will vary across organizations, there are three broad categories: (1) increasing employee engagement and effectiveness; (2) reducing the elements of risk faced by the corporation; and (3) providing an antidote to flawed or toxic leadership.

Increasing Employee Engagement and Effectiveness

Courageous followers are invested in the organization and care deeply about its direction and success; they are committed and engaged. This transcends the "feel-good" (albeit important) areas of, say, general morale and employee satisfaction, and translates ultimately into measurable economic payoff. More specifically, an economic payoff arises from the increase in the retention rate of high-performing employees and the improved ability to raise the talent bar with qualified new hires.

Courageous followership improves retention in an organization because it results in a fundamental shift in an individual's perspective. I have seen the shift, and it can be quite powerful when, for example, an individual moves from a passive mode ("I'm an employee") to an active mode ("I'm a steward of the business"). Individuals progress from believing that they can neither effect change nor improve their working conditions to knowing that they are responsible for, and can effect change in, their working environment, including their relationships with senior leaders. In short, positive changes in culture will shift an employee's focus from basic needs to higher-order concepts relating to personal achievement and self-actualization. These changes lead to higher daily engagement and a general feeling that one's work has purpose and meaning, two prerequisites for higher employee satisfaction.

A tangible result of this shift is that corporations who develop this type of culture will find themselves in the enviable position of having better talent gravitate to them during the recruiting process. This last point is especially important as workforce demographics and preferences change, particularly if there are shortages of qualified candidates needed to fill open positions. Demographic shifts in the next ten to twenty years will be huge, as baby boomers—who are in senior leadership positions currently—retire in record numbers. This will make way for the next generation of leaders, those in the twenty-five- to forty-year-old demographic. Fostering courageous followers who will become the next wave of leaders will confer significant advantage to corporations that are mindful of this dynamic.

Reducing the Elements of Risk Faced by the Organization

A key element of corporate survival is to reduce or mitigate the risks faced by the corporation, regardless of whether they are of a competitive, economic, or legal nature. A culture of courageous followership helps a corporation inoculate itself on a daily basis from these risks by supporting individuals who believe in "doing the right thing" and who are actively engaged in building, promoting, and safeguarding the organization.

From a competitive perspective, individuals on the front lines are closer to client feedback and to actions taken by the competition. Consequently, these individuals are able to see patterns develop before formal, empirical evidence may reach a senior leadership team in the form of statistical analyses or slick PowerPoint presentations. This is true even in today's accelerated reporting environment and with sales organizations' ability to mine relevant data quickly and in depth. If a culture of courageous followership exists, those on the front lines are likely to share their opinions. From an economic perspective, companies reduce their risk when their people make better business decisions. Such decisions clearly stem from diversity in thought and diversity in approach; this diversity will help prevent insular thinking (groupthink) that leads to poor or suboptimal decisions.

Legal risks are in a league by themselves. As we have seen over the past decade, there are significant and even catastrophic consequences when individuals and organizations make poor decisions. In my industry, these negative outcomes are well documented, and they resulted in the failure of one of the Big 5 public accounting firms and in additional rules and regulations by professional and governmental organizations. Although it may be convenient to apply a "bad apple" framework to these situations (isolating the poor decisions and bad behaviors with a single individual), it is rarely accurate to do so. In short, courageous followers who operate in these environments facilitate the right behaviors—and confront poor behaviors—at crucial times. They are willing to raise their hands and speak up for the greater good of the firm when they see signs of inappropriate behavior.

Providing an Antidote to Flawed or Toxic Leadership

This is arguably the most visible of the benefits arising from a strong culture of courageous followership. You can no doubt draw on your own experience to visualize a particularly poor or ineffective leader and reconnect with the negative impact this leader had on you, your colleagues, and the organization. Although anecdotes of toxic leadership provide the most colorful (albeit extreme) examples, the most important benefits to the organization will arise from building and improving relationships with the much larger number of leaders who are not toxic, but who have very human limitations and personality flaws and who overreact to the pressures they face. On the basis of my twenty years of professional work experience, I believe that this latter group comprises the majority of the leaders employed by corporations. When we improve the effectiveness of these leaders, they make better decisions (or at least make fewer bad decisions), and there is an increase in the overall morale of these leaders' teams, groups, or divisions.

BARRIERS TO BUILDING A CULTURE OF COURAGEOUS FOLLOWERSHIP

In an ideal world, corporations have values and a purpose that resonate with and motivate their employees. These corporations also have leaders who are committed to creating a positive work environment by providing ample opportunities for the employees in their organizations to grow professionally. In this ideal world, individuals are passionate about their careers, feel a strong sense of purpose in an organization, and are grounded in both personal and corporate values. If this were the existing reality, there would clearly be minimal (if any) barriers to fostering a culture of courageous followership within an organization. As we move away from these ideal conditions, however, barriers to fostering a culture of courageous followership inevitably arise.

When corporations are operating at their peak, they provide a clear and compelling vision for their employees, are sincerely concerned about their employees' development, and proactively foster a culture of courageous followership. In reality, corporations may be at a low or high point along any of these axes. Corporations may not only lack receptivity to the concept of courageous followership but even foster a culture in which practicing courageous followership does not seem to be a viable option. In reality, corporations fall short of ideals. A less than optimal situation is made worse in the face of pressures created by competitive threats, demands of investors, and changes in the regulatory environment.

From the perspective of the corporation, barriers that frequently arise in conversations about the topic include the existence of poor leaders (ineffective and uninspiring leadership), the celebration of individual leaders (to the exclusion of teams and other contributors), and a lack of clearly articulated values and purpose. Although these factors may be outside the usual scope of influence of those who desire a culture shift based on the concept of courageous followership, they are not insurmountable.

The most expedient culture change would be initiated and supported by senior leadership, but this is not a prerequisite for making progress toward culture shift. In fact, in some instances, visible support from the top might be damaging initially if employees have credibility or trust issues with the senior leadership team.

A factor that may diminish senior leadership support is that initiatives of this type do not readily lend themselves to numerical analysis and supporting metrics, such as return on investment. It also may be difficult to determine what "success" means in this context. It should therefore come as no surprise that given these factors and the reality of limited resources and investment dollars, initiatives focused on courageous followership may be difficult to launch or scale up unless these types of issues are specifically addressed and overcome.

Most important, though, is that without addressing the issues from the perspective of the individual, success will be limited at best. Like companies and leaders, employees fall short of the ideal. There are differences in how seriously they take their careers, in whether they are just entering the workforce or close to leaving it, in their positive or negative past experiences with leaders, and in how dependent they are on their employment with the company as a source of income. The fundamental barrier for the individual is that acting courageously involves taking risks. Whether these risks are real or perceived is moot—this distinction is irrelevant when viewed from the perspective of the individual. In an ideal world, acting courageously and doing the right thing should be reward enough, but these concepts ring hollow when loss of employment could result in missed mortgage payments or lost health care benefits. Those less devoted to the company or leader may ask the question, "What's in it for me?"

CAUSES FOR OPTIMISM AND PERSISTENCE

As I move to address the barriers to implementation in the final section of this chapter, the following considerations provide a foundation for optimism and the energy required for sustained efforts in this area.

- Outcomes are not binary; implementation does not have to be an all-or-nothing proposition. There are benefits along the way, and the gains achieved are worth the investment.

- Trying to create a courageous followership culture for an organization of several hundred, several thousand, or even tens of thousands of employees is a daunting task. Instead of attempting to "boil the ocean," as the saying goes, identify small teams or small groups within an organization that are receptive to the idea. Gains can be made in these areas and then leveraged across the organization.

- Consider these questions: "What is the alternative?" and "Is the status quo really acceptable?" Simply pondering these questions may provide the motivation to find creative ways to foster a courageous followership culture within an organization.

In my case, developing a culture of courageous followership proceeded rather slowly, and our successes occurred on a relatively small scale during the first few years of our efforts. A rather large step forward occurred approximately three years after our initial design and implementation efforts began: our learning leaders embraced the concepts, saw their importance to the firm, and ultimately made relevant content available to all of our North America–based personnel.

QUESTIONS TO CONSIDER IN DEVISING AN INITIATIVE

Before designing an initiative for culture change, it is imperative to examine the following questions:

- What are your short-term, intermediate, and long-term goals for this initiative?
- Is there senior leadership support for this initiative? What level of receptivity to the concept do you think you will find or can develop?
- What is the business case (value proposition) that can be made to support the initiative?
- Is there a general perception within the organization that senior leadership is credible and can be trusted?
- Who are the influencers (individuals with reach and leverage) below the senior leaders in the organization? Will they be receptive to these ideas?
- Are there subsets of employees (for example, teams or divisions) that may be more receptive to these ideas and that perhaps could be used to pilot certain items?
- How well articulated are the company's values and purpose? Do employees embrace them?
- What is your level of influence within the organization? Who would be your allies in the development and implementation of a courageous followership initiative?
- How will you and your organization be able to reinforce the concepts "on the ground" on a daily basis?

This list is by no means exhaustive. Just asking these questions may well spawn others. It may take weeks or months to fully address them all. I cannot overemphasize the importance of addressing these issues prior to the creation of any content or the implementation of any programs. The answers you develop will have a direct impact on how you choose to design your initiative and to develop and implement the corresponding learning curriculum.

STRATEGY AND IMPLEMENTATION

As with other initiatives, you will achieve optimal engagement with the creation and adoption of a corporation-wide "umbrella" under which the learning content fits, so that the content is not viewed as a one-off, flavor-of-the-day initiative that—like so many others before it—generates the skeptical sentiment of "this too shall pass." For example, you will achieve optimal effectiveness if there is an alignment of incentives and rewards with desired behaviors. Alignment should also be pursued with larger cultural change efforts that already enjoy a high level of broad support. Can you effectively roll out courageous follower initiatives without these alignments? Of course, but you will have to be more creative and more targeted to selected audiences. Absent alignment, the time required to embed courageous followership in your corporate culture will significantly increase.

As with all learning content, several options exist for its dissemination. These include various means of content delivery, from reading background materials and raising awareness to holding webcasts and offering classroom-based learning and similar interactive events to introduce and reinforce higher-order concepts and application. However, unlike just-in-time technical skills or "soft" skills such as those needed for presentations, the courageous follower concepts require more time and effort to convey effectively and to reinforce.

Effectiveness in delivery is directly correlated with how passionately instructors and those responsible for implementation believe in the concepts themselves. What also matters is that company-specific examples, including corporate storytelling and company-specific case studies, are incorporated into the curriculum and course materials. Although there are some extremely powerful examples provided in Chaleff's book, without company-specific content and examples, it is likely that individuals will fail to fully engage with the material.

Ultimately, however, the most effective way to institute a culture shift with respect to the courageous follower concepts is to identify influential individuals and engage them on a one-on-one basis, with dialogue, training, and coaching. Creating early adopters will allow you to leverage their experiences and their passion. How do you identify those who are receptive? First, you probably know at least a few individuals who already live with these values. Second, you can gauge interest at a training program or other events where the content and ideas are introduced and you are able to observe reaction and buy-in. Some will likely approach you afterwards or in private, and share such comments as "Hey, this was great!" or "It was a long time in coming . . . and we really need this."

Even if there are negative reactions ("This will never work" or "Leadership doesn't care about this" or "I have real work to do—let me get back to it") you have the ability to engage these individuals in a constructive dialogue. Learning about the objections and squaring off with them will allow you to further customize your approach and learning content for future offerings. Best-case scenario? You are able to convert an influential naysayer—who then becomes one of your most influential champions.

CONCLUSION

Those responsible for the creation of a culture of courageous followership should be under no false impression that even with full support of senior leadership, an ample budget, and appropriate resources for implementation that adoption and application of these concepts will be expeditious or received by all with open arms. However, the rewards for successful implementation are significant and can provide firms with competitive advantages, lower risk profiles, and significant economic benefits from improved employee engagement.

Developing Great Leaders, One Follower at a Time

Rodger Adair

O nly within the last few decades have researchers and scholars started to focus seriously on the enigmatic majority (followers) in organizations. This chapter focuses on this enigmatic majority that makes up the bulk of the workforce, the real engine behind multiple economies around the world. This chapter will look at followership strengths and weaknesses, how the pieces of "organizational puzzles" fit together to create teams and workgroups. In addition, this chapter will attempt to identify the different followership perceptions using a new model called the 4-D Followership Model. By the end of this chapter, you should understand how each follower fits into groups, establishing a firm foundation of followership and developing great leaders, one follower at a time.

We all recognize that the world would become total chaos if every person demanded to be in charge. We would have no societies, no governments, and no progress. Simon and Garfunkle's lyrics, "I am a rock, I am an island" would be commonplace; cooperation and teamwork would not exist. Language would never have developed if each of Earth's inhabitants had insisted on his or her own way to communicate. Although I have described an extreme situation, it portrays what the world could be like if no one allowed anyone else to lead him or her.

Schools teach children to sit still, be quiet, listen, and obey. They must not interrupt, disrupt, or even become too curious. Children must follow the lesson plan as the teacher presents it. Some fall into this peg hole easily, whereas others resist. These resisting children typically break out of their scheduled regimen of subordination, leading other children, role playing, and pretending to be in charge of some adventure. Many children express their desire to lead, whereas others openly wish to continue their role as follower.

In Phoenix, Arizona, a new Ford Explorer truck sported a license plate that read, "NO1HLPD," which seemed to translate into "No One Helped." The profound arrogance of this statement struck me. No matter what this license plate refers to, the statement cannot be true. Of course someone helped! Assuming the license plate was bragging about financial independence, a whole host of people (customers, coworkers, suppliers) helped along the way. If this license plate was talking about the buying of the truck itself, then who taught this driver how to safely control a vehicle? Who made the vehicle? How could this driver afford this truck without a job? Where did the skills come from to qualify for that job? Who gave this driver the opportunity to test-drive the truck prior to the purchase?

Many leaders stand in front loudly proclaiming, "NO1HLPD!" when discussing accomplishments and successes. This has been drilled into their minds since childhood.[1] Our schools of advanced learning still profess this today. Two false mantras are being taught today in business schools: first, that followership is a part of leadership; second, that attaining a leadership position is the best way to measure success within the ranks of an organization. Both of these have received so much airplay that they seem to have become reality. Yet employees do a great deal more following than leading, even as leaders. For the most part, followership behaviors drive tactical successes. Leadership talents and skills propel strategic accomplishments.

Despite the volumes of writings illuminating leadership, most people have yet to understand the very fabric of this discussion. Followership is *not* a part of leadership—leadership is a part of followership. All people begin with the foundation as a follower and build up from there. A house must sit on a solid and firm foundation to withstand the elements outside. A strong house will last no longer than the foundation. To some degree, each person still maintains that status of follower. As long as this foundation holds, the ability to lead will flourish.

The research for this chapter began with my asking three critical questions about followership principles: (1) When are employees followers, and when are they leaders? (2) Can people occupy the space of both realities simultaneously, or do they exist in only one role at a time? (3) What kinds of followers are out there, and are these types measurable? Can we classify styles of followership?

Merriam-Webster Online defines followership as "Following, the capacity or willingness to follow a leader." This definition seems too vague and broad for research purposes, so I needed to find one that suited the depth to which I hoped to go to find answers to this chapter's questions.

Joseph Rost provided the best definition of leadership: "Leadership is an influence relationship among leaders and followers who intend real changes that reflect their mutual purposes."[2]

This leads to a parallel definition that can apply to followership: "A follower shares in an influence relationship among leaders and other followers with the intent to support leaders who reflect their mutual purposes." This would mean that collaborative employees (followership) would be the very support system leaders need to lead effectively.

I need to place a small disclaimer here. In a presentation at a recent conference (and in Chapter Three of this volume), Dr. Rost stated that he does not support the term *followership*.[3] Leaders and followers cannot be separated. He played a segment of the John Lennon song "Power to the People," demonstrating the intertwined relationships of leaders and followers. In application, this is true. However, when looking at leaders and collaborators, researchers view this relationship as two different sides of the same coin, but they have stared so long and hard at the leadership side that most have no idea what sits on the other side of that coin.

A study of followers, followership, collaborators, or even collaborator-ship indicates an initiative to finally look at the enigmatic masses that sit in the dark shadows of organizations. *Followership* is a conjured term, but it gives the average reader a mental picture with which to work, so I choose to use it.

ENIGMATIC MAJORITY

A consistent theme keeps surfacing throughout the research and writings about both leadership and followership. Some researchers and scholars indicate that employees should always be leadership bound. They believe that everyone wants to have the opportunity to be a leader in one way or another, and that leaders need to give followers that opportunity.[4] But some people feel punished for trying to participate, then when given the opportunity to lead, they shy away. Managers bypass other employees thinking they do not want to take on the mantle of leadership when in these employees' hearts they want the opportunity to excel, though they may be afraid of repercussions. Still others do not want to take on a leadership role in the workplace, yet take on this role in social, community, or family settings. Why at times do people prefer to follow?[5] While reading the available literature, I created a list of twelve perceptions (not all-inclusive) that employees may have of themselves as followers; these may influence their choice.

Followership Perceptions	"Why do I choose to follow?"
Personal values	"I'm not the chosen leader, and I will respect that."
Economic status	"I make more money doing than leading."
Personal goals or focus	"I don't have time; one day I plan on being . . ."
Humility	"Why should I be in charge? I'm no better than . . ."
Lack of confidence	"I don't feel I am good enough to lead."
Fear	"What if I fail, or give bad directions?"
Ignorance or lack of comprehension	"I don't know how to take charge."
Lack of trust	"You have to pull a fast one to get promoted here."
Lack of feeling of inclusion	"I'm not part of their clique."
Lack of conviction	"It is not something I'm interested in now."

| Comfort or complacency | "I'm happy here. I don't need the headaches." |
| Perceived social status | "I'm not even in their league." |

Many employees (followers and leaders alike) use these excuses. While in this mode, employees seek to avoid becoming part of leadership, or higher levels of leadership, when their values (organizational, personal, or both) differ from those of the leadership or the organizational culture at that time. They decide that they do not want to lead that group of people, even if they have held leadership roles previously. Some would gladly lead others again when given the right opportunity. Realizing that employees exist in different categories of followership and leadership mind-sets all the time, I concluded that a way to measure these categories had to exist. The trick was to understand how these mind-sets would look on paper, which would serve both to easily identify and to clearly explain their relationships in the workplace. Considerable reading and observation on the subject of followership led to the development of the 4-D Followership Model.

Building on the prior personality typing of such researchers as Carl Jung, William Moulton Marston, and Walter Clark, I have identified four basic patterns of employee behaviors in an organization. Most of the literature and research supports this assertion without putting a graphic tool in place to visualize the concept. The 4-D Followership Model attempts to explain the basic roles occupied by millions of people inside thousands of organizations large and small, for-profit and nonprofit alike. Before we look at the model, we need to examine a key organizational puzzle to understand the model's descriptive value.

ORGANIZATIONAL PUZZLE

Organizations succeed or fail on the basis of the input and output of their people. However, employees succeed or fail based on the function of leader-follower relationships. These organizations measure success in one of (or in a combination of) three ways. First, companies measure success through financial growth and standing. Second, they evaluate the effectiveness of the leadership role within the ranks. Third, they measure success in terms of their ability to compete with (and conquer) the competition. It is here within these three measurables that the root of organizational change takes place. It is here that the organizational puzzle begins to take shape. Yet most people miss the followership piece that completes the organizational puzzle.

When managers focus on systems, they deselect the people and their needs. However, by focusing first on people, they in turn deselect the system. Managers and leaders tend to look at processes, costs, revenue, and end quality as prime qualifiers of success or failure. In focusing on those elements, they subordinate employee values, trust, attitudes, and relationships for the good of the company. To compensate, managers begin looking at their people from a leadership lens to fix those employees affected, thus deselecting the system at that point to focus time and energy on their people. What results is a mess of selecting and deselecting back and forth.

By balancing the focus equally on the organization and the people (and what these relationships might imply about the societies that constructed them), organizations are in constant conflict between continual change and perpetual stability.[6] One end of the spectrum satisfies organizational needs; the other end satisfies individual needs.

Organizations	People
Focus on change	Focus on stability
Continual growth	Pursuit of leisure
Seek for success in instability	Try to make job part of stability
Reward for growth through change	Seeks rewards for mastering processes

Lawrence (Lawry) de Bivort has noted, "Organizations often blame employees for having inadequate attitudes when in fact those attitudes are appropriate responses to organizational and societal problems."[7] We might also define "appropriate responses" as typical or common responses. And when people have been pressed long enough, their reactions become habitual.

When organizations implement change (whether focusing on market share, cultural communications, or restructuring), leaders often wonder why employees demonstrate stressful responses to the new change, often much more profound than anticipated. This stress can result from change itself. Stress can threaten an employee's sense of ownership on the job.[8] Feelings of ownership are a natural part of the human conditioning, a psychological reality of which many leaders seem unaware.

Some people react openly to stress, whereas others hold their emotions in; regardless of the type of response, everyone reacts to stress. In fact, individuals react to their perceptions of what the team expects of them as much as to their perceptions of what they expect of the team. What kind of baggage does an employee carry around in an organization? Is this baggage useful or detrimental to the processes assigned? What does this baggage (these appropriate or habitual responses) look like? Most often this baggage manifests itself in nonverbal communication.

Physical science theorizes that dark matter holds the universe together and that dark matter makes up as much as 90 percent of all matter in the universe; in much the same way, nonmanagerial employees make up a huge portion of the workforce, and the efforts of employees hold free enterprise together much the way that dark matter holds the universe together. Robert Kelley called this the organization in the shadows.[9]

If managers and leaders were to fall by the wayside, some employees could step up to the task and keep the organization alive. However, if employees were to resign en masse, management alone would not be sufficient to sustain the life of the organization. Followership is that dark matter that allows leaders and managers to direct activities. People are the foundation on which all organizations are built.

Leadership studies have become the focus for business and market research, whereas the study of human behavior in organizations gets relegated to the social sciences. Basically, the two are the same, yet many people devour leadership literature while passing up human behavior research as if it had no bearing on what makes organizations successful!

Some key social science research has looked at followers and followership under the names of workforce research, employee development, or human resource development. This research organizes the data for the use of managers and leaders, not the followers themselves. Focusing on followers as a distinct area of study entails looking at data that would be useful to both followers and leaders. This means establishing an active field of research that looks at human behavior from a follower's perspective first.

Companies have spent 80 percent of their time and research efforts looking at the 20 percent (leadership) within organizations, while spending barely 20 percent of their time and energy focusing on the other 80 percent (followers). Most training budgets support only 20 percent of the organization, leaving the other 80 percent in the shadows. It is time to turn on the lights to see the real talent within organizations, the real success, the real heart and soul that drive economies around the world.

4-D FOLLOWERSHIP MODEL

The model, illustrated in Figure 11.1, is a visual representation of how employees view themselves within the workforce—not just how they feel about their current positions, but how they express their appropriate and habitual behavior patterns within their respective organizations and positions. Considering the quadrant principle, we can see four distinct employee characteristics.

1. **Disgruntled** employees typically have been slighted (whether from an actual or perceived event). They have decided that this organization is of little value to them and that they are of little value to the organization.

2. **Disengaged** employees see the value of keeping their present job and will do the minimum to ensure continued employment. These employees do

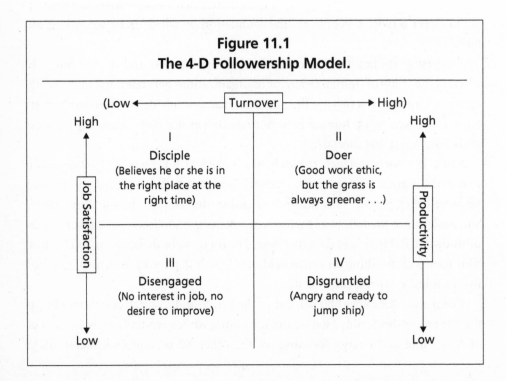

Figure 11.1
The 4-D Followership Model.

not buy into the company's mission or purpose. These employees' attitude could reflect either a personal issue or a cultural issue pervading the organization as a whole, but in either case, it hinders the individual's progress within this person's position.

3. **Doer** employees are motivated, excited to be part of the team. They are enterprising people, and overall are considered high producers. The only real issue with these employees is that no matter where they go in an organization, the grass always looks greener elsewhere. Turnover for career advancement is commonplace.

4. **Disciple** employees feel engaged; they are highly productive and plan to stay with the organization for a long time. There is little that will convince these employees that they are not in the right position at the right time. However, being team focused may mean that they miss great opportunities to excel individually as they help others along the way.

The next few paragraphs are an explanation of the 4-D Followership Model. Keep in mind that these descriptions are examples of single-minded employees who do not share traits with other quadrants. In reality, people cross boundaries daily and share many traits (both positive and negative) among all four of the quadrants. Yet people's most natural perceptions and tendencies fall within quadrants I or II (Disciple or Doer). When stress rises, behavior will move from the natural quadrant (I or II) to one of the stress quadrants (III or IV). Or, as is so often the case, employees share adaptable traits with the neighboring quadrants.

Quadrant I: Disciple (Focus: Serving Others' Needs)

This quadrant is a natural place for many followers and leaders to be. The employee who perceives work from this quadrant could easily be called the company person. These employees sacrifice for the good of the company, at times even becoming martyrs. These are employees of whom we all dream. They are loyal and committed to the mission, they are willing to work extra hours with a smile, and they hope to better the organization as a whole through their efforts. They are fully engaged in their work.

Sound a bit Pollyannaish? To most people this is an unreal state of mind—but these employees do exist, even if for a few days; they are there in your organizations, sometimes receiving the appreciation they deserve but often getting laughed at, stepped on, laid off, and deprogrammed away from believing that commitment and hard work can get them anywhere. Who is doing such damage to these angels of productivity? Well, you are. Your systems, your processes, and your employees are doing it. You are all doing it to each other when, inadvertently or not, you deselect the people.

The following are expected identifiable attributes and attitudes of the disciple:

- Inclusive (invites others to participate and share talents)
- Open-minded (willing to learn from others, engage in self-development, build the skill base)
- Adaptable and forgiving (easily accepts guidance from multiple leadership styles)
- Friendly (engages in open and progressive communication)
- Integrity (consistency, honesty)
- Strong work ethic (determination and productivity)
- Team player (collaborator; spotlights others' talents and helps others)
- Follow-up and follow-through (keeping on task even when others slack off)

Quadrant II: Doer (Focus: Serving Own Needs)

This quadrant is also a natural place for many followers and leaders to gravitate. Employees who perceive work from this quadrant could easily be called go-getters, productive, even aggressive. They have a strong commitment, and they seem like the disciples you were intent on hiring in the first place. They have a great work ethic. What could be better? Well, doers are always on the move: around, up, or out. The typical attitude of a doer is, "The grass is always greener," ensuring that their resumes are continually updated. They typically do not desire to stay with one job for too long. Retaining doers in an organization may mean finding new opportunities with bigger and better projects for them to keep them excited, as they are more loyal to their career aspirations than to the organization they currently work for.

The following are expected identifiable attributes and attitudes of the doer:

- Competitive (may be inclusive when it serves a need)
- Partially open-minded (on the lookout for better opportunities)

- Adaptable (easily accepts guidance from multiple leadership styles)

- Engages in selective communication (seeks first for own opportunities)

- Integrity (may or may not be an issue)

- Strong work ethic (seen as a way to get ahead)

- Conditional team player (collaborator; spotlights own talents and may help others)

- Follow-up and follow-through (keeps on task even when others slack off)

Quadrant III: Disengaged (Focus: Passive Reactions to Stress)

Disengaged is one of the two stress quadrants. When employees feel pulled away from their natural quadrant, they exhibit symptoms of stress. This quadrant identifies the passive response to stress. It may be difficult to observe at first, but grows quietly until it becomes difficult to control.

So much has been written of late about this kind of employee that I can add little, except to say that some people come to an organization with the intent to survive, whereas others come with the intent to thrive. Most employees begin as either disciples or doers, but soon realize that their expectations and reality were not quite in harmony with each other. Yet disengaged employees may become so detached that they just want to exist without expectations to lead, follow, or get out of anyone's way. Disengaged employees justify their behavior by questioning the organization's loyalty to them.

The following are expected identifiable attributes and attitudes of the disengaged:

- Noninclusive and nonresponsive (does not invite others to participate, holds talents inside)

- Not open-minded (does not want to learn or grow, yet not truly closed-minded)

- Not adaptable (dreads change)

- Engages in guarded communication (sees communication as a win-lose scenario)

- Integrity (may or may not be an issue)

- Weak work ethic (disinterested in the work, organization, or both)

- Solo player while thinking he or she is a team player (avoids any attention, positive or negative, about own accomplishments)

- Little to no follow-up and follow-through (difficult time performing well)

Quadrant IV: Disgruntled (Focus: Active Reactions to Stress)

Disgruntled is the other of the two stress quadrants. Again, when employees feel pulled away from their natural quadrant, they exhibit symptoms of stress. This quadrant identifies the active response to stress. This behavior is easy to identify early on, and may be difficult to satisfy consistently. Some leaders and managers feel tempted to acquiesce to the vocal, aggressive employee. By catering to disgruntled traits, we validate negative behavior and open a Pandora's box from which more behavior will flow.

There is plenty of literature about disgruntled workers. Unfortunately, most are news clippings about the aftereffects of raging incidents. Fortunately, the vast majority of disgruntled employees are merely upset, with chips on their shoulders, and they are looking to leave their company. Some of these employees may be natural leaders who have not been given adequate opportunities to develop their talents, or have been punished for attempting to do so. These employees tend to be more reactive and ready to jump ship to find another organization with which to work. When the organization no longer provides attractive incentives or opportunities, these individuals' attitude deteriorates into, "Any place is better than here."

The following are expected identifiable attributes and attitudes of the disgruntled:

- Noninclusive (may be hyper-responsive, destructive, or both)

- Closed-minded (unwilling to listen to opposing viewpoints)

- Not adaptable, not forgiving (refuses to accept guidance from multiple leadership styles)

- Engages in combative communication (often escalates to an emotional level)

- Integrity (may or may not be an issue)

- Work ethic suffers (focused on negative emotions, not productivity)

- Solo player and proud of it (refuses to cooperate with team efforts)

- No follow-up or follow-through (has difficult time performing well)

PRACTICAL APPLICATION

Anecdotal evidence shows that the population group in each quadrant changes with succeeding generations. In the 1940s and 1950s, people were told that their jobs were good and that they should be glad to have them, and those who believed this could have been called the disciples of their organizations. In the 1960s and 1970s, the next generation grew very dissatisfied, even disgruntled with the establishment. By the 1980s, the disengaged worker overpopulated the workforce. Today, with the advent of rapid transit, rapid communication, the Internet, and a variety of other life-changing, barrier-smashing technologies, it seems that the doer has been the dominant employee base since the mid-1990s.

With this new understanding of the 4-D Followership Model, group members can identify and predict their own behavior and those of other followers and leaders. They can identify where individuals currently reside within the quadrants and determine the most suitable motivational strategies and organizational cultural actions and decisions to move valuable employees closer to their natural quadrants.

In exploring followership alignment, I recognized that people gravitate to a basic perception that they exhibit in their workplace behavior. The status quo comes into play when some followers make every possible effort to maintain it. Others stretch and expand their horizons, exerting their adaptable nature to try new and exciting things. Both kinds of employees can be invaluable to the success of an organization. When employees have found their aligning quadrant, they will be more productive. Employees in the doer quadrant will become most valuable in ways that employees from the disciple quadrant cannot, and vice versa.

The first information pressed into the human brain is the strongest, the source of the basic reactions exhibited in both productive and stressful situations. This translates to the natural quadrant that employees tend to move toward depending on the level of stress or opportunity facing them. This is what I call followership alignment.

People teach that the status quo is a bad place, a stagnant region in which talent decays and progress atrophies. They spend much of their time working to find alignment, but they rarely understand which is their natural quadrant and how to operate from within it. The following two examples of employee behavior will show how these behaviors fit into one of the four quadrants of the 4-D Followership Model.

John Bean's Typical and Current Behavior

In this first scenario, look at the historical or typical behavior of the main character, John Bean, then compare it to his current behavior. Apply the 4-D Followership Model to create valid and lasting interventions and solutions.

John Bean's Typical Behavior   John Bean has been with his organization for several years as an IT specialist. He knows the politics and the "ins and outs" of the culture, and he typically acts excited when he uses these connections to benefit the team (through a loose network of friends outside the team). John has always been a highly productive and industrious employee, accomplishing more than most would have expected from his laid-back demeanor. He is very supportive of his team members and enjoys participating in discussions as much as he enjoys working alone.

John Bean's Current Behavior   Of late, John's new manager has decided to hold the team on a tight leash. She believes that empowering others requires constant feedback. John adapted to this change at first. Lately, however, he seems less accepting of this new accountability, calling the manager Big Sister behind her back. Under the new conditions, his manager expects him to involve her in all of his communications with his established network. Predictably, he has not sought their assistance as much lately. John has scaled back his active participation in meetings. It seems that every time he shares an idea with the team, the new manager gives him that idea as an assignment and expects him to have an update ready for the next meeting. By now, John feels too busy to add anything to his schedule. He used to be a very productive employee, but his completion rate has become sporadic, he talks less to team members, and his once infectious motivation now seems absent.

Applying the 4-D Followership Approach to John Bean

Identify Natural and Stress Quadrants   Which quadrant fits John's typical behavior, and which one fits his current behaviors? From the information we have, we can easily classify John as a natural disciple. He enjoyed the team atmosphere as well as providing solutions for others' successes. He is now disengaged.

Compare Typical and Current Behaviors   What happened to John Bean, and what can he do to become a star employee once again? Note that this path to improvement cannot be a training program or even a strategically placed intervention. John's return to his typical behavior must begin within. As a disciple, John hopes that he will be allowed to serve the team's needs, to be a quiet hero. When this opportunity is restricted, John takes the passive route and becomes disengaged. He does not want to leave his job, and he reacts appropriately to the situation as a passive disciple.

Implement Potential Interventions and Solutions   What could John's manager do to help him get back on track? If she understands how John views his role as a member of the team (using the 4-D Followership Model), she could realize that John's need to serve is accompanied by a strong need to do it on his own terms. As John's manager, she could return autonomy to John and allow him to serve as he has in the past. This may not sit well with her management style—thus the conflict. At this juncture, both John and his new manager need to stretch and give what they can. By recognizing what John is unwilling to give, his manager can see how far she herself should stretch to make this business relationship work. By seeing his manager make good-faith efforts to support his natural style, John can make good-faith efforts to meet her.

Mark Mook's Typical and Current Behavior

In this second scenario, compare the typical behavior of the main character, Mark Mook, with his current behavior. Then apply the 4-D Followership Model to create valid and lasting interventions and solutions.

Mark Mook's Typical Behavior   Mark Mook loves dealing with people, whether he is talking one-on-one or with large groups. He has this knack for getting what he wants from practically every conversation he has. His energy can be overwhelming at times, but he does very well in the sales arena. He is very good at giving direction respectfully, and has had three happy direct reports for years now. Mark is competitive, sticking persistently to a client until he gets the sale. He gladly shares the successes with his team, but rarely acknowledges the successes of other teams in his division (unless he uses them as the team to beat).

Mark Mook's Current Behavior   For the past three months, Mark's sales numbers have slowly dropped in response to largely unavoidable changes in the economy; his stats are now just above average for the organization. This has caused visible frustration for Mark and his team. He seemed to be resisting helpful suggestions from his manager, implementing them with vocal reservations. This month he began demanding that his team work an extra twenty hours each week to catch up to the top team in the company, causing significant upset. When Mark's manager discovered this, he had a private meeting in Mark's office. The team reported that they could hear only Mark, who was yelling about needing to get back on top. Mark had a few choice words for his boss's leadership style as well.

Applying the 4-D Followership Approach to Mark Mook

Identify Natural and Stress Quadrants   Which quadrant fits Mark's typical behavior, and which one fits his current behaviors? From the description of the situation, we can say that Mark seems very energetic, excited, and competitive. Numbers and status are important to him, and as a strong-willed doer, he will try to get what he wants at any cost. His current behavior indicates that he seems to have a hard time coping with the impact of average sales numbers on his self-esteem. Everyone hears it, and everyone sees it. As a disgruntled manager, he can be difficult to work with.

Compare Typical and Current Behaviors   What happened to Mark Mook, and what can he do to become a star employee once again? Like John, Mark must change from within. From his current perspective, the best solution would be to get those numbers back up. In the face of reality, Mark needs to accept that he will not always be number one. Until he realizes this, everyone suffers, and an undesirable situation is made worse.

Implement Potential Interventions and Solutions   What could Mark's manager do to help him get back on track? Understanding that Mark is an active doer will not by itself solve the team's headaches. To Mark (as an active doer), his need to succeed comes first, even at the cost of relationships. The manager needs to know that this disgruntled behavior is Mark's typical reaction to stress. In recognizing this, the manager can decide far in advance what he will and will not tolerate in workplace behavior and make this clear. As a doer, Mark may leave, or he may perceive the challenge to improve his team's performance without transmitting undue stress as a growth opportunity, which doers thrive on. Conversely, in his role as a follower familiar with the 4-D model, if Mark perceived that his manager had become either disgruntled or disengaged, Mark could use his considerable energy and persuasiveness to help restore the manager's natural typical style.

SUMMARY AND CONCLUSION

Existing thought on followership leans toward leadership, and research on the topic is derived from leadership principles. There is so much interplay and crossover between leadership and followership that the two cannot be studied completely independently of each other. The 4-D Followership Model is not a complement to older thoughts on this subject, nor is it antagonistic toward them. This model takes followership in a new direction, placing it in a new light with a reorganized taxonomy, seeing it as the framework that builds leadership, not as an effect thereof.

Whether we define followership as a role or a behavior, employees can occupy both follower and leader roles simultaneously. Whether we call employees followers or collaborators, researchers can use the 4-D Followership Model to type employees' behavioral patterns and determine their strengths and weaknesses (as well as potential stressors). Such understanding and use of the model should help followers who aspire to greater leadership roles do so, and should help leaders develop other leaders one follower at a time.

Getting Together

Gene Dixon

A charming consequence of being an engineer is a unique propensity to make everything into a literal graphic mental image. Having accepted my first organizational leadership position, this became very discomfiting when my new boss said to me, "So, are you ready to take names and kick ass?" in more of a command tone than as a question. I immediately created two mental images of a manager's role in industry: the first of the grammar school student who always got assigned to write down the names of students who misbehaved while the teacher "stepped to the office" (when, of course, she was off to smoke a cigarette). The second image was one of my fellow workers bending over and grabbing their ankles while a supervisor walked by kicking their behinds, no exceptions, no excuses, no explanations. Yes, that was old-school "leadership."

I had another reminder of my frailty when shortly after the shocking events of 9/11, I read the following in an editorial in *Government Executive* magazine: "We knew, here in Washington, that danger was at hand long before 9/11. We knew that our government was not prepared. We knew that preparation would entail hard work and more money and politics beyond the partisan. But in our deep suspicion of government, in our determination to shrink it, not to spend a penny more of our money on it than absolutely necessary, in our reluctance to tackle political obstacles, we overlooked the warnings and did too little."[1] My mental image generator burnt out its bearings with thoughts of careerists running around D.C. with knowledge and closed lips; of politicos so intent on pork at home that the country was lean on preparation, and members of Congress focused on elections and not on the people's business; it was self-preservation over national protection. That's my image. Maybe you get some visions too.

If we are not the president (and there can be only one), then the rest of us can be, in a way, classified as followers. If we're not taking names and kicking someone, at least some would say we really are followers. If that is anywhere near true, then perhaps as Boccialetti says, "In any effective and healthy organization there must be a tacit, if not explicit, understanding that it is everyone's job to help make others competent and to do what needs to be done to avert serious harm and assure effective outcomes."[2] In other words, it really is up to us, the nonleaders, the followers, to make the organization effective, to achieve the mission and vision, and in a broader sense, to protect the nation. As a leader or a follower, we are destined to contribute.

LEADERS AND FOLLOWERS: HOW WE GOT HERE

Before the nineteenth century, leadership was the realm of the craft guild. Master craftsmen lorded over apprentices with great autonomy. "Great men" controlled politics and economies. With the nineteenth century's Industrial Revolution, family farm workers moved into cities where industries were expanding. Workers with the highest skill levels were made managers, an adaptation of the guild model of the previous century. Labor was cheap, jobs were plentiful, and the twentieth century began with a dominant theory of management that held a low opinion of the workers' motivation, maturity, and abilities. This is probably the source for the take-names-kick-ass modus operandi of my earlier boss. "Great men" controlled the destinies of the working class.

In the 1920s, Frederick Taylor introduced a scientific, rational management model—"the one best way." Managers refined "the one best way" and directed the task be completed accordingly.

The end of World War II invigorated management-by-fiat as soldiers, highly versed in chain-of-command models, returned to the workforce. During the

1950s and 1960s, management became a profession, and that profession required education. Leadership was the domain of the "guys at the top" (gender diversity being unheard of at the time), a mind-set that resulted in ever-diminishing individual responsibility at the lower organizational levels. Obedience was the key to advancement. Pay incentives controlled productivity. The cost of job security for employees was paid in company loyalty. The "good old days," some might say.

By the time baby boomers dominated the workforce in the 1970s, the "not my job" attitude born of the "me first" mentality was firmly ingrained in the workforce. Professional managers responded with such controlling techniques as quality circles, pay-for-knowledge, self-managed work teams, union representation on director boards, and profit sharing.

The 1980s featured the birth of the information blitzkrieg. Technology was no longer confined to automation. Managers were inundated with information but continued decision making by "gut feel." Management theory's search for excellence reverted to a psychological, one-best-way management model, this time with eight steps. Great men were once again sought as corporate leaders in order to mitigate the impact of information overload. The mega-rewarding of the toxic leader began. CEOs were commended for being calculating, decisive, and neutronish. Jack Welch in essence told everyone that an overburdened, stretched-out executive is best because that executive doesn't have time to meddle, to deal in trivia, to bother people.

During the 1990s, as markets were turned more global than the cotton cartels of two centuries back, competition moved from the national level to the international level, and corporate boards of directors became both "team" and "leader" focused. The combination of need for corporate leadership and the need for employee involvement—heart and hand—resulted in new programs for controlling the worker through employee empowerment, job reengineering, right-sizing, doing more with less, and using black-belted, total-quality leaders at every organizational level. Toxic leaders began laying the foundations that would ultimately necessitate the Sarbanes-Oxley Act in 2002.

Now the world is complex and faster paced. Nominating committees, not the CEO, pick directors. Boards are more susceptible to shareholder pressure. Information is available from any keyboard allowing every employee to participate in the global marketplace of ideas, information, and news—sometimes as an employee, sometimes as a citizen, and often as an independent entrepreneur and competitor with instant global market access. Leaders are no longer in complete control of the employee-employer relationship. Employees are discipline-loyal, not employer-loyal. The technologically skilled auction their services on the Internet. Employees are virtual. Organizations are ethereal. Competition now includes the third world. Organizations are executing on relevant—not necessarily complete—information in order to keep up. Corporate leaders are sought who will bring a vision of stability to the chaos of stay-at-home workers, electronic monetary exchanges, and growing environmental awareness across all communities.

HOW DO YOU LIKE ME NOW?

Where does this management history take us? It's sort of like the country song "How Do You Like Me Now?" where the high school heartthrob who rejected her would-be suitor now has to deal with the singer's success.[3] In management theory, we are basically a product of where we have been. When you consider all the history of management, you can also recognize a love affair with leadership. America particularly has a preoccupation with leadership. Rost tells us that leadership is a process and has as its constituent components leaders and followers.[4] It makes sense to study both components. While starting my research on followers, I recall contacting a principal in a firm that manufactures and sells office furniture. After I explained my premise for the follower study, his terse reply was something to the effect, "I don't want followers in my organization. I don't want the word 'follower' used in my organization. Here we want everyone to be a leader. All of our people are leaders." I thought that was really a bold statement for a CEO. It implied that everyone is a CEO in that organization. He probably wouldn't have liked that. We exchanged a few more sentences before I realized he was to be of no help, but his words hung over me like a dark cloud. Again, following my engineering tendencies, I envisioned what his company's organization chart must look like (illustrated in Figure 12.1). I devised this chart purely for my entertainment—it was therapy after that depressing phone call.

During the course of my research I experienced one other occasion when a corporate "leader" told me he wanted an all-leader organization. He essentially said that the concept of followers was the antithesis of the TQM concept of leader. I'm not sure what that means, but it really sounds like he misunderstood the concept of followers. MacKenzie has observed that considering all the time, enormous human resources, and money spent on promoting leadership and learning, the

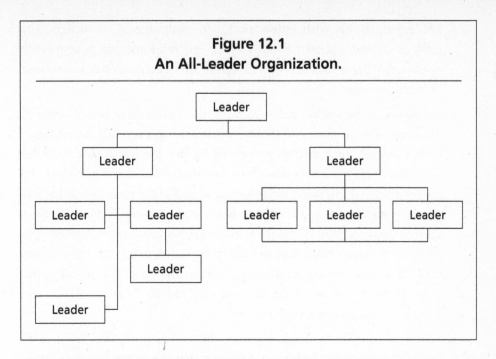

Figure 12.1
An All-Leader Organization.

ROI has been low.[5] I believe, from observation and research, that our organizations contain leaders, managers, followers, and subordinates, with the obvious pairings.

INALIENABLE TRUTHS

Sometime in my research, I ran across a set of ideas that I've massaged and compiled into what I call inalienable truths of leadership (listed in Exhibit 12.1). These are not original to me, but when I stylize them in my words, they're a little sexier and easier to understand.

Exhibit 12.1
Inalienable Truths of Leadership.

1. Leaders exist only with followers.
2. Followers do the work.
3. Followers provide feedback.
4. Management research does not appreciate followers.

---

1. **Leaders exist only with followers.** No followers means no leaders. This really is common sense for most of us, but reinforcement is apparently necessary. What it means is that followers are to be respected, maybe even honored, because . . .

2. **Followers do the work.** Leaders may get their hands dirty, but followers do the work.[6] That is not a bad thing; it's just a thing. I recently interviewed a plant manager for a chicken processing facility. He was quite proud that when the chicken catchers thought it was too hot to catch the chickens, he, his HR manager, his engineering manager, and other members of his staff spent the night going to the chicken house and catching chickens. He was a leader who understood what it means to get his hands dirty. Normally, he spent his fourteen-hour days in such things as plan, do, act, check. When needed, however, he caught chickens. You can almost see the morale in that organization when they processed the chickens the boss caught. (Maybe there is a management axiom in that.)

3. **Followers provide feedback,** sooner or later, overtly or covertly.[7] Back on the dairy farm as a growing lad, I learned that the dairy cows understood respect. If you approached them gently and considerately, your job was easier, and their production went up. Less stress meant more milk. In a way, those cows taught me the lesson of feedback. When the cows were comfortable, their feedback was greater production. On occasion I've remembered that fundamental truth when working with people.

4. **Management research does not appreciate followers.** The trend is changing, but generally management researchers like to study the boss and not the subordinate, the leader not the follower. Although there is still a relative dearth of studies that recognize followers as vital players, there is progress.[8] And research is moving from tips and techniques for manipulating employees to interrelationships, behaviors, and attribute (leader-member) exchange (aka LMX) between leaders and followers.

These inalienable truths take us beyond the all-leader organization chart. What they imply is the need for a leader and follower organization chart, as illustrated in Figure 12.2. This is not a chart of managers and subordinates. No, this is a quantum leap beyond that. When leaders lead, followers follow. Middle-level positions are the problem in this arrangement, as it implies that there can be only

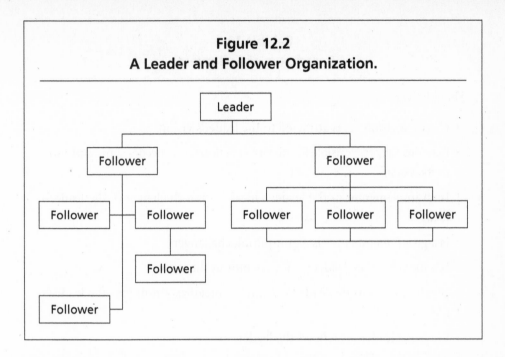

Figure 12.2
A Leader and Follower Organization.

one leader. For the moment, let's accept that shortcoming and note that the leader and follower chart is not a panacea. It is a work in progress. Works in progress usually have a few problems or paradoxes that must be recognized, addressed, and sometimes accepted.

PARADOXES

What do the truths mean? They mean that followers are an important part of leadership and organizational effectiveness. They also mean that the concepts of following and followers are concepts fraught with paradoxes, listed in Exhibit 12.2.

For instance, Chaleff would tell us that a follower has a clear internal vision of service to the organization, to the mission, or to humanity, while simultaneously he or she is attracted to a leader who articulates and embodies the external manifestation of the organization or its mission.[9] This in a sense is the opposite, or a corollary, of inalienable truth 1; in this case, without leaders there are no followers. A second paradox is that followers remain fully accountable for their actions while relinquishing some autonomy and conceding certain authority to a leader. This is easily understood when another of my former bosses, upon noting my

---

Exhibit 12.2
Paradoxes of Followers.

The follower . . .

- Has own vision . . . is attracted to the leader's vision

- Remains fully responsible for his or her actions . . . concedes some authority to the leader

- Is an implementer of the leader's ideas . . . is a challenger of the leader's ideas

- Is a group member . . . is a groupthink challenger

- Is a mentee of the leader . . . is a mentor to the leader

- Breathes life into the leader's vision . . . breathes vision into the leader's life

- Leads the leader . . . follows the leader

Source: Adapted from Chaleff, *The Courageous Follower.* (2nd ed.) San Francisco: Berrett-Koehler, 2003.

---

creativity on a project, stated "If I go down, I'm taking you with me." The creativity was appreciated (to a degree) by him and my grand-boss, but it was risky. I was certainly accountable, but the responsibility was not solely residing with me. My boss, a likable fellow to be sure, would have to bear some culpability.

Chaleff also tells of a third paradox, a central dichotomy of followers—the need to energetically perform two opposite roles: implementer and challenger of the leader's ideas. Although it is usually the role of a team's coach, not the role of the player, to push to improve the team, this paradox parallels the next paradox and is obvious when put in a team perspective: be a team player while improving the team. When on a high school football team, the defense would practice against the offense. It was a small school, so the starters played both ways. I have distinct memories of how the starting line reacted when the second string practiced hard in an attempt to keep the starters sharp. After each play, the practice squad had to learn to bob and weave, as Ali used to say; there were some punches thrown to slow the practice squad down. Sometimes pushing to improve a team's performance is not as well received as it was intended. There is inherent tension between the identity a follower derives from group membership and the individuation required to question and creatively challenge the group and its leadership.[10] (By the way, we had only a respectable, not stellar, season that year.)

A similar paradox: followers often benefit from the leader as mentor, learning crucial things, yet at the same time they must be willing to teach the leader. The role of a leader is primarily to lead. Secondary roles include teaching followers to become teachers of followers, a real leadership task. The role of the follower is not only to learn but to learn to teach. Followers teach their peers, new followers, and, perhaps most important, the leader. What do followers teach leaders? Think about what a leader needs to know: what is the follower doing with leader expectations; how are leader expectations being implemented; and why are they implemented that way? Essentially the follower must teach the leader how the leader is being effective or ineffective. This really is a matter of part cart and part horse and leads to the next paradox: at times, followers need to lead from behind (forget the view), breathing life into their leader's vision, or even vision into the leader's life.[11] Still, the idea that a follower has leadership responsibilities should not be foreign or strange. It is the followers' responsibility to "tweak," to personalize the vision for peers and others in the organization, which is described as leading from behind. It is the process of sanding down the conceptual vision into executable mechanisms that are really the follower's piece in leading from behind.

This paradox of leading from behind also leads naturally into the last paradox: senior (as in tenure) followers often are important leaders in their own right and must integrate within themselves the perspectives of both leadership and followership. Bottom line: as followers gain experience in working with the leader, their peers, and the organization, they become de facto sounding boards for the less experienced; counselors whose mission and vision compass has stronger, more reliable bearings and an ability to weather storms of conflict. These followers are leaders in helping the less experienced hold their course in achieving the leader's expectations.

SO MANY PARADOXES, JUST ONE PARADIGM

Getting together for leaders and followers is a process of understanding each other. Assuming that others have done a reasonable job of laying the groundwork for understanding leaders, the effort here is to understand followers. In reality, followers dominate all organizations; Kelley reports that 10 percent of who we are and what we are represents leadership skills.[12] That leaves 90 percent for other activities: follower roles, behaviors, and actions—getting our hands dirty by getting things done. The traditional image of a follower conjures up sheep who unquestioningly and blindly obey the sheepherder's direction. That just doesn't make sense given where management history has evolved. In order to answer the "How do you like me now?" question for followers, a new paradigm is in order. Chaleff suggests that followers are to be understood and treated as partners, participants, coleaders, and cofollowers who are in pursuit of productivity in the organization.[13]

In his description of followers, Chaleff points out that the followers are engaged heart, mind, and soul in the commonly held purposes and vision of the organization. Followers hold purpose, beliefs, and desire for organizational success in common with the leader. In this sense, following can be conceptualized as a free-will gesture whereby the follower becomes steward of self, immediate peers, and the organization. This conceptual description is based on five unique behaviors that lead to what Chaleff calls courageous followers: the courage to assume responsibility, the courage to serve, the courage to challenge, the courage to participate in transformation, and the courage to take moral action.

Assume Responsibility

> *You didn't have to do that.*
>
> Joe Beam, founder and CEO,
> Family Dynamics Institute

Courageous followers assume responsibility for themselves and the organization. They do not hold a paternalistic image of the leader or organization; they do not expect the leader or organization to provide for their security and growth or to give them permission to act. Courageous followers discover or create opportunities to fulfill their potential and maximize their value to the organization. They initiate values-based action to improve the organization's external activities and its internal processes. The "authority" to initiate comes from the courageous follower's understanding and ownership of the common purpose, and from the needs of those the organization serves.[14]

Joe Beam is founder and CEO of Family Dynamics Institute (FDI). FDI is a nonprofit organization dedicated to helping families work. A few years back, as

Joe was evolving the concept behind FDI, he did some work on another concept he had developed called Life Balance, a program of empowerment for people struggling to keep their life's demands in relative balance.

While working with a potential collaborator, Joe had arranged for a presentation to about fifteen hundred people in order to judge receptivity to the concepts of the Life Balance program. Joe, a renowned rhetorician, was to be the presenter. The presentation was a part of a larger conference of ten to twelve thousand people, at which Joe was also a keynote speaker. Joe and the potential collaborator had agreed to meet at the presentation room at a certain time to set up the room, distribute handouts, and work out last-minute logistics. Joe arrived at the appointed time and found the chairs arranged, the handouts distributed, and the sound system ready. This gave Joe the opportunity to relax and collect his thoughts for a few minutes before his presentation. The potential collaborator had assumed responsibility for the room, the setup, and the logistics.

"What did you say to him, when you saw all the physical work was done?" I asked Joe.

"I told him, 'You didn't have to do that,'" Joe replied.

"And what did he say?" I asked.

"He said, 'I'm a better second. You're the focus today. This was my part.'"

I don't know about you, but that vignette makes me want to call HR and tell them to hire the guy. This "second," this "follower," demonstrated an ability to choose his response to a situation that could better the mission at hand. Followers like this are committed to personal performance and professional responsibility, and are dedicated to the mission of the organization.

Serve

Dottie will have taken care of it.

Dr. Jerry Westbrook, UAH Professor Emeritus,
University of Alabama in Huntsville

Courageous followers are not afraid of the hard work required to serve a leader. They assume new or additional responsibilities to unburden the leader and serve the organization. They stay alert for areas in which their strengths complement the leader's and assert themselves in these areas. Courageous followers stand up for their leader and the tough decisions a leader must make if the organization is to achieve its purpose. They are as passionate as the leader in pursuing the common purpose.[15]

Dr. Jerry Westbrook, founding chair of the Engineering Management Distance Education program at the University of Alabama in Huntsville tells of his administrative assistant's dedication to service. Jerry says, "We were on our way to the airport when one of the faculty members said, 'I don't remember making plane reservations.' I simply said to her, 'Dottie will have taken care of it.' When we checked in at the counter, the needed tickets were waiting." Dottie was the department's go-to person, and even when someone didn't go-to, Dottie got it done. Dottie really did have the spirit of serving the leader.

When followers serve, they conserve the leader's energy. Followers solve the mundane, repair what's broken, and take care of the follow-up, all without being asked. They provide a continuous review to achieve balance in a communication system so that all levels are touched in a timely way, in all directions, without overburdening the leader or the organization.

Challenge

> *I listened and realized she was right.*
>
> Jim Lewandowski, Saturn Corporation, retired

Courageous followers give voice to the discomfort they feel when the behaviors or policies of the leader or group are in conflict with their sense of what is right. They are willing to stand up, stand out, risk rejection, and initiate conflict in order to examine the actions of the leader and group when appropriate. They are willing to deal with the emotions their challenge evokes in the leader and group. Courageous followers value organizational harmony and their relationship with the leader, but not at the expense of the common purpose and their integrity.[16]

Jim Lewandowski, founding vice president of human resources for the Saturn Corporation, says that Saturn was founded on two principles: teams and consensus decisions. For Jim and the other managers, living these principles required a significant change in their behavior. As Jim describes the start-up, traditional GM leaders (read managers) were to become followers, and the followers (read labor) were the leaders, requiring a significant shift for labor union behavior. Jim sums up this part of his story as a process that is easy to preach, hard to live.

Jim learned this the hands-on way: "One day, a woman stormed into my office. She had seen the 'other way' of managing. She transferred from Texas where she had been a union bumper installer at the Buick division. She was now part of a thirteen-member Saturn team. When she spoke, she almost shouted, 'Did you have anything to do with . . .'"

Jim continues, "I had made what I thought was an innocuous decision, well within the authority of any vice president of HR in any GM division. But it was not the Saturn way. She was upset, crying, and accused me of betraying her, the team, and Saturn. Adding further insult, she had heard about the decision from one of her customers (another Saturn team)."

When Jim told me this story, I could see a definite change in his intensity. "My initial reaction was anger. This woman was challenging my authority and my position. I was a GM VP. I wanted to throw her out. But I was not in Detroit. I listened and realized she was right. I had to admit my guilt. I called a team meeting and apologized. It is easy to revert."

Although it needn't be done this dramatically, courageous followers are willing to initiate confrontation in order to cause an examination of the actions of the leader or their peer group when appropriate. They work hard to keep the leader consistent in word and in deed and thereby create mutual trust.

Participate in Transformation

> *In creating an operator-centered approach to shift management, we effected a change that benefited our operators the most.*
>
> Buddy K., manager, HR operations

When behavior that jeopardizes the common purpose remains unchanged, courageous followers recognize the need for transformation. They champion the need for change and stay with the leader and group while they mutually struggle with the difficulty of real change. They examine their own need for transformation and become full participants in the change process as appropriate.[17]

I liked Buddy K. the first time I met him. He was a potential hire fresh out of the required military service following his graduation from West Point. New blood that understood leadership the military way. I anticipated learning a lot from him. I hoped it would be two-way.

After many years, Buddy commented on changes we both had championed: "In creating an operator-centered approach to shift management, we effected a change that benefited our operators the most." Both Buddy and I had been intent on changing the status quo. Buddy was the antithesis of Tim, my shift supervisor.

Tim and I worked a rotating shift arrangement and spent a lot of time together in the control room of a production nuclear reactor. On the back shifts, when normal people are at home with their families, Tim and I were kings of our worlds. Tim came up through the ranks and knew the process as well as any seasoned veteran. I was the engineer-turned-manager, kind of new, but had been on operations side as a manager for a couple of years. This was heady stuff for a young manager. Tim was the perfect number two. Almost.

The shift crew had nine operators; five sat at the controls, and four were scattered around the building monitoring equipment that was not monitored in the control room. The process had six 3,400 horsepower pumps to circulate water through the main system. Starting those pumps was considered a critical operation that required attention to detail. That was Tim's forte. It was tradition for the shift supervisor to sit at a desk in the control room and read the standard operating procedure to the operators as they pushed the switches to start the pumps and align the valves. This was the management system Tim knew. The boss tells; the operators do. It was a system needing change. Tim was an obstacle to change. The operators had told me they were ready for change. They could read the procedure. They could set the controls. They could manage this work themselves.

One night, when it came time to start the pumps, Tim positioned himself at the control room desk and spread out the procedure. Just before he started calling out the steps to the control room crew, I called him aside, "Tim, let the operators do it."

"Do what?" he replied.

"Let the operators run the procedure."

Tim said, "They can't do that."

"Why?" I asked. He mumbled a few things, and we sparred for a few minutes before Tim concluded that I was not going to back down. He fumed off to hand the procedure to the operators and went to get a second copy for himself to use as he observed—policed may be a better word. He was intent on catching a mistake to prove that he was right. Tim wasn't happy. You know the rest of the story. The operators started the pumps without incident. Tim was shocked to the point of saying, "This makes sense and is a whole lot easier on me." The next time we started pumps, Tim smoked a cigarette.

Tim was a quick learner and soon began looking for opportunities. The next time we decided to transform the operation from the old way to something more empowering, Tim was eager to turn control over to the operators. They knew how to do the work; they needed a transforming agent to let them do the work. Tim the Transformer—I like that.

Transforming followers are willing to put themselves on the line, and they believe that others, especially the leader, should do the same. Transformations may be personally oriented for the leader or follower; process oriented to break the mold of "we've always done it this way"; or goal oriented, as in goals to reduce emissions.

Take Moral Action

I had to leave.

Dr. P (withheld by request)

Courageous followers know when it is time to separate from a leader and group. Self-growth or organizational growth may require a courageous follower to eventually leave even the most enlightened and effective of leaders. When leaders are ineffective or their actions are detrimental to the common purpose and they are not open to transformation, the need for separation becomes more compelling. Courageous followers are prepared to withdraw support from destructive leaders and even to disavow or oppose them, despite high personal risk.[18]

When Dr. P took over as plant manager of a plating operation in West Virginia, he was aware of some hazardous waste issues and had started treating the hazardous waste and gathering information on the extent of on-site dumping. He notified his superiors at headquarters, who authorized him to proceed with what had to be done. He called the West Virginia Department of Natural Resources (DNR) for recommendations. The DNR came, inspected, reported, and recommended as any regulator would. When the recommendations came, Dr. P notified his boss, who said, "Do nothing. That's what lawyers are for." When the DNR found out, they returned, in force (six or seven carloads), armed, with a warrant and $250M in fines and $250M in cleanup estimates. Dr. P once again contacted headquarters. The lawyers spoke with the DNR rep without identifying themselves as lawyers, an inexcusable breach of protocol. The warrant was executed, and Dr. P opened up the plant to the inspectors. What else could he do?

There was one other thing Dr. P could do. Dr. P says that the blatant disregard for environmental ethics and protection of people as well as natural resources was too much: "I had to leave."

Oftentimes, leaders and followers wrestle with their choices. The easy way is not always the best way, particularly when the impacts are significant, whether in terms of money, quality of life, or impact on the future. When the wrong choices are being made despite a follower's efforts to influence a leader's thinking, moral action is required. Loyalty to mission, vision, and humanity drives moral action. Moral action is necessary to maintain consistency between the actions of the leaders and the organization and the fundamental values of citizenship.

THE BIGGER PICTURE: RISKS IN LEADER-FOLLOWER RELATIONS

Followers in a real sense are strong organizational players. The followers demonstrating the behaviors I've described are self-managing—maybe some would say self-leading. This chapter is not about personal leadership; it is about organizational leadership and its components, leaders and followers. It may not be apparent, but not all leaders and managers like having self-managing followers or subordinates. Command-and-control managers would rather have sheep or yes-people. The best that good followers can do in this situation is to protect themselves with a little career self-management—that is, to stay attractive in the marketplace. The qualities that make a good follower are too much in demand to go begging for long.

NO FREE LUNCH

There is a downside to being a courageous follower. Think about what we might call the Lewandowski factor. Here was an organizational follower who challenged. When she got angry enough, she spoke up. Preferably, followers will speak up before emotions build to the point of explosion, but it happens. Speaking up is the follower's vehicle for expressing ideas, solutions, critical perspective, opinions, or feelings; it is the key to challenging. An unspoken challenge is no challenge.

Communicating with the leader allows for direct and uncensored exchange, what Senge would label dialogue.[19] Speaking up requires the follower to develop the capacity to take the risks necessary to say what he or she actually thinks and feels. In engineering, we call that risk accepting. The opposite is risk avoidance; if sheep had the intelligence to know better, they would avoid the wolf's neighborhood. Followers know better, overcome the fear, and accept the risk, not because the grass is greener necessarily but because it is ethical; it is the right thing to do. There is no free lunch.

The strength to persevere when confronted with fear or difficulty is often crucial to the development of a collaborative leader-follower relationship. Speaking up to or against someone with more power and authority always entails the risk of being demeaned, feeling inadequate, being attacked, or even losing one's job. The hierarchical character of the leader-follower collaboration heightens the follower's need for courage. As the relationship develops, the need for courageous acts might decline, but in a hierarchical world, it never disappears.

In a world in which followers are implicitly competing for the jobs of those above them, it is difficult to expect people in leader-follower relationships to freely discuss the limits of each other's skills. At an early stage in my career, I asked my manager for a critical review of my personality and my skills. He was a man about my age. We were both less than ten years out of college. I intended this to be a growth opportunity for me and me alone. This was a beyond-the-corporate-performance-evaluation assessment. Imagine my surprise when he turned the tables by saying, "I'll do this for you if you'll do the same for me." At that time, I confess, I didn't have the personal strength to hold up my end of his proposal. If such a conversation were to have taken place, it is tantalizing to imagine the progress we both could have made. Imagine: a conversation that was so open that it could be free of concerns about the misuse of information in the highly charged promotional sweepstakes always at play. It would be a rare gift, indeed, but not beyond the scope of a purpose-driven, courageous leader-follower relationship.

At the same time, however, this same kind of open environment raises concerns about exploitation. There is a risk that should the leader be too engaged in finding a place further up the hierarchy, he or she may be tempted to present collaborative work as individually conceived. This is an example of the potentially risky, corrosive, or even toxic effects of "standard" organizational practices in a collaborative leader-follower relationship. Although there are no simple remedies, acknowledging that such forces exist and may affect relationships allows the courageous follower to take appropriate, rather than naive, risks.

All humans have weaknesses and limits, but there are few of us who are totally comfortable with the personal consequences of this notion. We find it difficult to take an intensive, systematic, and public look at our weaknesses. Being reminded of our weaknesses by others is stressful at best. For leaders there is the additional hazard in acknowledging weaknesses and limitations. A look at toxic leaders from the last five years and our collective reaction to them when exposed shows us that organization members tend to require perfection in leaders and put pressure on the leader to hide or cover up shortcomings. We have a natural inclination to shy away from scrutinizing personal weaknesses. When combined with the organizational pressure for perfect leaders, this robs leaders of some significant self-understanding and followers of a chance to form a collaborative (and challenging) relationship that is good for leader and follower.

Despite their best efforts, leaders sometimes require rescue—a "pulling from the burning house." A courageous follower can be especially helpful in that rescue. But a leader has to permit the rescue. Permitting a rescue requires an understanding that allows personal weakness and limitation to coexist with personal strength and recognition of the expanding potential of followers who can help. Let's face it: Super(wo)man we are not (despite the old school management training that says we are). And even if we are, there is plenty of kryptonite to go around for all. It is the mutual coexistence within the leader-follower relationship and the intrinsic complementary strengths and weaknesses that require the leader to follow (at times) and the follower to lead (at other times).

LET'S GO BACKWARD . . . AND FORWARD

This chapter began with a brief review of management history that led to an all-leader organization paradigm. I hope you found some of that informative and to some degree humorous. Maybe your creative process brought back some memories. But let me restate a serious thought from MacKenzie: "For all the time, enormous human resources, and money spent on promoting leadership and learning, our ROI has been low."[20] The question is, where or how can organizations earn a better ROI?

After the history review, we explored the idea of courageous followers. Next there was a discussion about leader-follower relations. Let's go one step forward.

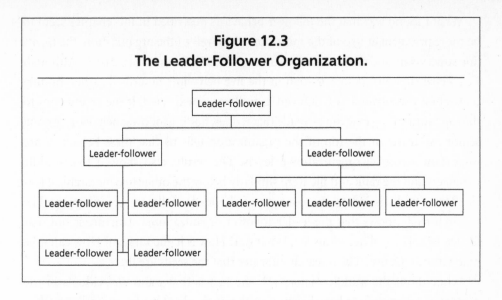

Figure 12.3
The Leader-Follower Organization.

Organizations are organisms. The creativity, inventive agility, passions, and majestic complexity that make up a company are always in flux.[21] The role of leaders and followers within an organization, what Rost would call the "leadership process," is a role of making the organization effective.[22] The all-leader paradigm is whimsical and unworkable. The traditional organization chart, positional in nature, brought us through the industrial age and into the information age of industry. The leader and follower organization chart has some academic appeal and seems to work well with current research models. The global, flat-world age, however, requires something new, something different. I call it the *leader-follower organization* (see Figure 12.3).

WHERE DID THAT COME FROM?

I get a lot of reactions when I talk about the leader-follower chart and the corresponding leader-follower organization. In my research studying follower behaviors as they relate to organizational hierarchy, I surveyed over three hundred technology workers (okay, engineers) and others who use technology in some way to get their jobs done.[23] The survey included exempt workers and nonexempt—tradespeople and craftspeople and professionals—and included every hierarchical level, from repair technicians to CEOs. Some data were gathered from government sources, some from government contractors, and some from both nonprofits and for-profit companies. It was a very diverse mix.

What I found was that the follower behaviors described in this chapter seem to be more prevalent at two of the most opposite levels of the organization, the front-line supervisors and the senior executives and CEOs. I was surprised, too. Although I expected supervisors to rate high in the five behaviors described earlier, finding that senior executives and CEOs did as well was unexpected. If the cream rises to the top, and a strong case can be made that it does, finding follower behaviors among senior executives at the top of the organization tells us that these behaviors are important across all organizational levels. The results also showed that middle managers and the rank and file were similarly below the other two hierarchical levels. These findings led to the concept of the leader-follower organization. The research really shows that the leader-follower organizational structure is not that far-fetched. The real questions are, What is it? How is it encouraged? How can it be made more effective? The research indicates that the seeds are there.

What about the middle managers? The fact is that many individuals in the middle of organizations have been given the dual role of leader and follower. It is never articulated this way, but it shows up functionally in job descriptions and performance review criteria, using different language that captures the minimal actions of each role, not the rich actions if the roles are being performed in exemplary fashion. Because these managers are pulled both ways and maybe because they are caught in the swamp of the middle ranks, perhaps the courageous follower within has gone dormant, or perhaps the courageous followers have been promoted out.

THE LEADER-FOLLOWER ORGANIZATION

The leader-follower organization is the organic state in which all organization members are capable of transitioning between leading and following throughout the scope of their responsibilities. Yes, this is idealistic. It is hard work. I believe it is possible. I believe that it is happening even though it is not necessarily recognized. The dual roles of a person who is both follower and leader demonstrate an art form whereby the individual moves fluidly between these roles and remains consistent in his or her treatment of others. This is based on Chaleff's idea of partnering.[24] Two fundamental ideas capture the leader-follower organization: (1) by staying aware of our reactions to those we follow, we learn to be more sensitive to our effect on those we lead; and (2) by staying aware of our reactions to those we lead, we learn to be more sensitive in our efforts to support those we follow.[25] This leader-follower organization is created when followers are granted status equivalent to leaders and are nurtured, respected, and rewarded according to responsibility and contribution, not position. It sounds easy when explained that way. It would take a book (or two) to fill in the blanks—it's a little beyond the scope of this effort. Saving that for another time then, let's ask, How does this organization work, and how is the leader-follower organization effective?

According to Chaleff, an organization is a triad consisting of leaders and followers joined in a common purpose.[26] The purpose is the atomic glue that binds the organization together. It gives meaning to the activities associated with fulfilling the organization's mission and vision.

Followers and leaders both orbit around the purpose and values of the organization; followers do not orbit around the leader. In the leader-follower organization, this orbiting is blended into a cloud of leaders and followers in balance (see Figure 12.4). At the heart of balance is the dual nature of the universe—I and other, leader and follower—and the necessity for relationship. Genuine relationships will not tolerate extremes, which become abusive.[27] The key to personal balance for leaders is the quality of their relationships with followers. Honest, open

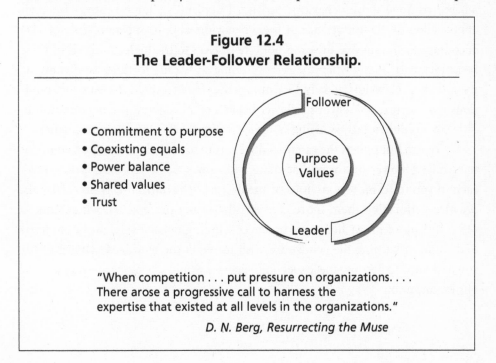

**Figure 12.4
The Leader-Follower Relationship.**

- Commitment to purpose
- Coexisting equals
- Power balance
- Shared values
- Trust

Follower

Purpose
Values

Leader

"When competition . . . put pressure on organizations. . . .
There arose a progressive call to harness the
expertise that existed at all levels in the organizations."

D. N. Berg, Resurrecting the Muse

relationships will provide a steady stream of uncensored feedback and challenge behavior in two directions. It is only through this dialogue that leader-followers can accurately perceive and modulate their behavior.

EPILOGUE

Remember that earlier I stated something about cream rising to the top? Actually, there is good reason to believe that this is true and that research-based validity exists to support the "rising." It makes sense then that regardless of the organizational type, those who are promotable would be those who demonstrate the courageous follower behaviors. That is a convoluted way of saying that as more of the cream rises, there is a stronger talent base from which to select. The extreme is an organization where everyone is promotable. The opposite of a nightmare has to be an organization where everyone is promotable.

With that background, I'll offer some conclusions. First, although I believe that all individuals can improve both the satisfaction they derive from their jobs and their contributions to their organizations through "putting on" the courageous follower behaviors, those who aspire to senior management positions are particularly advised to hone those behaviors. Second, I applaud senior executives for their appreciation of the importance of these behaviors and, in applauding them, also encourage the senior executives to hold themselves to the high standards of these behaviors, particularly when the risks of doing so require fortitude and commitment to these behaviors. Finally, I encourage the effort required to create the conditions that nurture courageous follower behaviors throughout the organization in order to serve as an early warning system, a reality check, for any given situation.

My research supports the essential dual nature of the role and responsibility of the leader-follower in a way that transcends any specific job description. I ask each of you to be more conscious of the desired behaviors and, as professionals, practice performing them more consistently, as any professional who wants to reach the top of his or her game practices winning behaviors. Gandhi observed that we must become the change we wish to see in the world. My challenge for you and me is to become the leader-followers we would like to see at every level of our organization.

The Pitfalls and Challenges of Followership

From the very outset, the field of leadership has been characterized by a positive, even romantic, bias.[1] The Great Man theories
of leadership set the tone early on, and subsequent work has simply
picked up the beat. Consequently, the long shadow of positive leadership has obscured two related phenomena: first, toxic leadership,
and second, the pitfalls and challenges that followers face when they
find themselves caught in the grip of a bad leader.

This third part of the volume addresses those pitfalls and challenges. Why we tolerate toxic leadership in the schoolyard, in cyberspace, in the workplace, and in
the political arena does not yield to a simple answer. In this section, the four
researchers and one practitioner who train their lenses on different aspects of this
troubling phenomenon raise many uncomfortable questions. They also present
us with possible solutions to the problems that arise when followers awaken to
the realization that their leaders are far from heroic role models.

Beginning with the internal forces that play a major role, this section examines
the normal, but unconscious, psychological and existential factors that entrap
often well-intentioned followers who must deal closely or remotely with toxic
leaders. Their yearnings for heroism and immortality make followers exceedingly

vulnerable to the illusions and inducements—such as safety and significance—that bad leaders offer. Seeking meaning and exhilaration in their lives, followers often unwittingly join bad leaders' grand enterprises, even when they lead to demonic ends.

When we shift to the early, external landscape of the schoolyard and cyberspace, we witness the seedbeds of toxic leadership, where young bullies strut largely unimpeded. Here our attention is called to the critical role of bystanders, both children and adults, whose objections could short-circuit the first emergence of toxic leadership. When bystanders step out of their follower role to intervene, bullying behavior can be stopped in its tracks.

Challenging the authority of good, never mind bad, leaders is an awesome task. What is the role of authority, and how are we programmed to acquiesce, sometimes even against our better judgment? What are the appropriate and inappropriate implications of the famous—some would say infamous—obedience experiments, conducted by psychologist Stanley Milgram? One challenge demands understanding how we followers add gravitas to improper directives by attributing them to powerful institutions and culture, rather than to fallible, toxic, human leaders.

Despite the awesome barriers to defying and denouncing bad leadership, some individuals, nonetheless, take on the formidable task of whistle-blowing. Whistle-blowers, who refuse to give up their responsibility to the world beyond the organizations in which they work, protest and expose immoral, unethical, and illegal behavior. These stalwart individuals, representing the larger, external social order, consistently bear the wrath of bad leaders and their followers, even those who were fellow sufferers. In this section, we explore the challenges that whistleblowers take on and the pitfalls that they commonly encounter.

Despite the serious issues that followers face in their interactions with toxic leaders, we are not without hope. Because of structural changes in the American family, as well as in the workplace, followers are less and less likely to see themselves as part of an authoritarian hierarchy. Contemporary workers, many the products of two-income families or families headed by single working mothers, are more likely to display an "interactive" social character, stemming from their experience with siblings and peers in day-care centers and schools. Consequently, they tend to network, mediate, and negotiate with their sibling-like peers, rather than simply follow orders cascading down the hierarchy.

Recognizing that the emperor has no clothes or, worse yet, is the devil in disguise is both disillusioning and disquieting. Yet by relinquishing our illusions that leaders are the ones we should rely on to carry the burdens of society, new, more constructive possibilities emerge. "Disillusioning leaders,"[2] those who dispel our romance with leadership, may do us a great service. In fact, they may even point the way for us followers to assume our rightful responsibility to share the burdens we now leave to imperfect human leaders.

Following Toxic Leaders

In Search of Posthumous Praise

Jean Lipman-Blumen

Cultural anthropologist Ernest Becker proposed that the human condition, beset by our awareness that we all inevitably die, evokes both a terror and denial of death.[1] In this chapter, I would like to build on Becker's insight by proposing that, to cope with our existential angst, most of us choose to live by illusions. We seek illusions that lull our existential anxiety, reassure us that we are safe, even convince us that we shall attain immortality, which, as Napoleon Bonaparte argued, exists only "in the memory in the minds of men." We might even think of immortality as posthumous praise. Our choice to live by illusions leaves us susceptible to dream merchants, who often appear

This chapter draws and expands on several of my previous publications, including *The Allure of Toxic Leaders*. New York: Oxford University Press, 2005; "Toxic Leadership: When Grand Illusions Masquerade as Noble Visions." *Leader to Leader,* Spring 2005, pp. 29–36; "Our Existential Vulnerability to Toxic Leaders." In D. Liechty (ed.), *Death and Denial: Interdisciplinary Perspectives on the Legacy of Ernest Becker.* Westport, Conn.: Praeger, 2002; and "Toxic Leaders and the Fundamental Vulnerability of Being Alive." In B. Shamir, R. Pillai, M. C. Bligh, and M. Uhl-Bien (eds.), *Follower-Centered Perspectives on Leadership.* Greenwich, Conn.: Information Age, 2006.

in the guise of toxic leaders, leaders who leave us worse off than they found us.

In this chapter, after briefly defining "toxic leaders," I discuss how we fall victim to them, particularly why we cling to the myriad illusions they toss us as lifelines in our uncertain, unfinished, and unfinishable world. After that, I focus on two related, central illusions that toxic leaders offer us as dangerous, seductive gifts: first, that we are "the chosen," and second, that we are at the center of action. In the next section, I explore the relationship among our existential anxiety, the exhilaration of being at the center of action, and the thrill of war. The chapter turns to a discussion of the euphoria of war and what we can learn from it. In this section, I also differentiate between two sources of exhilaration: the grand illusions of toxic leaders who often draw us into their destructive enterprises, and the noble visions of non-toxic leaders who offer us opportunities to contribute to the world. The chapter concludes with a few thoughts about how we might transform our exhilaration and anxiety into positive forces to help free us from the allure of toxic leaders.

A BRIEF DEFINITION OF TOXIC LEADERS

My central interest is in the *followers* of toxic leaders, not toxic leaders themselves. Yet to create a shared understanding of the context in which followers fall into the clutches of toxic leaders, let me try to define toxic leaders briefly.

I am not speaking here of commonplace authoritarian bosses, corrupt political leaders, abusive parents, or even overbearing spouses. For our purposes, toxic leaders are those individuals who, by virtue of their "*destructive behaviors* and *dysfunctional personal characteristics/qualities,* generate *serious and enduring poisonous effects* on the individuals, families, organizations, even entire societies they lead."[2] Toxic leaders span a broad spectrum, too broad for us to elaborate in this allotted space. Suffice it to say that toxic leaders come in various sizes and shapes, distinguishable by different degrees of intensity, intentionality, and impact. Moreover, they may be toxic in some situations and not in others, and they may be toxic in a given situation at time 1 and not in time 2. To make the matter even more vexing, because of the multidimensional grid that toxic leaders inhabit, my toxic leader may appear to be your ideal leader.

Yet the bottom line is this: toxic leaders generally leave us worse off than they found us. The intent to harm others or to enhance themselves at the expense of others distinguishes seriously toxic leaders from the careless or unintentional toxic leaders, who also may cause significant negative fallout.

WHY WE FOLLOW THEM

Having studied toxic leaders for many years in different situations, I come back to the question that first set me on this path: *Given that we recognize toxic leaders for what they are, why do we not only tolerate but often prefer and sometimes even create them?*

True, now and then, whistleblowers, such as the FBI's Coleen Rowley, puncture the illusions that toxic leaders spin. Despite our applause for their bravery, those whistleblowers almost always incur a heavy penalty.[3] Occasionally, but only occasionally, we rise up *en masse* against toxic leaders and kick them out.

Too frequently, the majority of followers acquiesce to toxic leaders, many because the ticket to escape is too costly, whether the coinage be psychological, existential, financial, political, or social—or, in the worst of all cases, an overpowering mix of these currencies. Mostly we simply hang on, waiting for others to oust them. So, too often, toxic leaders hang on as well—and usually for as long as they choose—leaving destruction scattered in their wake.

I come not to blame the follower/victim, but to help liberate those of us who become entrapped by toxic leaders. To do so, we must lay bare the web of forces that tempts us to accept these characteristically charismatic leaders who undermine our social institutions and sometimes our very lives. By failing to examine the factors that render us painfully vulnerable to toxic leaders, we condemn ourselves to remain in their thrall.

HOW WE FALL VICTIM TO TOXIC LEADERS: THE SHORT VERSION

Complex forces within ourselves and society compel us to search for leaders in general, not just toxic leaders, despite their long history of disappointing us. There is not space enough in this chapter to elaborate on these complicated forces—that is, our *internal* psychological and existential needs, as well as the *external* sociological, political, and historical conditions—whose dynamic interaction leaves us susceptible to toxic leaders.

Let me simply say that as we mature, we bring an intricate and unique set of existential and psychological fears and needs to our interactions with the world around us. Our existential concerns focus mainly on our fear of death and our yearning for immortality. One can identify a long list of psychological fears and needs, but the most relevant ones for our discussion are parental transference to authority figures;[4] the need for security and certainty; the need to feel chosen; the need for membership in the human community and its counterpart, the fear of ostracism, isolation, and social death. Add to those the fear of personal impotence vis-à-vis a toxic leader, the desire to commit to a noble vision, the need to be at the center of action, and the need for self-esteem and achievement. In our confrontations with our complicated universe, all these personal factors are at play, and, in those encounters, we deal successfully with some and less so with others.

The success or failure of our interactions with the wider world has important consequences for our vulnerability to leaders. If we "succeed"—when we reach or surpass our society's norms—we are acclaimed heroes, and our self-esteem grows. Then, we look to ourselves as leaders. If we fail, we tend to turn to others as our leaders and heroes (we frequently don't differentiate between the two) to bring meaning and a sense of safety to our lives. At a primal level, this connection also assures us that we shall transcend death—if not physically, then at least symbolically.

Here let's focus on just one small, very limited piece of the puzzle: our anxieties about life, death, and immortality, and the illusions we gladly accept to buffer us from them.

TWO ASPECTS OF THE HUMAN CONDITION: EXISTENTIAL ANXIETY AND SITUATIONAL FEAR

We have already noted that existential anxiety lies at the core of the human condition. It takes nourishment from two sources: the *certainty* that death is inevitable and the *uncertainty* of its particular circumstances. Eliminating either source is nigh impossible.

Nor is our existential anxiety the only wellspring of our angst. The world around us creates daily chaos, uncertainty, and turbulence that arouse what Hungarian sociologist Elemér Hankiss calls "situational fears."[5] Beyond that, the particular historical moment in which we live adds its own special terrors, be they smallpox in an earlier time or mad cow disease and suicide bombers today.

Constantly confronting our anxieties—existential and situational—could leave us both paranoid and paralyzed. So we tend to drown our fears, particularly our existential dread, in the sea of our unconscious. From that unseen and silent depth, they direct our search for eternal life, security, certainty, and heroism toward leaders, both divine and human.[6]

Archival footage of dedicated thousands marching past draped swastikas or hammers and sickles, or smaller groups in Klansmen's robes, demonstrates the complex power of toxic leaders. It conveys their ability to coerce as well as our need to stave off our dread through activities that eclipse our deepest subconscious fears. Contemporary footage of tens of thousands amassing for pilgrimages or holy blessings, whether drawn by toxic or nontoxic leaders, also signifies the power of these same deep wellsprings.

A THIRD ASPECT OF THE HUMAN CONDITION: OPENNESS TO LIFE'S POSSIBILITIES

Another, perhaps more salutary aspect of the human condition also affects our yearning for leaders: our awareness of the infinite possibilities through which we can find and create meaning in our lives. This awareness of endless opportunities allows us to envision sublime, heroic destinies.[7]

Besides, we humans have always lived in an unfinished and unfinishable world, where today's knowledge is unraveled and respun by new discoveries, demanding still newer knowledge and newer discoveries. In one era, we believe cancer is a response to pesticides. In another, inflammation looms as the possible key to unlocking that dread disease. This unfinished and unfinishable world confronts us with limitless challenges in each new era, setting and resetting the stage for heroic action.

BEWARE LEADERS BEARING GIFTS AND GRAND ILLUSIONS

If we are to live our lives and "do our thing," we must somehow maintain the belief that life is both meaningful and under control—if not under our own control, then under someone else's. So we seek meaning and a controlled world from leaders, whom we agree to obey in exchange for their reassuring gifts of meaning and security.

But beware leaders bearing gifts of unfulfillable promises, grand illusions—such as the guarantee of safety and immortality—that they offer us, presumably without cost. In fact, those "gifts" of an impossible level of security and eternal life that toxic leaders promise usually come at an exorbitant price: our own or others' freedom.

One brief example: the charismatic Reverend Jim Jones promised members of the Peoples Temple in California a life of spiritual peace and meaning if only they would follow him to an isolated ranch in Guyana on the northern edge of South America. Jones preached a belief in "Translation," whereby he and his followers would all die as a group but subsequently live a "life of bliss" on another planet.[8] The story of their eventual mass suicide at the urging of their toxic leader is too well known to bear repeating here.

Leaders who offer us such unredeemable gifts have taken a giant step toward toxicity. Joining up with such leaders may temporarily reduce our anxiety, but that also predisposes us to tolerate even more pernicious behavior.

These two consequences of our human condition—our recognition of the *infinite* possibilities waiting to be explored, joined to our awareness of the *finite* limitations imposed by certain death—induce two profound emotions: exhilaration and desolation. These contradictory emotions, linked to related cognitions, frame our behavior, our yearnings, our vulnerabilities, our dreams, our struggles, and our strengths.

The need to reconcile these forces creates a fierce tension. From that same seedbed grow many of our expectations for ourselves and for the leaders whom we choose to follow.

LEADERS OFFER ILLUSIONS: OUR LIFELINE IN AN UNCERTAIN WORLD

Our uncertain world, filled with chaos and challenge, also offers us a tempting "fix": leaders who throw us lifelines baited with illusions. Leaders who create illusions that lull our anxieties help us bear the unbearable, those heartbreaks of life, by appearing to lend them meaning. Sadly but comfortingly, these illusions blunt our painful encounters with reality. Thus we readily trade the sting of authentic experience for the balm of illusions that buffer us from fear and misery.[9]

Probably the most irresistible and unfulfillable illusion toxic leaders offer us is that we can escape death, either physically or symbolically, but only if we follow them. Living on symbolically constitutes immortality, as it is not just death that we fear but the obliteration of our contributions to the world. Thus leaders who vow to protect us from death—either physical or social death—by helping us leave our mark on life through their larger-than-death projects—take strong hold of us.

One avenue to the posthumous praise that immortality brings is a heroic performance often commissioned by the leader. And it is routinely through "grand performances"—such as war—that leaders also identify the heroic, if illusory, path to a meaningful and memorable life.[10] Consequently, those leaders who show us how to act so heroically that our achievements not only satisfy our own yearning for meaning but also ensure that we live on forever in the memory of others—regardless of the profound destruction and suffering wrought by their toxic projects—have a particular allure.

TWIN ILLUSIONS: BEING THE CHOSEN AND BEING AT THE CENTER OF ACTION

Being the Chosen

We humans have a deep need to feel chosen. We also need to feel that we belong to an elite group, be it the exclusive country club set or the leading gang on the block. As Freud suggested, sibling rivalry is a fundamental part of that dynamic. Leaders who instinctively understand this need wield a formidable tool. The concept of belonging to the chosen group—be it the Peoples Temple, the elite social set, a particular religion, Ivy League graduates, or Enron executives before their fraudulent practices unraveled—has immense appeal to us humans. The promise of an honored place, with all the accompanying perks, here or in the hereafter (or both), can make us readily forgo our freedom and follow the dictates of even the most toxic leaders.

Although the illusion that we are the chosen is both potent and comforting, it also holds serious dangers. Many religious and ethnic leaders have fed their followers' hunger for security and meaning with the assurance that they alone are the "chosen people," blessed with a special relationship to God and a singular destiny. From earliest Biblical times to the present, religious leaders have assured their followers that they are the chosen, endowed with special, possibly divine gifts of grace. Such leaders draw a sharp line between the "chosen" and the "other" or "nonchosen." The leader may even advocate the chosen's obligation to rid the world of the "other's" polluting taint, be it commercial, political, or religious.

A prime maxim of salespeople dictates that they must convince themselves first before they can convince others. We witness a similar phenomenon in leaders, both corporate and political, who fervently believe that their product or policy is the only one worth supporting. They see no middle ground. They buy wholeheartedly into the illusions they offer others. Corporate leaders, intent on destroying, rather than competing or collaborating with, their market rivals, whom they perceive as the "other," demonstrate this perilous confusion. Ideologues and fundamentalists in different arenas display a similar bent.

When we feel we are the chosen—that our company or our religion or our institution alone deserves "Olympic gold"—there are at least four possibilities for imposing that "truth" on others: absorb, convert, marginalize, or simply eliminate them. The history of religion is fraught with such examples. The corporate world has its own version, commonly referred to as mergers and acquisitions or hostile takeovers.

Moreover, psychologists have demonstrated that the most effective way to create cohesion within group A is to recognize an "other," presumably group B, particularly a hostile group B.[11] Although the "other" may react with anger, that simply reinforces the chosen group's conviction that its own claims are legitimate.

Membership in the Center of Action

Membership in an elite group, like the chosen, also offers many benefits. It allows us to feel that we are at the center of action, where important people—leaders and their minions—congregate to make important decisions. Momentous action takes place at the center, where, as anthropologist Clifford Geertz suggests, "Leading ideas come together with . . . leading institutions to create an arena in which the events that most vitally affect its members' lives take place."[12] Being at the very center of things is exhilarating. In that space, we feel most engaged, most sure of our significance and, thus, of success in our bid for immortality.

Leaders who invite us to join them at the center of things promise to let us touch the very heartbeat of life. They connect their followers to power and meaning in ways that add significance and exhilaration to their lives. There, followers vicariously experience the leader's power and thereby can feel powerful and heroic themselves.

When following the leader brings us to the very center of things, our lives take on increased relevance and meaning that cannot be eroded even by physical death. Conversely, being exiled from the center, isolated from the chosen, constitutes social death, a life without import, a life unworthy of immortality, of posthumous praise.

The center of action offers another attractive reward: it is the repository of the latest knowledge. Being at the center diminishes our fear of the unknown and the unpredictable as we witness the creation of the newest "truth." The latest scientific, political, and military knowledge all gravitate to the center, where their bearers are honored with a plethora of medals and prizes.

New knowledge creates an illusion of increased safety and control over the unknown and the unwanted. At the center, we hail the discoverers of recent knowledge as heroes. Even when we are not the actual creators of that knowledge, by rubbing shoulders with those who are, we can partake in the illusion of increased safety, control, power, knowledge, and vicarious heroism. Knowledge leaders can ease our transition from a crumbling faith in current "truth," now exposed as illusory or false, to an energizing and comforting belief in emerging knowledge, even if that, too, eventually will be overwritten and exposed as faulty.

Still, such advances in knowledge are not without their dangers, particularly from entrenched leaders whose own illusory beliefs now lie shattered. These established "truth holders" often resist new explanations, vilifying the bearers of new knowledge, like Galileo or, in more recent times, the scientists who voiced early warnings of global warming.

New knowledge may also threaten the followers' security because it destroys the old beliefs that gave structure and meaning to their world. Thus they commonly become the snitches, taunters, and executioners of the inquisition launched to destroy the heretics. Toxic leadership can be enabled by toxic followership.

Yet human curiosity propels us forward. Gradually, additional pieces of confirming information fall into place, creating the paradigm shift so aptly described by Thomas Kuhn.[13] The new knowledge provides better models, replete with their own illusions, at least until the next cycle begins.

COSTS AT THE CENTER

Although the center has a strong gravitational pull, it also has its costs. For one, periodic quakes can liquefy its seemingly solid ground into molten toxicity. For example, congressional representatives, unaware that their elite club of elected officials and lobbyists is gradually succumbing to corruption, periodically find that center a direct route to prison. The obsession to remain at the center, where leaders congregate, may blind us to the steep price we often must pay: tolerating or even becoming toxic leaders ourselves.

Let me touch briefly on just three additional dangers. First, being at the center can create a treacherous addiction. In that charmed circle, we socialize on a first-name basis with the great and the powerful. To maintain their standing at this center of the world, the chosen must often suffer grave consequences.

For example, when we, as the chosen, are asked to remit our center "dues" by engaging in toxic behavior, we may be so addicted that we easily rationalize our acquiescence. Or we may be beholden to the people who ask that of us, like Betty Vinson, a forty-seven-year-old accountant and senior manager at WorldCom's accounting division, trapped in an $11 billion fraud. Vinson's WorldCom boss, Buford (Buddy) Yates, her former colleague at Lamar Life Insurance, asked her to make false entries, rationalizing illegitimate behavior as toxic leaders frequently do. Friendship and a sense of indebtedness pushed Vinson to accede reluctantly. Over a period of eighteen months, Vinson falsified profits to the tune of $3.7 billion. Vinson's penalty was steep: five months in prison and the devastating impact of the trial and sentence on her family, social relations, career, and reputation—the rippling fallout from following a toxic leader.

There is a second hazard at the center of action: the center may mean existing in a frenzied, tormenting culture, an exceptionally competitive, sometimes unethical climate, where only the toughest survive. Enron, in its heady rise to dominance in the energy trading sector, generated such a culture. Enron created a community where survival was proof that one "had the right stuff," even when having the right stuff meant crossing the toxic line. Former CFO Andrew Fastow and COO Jeffrey Skilling, majordomos of Enron's corrosive culture, have now joined the prison population.

Sometimes those at unethical centers may not be asked to engage directly in toxic behavior, only to look away as others do so. Yet as Martin Luther King Jr. reminded us, "He who passively accepts evil is as much involved in it as he who helps to perpetrate it. He who accepts evil without protesting against it is really cooperating with it."[14]

Consider still a third, less obvious peril at the center: at times, leaders at the center, despite impressive credentials, simply are in over their heads, lending additional credence to the Peter Principle. Given the restrictions on center membership and the delusions of grandeur often entertained by those at the center, such leaders rarely reach beyond their charmed circle for counsel or correction. When groupthink, that premature rush to consensus, infects a power center, the likelihood of disastrous decisions and crisis escalates sharply.[15] Almost daily, we witness toxic leaders in business and government who recast unwelcome counsel and alternative diagnoses to fit their own unshakeable, but quite mistaken, judgment.

EXHILARATION, ANXIETY, AND WAR

The center has its plus sides too, of course. It can put us in touch with authentic existence, an ideal described by several prominent philosophers.[16] Such authentic experiences are exhilarating. They make us feel intensely alive, even heroic. Yet exhilaration can itself be problematical. It is uncommonly tantalizing, and it can flow from toxic, as well as more positive, sources.

Even war—or perhaps especially war—can be intoxicating, a grand military war to "end all wars" or to put us in control of the world. But athletic wars, gang wars, and industrial wars can also make our adrenaline run. At a minimum, war forces us to confront our anxieties and put them to conscious use. Our desire for elation, spurred on by our unexamined longing to be heroes, can leave us responsive to the toxic leader's dark call to battle, to unjust wars, and even to genocide. War may be the quintessential case of the grand illusion, disguised as a noble vision that the toxic leader identifies as the road to immortality.

Through the lens of time, many war veterans remember their battlefield experiences as the most thrilling moments of their lives. They recall how their terror of death broke through their unconscious, taking form as life-sacrificing dedication to their buddies and visceral hatred for the enemy, fused to a full-hearted commitment to a grand cause. Sadly enough, hate can inspire what passes for heroism in many societies.

There are other lessons that war teaches us about anxiety, heroism, grand illusions, immortality, and toxic leadership. In war, we can feel totally alive and energized because our repressed terror of death, that existential anxiety, breaks through the armor of our unconscious. It is then that we allow ourselves to feel that anxiety, heightened by the situational fears that war provokes. When that occurs, we can put our anxiety to constructive use to order our priorities, to clarify our vision, to point us in the right direction, to protect us, and sometimes to infuse us with uncommon strength.[17]

If, in nonextreme situations, we could confront our existential and situational anxieties—instead of feeling their control but not knowing their source—we probably could live our ordinary lives with a far greater sense of exhilaration and purpose. Confronting our anxieties, painful as that might be, would allow us to use them more constructively and creatively. As I have noted elsewhere, "Acting *despite* fear and trembling is one definition of courage, the very stuff of true heroism. Then we are most likely to take risks, to act as our own leaders, even to reach for the stars."[18]

If we could face our anxieties and stare them down, we could feel exhilaration without fear, as for example in the "hot groups" that Harold J. Leavitt and I studied.[19] Those hot groups, facing major obstacles and immense challenges, even danger, nonetheless felt totally alive, excited, heroic, and significant. There was little doubt in their minds that their lives had important meaning, not just to themselves, but to society.

TWO TYPES OF EXHILARATION

Elsewhere, I have differentiated between the exhilaration that comes from noble, life-affirming causes of constructive leaders and the excitement that flows from grand illusions that toxic leaders ask us to engage in or merely endorse.[20] So, here, let us consider very briefly four possible ways to distinguish between the two.

First, the toxic leader's grand illusion envisions an "unattainable Nirvana," "a grandiose dream of an unrealistic future that [is] unconditionally positive"[21] and poses little risk for the followers, provided they do as the leader says. Hitler's Thousand Year Reich is perhaps the archetype of the unattainable, improbable vision of a toxic leader. By contrast, John F. Kennedy's proposed lunar expedition, though fraught with risk, had more scientific foundation at the time he suggested it than the stunned American public realized. The benefits of that round-trip voyage to the moon would enhance the entire world, not just the United States.

Second, the toxic leader's grand venture usually positions him or her as an omnipotent savior, commanding docile followers, who largely play the role of infatuated observer or unquestioning tool of the "master." Just witnessing the exploits of the savior provokes their exhilaration. By contrast, the nontoxic leader requires immense, well-conceived, and cooperative efforts from followers, discriminating exertion that infuses them with unexpected self-confidence and heroic excitement.

Third, the grand illusion of the toxic leader pictures an idyllic world, untainted by the nonchosen. It is a vision of the world that calls not for vigorous self-improvement by followers, but an all-out jihad by the followers to eradicate the impure "other." Measure that against the constructive leader's noble enterprise, designed to help humankind or lift up the weakest, smallest, or poorest in our midst. No harm to others is involved, nor is one group enhanced by diminishing another.

Fourth, toxic leaders' grand illusions represent evil as a moral action. One example: Gestapo leader Heinrich Himmler congratulating the SS members on their extermination of millions of people as a "glorious page" in German history.[22] By contrast, the nontoxic leader articulates a vision that elicits the best in his or her followers, from integrity, altruism, and compassion to creativity and imagination.

True, toxic leaders' grand illusions pump our veins with pulsating excitement, but so can the life-affirming noble enterprises of nontoxic leaders. Both involve letting our anxiety surface; however, the purposes to which each puts the anxiety are vastly different. It is for the followers to ferret out the wellsprings of their exhilaration: Does their euphoria flow from a narrow self-interest and hatred or from a larger, altruistic, and compassionate dedication to those beyond their own circle of family, friends, and fellow believers?

Yet anxiety continues to bedevil us. Confronting and defanging our anxiety could sharpen our direction and invigorate us, even if we cannot count on complete safety. Then we might live intensely, indeed with great exhilaration, without the stimuli of enemies and daily wars, small and large, and without falling under the sway of toxic leaders.

One answer to the human condition calls for freeing ourselves from anxious subservience to, as distinct from knowledgeable support of, *all* leaders, not just the toxic ones. This, coupled with the necessity to take action despite our fears, may be the best hope we have in the long run. In fact, this strategy may just provide the most important route to finding, even creating, exhilarating meaning, as well as memory in the minds of future generations—that posthumous praise we all unconsciously seek.

What Can Milgram's Obedience Experiments Contribute to Our Understanding of Followership?

Thomas Blass

On June 1, 1962, Claude Buxton, the chairman of Yale University's Psychology Department, received the following letter from a junior faculty member:

Dear Claude,

I wish to announce my departure from the Linsly-Chittenden basement laboratory. It served us well. Our last subject was run on Sunday, May 27. The experiments on "obedience to authority" are, Praise the Lord, completed.

In the end it took almost a thousand subjects and twenty-four experimental conditions in Bridgeport and New Haven to answer the several questions that inspired the research. At this point the findings look very strong, but need to be written up in a clear and intelligent fashion. The year ahead will pose an exciting challenge at the level of thinking and writing.

The day before, the Israeli government, after a long trial, carried out Adolf Eichmann's death sentence for his role in the murder of a large proportion of European Jewry, presaging a more substantive connection that was to be made later between these experiments and the behavior of the Nazis during World War II.

The letter writer was a brash and energetic twenty-eight-year-old junior faculty member driven to make his mark with a distinctive piece of research.[1] As he wrote an old friend soon after arriving at Yale in fall 1960, he was ruminating about designing the boldest and most significant research possible. His name was Stanley Milgram, and it was barely two years earlier that he had received his PhD in social psychology from Harvard's Department of Social Relations, with his dissertation chaired by that giant of American psychology, Gordon Allport. It was an ambitious piece of research, requiring spending almost two years in Europe comparing conformity levels in France and Norway using a modification of the Asch conformity paradigm.

And indeed Milgram succeeded in making his mark with the obedience research. Although he had just begun his academic career, and would go on to do other innovative research, it would always be overshadowed by the obedience work. Of the 140 or so talks he gave during his career, more than a third dealt with obedience. He was still giving invited talks on obedience in 1984, the year he died. It remains his best-known and most widely discussed work; many consider it one of the most important psychological works of the latter half of the twentieth century.

Some have equated the importance of his work with that of Sigmund Freud. But Milgram was no Freud. He did not attempt an all-encompassing theory of human behavior. No "school" of thought bears his name. Whereas Freud, of course, focused on childhood and intrapsychic determinants of human behavior, for Milgram—following in the footsteps of Kurt Lewin, the father of experimental social psychology—the primary causal explanation for a person's actions was to be found in the here and now—in the immediate, concrete social situation. However, Milgram was similar to Freud in that both of them have led to profound alterations in our thinking about human nature.[2]

As many, if not most, readers probably know, in his obedience experiments Milgram made the startling discovery that a majority of his subjects—average and presumably normal community residents—were willing to give a series of increasingly painful and perhaps harmful electric shocks to a protesting, screaming victim simply because they were commanded to by an experimental authority.[3] They did this despite the fact that the experimenter had no coercive means to enforce his commands and the person they were shocking was an innocent victim who did nothing to merit such punishment. Specifically, the subjects were participating in an experiment supposedly investigating the effects of punishment on learning. The centerpiece of the laboratory setup was a very realistic looking, but actually fake, shock machine. Its front panel had a row of thirty switches, which, when pressed, would deliver increasingly intense shocks, ranging from 15 volts to a maximum of 450 volts. The task of the subject was to teach another subject to memorize a list of adjective-noun pairs by shocking him every time he made a mistake and to increase the voltage one step at a time on each subsequent error. The learner was actually in cahoots with the experimenter and did not actually receive shocks, only feigning his suffering. For the subject-teachers, however, it was a very real and gripping experience. The results: about two-thirds of the subjects fully obeyed the experimenter, progressing to the maximum 450-volt shock.

These groundbreaking and controversial experiments have had continuing and enduring significance because they have shown with stunning clarity that ordinary people would follow destructive orders, even without hatred toward their victims. People generally assume that there is a direct line between the kind of individual a person is and the nature of his or her actions, but Milgram showed that it doesn't take evil or aberrant persons to carry out actions that are reprehensible and cruel. Milgram's experiments have reshaped our conceptions of individual morality: Although we would like to believe that when saddled with a moral dilemma we will follow the dictates of our conscience, those experiments have taught us dramatically that if we find ourselves in a concrete situation that contains powerful social constraints, our moral sense can readily be shunted aside.

Milgram apparently thought that there would always be some people who would say "we knew it all along" when learning about his demonstration of extreme obedience. To short-circuit that kind of reaction and to highlight the revelatory nature of his findings, he would describe his experiment to various groups and ask them to predict how many participants would be fully obedient. In all cases, the predictions vastly underestimated the actual results.[4] For example, a group of psychiatrists predicted that fewer than 1 percent of a group of one thousand participants would be completely obedient. Here is how Milgram described this finding in a letter to a fellow social psychologist: "Recently, I asked a group of 40 Yale psychiatrists to predict the behavior of experimental subjects in a novel, though significant situation. The psychiatrists—although they expressed great certainty in the accuracy of their predictions—were wrong by a factor of 500. Indeed, I have little doubt that a group of charwomen would do as well."

One of the unusual aspects of Milgram's obedience research is the degree to which disciplines outside of psychology have found it relevant. One can find it discussed in publications devoted to topics as wide ranging as philosophy, medicine, economics, Holocaust studies, education, accounting, and political science. It has even appeared in anthologies of English prose.

In fact, the influence of the obedience experiments goes beyond academia, permeating contemporary culture and thought. Their impact has ranged from the superficial to the serious, and points in between. For example, a few years ago, I discovered a French-German punk rock group named Milgram. In 1986, the British musician Peter Gabriel, a serious admirer of Milgram, paid tribute to him by recording a song titled "We Do What We're Told (Milgram's 37)."

Milgram's work has also captured the dramatic and literary imagination. In 1976, CBS aired the film *The Tenth Level,* a made-for-TV drama starring William Shatner as the Milgram-like character. According to the writer of that drama, George Bellak, the film caused almost as much furor as the experiments themselves. When he first presented the idea to a group of TV executives, many were outraged by it; one even called it "Godless." Even after he completed the film for CBS, it took about a year to cobble together enough willing sponsors. Major sponsors like IBM and GM did not want to touch it with a ten-foot pole. Nevertheless, it received honorable mention at APA's Media Awards in 1977.

Early on, British playwright Dannie Abse produced a play, *The Dogs of Pavlov,* inspired by the research.[5] Since then, there are at least half a dozen plays that I know of that have been written, or are in progress, based on the obedience studies. The most recent one is an off-Broadway performance presented in the summer of 2006, titled *The Answer Is Horse*—an engaging and insightful production conveying the contemporary relevance of Milgram's research. And several years ago, Canadian writer Eileen Coughlan published a very clever murder mystery titled "Dying by Degrees," which has a plot built around a sinister version of the obedience experiment.[6]

There are also contemporary cultural influences of a more serious, consequential sort. Clearly the potential connection that is of the greatest consequence is the one between the obedience experiments and the Holocaust. An attempt to shed light on the Nazis' destruction of European Jewry was one of the driving forces that led Milgram to study obedience.

Milgram saw his findings as providing the scientific underpinnings for Hannah Arendt's concept of the "banality of evil"—that the abhorrent acts of the Nazis were carried out in the name of obedience and not out of hatred toward their victims.[7] My own view is that Milgram's approach does not fit the whole range of horrors comprised by the Holocaust. Although it might account for the dutiful train conductor who transported thousands of Jews to Auschwitz as routinely as he might deliver bushels of apples from one German city to another, it does not account for the unspeakable, inventive cruelties of the Nazi concentration camp guards. They must have come from within.

Another important domain where the influence of obedience experiments is discernable is the U.S. Army, which apparently has taken the lessons of Milgram's research to heart and acted on them. A military psychologist named Lieutenant Colonel Dave Grossman told me something that I found absolutely astounding: when he was undergoing officer training in the early 1970s, he was shown training films instructing soldiers on how to *disobey* illegitimate orders. He described this to me as "a true revolution in military history," which he said is directly traceable to Milgram, as well as to the My Lai massacre.

Yet another important domain of human activity where the obedience experiments have had an impact is the legal profession. According to Lexis/Nexis, the online bibliographical database, Milgram has been cited in over two hundred law reviews and several Supreme Court briefs. A frequent argument contained in these sources is that laws limiting police searches to instances where there is cause are essentially toothless. Drawing on Milgram's findings, they argue that given our extreme readiness to obey authority, a person is not very likely to question a police officer's right to search him or his house when he is requested to.

Over the years, as I kept discovering more and increasingly diverse uses of the obedience experiments, I would occasionally ask myself, "Why have these experiments had such wide appeal and influence?" I finally concluded that it is because in his demonstration of our powerful propensity to obey authority, Milgram has identified one of the universals of social behavior—transcending both time and place—and people intuitively sense this.

I have done two data analyses that provide at least some modest evidence for this assertion. In the first, I took all of Milgram's standard obedience conditions and all the replications I could find conducted by others and ran a correlation between when a study was done and the degree of obedience it yielded. There was absolutely no relationship: the correlation coefficient hovered near zero. That is, although there is some variability across studies in the degree of obedience they found, that variability is not at all a function of how long ago or how recently the study was conducted.

In a second analysis, I again took all of Milgram's standard conditions and replications by others and compared the degree of obedience found among the studies conducted in the United States with the degree found in the studies conducted in other countries—such as Spain, Austria, Italy, and Australia. Quite remarkably, the outcomes of the two groups of studies turned out to be very similar. The average obedience rate among the experiments conducted in the United States was 61 percent; rates of obedience found in studies conducted elsewhere averaged 66 percent. A one-way ANOVA showed that this difference between the two groups of studies was not significant.[8]

I have sampled from a wide variety of uses that have been made of the obedience experiments. My aim in this chapter is to add to that array by showing what the obedience experiments and Milgram's views about them can contribute to our understanding of followership.

To pave the way toward that understanding, I would like first to make clear what the experiments *do not* tell us about an individual's extreme readiness to follow a leader's orders.

First, they do *not* tell us that humans are by nature mean and nasty, with bottled-up, hostile impulses that normally cannot be expressed because of societal constraints. According to this view—rooted in Freudian thinking—the experiments are about aggression and not about following orders. The experimental authority has merely created a permissive environment for uncapping normally repressed aggressive tendencies. So when a follower carries out a leader's malevolent orders, those orders are really a smokescreen to hide actions that the follower would have been willing to do even without the orders.

Milgram effectively demolished this alternate view by conducting a most theatrical and clever variation of his basic experiment.[9] The experiment begins and unfolds in the usual fashion with the learner getting increasingly strong shocks for each mistake, accompanied by stronger and stronger cries of protest from the learner. At 150 volts, the experimenter abruptly turns to the teacher and tells him that they are going to have to stop because he is worried about the learner, whose reactions seem to be unusually strong. Suddenly, the voice of the learner is heard from the next room, protesting the experimenter's decision. He says he wants to continue to the end; his friend who had previously been in the experiment went all the way, and he is not less a man than his friend, so he doesn't want to stop now. The naive subject is now faced with a conflict: Whose wishes should he follow? The result: not a single subject continued beyond this point. If the opportunity to vent pent-up hostilities were the driving force for the subject's behavior, he would have continued: What better excuse could he have than permission from the person he was supposedly hurting? Yet no one went any further, clearly demonstrating that it was the authority's orders and not any aggressive tendencies that governed the subject's behavior.[10]

Second, the extreme obedience Milgram found tells us nothing about the power of *coercive* leaders to influence their followers. We didn't need Milgram to tell us how difficult it is for workers to defy unethical or malevolent orders when management can, and is likely to, punish disobedience. We *know* this—which is why whistleblowers merit our admiration. As Milgram put it: "Our studies deal only with obedience that is willingly assumed in the absence of threat of any sort, obedience that is maintained through the simple assertion by authority that it has the right to exercise control over the person. Whatever force authority exercises in this study is based on powers that the subject in some manner ascribes to it and not on any objective threat or availability of physical means of controlling the subject."[11]

Third, the experiments do not tell us that authorities are all-powerful beings whose grip on their subordinates is absolute and total. The term "blind obedience" that is sometimes used to refer to Milgram's findings is misleading in this regard, because it conveys a simple, reflexive, uncritical yielding to the authority's wishes by almost all his followers. Readers who have seen Milgram's black-and-white documentary, *Obedience,* know how wrongheaded this characterization is. The stop-and-go behavior, the visible signs of stress, the need to use verbal prods by the experimenter—all convey deep conflict, rather than reflexive compliance. And, in fact, about a third of the participants resolve the conflict by exercising critical judgment and not following the leader. In this regard, Milgram once wrote, "It may be that we are puppets—puppets controlled by the strings of society. But, at least we are puppets with perception, with awareness. And perhaps our awareness is the first step to our liberation."[12]

Let us now turn to what Milgram's research ideas *can* contribute to understanding and conceptualizing followership. First, of course, is the unexpected enormity of the basic findings themselves. And lest we think that his findings are only narrowly applicable to the one-person-to-one-person authority structure of experimenter and subject studied in his laboratory, Milgram explicitly, and with palpable pessimism, connects his results to organizational life in which the hierarchical social structure typically consists of leaders and multiple followers: "Each individual," he wrote, "possesses a conscience which to a greater or lesser degree serves to restrain the unimpeded flow of impulses destructive to others. But when he merges his person into an organizational structure, a new creature replaces autonomous man unhindered by the limitations of individual morality, freed of humane inhibition, mindful only of the sanctions of authority."[13]

And how does this transformation take place? What mediating mechanisms result in an individual's willingness to follow a leader's reprehensible orders when he would not normally behave this way when acting under his own steam, as an autonomous individual? Milgram argues that when people accept the legitimacy of an authority—that the person in charge has the right to prescribe their behavior and that they in turn feel an obligation to do so—certain internal changes take place.

The first change that makes destructive obedience possible is accepting the authority's definition of the situation, of reality. The follower comes to see things through the eyes of the leader, so to speak. As Milgram put it, "With numbing regularity good people were seen to knuckle under the demands of authority and perform actions that were callous and severe. Men who are in everyday life responsible and decent were seduced by the trappings of authority, by the control of their perceptions, and by the uncritical acceptance of the experimenter's definition of the situation, into performing harsh acts."[14]

A Vietnam veteran who was a student in one of my social psychology classes told of an incident that illustrates this process. He was a member of a unit patrolling the coastline. He saw a boat approaching in the distance. As it got nearer, he realized that it was only a fishing sloop and, therefore, presumably harmless. The officer in charge asked him, "What are you waiting for? Blow it out of the water."

"But it's only a fishing sloop," the soldier replied.

"No," said the officer, "it's a gunboat."

The soldier blew it out of the water.

The second internal change that makes people receptive to destructive commands, according to Milgram, is a shift in responsibility from the follower to the leader—what he called the agentic shift or entry into the agentic state. Now the subordinate's main concern is how well he will do his job—he is no longer concerned with the morality of his actions. He has relinquished that judgment to the leader. By pointing to relinquishing of responsibility as a bridge that can lead to obedience without moral limits, Milgram can alert followers to try to block this tendency and to realize that being a good organizational citizen does not require that followers put their sense of responsibility on ice. Of course, this is facilitated by leadership that promotes an organizational culture that doesn't make blind obedience the prime value, where the exercise of critical judgment is expected and even encouraged, and where constructive questioning is acceptable.

Milgram's work can also alert us, or at least remind us, of the importance of the social situation—rather than inner attributes such as personality or character—in determining the way a follower responds to leadership. An important lesson that Milgram's experiments teach us is how much of our behavior is a product of the characteristics of the immediate situation, which can override our personalities. As Milgram put it rather strongly, reflecting not only on his own work but on social psychology as a whole, "The social psychology of this century reveals a major lesson: often, it is not so much the kind of person a man is as the kind of situation in which he finds himself that determines how he will act."[15]

And, in fact, the main reason Milgram carried out over twenty different experimental variations was to identify the specific alterations in the immediate situation that increase or reduce obedience. One such variation has special relevance in these times of revelations of massive corporate wrongdoing set into motion by corrupt leadership.

In this experiment, the naive subject is part of a three-person teaching team, the other two people being confederates. Their job, like that in the other experiments in the series, is to teach the learner a list of word pairs using incremental shocks as punishment for each error. One confederate is given the job of reading the word pairs, the second announces whether or not the learner's answer is correct, and the real subject administers the shocks. In the midst of the process, the two confederates drop out—one at 150 volts, the other at 210 volts—because of their concern for the learner. The results—first reported in an article aptly titled "Liberating Effects of Group Pressure"—only 10 percent of the subjects ended up being completely obedient.[16] The rebellion of peers dramatically weakened the authority's grip. Milgram noted, "Of the score of experimental variations completed in this study, none was so effective in undercutting the experimenter's authority as [this one]."[17]

This variation suggests a potentially powerful antidote to objectionable authority. For the conscientious follower who, let's say, is employed by a company whose management has issued immoral or illegal orders for the employees to carry out, it would be best to find allies among coworkers who share his or her perceptions and are willing to join him or her in opposing the malevolent directives. It is tremendously difficult to be a lone dissenter, not only because of the strong need to belong but also because—through the process of pluralistic ignorance—the compliance of peers (that is, the other employees) makes the ordered actions seem acceptable and leads the follower to question his or her own negative judgment. The pervasiveness of this difficulty of being a lone dissenter, of deviating from the group, was driven home to me by a very recent study showing that even people of the highest stature are not immune. In an ingenious archival study, Granberg and Bartels analyzed the voting patterns among the justices of the U.S. Supreme Court from 1953 to 2001.[18] They found that the eight-one split was the least common, occurring in only 10 percent of approximately four thousand decisions.

The step-by-step escalating shock procedure in Milgram's experiments also contains an important message for followers, although admittedly it is one that is not that easy to implement. Followers should try not to even *start* to comply with requests from above that they feel even *slightly* uneasy about. As in Milgram's experiments, acquiescing in carrying out actions in an organizational hierarchy that are only mildly objectionable is often the beginning of an escalating process of entrapment, in which, one step at a time, the actions become more and more objectionable. The further along the continuum of destructive acts, the harder it is to extract oneself from the commanding authority's grip, because to do so is to confront the fact that one's earlier acts of compliance were wrong. When social psychologists Andy Modigliani and François Rochat conducted a content analysis of subject-experimenter dialogue in one of Milgram's experimental conditions, they found that the earlier the subject started questioning or resisting the experimenter, the more likely he would end up ultimately defying him by not going to the end.[19]

Another important message for followers can be derived from yet another technical feature of Milgram's laboratory procedure—namely, the creation of a psychological force that Milgram referred to as "counter-anthropomorphism." This term is meant to denote a process that is the direct opposite of anthropomorphism—the primitive tendency to ascribe human qualities to inanimate objects. Counter-anthropomorphism, according to Milgram, is "the countervailing tendency . . . of attributing an impersonal quality to forces that are essentially human in origin and maintenance. For some individuals, systems of human origin are treated as if they existed above and beyond any human agent, beyond the control of whim or human feeling. The human element behind agencies and institutions is denied."[20] The technical detail in Milgram's procedure that evokes or heightens this tendency is "The experiment *requires* that you continue," one of the prods used by the experimenter to get the subject to continue shocking the victim. This tactic of creating a psychological force that seems to transcend the personal can blind the subject to the human origins of the unwanted orders and may serve as a deterrent to questioning or defying those orders. As a subject quoted by Milgram kept muttering to himself, "It's *got* to go on. It's *got* to go on."

Milgram's observations in his lab suggest that contemporary followers within organizations should be on guard against similar kinds of word tricks that can occur in organization life. When a follower who questions problematic directives is met with "It is company policy" or a similar retort, he or she should recognize that Milgram's counter-anthropomorphism is at work. With this awareness, the follower will not be deterred in probing for the human source of the objectionable orders, thereby enhancing the possibility of opposing and even derailing them.

In a thought-provoking review essay titled "Are Corporations Evil?" the legal scholar Douglas Litowitz notes that this process of mystification, identified by Milgram and used by his experimenter, in which commands originating with humans gain added power to entrap when the sources of those commands are depersonalized, is especially relevant to very large corporations.[21] Here's how he put it:

> All of the institutions involved in the [recent] corporate scandals were large and impersonal. . . . It is no coincidence that the scandals involved massive companies. When an institution reaches a certain critical mass, the lowly individual worker cannot peer around the curtains to see fallible human beings pulling the strings—the institution begins to loom large as if it had a life and a force all its own. . . . [W]hen the institution in question is a multinational colossus and the order is filtered through a series of middle men, . . . there is only a stark choice between obedience and losing your job. The obvious decision is to keep your position and rationalize your conduct as mandated by some mystical, invisible, immortal entity—the "firm" or the "company."[22]

CONCLUSION

There is typically a gray cloud of gloom hovering over any discussions of Milgram's research and its pessimistic implications for superordinate-subordinate relations and, more generally, for our conceptions of human nature. This is not surprising, as Milgram himself repeatedly and almost exclusively drew troubling implications. For example, he wrote that "ordinary people simply doing their jobs and without any particular hostility on their part can become agents in a terrible destructive process. Moreover, even when . . . they are asked to carry out actions incompatible with fundamental standards of morality, relatively few people have the resources needed to resist authority."[23]

But Milgram also recognized that a necessary element of civilized society is the presence of hierarchical structures of authority. As he wrote in a letter to his former student Alan Elms in 1973: "We do not observe compliance to authority merely because it is a transient cultural or historical phenomenon, but because it flows from the logical necessities of social organization." In fact, even in the introduction to his first journal report on his findings, Milgram recognized the positive side of obedience, writing that "obedience serves numerous productive functions. . . . Obedience may be ennobling and educative and refer to acts of charity and kindness, as well as to destruction."[24]

If so, why was his work so one-sided? Why did he limit his research only to the darker side of obedience? He essentially answered this question in a letter to Solomon Asch, his scientific mentor, just before embarking on his obedience experiments in the summer of 1961, in which he outlined his plans: "Certainly obedience serves numerous productive functions, and you may wonder why I focus on its destructive potential. Perhaps it is because this has been the most striking and disturbing expression of obedience in our time"—referring undoubtedly to the Nazis' genocidal program aimed primarily at European Jewry.

However, once he felt that he had probed the destructive side of obedience in sufficient detail, he was ready to turn his attention to its positive aspects. All of Milgram's obedience experiments were funded by the first of a series of three grants from the National Science Foundation (NSF), beginning in the summer of 1961. Milgram submitted a continuation grant proposal to NSF in early 1962, after he had completed almost all of the experimental conditions dealing with destructive obedience. One of the proposed experiments he listed in that grant proposal was titled "Constructive Obedience." Although he hadn't yet come up with a concrete procedure, he expected that "a simple significant situation can be set up in which a subject can be commanded into socially commendable acts as much at variance with his customary standards of behavior as the inhumane acts we have seen so far." The grant proposal was only approved in modified form with reduced funding, so Milgram never did carry out such an experiment. Nonetheless, that he planned such an experiment is informative, because it implies that Milgram may have thought that the unexpected strength of the obedient tendencies he had discovered so far was just one part of a more general, full-spectrum predisposition.

To the extent that my argument is correct about Milgram's belief that our propensity for extreme obedience can take constructive forms and not just destructive ones, Milgram's work can provide us with some concrete, optimistic implications for the nature of followership and the leader-follower relationship.

To illustrate this—and to help me end this chapter on a positive note—let me quote from Paul Pfeiffer, the editor of a magazine published by the Larson Allen business consulting firm in Minneapolis, who insightfully extracts this kind of rarely recognized, hopeful implication from the Milgram experiments:

> Milgram's experiment suggests that few people will defy authority even pressed to an ethical extreme. Casting Milgram's findings in a positive light might suggest that an ethical leader can . . . take advantage of a position of authority to push a team toward increased productivity. The dynamic already exists: you lead; we will follow. And if leaders recognize that they possess significant power before they enter the building, and if they can believe that those who work for them are more eager to follow than resist, then organizations, as well as leaders and their employees, are poised for a great leap forward.[25]

What Kind of Leader Do People Want to Follow?

Michael Maccoby

We urgently need leaders, but it has become harder than ever to get people to follow. To explore why this is so and what we can do about it, this chapter addresses the following questions:

- Why do we have such an urgent need for leaders?
- Why do people follow a leader or resist being followers?
- What kind of leader will be most effective at the present time?

THE NEED FOR LEADERS

To answer these questions, we need to be clear about the definition of a leader. Many commonly used definitions don't hold up to analysis. Leaders are sometimes defined as visionaries, but many visionaries have no followers. Indeed, there are visionaries in mental hospitals. Leaders are sometimes defined as people who set goals or motivate people, but increasingly teams also set goals and motivate themselves. Leaders are sometimes defined as people who influence others to change their behavior, but so do psychotherapists and philosophers.

The ideas presented in this chapter are further developed in my book *The Leaders We Need*. Boston: Harvard Business School Press, 2007.

One definition of a leader is irrefutable: a leader is someone people follow. Although this definition may seem too simple for some academics, it raises the difficult questions of *why* people follow a leader and *how* people follow. This definition implies that leadership is always a relationship between leaders and followers. If someone is in a leadership role but people don't follow, that person is not a leader. Consequently, if you are someone people want to follow, you can't just give your leadership to someone else. You can delegate management, which is a collection of functions, such as budgeting, scheduling, hiring, and evaluating. But you can't delegate the quality of a relationship.

A generation ago, people questioned whether leadership was needed, especially in organizations. They argued that whereas management was rational and predictable, irrational leaders could take people to dangerous places. Why is leadership so urgently needed now? The answer is that a generation ago, large U.S. companies controlled markets, and the job of manager was to keep the corporate ship on a straight course. But now, in a time of uncertainty and constant change in the business environment, leaders are needed to adapt and transform organizations. Furthermore, only leaders can establish trust in a workforce that is highly diverse in terms of race, gender, age, national cultures, and social character. Leaders are also needed to create collaboration between departments and functions, between companies, and between companies and governments.

Only effective political leadership can mobilize the public to gain energy independence with alternative nonpolluting means, health care for all Americans, effective public education that prepares children for a demanding global economy, and support for a foreign and military policy that protects the national interest.

We can better understand the urgent need for leadership and the attitudes of key followers in the context of historical changes in the nature of work and the emotional attitudes shared by the new generation of technical and professional employees. I approach these changes from the point of view of a psychoanalyst and anthropologist. As a psychoanalyst, I focus on the personalities of leaders and the motivation of followers, which is sometimes unconscious. As an anthropologist, I view leaders and followers in a cultural context that considers such factors as work, family structure, and values. A basic assumption is that in any culture, children are raised to have the attitudes as well as skills that prepare them to prosper.

Let's look at how the American culture has changed, and with it, the personal qualities required. In the middle of the nineteenth century, 70 percent of the U.S. labor force worked in agriculture and mining. Today, that number is less than 2 percent, and the dominant type of agriculture that produces enough to feed this country and also export food is no longer individualistic family farm labor, but rather a highly industrialized mode of production. Manufacturing and service work each involved about 15 percent of the mid-nineteenth-century workforce, but whereas manufacturing peaked at about 30 percent in the 1950s, services continued to rise and includes now about 80 percent of the labor force. However, services is a broad category that combines all kinds of knowledge work, professional services, and simpler retail or cleaning services. Once the new workplace is disaggregated into its knowledge and service labor forces, the urgent need for leadership becomes much clearer.

Figure 15.1 shows a way of describing the knowledge-service workplace as bounded by knowledge work on the vertical axis and service work on the horizontal axis. Each axis goes from low- to high-paid work. The highest-paid

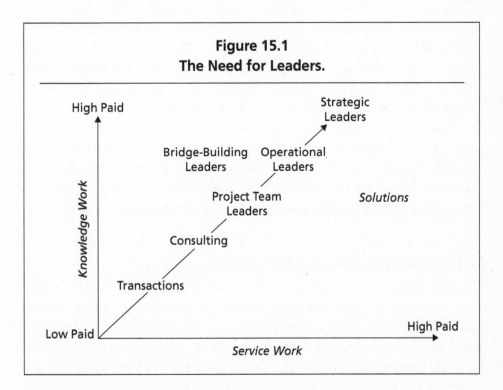

**Figure 15.1
The Need for Leaders.**

knowledge work might describe inventors; lower-paid work includes programmers and researchers. The highest-paid service work might describe a professional athlete or performer; low-paid service jobs include cleaning hotel rooms, gardening, and janitorial services. Between the knowledge and service axes is the vector of *solutions*. It describes work that translates knowledge into service, thus producing solutions for individual customers and businesses. Low-paid solutions work includes transactions like sales or check cashing in a bank. Higher-level solutions result from consultative work by legal, financial, and medical consultants who can use information technology to make their work more productive. Teaching also fits on this vector. At higher levels are the different types of leaders who must integrate all the work in this space.

Knowledge workers are continually automating transaction work. They have replaced telephone operators with electronic switching, bank tellers with ATMs; and they are now replacing store clerks with automatic checkout devices and Internet shopping. Increasingly, consultative advice—financial, medical, legal, and so on—is also being programmed on the Internet. However, the technical knowledge workers have to be organized and led by project team leaders. And as companies like IBM, Siemens, Nestle, and GE provide complex technical solutions for business customers, they need bridge-building network leaders to create collaboration between different departments and functions. The overall success of these companies depends above all on effective strategic leaders who determine purpose, and design highly motivated social systems.

Clearly the evolving knowledge workplace urgently needs leaders in ways that were not so essential in the more stable industrial bureaucracies in a less volatile business environment. But as work changes, so does the social character—the emotional attitudes of the key knowledge workers these leaders need to organize—and as a result, attitudes toward leaders are also changing.

THE CHANGING SOCIAL CHARACTER

The social character, a concept first proposed by the psychoanalyst Erich Fromm, refers to that learned part of personality that is shared by people in a culture or social class.[1] Social character is formed by family, school, and workplace to be adaptive to that culture and particularly to the dominant mode of production. In our culture, the social character has been changing as experience of both work and family changes. Fifty years ago, the dominant companies were huge, market-controlling industrial bureaucracies. In companies like GM, Ford, AT&T, IBM, RCA, and DuPont, employees expected lifetime employment and in turn felt loyalty to the company, which gave them a sense of identity as well as security. Almost all managers of the major companies were white men, and the white male employees saw their bosses in the image of paternal authority.[2] This feeling of protection as a member of the corporate family made it relatively easy for managers to get their subordinates to follow.

At the height of the bureaucratic industrial age, over two-thirds of American families had only one wage earner, the father. Now fewer than 20 percent of families are like these; the most common family has two wage earners, and there are actually as many families headed by a single woman as there are traditional families. In the bureaucratic industrial era, children grew up with the idea that boys were the wage earners and girls were the homemakers. Now, both sexes expect to be wage earners and aspire to be leaders.

The bureaucratic social character fits the hierarchical, uniform roles of the industrial bureaucracy. This social character still describes a significant percentage of the workforce. It is inner directed with the precise, methodical approach to tasks that Freud called the obsessive personality. The bureaucrat's values emphasize stability, organizational loyalty, and autonomy within the hierarchy. The model boss is the "one-minute manager" who gives you an objective, leaves you alone to get there, and grades your results.

Now, in the age of knowledge work, there is a different culture. Managers and employees are diverse in terms of sex, race, and social character. Children grow up seeing women as wage earners and in positions of authority in the workplace, as well as in the family. At an early age, children are sent to day-care centers where they learn to get along with strangers; they must develop interactive skills. Peers, siblings, and caretakers become as emotionally important to them as parents, and when they arrive in the workplace, there is no quick bonding with father figures. In fact, children from more affluent families grow up seeing guilty parents as scurrying around serving them, trying to make up for their absence. It's hard for these parents to say no to these children, and when the adult children reach the workplace, their attitude toward authority figures can be ambivalent, demanding, or rebellious. Furthermore, in contrast to the bureaucratic social character, those of the interactive social character neither expect a company to provide lifetime employment nor feel they need to be loyal to the company. Rather, they see themselves as free agents, ever ready to leave for a better deal. They expect continual change and look for the opportunities change offers.

The new interactive social character is also formed by the constant and instant interaction offered by wireless telecommunication and the Internet. A study by Beck and Wade reports that over 80 percent of technical professionals age thirty-five or under have grown up playing video games and that the heavy video gamers bring to the workplace attitudes forged by their gaming antibureaucratic experiences.[3] They view continual competition as the natural state, but they think roles in the workplace, as in the game, should be structured. They are not put off by making mistakes, because they believe it is always possible to get the right answer by trial and error, at work as in video games. They believe all rewards should be based on results, not on role or seniority, and that if need be, they can always take charge. For them, leaders are irrelevant and often evil.

The interactive social character and especially the video gamer variant present a big challenge for leaders. The contrast between the bureaucratic and interactive social characters, the forces shaping them, and their ideals are summarized in Figure 15.2.

Figure 15.2
The Bureaucratic and Interactive Social Characters.

	Bureaucratic	*Interactive*
Ideals	• Stability • Hierarchy and autonomy • Organizational loyalty • Producing excellence	• Change • Networks and independence • Free agency • Creating value
Social character	• Inner directed • Identification with paternal authority • Precise, methodical, obsessive	• Other directed • Identification with peers, siblings • Experimental, innovative, market oriented
Socioeconomic base	• Market-controlling bureaucracies • Slow-changing technology • National markets • Employment security • Traditional family	• Entrepreneurial companies • New technologies • Global markets • Employment uncertainty • Diverse family structures

WHY PEOPLE FOLLOW LEADERS

People follow leaders for both conscious and unconscious reasons. The conscious reasons are well known: hopes for money, status, power, new skills, and being part of a meaningful enterprise. The fears are of missing out on these good things, which economists commonly call incentives. The unconscious reasons for following a leader lie outside our awareness and control, but they can be even stronger than the conscious.

One of Sigmund Freud's most useful discoveries was the concept of transference. When his patients started falling in love with him and treating his every comment as a profound truth, Freud was wise enough to realize that this idealization had its roots in unconscious memories from childhood. Freud's patients were emotionally regressing to a childhood condition where father was an all-knowing protector. Transference meant projecting this image onto the analyst, and Freud proposed that this process also explained attitudes of followers to leaders. Particularly when people feel frightened, they will follow leaders who promise to protect them, transferring on to them these unconscious infantile attitudes and emotions.

But once people no longer believe in a leader, transference can turn negative. In this regard, the transferential feelings toward George W. Bush and Dick Cheney, forged in the anxiety after 9/11, dissolved in the aftermath of Katrina and the fiasco of the war in Iraq.

For the bureaucratic social character, the father transference tied younger employees emotionally to their bosses, who typically played the paternal mentoring role. Studies showed that the relatively few female managers who rose up the hierarchy of industrial bureaucracies were closer to their fathers than to their mothers.[4]

For interactives, growing up in families where both parents are at work and emotional support is found with peers and siblings, ties to sibling figures at work may be as strong as or stronger than paternal transferences. This can have the advantage of building more cohesive project teams, but it also makes leadership a tough challenge.

LEADERS FOR THE NEW CONTEXT

Interactives don't like the idea of just being followers. They prefer leaders who facilitate collaboration, such as Dee Hock, who created the Visa network, and those who express a purpose that has meaning for them, such as Art Levinson, CEO of Genentech, who creates the context in which they can participate in seeking cures for diseases.

Celebrity CEOs typically say that people follow them because of their flaming passion and strong beliefs. They boast about how they fire up the troops by communicating a powerful upbeat message. But this image of leadership is behind the times. A recent survey of one thousand employees indicated that they are not impressed by inspirational bosses. Writing in the *Financial Times*, Alison Maitland states, "What employees really want, according to a new survey, are straight-talkers who keep them up to date with bad as well as good news. They also want leaders who stay true to themselves instead of putting on a performance or preaching through PowerPoint."[5]

When leaders gain collaborators who share their purpose, the most effective approach to leadership is involving the collaborators in decision making. But when leaders have employees who resist their attempts to create needed change, they have to choose among different approaches.

Some leaders try to solve the problem by avoiding leadership, redesigning the organization to isolate or get rid of resisters. A traditional approach to leadership is the benevolent despot who forces resisters to follow with threats sweetened by promises of rewards for compliance. This approach, highly favored by the Chinese managers I've interviewed, works especially well if change brings positive results. Then the resisters become willing collaborators. However, despotism, even when it's benevolent, can also provoke resentment and unenthusiastic compliance.

The ideal approach to resistance, especially from interactives, is modeled after the doctor who is able to persuade reluctant patients that it's in their interest to change their way of life. For example, the effective doctor shows the patient with diabetes that his diet is putting his life at risk and that to be healthy, he needs to change what he eats and to manage his own condition. Of course, the threat is implicit that if the patient refuses to change, the doctor will stop treating him, and his condition will get worse. The doctor will listen to the patient's resistance, but answer arguments against changing with data and clear logic. A good doctor can usually turn a reluctant patient into a willing collaborator, and that should be the goal of a leader with resistant followers.

The answer to the question, What kind of leader is most effective? is that it depends on the context, the moment in history, and the social character of the people. What has made the need for leaders so urgent at the present time are the challenges to business and governments that can be met only with effective leadership. What has made leadership so difficult is diversity in the workplace, the mix of both bureaucratic and interactive social characters, and, in global companies, their cultural variants. Yet the challenges of our time require collaboration as well as leadership, and the interactives are natural collaborators. To be effective, would-be leaders should ignore much of the advice about gaining followers that made sense in the past and instead focus on expressing clear purpose and practicing an open, interactive, and persuasive style of communicating a meaningful purpose that gains willing collaborators.

Bystanders to Children's Bullying

The Importance of Leadership by "Innocent Bystanders"

Lorna S. Blumen

One of the most exciting ideas to come from leadership theory suggests that leadership and followership are neither dichotomous nor mutually exclusive. Rather, leadership and followership are dynamic roles, existing on a continuum. Instead of conceptualizing leadership as a commission, appointed or elected, and restricted to a select few, we must reframe and recognize that we *all* have the ability and, more important, the *responsibility* to be *both* leader and follower, as the situation requires.

One's individual place on the leadership-followership spectrum varies over time. Yet even while occupying a position toward the leadership end of the spectrum, one needs concurrent followership qualities. Conversely, there are leadership skills required of followers, too. Just as we can identify examples of positive and negative leadership, so we can distinguish patterns of positive and negative followership.

We allocate many resources today—time, money, and effort—to identify and cultivate leadership skills in adults. Unfortunately, much of what passes for adult leadership "development" is actually remedial retraining of poor interpersonal skills and bad behavior patterns that have frequently persisted since childhood. Isn't it cheaper and easier to build incremental leadership and followership skills in our children as they grow, rather than having to instill these skills *de novo*, once adults find themselves in leadership positions?

While considerable resources are spent in the elusive "leadership quest" for adults, far less is targeted where it could actually do the most good. Few resources are devoted to the development of children's leadership skills. Virtually no resources are allocated to the development of constructive followership skills, encouraging the active support of positive leadership and the active rejection of toxic leadership.

Nowhere is this lack of skill development more evident than in our continuing, escalating problems with bullying. In this chapter, I shall concentrate specifically on children's bullying and the role of the bystander, the "follower." I'll examine the contributions of both adults and children as bystanders to children's bullying. I don't risk dispelling the suspense of this chapter by stating that most bystanding activities are negative acts of followership. And although this chapter's focus is on children's bullying, the discussion applies squarely to adult and workplace bullying, too.

BYSTANDERS TO BULLYING: OLD IDEAS HINDER US

The role of the bystander to bullying is widely misunderstood. Most people still believe that if they are neither the bully nor the target, then they are not involved. Hence the ubiquitous explanation, "I was just an innocent bystander." Nothing could be further from the truth. **There are no innocent bystanders. Failing to intervene to stop the bullying of others makes us silent colluders,** accessories to the act, and nearly as culpable as the bullies themselves, for doing nothing to prevent or deflect the terrorizing of another human being.

Removing "doing nothing" from the acceptable list of options thrusts us out of our comfort zone when we wish to assure ourselves of our lack of guilt at bearing witness to the exploitation of another without offering help (and we've all done this). The rest of this chapter asks us, children and especially adults, to reexamine and redefine "doing nothing" as acts of abandonment of others, particularly children, desperately in need of our help and guidance. Ironically, it is the power of the bystander (yes, power) that can quickly end acts of bullying aggression. Before proceeding, let's set the context for our further discussion of leadership, followership, bullying, and bystanders.

CHILDREN'S BULLYING: WHAT IS IT, AND WHY IS IT "STILL" A PROBLEM?

To understand the power inherent in the role of the bystander to bullying (the follower), we must first understand the larger contextual framework of children's bullying, in which these events of bystanding are embedded. A brief review follows.

Despite much discussion, some money, and the appearance of numerous "antibullying" programs over the past decade, bullying is still a big and growing problem today. Here are a few reasons why:

- **We still have incomplete and inconsistent definitions of bullying.** We all operate under our own definition, which leaves us unsure whether an unkind, malicious, or hurtful act qualifies as bullying. Uncertain, we remain frozen in inaction. As a result, most bullying goes unrebuked and uncorrected.

- **We focus too narrowly on the bully and the target, and don't focus enough on the crucial role of the bystander.**

- **We overemphasize remediation—what to do when something goes terribly wrong—and underemphasize prevention.**

- **We concentrate too much on the children involved, and concentrate far too little on the role of adults in kids' bullying.** Adults are major contributors to kids' bullying. We teach it, permit it, and fail to prevent the bullying in the first place.

- **We think it's a "normal" part of growing up or a "normal" part of adult life.** Bullying may be a long-standing part of child and adult life, but that doesn't make it right or inevitable.

- **Everyone wants the "magic wand" or "magic bullet" approach to solve the problem today.** Bullying prevention and bullying repair are problems that require lowlevel but consistent long-term attention and intervention. We must identify and correct problems at an early stage and prevent further recurrence or escalation.

- **The background level of rudeness and in-your-face aggression has increased in everyday social interactions,** for adults and children, providing an easy scaffold on which full-scale bullying is subsequently erected, step-by-step. This incremental development makes it very difficult to detect the growing problem until it erupts into full-scale crisis.

- **The Internet and instantaneous communication technologies have provided us with both new avenues for cyberbullying and myriad opportunities for round-the-globe reporting of bullying activities.**
- **Bullying is often incorrectly labeled as a conflict,** and conflict resolution approaches are used to try to solve bullying problems. Conflict resolution skills are inappropriate and ineffective at solving bullying issues.

In reality, not only have we not "solved" the problem of kids' bullying, but we're only just beginning to work on it.

BULLYING: A DEFINITION WE CAN ALL USE

A complete discussion of bullying would dilute this chapter's concentration on the bystander. Nonetheless, a brief definition and discussion of the central components of bullying will help provide a common perspective and build a basis for responsible action.

Barbara Coloroso offers the following definition of bullying for simple (but not easy) use.[1] Bullying is characterized by

- A persistent one-way power imbalance: one child has all the power, one child has none
- The deliberate use of power and aggression by the bully against the target
- The intent to hurt the target—physically, emotionally, or socially (often a combination)
- The intent to cause fear, both in today's attack and through the threat of future recurrence
- Repeated attacks
- An intensity of attack that typically escalates over time
- An underlying attitude of contempt, entitlement, and lack of empathy on the part of the bully, who feels that it's acceptable to treat people this way

We commonly assume that kids' bullying is a school problem. That's an over-simplification. Kids' (and adult) bullying is a problem of social groups. Coincidentally, our children spend most of their time in social groups in the schoolroom or schoolyard. All solutions must encompass not only our children's behavior at school but also their (and our) behavior in all the arenas where children work and play—at school, at home, in sports, in other extracurricular activities, and in our communities at large.

THREE TYPES OF BULLYING

There are three types of bullying: *verbal*, *physical*, and *relational*.[2] With respect to gender differences, boys do more bullying, overall, than girls. Boys tend to use overt physical or direct methods to bully others. Girls' bullying is more verbal and relational, and often more covert.[3]

Verbal bullying is by far the most common form of bullying, for both genders. We have allowed it to become woven into the fabric of our society and our everyday lives. We hear it so often, we no longer pay attention. "Byotch," "Shut up," "Slut," "He's so gay," "Whatever," "Talk to the hand," "Loser!" are the beginning of an endless list of ways that adults and children speak disrespectfully and rudely in everyday conversation. Verbal bullying can be as simple as one word. Most of these verbal slurs do no physical harm, so we let them pass. There are three problems with that approach:

1. By reacting only when there is physical harm, we fail to recognize and protect our children from the emotional hurt and harm that come from verbal taunting.

2. We're teaching our kids that being rude and contemptuous is an acceptable way to deal with people.

3. By failing to stop this behavior at its earliest, least damaging stages, we provide the scaffold, the building base for further, escalated behavior that is even more harmful.

Physical bullying is the most easily recognized type. Physical bullying is the kind we visualize when we hear the word "bullying." We think of two boys fighting, one boy slamming another into a school locker. The full spectrum of bullying is far wider and more complex than this, and can include preventing a child from accessing his locker, hair pulling, "pantsing" (a common middle school prank), or sexual pinching, touching, and groping in the hallways between classes. We must revise our definitions and our mental pictures to allow us to recognize bullying when we see it and to intervene effectively to end it.

Although boys do more physical bullying than girls, girls do it too. Some shocking cases of girls' physical bullying have involved depraved threats and assaults, both verbal and physical. The horrifying death of fourteen-year-old Reena Virk in Victoria, B.C., Canada, is an example.[4] Reena was beaten to unconsciousness by a (mostly) girl gang of her school peers. Kelly Ellard, the ringleader, then held Reena underwater to drown. Shocking? Absolutely. An isolated case? Sadly, no. Although this case pulled the lid back on girls' physical bullying (verbal and relational bullying were also part of this story), it was not the first or the last case. Disappointingly little has changed since this case shocked the world in 1997, even as it is still making its way through the judicial system today. As heartbreaking as this story was, sadder still is the fact that adults have done little to prevent events like this from recurring.

Relational bullying, the third type of bullying, consists of threatened and real social exclusion and isolation. Whereas physical bullying is done primarily by boys, relational bullying is girls' special area of expertise. Relational bullying is about denying a girl access to social relationships. This is especially hurtful to girls, who value closeness and connectedness in relationships far more than do boys. "This table is for my friends," "You can't be our friend if you're friends with her," and "Do this, or I'll tell Stacy you called her fat" are the hallmarks of girls' relational bullying. Silence can also be used as a weapon, depriving a girl of an inclusive nod, smile, or "yeah." Girls are excluded from everyday and special occasion social events, leaving them isolated and ignored. Girls' relational bullying is often covert and, as such, kept from the view of adults until it has progressed quite far. Boys do some relational bullying, too, typically by spreading rumors, especially around physical size and sexuality.[5]

Another factor contributing to the severity of girls' relational bullying is the persistence of grudge holding by girls.[6] Relatively smaller acts of relational aggression become magnified as they persist for months and sometimes years, spinning out to encompass a wide circle of "friends" (bystanders-followers) beyond the originally conflicted pair. Adults, especially adult women, do a bad job of (or neglect) teaching girls to solve conflicts by expressing anger directly, working it through, and releasing the grudge. We need to set a better example by releasing our own adult grudges and teaching our girls how to do the same.

Cyberbullying is a new and developing weapon in the bullying arsenal, a hybrid of verbal and relational forms, delivered in a high-tech package. The incidence of cyberbullying is escalating rapidly. A recent study suggested that boys do more cyberbullying, in keeping with their generally higher rates of overall bullying,[7] although previous studies have shown that girls, with their generally higher verbal and writing skills, lead the way.[8] (This is *not* what I meant by leadership development in kids.)

Kids know how to sign on to the Internet with their friends' identities—the sharing of IDs and passwords happens routinely, despite parental and adult caution against it. For example, Brittney signs on to MSN with Sarah's ID. Posing as Sarah, Brittney says mean things about Shawna, who comes to school the next day and suddenly has no friends. Cyberbullying extends to the use of text messaging on cell phones and the use of digital cameras to post embarrassing, sexual, or severely edited photos or videos online. Adults are largely oblivious to their children's cyberbullying activities, as aggressor, target, or bystander, until a major crisis occurs (for example, when a suicide is threatened or completed, a Columbine-style death plot is uncovered, and so on).

BULLYING SYSTEM COMPONENTS: SPOTLIGHT ON THE BYSTANDERS

There are three components to the bullying system: *the bully, the target, and the bystanders.*[9] Any approach to reducing bullying must address the contributions of all system components—bully, target, *and* bystanders—and must contain both short- and long-term strategies.

My primary concern in this chapter is the bystanders. Bystanders are a very important part of the bullying system—in many ways the most important part. It's crucial that we understand that there are *no* innocent bystanders. *Bystanders to bullying are toxic followers*, enabling the bullying, whether the collusion is conscious or intentional.

Bystanders can be children or adults. Adult bystanders can be parents, teachers, coaches, or any adults who function as guides, mentors, and leaders to children. Bystanders can be active or passive—active, by cheering it on or by contributing verbal support ("Everyone talks that way," "Nobody invites her"), or passive, by allowing the bullying to proceed without intervening. Passive bystanders can encourage by watching bullying or by looking away, allowing it to happen. "I was just an innocent bystander," "We weren't doing anything," "Everyone talks that way," and "We were just kidding" are but a few examples of old-school bystander thinking.

Most adults would be appalled to think that they were actively colluding with, perpetuating, or extending the reach of a bully in our children's midst. We would strongly reject being labeled as a bullying follower "merely" by doing nothing. Ironically, that is exactly the role we are playing. By turning a blind eye, we become de facto followers, unwitting collaborators, and silent promoters of the very activity we deplore. As silent bystanders who fail to step into the leadership void and deflect the bully, we allow the bully's negative "leadership" to rule.[10] Our actions are causing results that are the *opposite* of our intent. The first step toward changing this is to become aware of the toxic contribution adults are making to the problem, conscious or not.

A final thought on the "We were just kidding" rationalization: this defense is often used by children to deflect adults' corrective actions. It leaves adults uncertain of the next step, and hence they often do nothing, again enabling the bullying to continue. We need to look beyond our children's stated intent in these situations. Instead, we must sensitize our kids to the *effect* of their actions (or lack thereof) on others.

CHILDREN'S BULLYING IS AN ADULT PROBLEM

It is tempting and easy to think that children's bullying is a children's problem. It is not. **Children's bullying is an adult problem.** Adults model rude speaking and bullying behavior to children far too often, in all of the following interactions:

- **The way adults speak and act to each other,** often when we think children aren't listening (but they always are)

- **The way adults speak to children,** often thinking they are acting in the child's best long-term interest

- **The way adults permit children to speak and act toward one another**

When adults model or permit rudeness, they are teaching their kids that it is acceptable to treat others with disrespect and contempt, and paving the way for bullying to follow. When adults bully kids, they are acting as toxic leaders. When adults allow kids to bully each other, they are toxic followers. These behaviors enable and perpetuate bullying.

In attempting to address bullying (and most social problems), we tend to focus too narrowly, only on the current crisis, the terrible end points, the Columbines and "bullycides," where extreme harm and violence have occurred. Instead, we need to have a wider view—to be willing to look at the road we traveled to reach the end point. We must count the incremental, scaffolding points along the way where we failed to stop the tide of bullying and, by our silence and lack of action, were complicit in the disastrous outcomes.

ADULTS AS BYSTANDERS TO KIDS' BULLYING

Adults are frequently passive bystanders to children's bullying. We know something's going on, and we fail to intervene. Sometimes we fail to notice—the background level of rudeness and confrontation in everyday life has desensitized us to seeing it in our kids. Sometimes we look away because it's uncomfortable or inconvenient to intervene. Unfortunately, doing nothing is not a neutral choice. We may choose to "do nothing" (and it is a choice). That may appear to be easier in the short term, but that act of ostensibly benign, silent followership has serious negative consequences that are much harder to repair later.

When we do nothing, we enable the bully to continue. We dismiss our kids' concerns ("What did you do to provoke him [her]?"). We intervene too late. We make lame excuses for why we didn't intervene. We hide behind twisted versions of "the rules" ("The bully has just as much right to be here as you," "The bus driver could have gotten into trouble for touching a child"—to explain why the bus driver didn't try to stop a group peer attack on a lone seventh-grade boy). The list goes on. When we adults do this, we create and maintain an environment that protects the bully. Even worse, we fail to solve the problem at its earliest, easiest stage, and virtually ensure that the later solution will be more difficult, more costly, and, at best, partial. There is no way to "fix" a Columbine.

A recent news story in Toronto, Canada, clearly illustrates the effect of half-hearted adult intervention.[11] A sixth-grade girl in a public school had been the target of verbal and physical bullying for three years at the hands of a female classmate. The child had sought medical attention for bruised ribs; the child's mother had spoken several times to the school and the school board. Eventually the school's solution was to give the targeted girl an adult bodyguard to shadow her every minute in the school.

All would agree that the problem has not been solved. If a bodyguard was the best solution they could devise, then it's the *bully* who should have the bodyguard, not the target.[12] Even worse, the adults had a vast array of excuses for why they had been unable to solve this problem in three years. School board officials were quoted and interviewed on camera with the following excuses (italic commentary is mine):[13]

"The bully has as much right to be here as the target."

> *Only if she's not hurting others.*

"We have a Safe Schools Action Team and programs coming out."

> *Binders with bullying lesson plans are not a substitute for working out real-life problems as they arise. Adults, schools, and school boards react to crises by producing a new set of binders and overrely on them.*

Here are several other problems with the bodyguard "solution":

- The solution makes the *target*, not the bully, responsible for the solution.
- Kids get the (accurate) message that adults will not protect them.
- By being assigned a bodyguard, the targeted girl is isolated from her friends, ironically placing her at *greater* risk for being bullied, if not at school, then out of school, in person, or on the Internet.
- Adults and children declined to be identified or to speak on camera about the problem, fearing retaliation, "afraid that their children would be targeted next."
- This was a long-standing problem—three years—and had become severe enough that other children had left the school because of it.
- If your child is in a situation like this for three years, after repeatedly raising and escalating the issue to the appropriate levels, the message is clear: remove your child. The school and school system have demonstrated their inability to handle the problem at this time.

Put simply, the adults are enabling the bully. The whole environment has been twisted inside out to accommodate the bully, resulting in a systematic, pervasive disregard of the right of a sixth-grade girl to be physically and emotionally safe at school. Instead of colluding up and down the line, adults and the other children should be putting kindhearted, supportive, yet firm and consistent pressure on the bully to change. Adults need to consider: What message are we giving our kids? How can we expect kids to make better choices and stand up for each other when this is the adult example?

The outcome could have been quite different had the adults and the other children in this environment realized, at the onset, the significance of their leadership opportunity. Seemingly small individual and group choices to stand up for the target, withdraw support from the bully, and relentlessly insist that every child has the right to attend school safe from physical and psychological fear and torment could have significantly changed the picture three years later.

BYSTANDERS' COSTS AND DILEMMAS

Bystanders don't escape without damage, either, even when they're not actively involved. Peer bystanders to kids' bullying feel unsafe, unprotected, powerless, and guilty. Guilt is not just for the bully. Talk to the surviving friends of children who have committed bullycide—kids who have committed suicide because they couldn't bear being bullied anymore or were frightened that the bully or bullies were going to kill them first. These surviving friends carry lifelong guilt, because they knew what was going on and did nothing about it, often at the insistence of the bullied child.

Clearly we have to teach our children to do a better job taking care of each other. In order to do so, however, adults must do a better job of identifying bullying problems earlier and correcting them before they intensify. Just because it's not your child being bullied today is no excuse for failing to come to the aid of another child in trouble. Tomorrow it might easily be your child who is targeted in an environment that leaves kids unprotected.

Further, learning is compromised for *all* children, not just the bullied targets, in environments where children fear for their safety or the safety of their friends. Avoiding trouble eclipses schoolwork as the daily objective. Like bullied targets, bystanders also experience stress and anxiety as witnesses to bullying and may exhibit many of the same school-avoidance fears and somatic symptoms.

Why don't bystanders intervene? Here are some top excuses and reasons given by bystanders:

- Bystanders fear retaliation or becoming the next target.

- The system currently ignores bystanders; all the attention is on the bully and the target. There is no pressure or expectation for bystanders to act. The actions of bystanders who *do* stand up are not valued or rewarded.

- Bystanders don't know how to solve the problem.

- Bystanders don't know how to confront the bully or the problem directly.

- Bystanders don't know how to solve and release the grudge (especially girls).

- Bystanders hide behind policies and rules, twisting them to justify not helping.

- There is peer pressure (real or perceived) to conform.

- Adult attitudes can be rigid, resistant to change, and defeatist.

  "What can I do?"

  "Wait till my kid grows up and sees the real world."

  "It's always been this way."

- Intervention won't help, or it hasn't helped in the past. Part of the problem is that our follow-through and consistency are poor. We use a one-time "correction" and hope it solves the problem permanently. It won't.

- Bystanders fear standing up to the bully alone—and with good reason. Research on toxic leaders and whistleblowers shows the price the lone crusader pays for trying to take down a toxic leader or bully boss single-handedly. The price is lost jobs, lost income, lost friends, threats, extreme stress, and extensive legal proceedings.[14]

- Bystanders don't understand the strength of group intervention to stop bullying and don't know how to mobilize the group to action.

- Bystanders seek protection or status by aligning with the bully (or at least not misaligning).

- Bystanders misjudge the seriousness of the incident. Often, the targeted child tries hard *not* to look upset. With verbal, relational, or cyberbullying, which don't produce physical bruises, the bystanders can convince themselves that nothing serious has happened.

BYSTANDER INTERVENTION IS THE KEY
TO ARRESTING BULLYING

The tragedy of bystander paralysis is that the key to both bullying prevention and control is in the hands of the bystanders or followers. **The single most effective tool for stopping a bullying attack under way is the intervention of bystanders.** Paradoxically, bystanders have the real, albeit nonpositional, leadership power for change in this situation. Research has shown that when bystanders intervene in a bullying incident, the bullying stops in half the time.[15] Bystanders must recognize their responsibility and demonstrate their leadership skills.

Adults can teach this to children. Adults must intervene earlier when they are witnesses to children's bullying. We must teach children that it is everyone's responsibility to look out for and protect one another, and that when someone's in trouble, the whole group should intervene. We must also teach kids the difference between teasing and taunting, to help them determine when the line has been crossed.[16]

This sounds easy in theory. The problem, however, as we know from work with whistleblowers, is that it is very difficult for a single person (child or adult) to stand up and go against the group, especially a group in the midst of a bullying attack. It would be an immense responsibility for a single child to shoulder. Further, a single intervening child is more likely to become a subsequent target. Our children's environments are currently not safe enough to insist that a child stand up in an individual act of positive leadership to oppose a toxic bully, who often travels with a group of toxic followers. It is critically important to work on making our children's environments safe enough to permit these acts of leadership. Achieving this goal will require purposeful adult teamwork, not just hope.

Much easier, safer, and attainable today is the shared responsibility of the entire group of bystanders to stand up and say, "Stop. We don't treat [or speak to] people that way," "That doesn't work here," "Stop or we'll call the teacher," or "He's having a bad day. Come play with us. When he's feeling better, he can come back, too." When the whole group of bystanders takes action, no one is singled out, and all are protected. Strength in numbers allows the norms of the group to prevail. A small group of kids, a nucleus, can start the process and then be joined quickly in an act of positive followership by the remaining children in the class (team, schoolyard, and so on). We can thus pave the path for individual acts of leadership, now set in a safe environment that encourages bystander action.

These same principles of group bystander intervention apply to relational bullying, too. "We can't leave anybody out," "Let's not talk about her behind her back," "I'm going to eat lunch with a group from my English class today," and "Let's work this conflict out and be done with it" are the building blocks of problem solving and inclusion.

CHANGING A FUTURE REQUIRES A NEW PAST

Although knowing how to intervene as bystanders to a bullying attack is important, the best solution is to prevent the attack from occurring in the first place. Unfortunately, that process must begin years before an actual bullying incident. It must start in early childhood, at home and when children first come together in social groups. We must teach the skills of social cooperation, social acceptance, and inclusion of every child. Children are welcome to have best friends and to like some people more and some people less, but we must insist that our children make room for everyone and be able to work and play with everyone. If we don't teach this when our children are small, they will not suddenly learn it in the pre-teen years, when bullying activity is at its peak.

The largest lever for change in bullying prevention today is to enable the bystanders. For that to happen, there must be an underlying support structure in place that makes bystander intervention the norm, not the courageous, risky exception. We can build that supportive structure by creating and fostering environments at home, school, and sports where taunting others is not permitted. We must confront the problem of bullying on both fronts—handling today's crises by teaching, empowering, and expecting participation from bystanders, while simultaneously committing the resources to prevention. We must both correct today's problem and reduce tomorrow's.

Prevention is more effective and less costly. The real challenge is to begin when children are young and for adults to continue to pay attention and provide gentle guidance, on a low level, for a long time (forever). Often we miss this chance because we don't think the problem is "serious enough," failing to recognize the building blocks. At the other end, once we do intervene, we often think (hope) that a one-time intervention is sufficient. Unfortunately, once a bullying problem has become serious enough to be raised to adult attention, it will require months—maybe years—of adult monitoring, with consistent boundaries and quiet enforcement. We simply need to pay more attention, retuning our desensitized eyes and ears to the warnings of incipient bullying. This can be done without extra programs, by making time to work through the real-life examples as they arise.

We must purposefully build new cultural norms against the abuse of power and the tolerance of abuse, in both adults and children.[17] Bullying is just one manifestation of this problem.[18] We must lead by example in our own lives, and reclaim power from bully bosses and other toxic leaders. It is crucial for adults to handle the adult bullying epidemic before we can serve as authentic role models for bystander power and responsibility in our children's lives.

Adults must also make a commitment to cleaning up our increasingly antagonistic, confrontational way of speaking to each other and to kids. We must re-create a demonstrable difference between "normal" conversation and bullying. Adults and kids must be able to tell the two apart. This also requires adult resensitization, to recognize and stop rudeness and exclusion before they build. We must be able to correct bullying without becoming bullies ourselves.

LEADERSHIP AND FOLLOWERSHIP: SKILL DEVELOPMENT FOR ADULTS AND CHILDREN

This leads us back squarely to the discussion of leadership development. Where and when do we spend the money and effort? How much do we spend to reclaim the adults? How much do we spend to prevent the adult problem by allocating the resources to our children?

How hard is it to undo and rebuild the faulty leadership skills of bullies, tyrants, and other toxic leaders who've been allowed to get away with their own, harmful leadership "styles," often for decades, without intervention? Can toxic leaders be retooled? I'll leave that question for researchers to answer. In the meantime, let's work to prevent these negative outcomes by instilling positive leadership and followership skills in kids. Prevention is cheaper and easier, requires less skilled practitioners, can reach a wider population, and has a better outcome with a higher probability of success. A small but significant change in our kids' behavior, carried forward to their maturity, can make a big difference in our adult home, work, community, and political environments.

ACTION STEPS ADULTS CAN TAKE TO STOP KIDS' BULLYING NOW

Here are a few straightforward things that adults can do right now to reduce kids' bullying. Although they are not difficult, all the steps require commitment and attention—every day, by all the adults in our children's world—parents, teachers, and coaches. Further, these actions are immediately useful in the adult world to reduce and control workplace bullying.

1. **Adults must lead by example.** We can change the toxic followership of ignorance and bystanding to active, responsible, accountable, positive followership and positive leadership. We must change our defeatist attitudes, recognize and use the power of group action, and stop tolerating bad leadership in our own lives and in our children's. We must learn to recognize the early building blocks of bullying, intervene sooner, and do so kindly but firmly. We must support our children to change, while bravely looking at and changing our own behaviors that enable or contribute to bullying.

2. **Spend most of our efforts on prevention.** Start when our kids are young to build empathy. We must insist on inclusion and model it for our kids. We must become resensitized to recognizing small-scale rudeness and taunting that encourage further acts of intolerance, disrespect, or bullying, and guide our children to more appropriate behavior. We must stop being passive bystanders and allowing our children to be passive or active bystanders.

3. **No tolerance for bullying.** Be alert to big and small acts of bullying. Intervene early. Don't ignore bullying or look away. Only by starting when our kids are young can we create environments safe enough for children (and adults) to stand up as individuals to oppose bullying. Positive leadership by adults will enable our children to contribute their own acts of positive leadership. In the meantime, we can insist on positive followership—children standing together to oppose bullying, or quickly joining to support a single child who has the courage to speak up to the bully. Not everyone can or will find the strength to stand alone, every time, but we can teach children to recognize, support, and protect positive leadership when it emerges.[19]

4. **Empower the bystanders.** Starting early, teach children that it is everyone's responsibility to look out for one another and to come to the aid of those who need help. Teach children the language of intervention ("We don't speak to people like

that," "That doesn't happen here," "You come with us. She's having a bad day," "Let's stick together and protect each other to stop bullying," and so on). Teach children to appreciate the power and ease of group intervention, how to withdraw power and support from a bully through words and actions, how to support positive leadership, and how to create environments that hold the bystanders accountable. Reward action and protection. When mistakes are made, use them as working lessons; teach the skills of apology and employ restorative, rather than punitive, consequences.

5. **Indoctrinate new students.** Schools have a built-in opportunity for change and a fresh start. Every year, the incoming class of students can be indoctrinated, from their first visit or first day of school, into the social rules and behavioral expectations of their new environment ("This is how we treat people here," "These are our expectations for your behavior, and we will enforce these rules"). Then, all school personnel must follow through.

6. **Find opportunities to demonstrate positive adult leadership and followership skills. Look for ways to teach and develop these skills in our kids.** There are opportunities for leadership at all levels in schools, families, and organizations. Many kids with strong personalities, showing tendencies to bullying, can be redirected into positive avenues for expressing their leadership skills. Teach children how to lead without abusing followers.

7. **Develop short- and long-term strategies.** Start with a few simple objectives (for example, teach young children simple bullying definitions and the concept of standing up for one another; pay specific attention to curtailing middle school girls' aggression). Build on successes. Be prepared to sustain the effort—it will take months to change bad situations. There is no substitute for sharpened attention and a small amount of intervention to prevent bullying and foster kindness and inclusion—daily, weekly, and monthly. Work through the real-life examples that arise every day, instead of encouraging overreliance on external bullying prevention lesson plans.

CONCLUSION

Adults can help children create environments of respect, inclusion, and acceptance of diversity that encourage bystanders to stand up for and protect a bullied target. We can teach children how to recognize the warning signs of incipient bullying and show them how to band together as positive followers. Ultimately, in the safe environments we will create, our children can become positive, individual leaders.

Adults must learn to intervene when they are witnesses to children's (or adult) bullying. We must teach this to our children—implicitly, by our example, and explicitly, in our real-life problem solving and in stories of heroes we admire. We can and must have high behavioral expectations for our kids and ourselves. Clearly articulated behavioral expectations, coupled with consistent, low-level adult attention and follow-through, will result in consistent, incremental change. We can make a big difference in three years. Choosing to do nothing will also make a big difference in three years—in the wrong direction. None of us has the individual power to solve this problem, but each of us has a responsibility to contribute to the solution.

By becoming more aware of our own behavior as adults and working first to change ourselves, we can develop better tools to help our children prepare themselves for their future in a world with far less bullying. We can actively support our own change from being unwitting toxic followers of adult and child bullies to becoming purposeful role models of responsible followership. Coincidentally, if we make these changes for the benefit of our children's futures, we will also have an enormous, positive impact on our own work and social environments today.

Whistleblowing as Responsible Followership

C. Fred Alford

The fate of the whistleblower is not the worst problem our society faces, but it illuminates many others. With the whistleblower, one sees not just the fate of the individual in mass democracy, but the fate of the individual in the organization that is situated in mass democracy. For a long time, people have worried about whether the large organization in which most people live their lives contributes to teaching democratic values. Richard Sennett believes that the values of the contemporary workplace are undermining the values of the rest of our lives.[1] The fate of the whistleblower takes these issues and heightens them, showing that the modern organization not only does little to foster civic values but also is committed to the destruction of the individual who displays them.

If my argument about whistleblowers is correct, the proponents of civil society are grasping at straws. Large organizations are not just undemocratic; they are the enemy of individual morality. Individuals who depend on these organizations for their livelihoods may become democrats in their communities in their off-hours, but there will always be something false and partial about their civic life. Large organizations, private and public alike, don't just control the political agenda. They are the political world that matters most to people's lives, that aspect of politics that controls your career, your paycheck, your health insurance, your mortgage, your retirement, and your family's economic security. Until there is room for the ethical individual in these organizations—until, that is, there is ethical commerce between the organization and civil society—the associations that make up civil society will have the quality of a hobby. Bowling with other people is better than bowling alone, but it is not real politics either.[2]

WHISTLEBLOWERS ARE NOT GENTLEMEN

The whistleblower is one who seeks to be a responsible follower and frequently ends up being a victim, pushed not just to the margins of the organization, but frequently to the margins of society.[3] In theory, anyone who speaks out in the name of the public good within the organization is a whistleblower. In practice, the whistleblower is defined by the retaliation he or she receives. Imagine that an employee observes an unethical or illegal act by her boss and reports it to her boss's boss. This is the situation more likely to get the employee into trouble. Rarely do employees get fired for reporting the misbehavior of subordinates.

Her boss's boss thanks her for the information and corrects the problem. She has performed an act of whistleblowing, but for all practical purposes she is not a whistleblower. She becomes a whistleblower only when she experiences retaliation. No retaliation, and she is just a responsible employee doing her job protecting the company's interest. This probably results in overstating the amount of retaliation experienced by whistleblowers. If the whistleblower is defined by the organization's response, then by definition most whistleblowers are retaliated against, and most of these severely.

Somewhere between half and two-thirds of the whistleblowers lose their jobs, according to several studies.[4] Intriguingly, whether the whistleblower goes first to the boss (or the boss's boss) or the media makes almost no difference in whether the whistleblower gets fired. Why would internal whistleblowing, as it is called, be so threatening to the organization that its consequences are virtually the same as for external whistleblowing: not just loss of a job, but in many cases a career? In creating the whistleblower, the organization is stating that there is a certain type of person it cannot tolerate in its midst. Not necessarily one who goes outside the organization, but one who appears to remember that there is an outside. One whistleblower put it this way: "I decided I needed to go back to work. I interviewed with the state of Texas, the city of Austin, and many industries. But nobody wants to hire former whistleblowers. They are all afraid of what we would do if we were asked to tell the truth about some problem."[5]

Zygmunt Bauman develops the systemic implications of the whistleblower's point when he states that all social organization "consists in subjecting the conduct of its units to either instrumental or procedural criteria of evaluation. More importantly still, it consists in delegalizing all other criteria, and first and foremost such standards as may render behaviour of units resilient to uniformizing pressures and thus autonomous vis-à-vis the collective purpose of the organization (which, from the organizational point of view, makes them unpredictable and potentially de-stabilizing). . . . *All social organization consists therefore in neutralizing the disruptive and deregulating impact of moral behavior.*"[6]

Above all else, responsible followership consists in intervening in this organizational normalizing routine, generally through an act of individuality, one that remembers that there is an outside to the organization and an inside to the person. This "inside" need not be understood as a rigid moral core. It is better understood as the capacity for dialogue: the ability to talk about what one is doing, a dialogue that takes place within the self and among others. That includes real others in the organization and imagined (real, but unidentified) others affected by the organization.

A GENTLEMAN'S AGREEMENT

A story in the *Washington Post* told of Duvon McGuire, a home insulation specialist who in 1988 served on a subcommittee of the American Society of Testing and Materials, which established the standards by which the FAA judged the safety of airline insulation. McGuire realized at the time that the standards of testing, holding the material over a Bunsen burner, were "meaningless . . . the technological equivalent of running your finger through a candle flame." Almost any material would pass. He fired off a memo to the subcommittee and eventually voted no when the subcommittee met to confirm the standards. Soon, however, he was persuaded to change his vote.

McGuire, now self-employed, said that under a "gentleman's agreement" with the subcommittee, he withdrew his negative vote in exchange for a promise that the subcommittee would revisit the issue, something that never happened. McGuire said that he never made any independent effort to contact the FAA, something he now regrets.[7]

Since 1988, several hundred people have died in aircraft fires whose spread and intensity have been attributed to the material originally tested by McGuire. Had McGuire been less of a gentleman, lives might have been saved. It is, in the end, the gentleman's agreement that the whistleblower violates, which shows how much the organization depends on such agreements. Or rather, the organization *is* such agreements, as the institution is the pattern of social arrangements over time.

Talking about what we are doing means breaking the gentleman's agreement, or rather acting as if it does not exist. Talking about what we are doing means talking about how what we do affects others. Talking about what we are doing makes these others present, as though they were represented in the discussion.

We live in a moral world. Not because people are good or because people always think morally about what they are doing, but because as human beings the categories of right and wrong are part of our natural moral environment. To talk about what one is doing is to make explicit the moral context that is always implicit. To talk about what one is doing is to bring to life one's own and others' "imagination for consequences," as one whistleblower who worked for the Department of Energy put it.

"I'm afflicted by my imagination for consequences. I just couldn't stop imagining what would happen if children climbed over the fence and played in the radioactive dust."

"What about your colleagues?" asked another whistleblower. "Were they too scared to protest?"

"I don't think so. They just didn't think about it, and no one wanted to talk about it. Site protection was not our responsibility."

To talk about what one is doing may be natural, but it is nonetheless no small deed. For the organizations where many whistleblowers worked, it was too much.

RESPONSIBLE FOLLOWERSHIP AS SELF-SACRIFICE

"When you blow the whistle, you become poison to the company," said one whistleblower. "Your presence makes them sick." The Greek term for the scapegoat is *pharmakos*, which means both poison and cure.

Whistleblower as Poison

As pharmakos, the whistleblower is poison to the unity of the organization, which wants to obliterate every memory that the organization also belongs to those outside its boundaries. In practice, this means obliterating individuals who remember the outside. One sees an example of how powerful this poison is in the decision of the IRS to fire Jennifer Long, the only one of seven agents who did not hide behind a curtain and did not wear a voice distortion mask (as the prisoners wore in Jeremy Bentham's Panopticon, his utopian prison, so that they would not be shamed) while testifying before Congress about abuses at the agency. The following Monday when she returned to work, said Ms. Long, every single manager was in her face with the same refrain: "You're not a team player."

The chairman of the Senate Finance Committee, William Roth, had warned the IRS not to retaliate against Long, and a year later he warned the commissioner in follow-up hearings. Two days later, on April 15, the Houston office of the IRS, where Ms. Long worked, fired her, after spending a year documenting thirty-three alleged shortcomings, including the failure to write neatly in her appointment book.

Senator Roth went ballistic, the new commissioner of the IRS saw red, and the story made the front page of the *New York Times*, which wrote about the "pathology of an ingrained culture" at the district office. Ms. Long will not be fired, and her supervisors will be punished, the reader is relieved to learn, but consider that her supervisors must have known that they were risking their jobs to take hers. They just couldn't stand it. They or she had to go, and this is one of the rare cases in which it was they, at least for now.[8]

Whistleblower as Cure

If the pharmakos is poison, he or she is also the cure. Not in the ethical sense. Rarely do the actions of the scapegoat stimulate others to stand up and be counted. The pharmakos is cure in the sense that the original scapegoat is cure. He represents what we all have learned about the organization, but cannot bear to know: that it will destroy us if we think about what we are doing and what is happening to us. So we hold our knowledge at a distance, in the mind and body of the scapegoat. That is, after all, the purpose of the scapegoat: not just to dispose of our sins, but to let us know them at a safe distance, so we might contemplate them as though they belonged to someone else.

It is a cruel distance, requiring not just the isolation of the whistleblower, but his isolation in the face of the togetherness of his tormentors. To be a whistleblower is to be without colleagues and friends. "I was never real popular," said one whistleblower. "I know what it is to sit by myself in the lunch room in high school. But I never knew what it was to be alone until colleagues I worked with for over twenty years wouldn't even look at me in the halls."

The original scapegoat, we recall, is not killed, but driven into the featureless desert after having had the sins of the tribe confessed before him (Lev. 16: 21–22). This fate is the cost of being an individual in the organization. To know means that one can no longer live among organized humanity, at least not in the organization one has been fired from, and likely not in any comparable organizations either. "Sister companies" is how one manager referred to comparable organizations. He used the term when firing a new researcher shortly after learning that she had been a whistleblower at another pharmaceutical company.[9] When all organizations are related, then being fired from one is akin to being ostracized by the tribe. In fact, most whistleblowers I interviewed, middle-aged professional men and women, never worked in their professions again.

Containing Individuality

René Girard argues that ritual sacrifice arose and is maintained by the need of the organization to contain the violence within, violence that threatens to engulf the organization in bloody, Hobbesian conflict: the war of all against all. The violence that the organization directs against outsiders and internal miscreants always threatens to overflow its bounds and engulf the entire organization. The scapegoat is sacrificed in the hope that the cycle of impure violence could be contained by an act of purifying, controlled violence: "The sacrificial process furnishes an outlet for those violent impulses that cannot be mastered by self-restraint . . . All concepts of impurity stem ultimately from the community's fear of a perpetual cycle of violence arising in its midst . . . The function of [sacrificial] ritual is to 'purify' violence; that is, to 'trick' violence into spending itself on victims whose death will provoke no reprisals."[10]

Girard is writing about the origins of sacrifice. What sacrifice looks like now, he says, is law.

One might imagine that my analysis mirrors that of Girard. In fact, I would argue that in important respects Girard has it backwards, always an interesting mistake. In spite of his profound insight into the importance of sacrifice in social life, Girard has made the mistake of most sociologists, the mistake of Thomas Hobbes: presuming that the problem is the anomic, presocial individual, always waiting for the breakdown of law and order so that he or she can run amok. Sacrifice ritualizes this anomic tendency, and so organizes it as a collective act against the one. In so doing, sacrifice protects order.

What if this has it backwards? Sacrifice serves not to contain and channel the ever present threat of individual violence, but the ever present threat of individual morality. It is this same morality that is the source of responsible followership, and it is against this disruptive moral behavior that sacrifice is mobilized. Sacrifice serves not to rechannel destructive violence. Sacrifice serves instead to rechannel destructive individual morality that might result in the breakdown of organizational control and hierarchy. Sacrifice is mobilized against thought in the name of organizational autarky or independence.

One might argue that Girard was right then, but not now. In the premodern era, before the rise of large-scale social organization, the leading threat was the outbreak of Hobbesian violence, the war of all against all. Today, the threat is the violence of the large organization itself. The Holocaust epitomizes this threat, which has made the twentieth century the bloodiest in world history.

PREVENTING AN EPIDEMIC OF ETHICAL BEHAVIOR

The trouble with this argument is that there was lots of large-scale social organization in the premodern era, including dynastic China and the Roman Empire. Furthermore, outbreaks of violence about which Girard writes, the war of all against all, are rare. It is almost always group conflict that threatens the social order, what the Greeks called *stasis*, intense factional conflict, like the Civil War in Corcyra about which Thucydides wrote, the inspiration for Hobbes (*History*, 3.69–85). In conditions of stasis, the real problem is who is in and who is out, and where to draw the boundaries? It is in this situation, the situation of most organizations most of the time, that outbreaks of individual morality are so dangerous. For it is the mark of individual morality that it speaks from a position at once inside and outside the organization.

In this circumstance, one who speaks from the outside is what Jean-Paul Sartre calls *visquex*, a viscous boundary crosser, outside and inside at the same time. The anthropologist Mary Douglas uses the term "slimy" to capture the fear of one who will not stay in his place. Or rather, whose place we do not even know.[11] It is what every organization fears most: that someone inside represents the interests of outside, that the organization cannot control its own boundaries, that it does not even know them. It is what Jennifer Long's supervisors meant when they accused her of not being a team player. The language is banal, but the sentiment is profound, reflecting the deepest fears of organizational man and woman.

This accounts, I believe, for that otherwise puzzling empirical finding, namely, that internal whistleblowers are about as likely to be punished as external whistleblowers. If you go to your boss with the problem, you are almost as likely to be fired as if you go directly to the newspapers. The whistleblower does not necessarily need to go public to get into trouble, because once he mentions his or her concerns he or she already *is* the public inside the organization. It is the only unforgivable organizational sin: to become the outside on the inside.

The purpose of sacrificing the whistleblower is to prevent the outbreak of an epidemic of ethical and moral responsibility that would threaten to engulf the organization, destroying its ability (or so its members fear) to maintain its boundless autonomy in a hostile world of other organizations, each competing for the same scarce resources: land, oil, grants, contracts, consumers, students. Sacrifice always aims at halting an epidemic, in this case of individuality, as though it could be spread by example. Perhaps it can. Its spread is halted by making the boundary between inside and outside as clear as possible. The real threat posed by the whistleblower is to remind the organization that it belongs to the larger world. In order to deter this way of thinking, the whistleblower must be moved to the margins: not just of the organization, but society. The task is complete not when the whistleblower is dismissed, but when he or she is unable to work in his or her profession, virtually unemployable at any "sister companies."[12]

CASE STUDY: ROBERT HARRIS AND THE DEPARTMENT OF DEFENSE

A not especially dramatic story about a whistleblower will help make this point. Most whistleblowers' stories are, by the way, not especially dramatic. Or rather, the drama is hidden, in the sacrifice of the pharmakos.

Robert Harris was a major in the U.S. Army before his retirement, when he became the chief procurement officer for a Department of Defense installation.

He continued working for the Army, but as a civilian. Within two years of assuming his new job, he won the secretary of the Army's Award for Outstanding Achievement in Acquisitions. Like many whistleblowers, he is a patriotic, conservative, middle-aged man who identified with the system. His father was a general, and he still believes that "an officer's word is his bond," what he calls the Old Army tradition. "I wasn't looking to make trouble. I had two kids in college, and I just wanted to see them on their own before I left the workforce."

Several years into his job, he was asked to write a purchase order for a sole-source contract. Evidently some Army colleagues had retired at about the same time as he, going to work for the consulting firm that recommended a sole-source contract be awarded to Armscomp, a manufacturer of specialized computing equipment.

I asked Harris if he thought the consultants were getting kickbacks from Armscomp. "Maybe, maybe not," Harris replied. "There wasn't a lot of money involved. Ten million, but for the Army that's peanuts. [The consultants] might have just been trying to help their buddies who founded Armscomp. [The consultants] were way out of their field of their expertise. They wanted their $30,000 a week as quick and easy as possible."

Harris convinced his commander not to issue the contract and, instead, to issue a solicitation for competitive bids. Less than a week later, the competition was halted by a telephone call from a general in the Pentagon, who said that if the contract was not let as originally written, the installation might not have enough work to justify next year's budget. Harris is certain that the consultants, all former officers, got a friendly senior officer at the Pentagon to make the call to his commander. Harris's commander quickly canceled the solicitation, but made no move against him, congratulating him on his "due diligence" and telling him it was time to drop it.

Harris didn't drop it. When the officer who canceled the solicitation ignored his faxes, Harris wrote to the secretary of the Army, contacted the inspector general (IG), and finally Senator David Pryor, whose congressional committee was interested in procurement fraud. A two-year investigation followed, but it was dropped when the Republicans won the 1994 election, and Pryor lost his chairmanship of the Senate Governmental Affairs Subcommittee.

Eventually, the IG found the contract award improper, but not illegal. As the computers had already been delivered, there was little else for the IG to do. Army investigators found no criminal bribe taking.

Harris's days at his job were numbered. He was given an evening shift, then transferred to a job sixty miles away, where he was told he could not use the telephone or fax. Soon he was denied access to the copier. His computer was confiscated. A series of bad efficiency reports followed. In a little less than two years he was fired. No one would ever talk to him about what he had done, or address his concerns that there might be a connection between his transfer, his bad efficiency reports, and his whistleblowing. Said Harris, "Once the IG's office was through with me, it was as though I didn't exist. I became a walking ghost."

Harris's story is typical. Matters of life and death were not involved. He was given an opportunity to back off, but did not. That Harris was not immediately fired is also the norm. Instead, he was put through a series of trials designed to enrage and humiliate him, perhaps just to ensure that he could not perform his job. When he did not, and after this had been documented over several consecutive efficiency reports, he was fired. There was, on the record, no connection between his blowing the whistle and his termination. Typical too was the refusal of anyone in authority to talk to him about any of this. Also typical is his reply to my question, "Why did you blow the whistle?"

> I honestly did not think of my having blown the whistle until the inspector general for the DoD audit team started telling me about the Whistleblower Protection Act. I was paid to use my skill and intellect to protect the taxpayers' purse. I was just doing my job. . . . I was absolutely ecstatic when I first convinced the [military installation] commander to compete for bids. When the assistant inspector general for auditing personally called and said he'd take my case, I was sure that it was all over, that my part was done. I didn't realize the brass was just waiting for the IG to finish his report before they retaliated.

In his forced retirement, Harris has established several Web sites that tell his story in excruciating detail. One contains the following statement: "A whistleblower on government contract fraud is most akin to the tree which falls in the forest trapping an animal of nature with no-one around—the falling actually occurred and the animal dies, but no one listened, no one helped the animal, and the cycle continues."

Still, Harris continues to tell his story. He seems convinced that if he can just find the right words to tell it, someone with the power to set things right will listen. It is a common delusion among whistleblowers.

SOURCES OF ORGANIZATIONAL POWER

The whistleblower, it is apparent, need not speak out in the name of the public within the organization in order to get into trouble. He or she need only speak as though he or she remembered his or her citizenship in the world, the fount [font] of responsible followership. To think and act in terms of this membership is to be a political actor in a nonpolitical space. Not because this space, on the margin of the organization, is not properly political, but because neither our political science nor our organizational theory can make much sense of this space.

The Cunning of Feudal Power

One reason for our inability to understand this space is that it is not supposed to be there; it does not fit into our theories, which generally look at the organization from the top down. In fact, the organization is more feudal than we know. Power is decentralized, and power is personal, located in the figure of the boss. As one whistleblower put it, "When you work for the agency, you don't serve the agency, you serve your boss. For all practical purposes, it's his fiefdom." It is a common perspective among whistleblowers, and the only question is how to take it—as the limited insight of the man or woman on the bottom looking up, or as a theoretical contribution? I take it as both.

To be sure, many organizations provide access to the central government of the organization, as it might be called. Even if appeals to this level are likely to get the whistleblower fired, this access still demonstrates that organizations are not feudal, but bureaucratic. Or does it? The second stage of feudalism (which flourished in the thirteenth century) also allowed such appeals. As one student of feudalism puts it, "the central government in some cases deals directly with rear-vassals instead of passing orders down a long chain of command. Royal law-courts play a great role in this reorganization."[13] What marks feudalism is not that there is no appeal. Nor does anarchy mark feudalism. There is nothing anarchic about feudalism.

What marks feudalism is that power is a private possession. What that means in the organization today is codified by Robert Jackall: (1) You never go around your boss. (2) You tell your boss what he wants to hear, even when your boss claims that he wants dissenting views. (3) If your boss wants something dropped, you drop it. (4) You are sensitive to your boss's wishes so that you anticipate what he wants; you don't force him, in other words, to act as boss. (5) Your job is not to report something that your boss does not want reported, but rather to cover it up. You do what your job requires, and you keep your mouth shut.[14]

The result is an organizational atmosphere, a "culture," in which private caprice serves organizational ends, somewhat like the cunning of reason that Hegel wrote of. Perhaps Adam Smith's invisible hand would be a more felicitous metaphor. The caprice of bosses serves the goal of "neutralizing the disruptive and deregulating impact of moral behavior" more effectively than any plan. Only, however, if the boss keeps his caprice within limits, but this too is compatible with the principle of vassalage.

Men with Guns

Civilization, says Norbert Elias, is a process of shifting powerful and disturbing emotions and experiences, such as sadism and violence, from the center to the borderlines of society. There they are not lessened or mitigated, but contained and stored up behind the scenes, in military barracks, police stations, and prisons, ready to be called on in times of unrest, and exerting a continuous threat to those who would challenge the regime. "A continuous, uniform pressure is exerted on individual life by the physical violence stored behind the scenes of everyday life, a pressure totally familiar and hardly perceived."[15]

Institutionalized violence and coercion are everywhere in ordinary public life, even if they are not generally recognized. What is remarkable about the organization, that entity in which the whistleblower works, is the way it draws on public power not just for private ends (a fact that has been known for centuries), but the way in which it uses public coercion to create a space in which it may enact an essentially public ritual, sacrifice, for a strictly private end, organizational autarky.

A surprising number of whistleblowers, about 30 percent of those I have listened to, have been removed from their offices, or not allowed to enter them, by men with guns: private or government security guards. The whistleblower does not forget the experience, frequently describing the gun in some detail. No whistleblower I have spoken with has been removed at gunpoint, but that hardly matters.[16] In no case have the men with guns been called as a last resort because the whistleblower refused to leave. The guns were a first resort. The gun is there, carried by the man who escorts the whistleblower to the door or prevents him from entering. That, or the gun is just a phone call away. In the last analysis, civilization rests on men with guns.

To be sure, a large proportion of the whistleblowers I spoke with had worked in government agencies with security concerns, such as the Department of Energy, the Nuclear Regulatory Commission, the Bureau of Engraving, and the Department of State. But a number of whistleblowers in private organizations reported similar experiences. Degradation ceremonies, they might be called: the whistleblower is summoned to his boss's office, fired, and taken to his old office in the presence of armed guards, who allow him to fill a cardboard box with mementos, such as family photos, but no papers, computers, or disks. Finally, he is escorted to the front door carrying his little box as though it were his coffin.

Capillaries Carry Blood and Power in Both Directions

These are not just degradation ceremonies. They are a type of public execution, designed to remind those who remain of the power of the organization to reach anywhere in a moment. All this does not make Michel Foucault mistaken about capillary power, as he calls it: power that migrates from the periphery to the center of society, from prisons and mental hospitals to the organizations in which we work and learn. In Foucault's model of power, often called disciplinary power, the power of knowledge and experts has replaced the naked power of the state.[17] The story of whistleblowers reveals a more dynamic reality, in which capillaries carry blood and power in both directions, so that we see at the margins more clearly the brutality, tyranny, and charisma of everyday life—sovereigns not in exile, but in waiting.

What is so striking about this power is the way that it can move the margin to the center in a moment, which is precisely what happens with the whistleblower: power moves from the margin to the center, moving back to the margin and carrying the whistleblower with it. Moved to the margins and rendered less visible, power has not therefore become more subtle. Power has just gone underground. Which means that it is able to emerge anywhere in an instant, but generally does not have to, precisely because we know it's there. From time to time, the whistleblower reminds us.

THE SACRED AND DREADFUL ORGANIZATION

Ours is a world in which sacrifice serves sacred purposes whose sacredness has long been forgotten. When we forget what we are doing, upholding a transcendent order, it does not mean that we are no longer doing it. It only means that we no longer know what we are doing. The sacrifice of the whistleblower could remind us, if we would let it.

If we remembered what we were doing, we might be less likely to treat particular organizations as though they were sacred. We might, in other words, be able to distinguish between particular organizations and the transcendent power of society. Expressed in terms of ideas attached to authors, we might be a little less likely to think about the sacred as Edward Shils does, and a little more like Emile Durkheim. For Shils, the sacred attaches not to the moral foundations of society, but to the power centers of society and their symbols, from crowns and limousines to men with uniforms and guns. This is why, Shils argues, an order from a superior is experienced (even if we no longer know it) not simply as a rational command, but as an utterance that shares in a transcendent moral order.

> [An instruction from a superior] is conceived as a "part" or an emanation of the cosmos of commands and judgments at the center of which is the supremely authoritative principle or a supremely authoritative role incorporating that principle. The particular incumbent of the role . . . is perceived as the manifestation of a larger center of tremendous power. What the "subject" responds to is not just the specific declaration or order of the incumbent of the role . . . but the incumbent enveloped in the vague and powerful nimbus of the authority of the entire institution. It is legitimacy constituted by sharing in the properties of the organization as a whole epitomized or symbolized in the powers concentrated at the peak.[18]

Disobedience becomes tantamount to sacrilege, though hardly anyone ever puts it that way. Whistleblowers don't put it this way either; they just feel in their bones what it is to be impure.

It might be helpful to think about the sacred more as Shils's predecessor, Emile Durkheim, did. For Durkheim, it is not the power centers of society, but society itself (what he calls the "conscience collective" in an early work) that is sacred.[19] Society is sacred not because society participates in a transcendent order, but because of the way individuals depend on society for the meaning and existence of their lives. It is in the awe-inspiring gap between individual and society that Durkheim locates the sacred. The more we talk about individualism, or even responsible followership, the less we shall know about them. That is not because individuals don't exist, and not because responsible followership is not of utmost value. They do and it is. Rather, we know less because we have become alienated from the dimension of the sacred that makes the individual and his or her acts worthwhile: his or her participation in this larger order.

Not even academics have much use for this aspect of Durkheim's thought these days. And surely it is the case that there is not much left of the sacred in our modern, rationalized world, even as Durkheim claimed to see its residue in such basic values as "Thou shalt not murder." If, however, we were to see the sacred in the basic values of society, not just its power centers, then it might be easier to see that challenging the organization may itself be a sacred act.

The sacred is not just power, but the conscience collective, the values that make this society a meaningful one to live in. It is these same values that the organization is organized to deny in the service of instrumental reason, as Bauman argues. To be a whistleblower is to assert the conscience collective in the midst of the organization. To be a whistleblower is to set one way of thinking about the sacred, the conscience collective, against another experience of the sacred: power. Only when we know this will we truly understand what is going on with the whistleblower.

In this superficially rationalized world, all the bits and bytes and flashing lights have blinded us to the power of the sacred in the midst of the social. Only when we regain some sense of what Durkheim called the conscience collective will we understand the terrible burden on one who would stand up against power in the name of a higher power. The conscience collective is represented by the responsible follower who remembers that he or she is not just a member of the organization, but of the larger society in which we all share.

PART FOUR

Followers and Leaders

Research, Practice, and the Future

There is a proliferation of books and journals that contain an ever-growing body of social science research on leadership. This leadership oeuvre is evolving into its own academic discipline, with areas of specialization, numerous courses on all types and aspects of leadership, comprehensive textbooks and handbooks, and professional organizations dedicated to leadership. But there is a dangerous limitation to this—one that has been mentioned frequently in earlier chapters of this book:

Despite the fact that followers are an essential part of the leadership equation, there has been very little research attention given to followership in comparison to leadership. Only a handful of pioneering courses on followership exist, and the number of consultants and other experts who focus on followership (many of whom are represented in this book) is miniscule in comparison to the vast and growing number of leadership experts.

The work reported in this final section of the book is a collection of research and applications of research from authors who represent that group of leadership scholars and experts who have been focusing in a serious way on followers and followership. For instance, authors Robert G. Lord and Michael A. Hogg for many years have advocated that followers play a central role in creating leaders and the construct of "leadership." Other chapters in this section examine specific aspects of how followers enhance value for groups and organizations. For example, authors address how followers contribute to and implement a vision for organizations, how followers make groups and organizations into creative entities, how followers support and challenge leaders, and how certain qualities and characteristics produce effective followers and followership. Despite these diverse perspectives on followership, we are just scratching the surface of a true understanding of the role that followers play in leadership and in understanding the dynamics of the leader-follower equation.

Followers' Cognitive and Affective Structures and Leadership Processes

Robert G. Lord

Contrary to the claims that followers have been ignored, the leadership literature has a long tradition of recognizing the importance of followers. Dyadic relations between leaders and followers have been viewed as a mutual influence process,[1] with leader behavior reflecting responses to subordinate performance levels as well as the attributions for subordinate performance made by leaders.[2] The potential of leaders to influence followers also depends on the idiosyncratic credit he or she has earned in followers' eyes[3] and the extent to which followers see the leader as fitting their image of what good leaders should be.[4] Some researchers, such as Meindl,[5] have even argued that leadership is a construction of followers, spawning numerous follower-centered studies of leadership.[6] Indeed, social psychologists have typically viewed leaders and followers as being engaged in a mutual exchange or transaction, in which both parties benefit and in which both parties are active contributors.[7] However, as noted by Hollander, the popularity of more recent transformational leadership approaches has tended to overemphasize the leader and underemphasize the follower contribution to this exchange process.[8] By reemphasizing followers' role in leadership processes, this book makes an important contribution, for particularly with the movement toward flatter administrative structures, "leaner" organizations, and telecommuting, followers are assuming more decision-making responsibility and are increasingly being asked to self manage their activities.

Effective leaders depend on followers and the self-leadership followers exhibit,[9] and this is particularly true in today's competitive, global economy. Ireland and Hitt also note that in the knowledge economy, many organization members must be capable of exhibiting leadership when the need arises.[10] As a consequence, leadership is a process that is widely distributed among formal leaders and their followers. Clearly, followers play many critical roles in making organizations successful, both individually and as members of larger collective structures.

The central premise of this chapter is that such follower effects can be understood by taking a closer look at followers as active, relatively independent agents in organizations. Followers interpret social processes and work events based on their own internal cognitive and affective schema, and followers' responses are guided by self-regulatory structures that are tied closely to their active self-identity. Political processes in business and government are also dependent on the meaning that followers construct. Thus followership is guided by the internal cognitive and affective schemas of followers, and leadership depends on followers' active construction of leadership perceptions using such schema.[11] Moreover, as stressed by complexity theories, more aggregated structures naturally emerge from individual units.[12] Consequently, over time, the individual-level perceptual, affective, and self-regulatory structures of followers are aggregated and transformed through social interactions into emergent, informal social structures that play central roles in organizational functioning. Such structures also provide meaning to social events and the individual's role in such events. Applying such reasoning to followership, Uhl-Bien and Pillai recently have proposed that followership as well as leadership is socially constructed at both the individual and group levels.[13]

This chapter discusses such follower effects in the context of followers' relation to their leaders. Specifically, four related issues are addressed. First, the chapter begins by discussing the effect of follower "sensemaking" in both affective and cognitive domains, where a critical issue for followers is making sense of social processes that include their leader as well as other followers. Second, the chapter addresses the role of followers' self-regulatory structures that guide their motivation and social actions. Third, recent insights from complexity theory are used to explain how more collective interpersonal structures can emerge from individual-level cognitive and affective schemas of interdependent agents, such as followers. Finally, the chapter examines the role of leaders in these processes. Leaders can influence the nature of follower cognitive and affective structures in multiple ways, yet they are also constrained by the social perceptions of followers and by the collective structures that spontaneously emerge in organizations.

INDIVIDUAL-LEVEL FOLLOWER STRUCTURES

Sensemaking

A fundamental insight provided by cognitive psychology is that people do not experience the external world directly. Instead, they experience it in terms of internal mental structures, or schema, that are activated by external stimuli or events. These mental structures, which are learned over time through individual and social processes, are a critical component of followers' contribution to the leadership process. Schema allow perceivers to construct appropriate interpretations of people and events, to grasp their own role in such events, and to appropriately generate behavior that is both consistent with the current context and with the perceiver's own sense of self. These structures also allow sensemakers to see patterns extending over time, connecting the past with the present and the future. In other words, they allow people to make sense of others and events and to use this sensemaking as a basis for action.

Sensemaking occurs as perceivers construct a framework for an event or action.[14] Because this is a basic aspect of how people know the social world and events in it, follower sensemaking is often automatic, occurring without awareness and without interfering with conscious thoughts, yet it is a critical part of the structure that organizes and binds leaders and followers. Sensemaking is a central component of leadership processes, one that is often associated with "sensegiving" by the leader, but it is the interaction of a leader's actions or visions with a follower's schema that actually gives sense to an event. Moreover, followers often need to make sense of events without guidance from leaders. In fact, in many fast-paced organizations, followers notice, make sense of, and adapt to change before leaders, who are more isolated from changing environments, are even aware of change.

Sensemaking has affective as well as cognitive components. A critical aspect of all perceptions of events or individuals is an appraisal of the potential harm or benefit to the perceiver. This appraisal produces either positive or negative affect, which then serves as a guide to approach or avoid the individual or event. When individuals identify with an organization, potential external benefits or threats to their organization can also produce personal affective reactions, which in turn guide potential follower responses. Thus the self-relevant emotions of followers can be a critical component of adaptation to changing environments. Surprise, for example, can be a critical emotion that directs individuals to process new information more fully.

Extreme events can also produce extreme emotions that can lead to the collapse of sensemaking. For example, Weick describes a collapse of sensemaking in the 1949 disaster at Mann Gulch, in which thirteen of sixteen smoke jumpers were burned to death by the sudden blowup of what they thought was a relatively small and easily contained fire.[15] Tragically, this collapse in sensemaking produced a failure on the part of the smoke jumpers to heed directions from their leader, which could have saved their lives and in fact did save his own life. This occurred not because the leader was wrong, but because his actions (lighting a backfire and lying down in the center of it) did not make sense to the followers, given the context and their state of panic. Although not as dramatic, injustice or disrespectful actions from leaders, particularly when in public, can also provoke extreme affective reactions in followers that restructure relations with leaders.[16]

The role of followers' perceptual structures in sensemaking related to leadership is perhaps best documented by the extensive research on implicit leadership theories that has occurred over the past thirty years. *Implicit leadership theories* (ILTs) are knowledge structures of perceivers that define appropriate leadership categories for them. This research has shown that it is the match of a leader's qualities and behaviors to followers' ILTs that allows followers to recognize an individual as a leader.[17] Because leaders emerge, in part, by fitting the ILTs of followers, leadership is a jointly constructed process in which both the conceptual categories of followers and the characteristics and behaviors of leaders play an important role. ILTs also guide our understanding of extreme organizational performance, which is often interpreted as resulting from effective or ineffective leadership.[18]

In sum, sensemaking by followers is a critical aspect of leadership processes that involves both an affective and a cognitive component, yet this process can also occur without much conscious attention on the part of followers. Follower sensemaking then provides a structure for further interactions, both with respect to task activities and with respect to acceptance and internalization of a leader's vision or compliance with a leader's attempted influence. The critical point to recognize is that this sensemaking process mediates between the qualities and actions of leaders and the responses of followers.

Self-Regulation

As well as having a rich system of perceptual categories for perceiving the world and other people, followers also have a rich cognitive and affective structure for regulating their own behavior. These structures involve self-identities, goal systems, and enduring affective orientations. Although traditional leadership theory represents leaders as the cause of many organizational outcomes, Lord and Brown have recently argued that it may be more helpful to focus on the followers, starting first with a theory of how they self-regulate and then asking how leaders can influence the self-regulatory processes of followers.[19]

Three ideas are critical for understanding how individuals self-regulate. One is that many cognitive, affective, and behavioral activities are influenced by goal-related feedback systems.[20] People compare feedback to their current goals to regulate the intensity of their effort and adapt their strategies to current contexts. The discrepancy between performance and goal structures is a critical motivational construct because, when discrepancies exist, people notice them and are motivated to bring performance back in line with goals. Goals also have an important effect on the accessibility of cognitive information.[21] As a consequence, the nature of followers' goals can affect how creative followers are or how carefully they process information.

The second critical idea is that goals often emerge spontaneously as a natural solution to sets of constraints.[22] These constraints can come from the current task context, social processes, salient leaders, other followers, information that is actively held in working memory, or from more complex internal networks of values and higher-level goals. Affect is also an important part of this process: positive affect elicits an approach-oriented regulatory focus; negative affect, such as anxiety, fosters an avoidance-oriented regulatory focus.[23] A person's active self-identity can also be a powerful source of constraints on goal emergence. For example, collective identities support the emergence of more collaborative, cooperative goals, and individual identities facilitate the emergence of competitive goals.

A third essential idea is that not all self-identities are active in any one situation. Markus and Wurf emphasized that the self is not a unitary whole, but instead is a confederation of selves that vary in degree of activation across contexts and time.[24] They labeled the currently active portion of the self the *working self-concept* (WSC). Follower WSCs differ in whether they emphasize differences from others, relationships with specific others such as leaders, or membership in groups and larger collectives. These individual, relational, or collective WSCs can reflect important chronic differences in followers as well as different cues originating in leaders, and they can profoundly influence the way that social transactions are structured.[25] Identities also have a dynamic quality: they continually shift within specific contexts, with identity construction being a mutual activity that reflects a two-way interdependence of leaders and followers.[26]

In short, in many contexts the goal-based self-regulatory systems of followers provide dynamic linkages with organizational tasks and roles and with followers' active identities. Followers' WSCs not only help regulate organizational behavior but also make task and social activities meaningful to followers, imbuing them with self-relevant value and affect. Along with sensemaking schema, these self-regulatory structures can also provide a basis for the emergence of more aggregated interpersonal structures, as explained in the following section.

COLLECTIVE-LEVEL FOLLOWER STRUCTURES
Complexity and the Bottom-Up Emergence of Structure

Recent work on complexity theory and leadership emphasizes that, like goals, informal structure in organizations can have an emergent quality, reflecting the combined effects of constraints that come from multiple individuals.[27] Further, just as individual-level goals reflect personal adaptations to work contexts, more macro-level structures can reflect an organization's adaptation to the environmental constraints that it faces. Because follower sensemaking and self-regulatory behavior help create patterns in individual thoughts and behaviors, they are also important building blocks for the emergence of more aggregated structures. Complexity theories emphasize the parallel nature of the emergence of intra- and interpersonal structures, as well as the cascading process in which larger and larger structures emerge from more micro-level structures.[28] In terms of leadership, individual schema and self-regulatory structures can influence the nature of dyadic relations that develop between followers and leaders, and dyadic interpersonal structures may set the stage for the emergence of a group structure, which in turn can lead to intergroup structures, and so on. For example, as Dragoni has emphasized, a leader's goal orientation (for example, learning versus performance orientation) can influence subordinates directly, or it can create a consistent group goal orientation that serves as a constraint on individual goal orientations.[29] Over time, such processes can also influence the emergence of more aggregated organizational structures. The enduring goal orientations followers bring with them to organizations can also have effects that are independent of leaders, affecting their own behavior and interactions with others.

An important point made by complexity theorists is that emergent structures need not be centrally directed, but rather can emerge from the local interaction of people (or the larger units of which they are members). Thus the emergence of structure does not need to depend on hierarchical leadership in organizations. Structures can develop from follower interactions that produce consistencies in affective orientations, goal orientations, or identity levels among interacting individuals. Ideally, these structures complement formal administrative structures in organizations, and they facilitate adaptation to changing environments. Indeed, in modern organizations with flatter administrative hierarchies, there is a great need for emergent informal networks to provide horizontal connections among employees and to supplement the more formal management hierarchy.[30]

This line of theorizing suggests that successful adjustment to organizational environments may be as much a function of successful followership as it is of successful leadership. This follower-based adjustment may be particularly important in organizations that emphasize technological innovation and knowledge development, which may occur at relatively low levels in organizations. In these cases, appropriate adaptive structures may emerge in more of a bottom-up than top-down manner. Indeed, it may not be possible for a top administrator, or any single individual, to fully understand the consequences of developing specific structures.[31] In such cases, leaders may not want to communicate a powerful vision of how the organization should adjust to the external environment, because such a vision may inhibit more appropriate follower-based adaptation arising at other levels in the organization. Thus, in complex organizations, leaders should not micromanage the emergence of structure.[32]

Followership and Structure Emergence

It is instructive to consider the implications of this perspective on complexity and structure emergence to understand the importance of followership in organizations. First, it implies that followers need to be more independent and proactive than is suggested by traditional leadership theory. Followers cannot just react with cooperation and enthusiasm to initiatives originating from the top of an organization. Passive, leader-directed actions are often too slow to be effective in the marketplace, often lagging rather than leading innovative developments. Second, information networks and other types of structures need to emerge as they are required, rather than in response to top-level initiatives. Leaders need to encourage such developments. As key agents in such emerging structures, followers may often act as leaders themselves; thus they need to be comfortable with the demands of this new role. Effective leadership, then, may be a process that is distributed across many organization members, as Ireland and Hitt maintain, and the emergence of effective organizational structures may depend on the proactive actions of many potential leaders.[33] In short, more dynamic and complex business and political environments can change the nature of leader-follower relations, requiring both new perspectives on how leadership occurs and an expanded view of the follower's role.

We can see the link between individual-level structures and emerging social structures quite clearly if we consider the effects of the active WSC on followers' leadership activities. Some individuals may have self-views as leaders that are central to their self-identity, making it easy for them to assume leadership roles when necessary. But for other individuals, a self-view as a leader may be peripheral, making it more difficult for them to assume leadership roles when necessary because they have difficulty activating a WSC that includes such a self-view. When self-views suggest that one can be an effective leader, one is likely to attempt leadership activities, developing a provisional identity as a leader and building a repertoire of leadership skills.[34] This proactive leadership activity, in turn, increases one's self-view as a potential leader, completing a positive feedback spiral that increases both the motivation and the capacity to lead. It is also important to recognize that because leadership is inherently social, the emergence of flexible leadership structure is constrained by many types of belief structures among followers as well as leaders. For example, beliefs regarding appropriate role activities for males and females can be important constraints on emergent leadership structures.[35]

LEADER-FOLLOWER DYNAMICS
Followers' Constraints on Leaders

In the previous discussion of sensemaking processes, I emphasized that sensemaking occurs when followers construct an internal framework for interpreting a social stimuli, such as an organizational superior. Thus followers' sensemaking serves as a powerful constraint on leaders' sensegiving. Ineffective supervisors may attempt to explicitly communicate messages or visions that do not provide effective interpretive frames for followers, either because the visions of the supervisor lag the realities confronted by followers or because followers do not perceive their supervisor as an effective leader.

As previously noted, lower leadership ratings tend to occur when leaders' traits or behaviors do not match the implicit leadership theories of followers. Followers also draw leadership inferences from knowledge of a leader's performance.[36] Both the inferential and the prototype-matching bases for leadership perceptions are enhanced when dispositional attributions are formed for a supervisors' activity.[37] Causal attributions are also based on the perceptual salience of potential causal sources; sources on which perceivers focus their attention or for which information is more available in memory are overrepresented in causal analysis. It is important to note that when followers take a more active role in responding to change and generating adaptive organizational structures, *their* actions rather than those of leaders become salient. Consequently, leaders who encourage effective followership may run the risk of not being perceived as being causally important. Thus their potential influence may be reduced because influence is tied to being perceived as a leader.[38] This is an issue that needs to be investigated by leadership researchers who are interested in followership. The bottom line is simply that how followers perceive potential leaders is an important constraint on social influence processes, and an emphasis on followership rather than leadership will have consequences in terms of a leader's social power and influence.

Leaders' Influence on Followers

Individual Level   Because different subordinate regulatory structures may be active at different times, one means for leaders to affect subordinates is to prime particular regulatory structures and thereby alter subordinates' WSCs. Lord and Brown provide an extensive discussion of this process.[39] I will simply note here that leaders can have effects on specific subordinates that operate through affective processes, through their encouragement of particular types of goals, or through their effects on active identities. Such effects can be explicit and may be carefully managed by leaders, or they may be implicit, being the result of other social processes. For example, social justice behaviors on the part of leaders may be of critical importance in making individual or collective identities salient in subordinates, in eliciting cooperative behavior from subordinates, and in eliciting positive or negative affective reactions.[40] Researchers interested in followership as well as leadership should address how leaders can affect these cognitive and affective structures of followers, paying particular attention to the possibility that the implicit approach of leaders may not fit well with followers' structures. The fit between a leader's and a follower's implicit theories may have important consequences for the nature of the exchange that develops between them.[41] The effects of leaders on followers have been a central focus of the leadership field, but what has not been so widely recognized is that these effects are mediated by the schema that are activated in followers. Thus they are a follower as well as a leadership process.

Collective Level   As previously noted, complexity theory maintains that structure spontaneously emerges from the interaction of units. This process occurs within individuals as they develop self-perceptions or perceptions of others,[42] and it also occurs as individual-level goals emerge from multiple internal and external constraints.[43] Emergent internal structures then form the basis for the emergence of more macro structures that connect autonomous agents in organizations: affective and informational networks develop,[44] and collective knowledge structures emerge from interrelated task activities.[45] It is important to recognize that rather than being centrally directed by formal leadership systems, such structures develop from local interactions, and no single individual may have a comprehensive knowledge of the adaptive structures that develop. Thus followers are the crucial component of such emergent structures, but leaders can still have profound effects that operate through followers.

As Marion and Uhl-Bien note, leaders do not control emergent processes, although they may manage them to a certain extent, in that their actions can function as a catalyst for the emergence of some types of structure, or can forestall the emergence of other structures.[46] Leaders can affect emergent structures in three important ways. First, when leaders attempt to construct a powerful image of the future and tie this image to specific types of actions or identities, they may affect the emergence of subordinate structures. Though often portrayed as having positive effects by leadership researchers, a transformational leader with an outdated vision may prevent the spontaneous development of more adaptive structures from the interactions of followers. Whether structure should flow from the vision of leaders or should emerge from followers in a bottom-up manner depends on where relevant knowledge is localized in an organization. When followers have more extensive technical knowledge or more current information on an organization's environment than top-level leaders do, structures that emerge in a bottom-up manner may have a distinct advantage.

Second, dyadic leadership activities can facilitate the development of more autonomous, self-directed followers; or, by being overly personal, leaders can undercut the development of leadership identities and skills among followers.[47] Further, because the self-views and identities that develop in conjunction with a particular leader are structures that are internal to subordinates, they can carry over to new potential leadership relationships,[48] having an effect that outlives a particular dyadic relationship. This process may then be compounded as subordinates interact with each other, facilitating or inhibiting the development of effective interpersonal structures. In other words, the nature of dyadic relations may create the conceptual and affective structures in subordinates that act as building blocks in constructing emergent structures in organizations. Small changes in orientations induced by leaders can create large changes in the structure that evolves, a phenomenon labeled *divergence* by dynamic systems theorists.

Third, leaders can have more subtle influences that merely bias the spontaneous development of internal and interpersonal structures.[49] That is, they may make certain identities, affective orientations, or goal structures more or less available by the subtle primes they provide to subordinates. For example, positive affect may elicit approach-related regulatory structures, whereas negative affect may foster avoidance-related structures. Because affect is contagious, leaders' emotions may infect subordinates, and subordinates may infect other subordinates with their emotions,[50] setting the stage for the emergence of very different types of self-regulatory structures when leaders express positive as compared to negative emotions. Affective structures can also cascade upward, with individual or dyadic structures evolving into stable group affective structures.[51] These three ways of guiding emergent structures vary in terms of their focus on leaders, with the first being leader-centered, the second being based on the nature of dyadic relationships, and the third being based primarily in the structures created by followers.

CONCLUSION

Although dramatic transformations in organizations or societies can indeed be created by insightful and charismatic leaders, this is probably not the most typical means by which organizations or societies develop. Instead, leaders may often operate through their effects on followers, or followers may assume leadership roles when necessary. Further, many critical collective structures in organizations emerge from the actions and relations created by followers. Formal organizational leaders certainly have an important role in catalyzing such processes,[52] but emphasizing a leader's role while neglecting that of followers is not likely to produce optimal theory or effective practice. A more balanced approach can enhance our understanding of followership as well as improve leadership theory.

Social Identity Processes and the Empowerment of Followers

Michael A. Hogg

This is a book about the role of followers in leadership. Although the majority of leadership research focuses primarily on the leader, there has been a growing interest in "followership" that acknowledges that followers may actually play a key role in leadership.[1]

This latter research tends to view followership as the active engagement of followers in helping the group achieve its goals—a view that was at least partly adopted in order to contrast with the more common view of followers as passive and compliant. Followership research has focused on followership styles (for example, star followers, alienated followers, yes-people) and followership motivations and paths (for example, the apprentice, the disciple, the comrade).

There is, however, another way to approach the role of followers in effective leadership—one that focuses on the fact that leaders and followers are, ultimately, members of the same group.[2] One cannot logically exist without the other, because their relationship is defined by membership in the same group and thus by possession of the same group or social identity. This approach focuses on social cognitive and social interactive processes associated with group membership and collective identity.

In this chapter I describe the *social identity theory of leadership*—a social psychological theory that focuses on the identity function of leadership. It describes how followers permit and help leaders forge an identity for the group and its members and how followers are transformed to define themselves and act in terms of this identity. This is an analysis of leadership that places followers very much in the driving seat of effective leadership, insofar as followers provide clear limits for what leadership behaviors and innovations they will approve of, endorse, and follow.

SOCIAL IDENTITY THEORY

Social identity theory has developed since the early 1970s to become a significant social psychological theory of group processes and intergroup relations.[3] One of its key insights, which distinguished it from other social psychological accounts of group processes and intergroup relations, was its emphasis on the role of social identity—that is, representation and evaluation of self in terms of shared attributes that define the group one belongs to, one's ingroup.[4]

In order to deal with the incredible diversity of humanity, the mind represents the social world in terms of categories of people (for example, men, Germans, psychologists, Latinos, Hindus, mechanics). The technical term for these representations is *prototype*—a prototype is a set of attributes (for example, attitudes, behaviors, dress, customs) that we believe characterize a group and distinguish it from relevant other groups. Typically people in one group agree on their prototype of their own group (ingroup) and of relevant other groups (outgroups). They often also exaggerate differences between their own group and relevant outgroups and exaggerate how similar members of a specific outgroup are to one another.

In situations where group memberships are salient (for example, we are involved in a group activity or intergroup encounter, we meet a stranger whom we know little about, we feel proud of our own group or despise a particular outgroup), we psychologically use category membership to configure perception, program behavior, and structure interaction. Under these circumstances, we relatively automatically categorize people as group members and assign them the attributes of our prototype of their group—we stereotype them and treat them as embodiments of their group rather than as unique individuals (a process that social identity theorists call *depersonalization*).

So, for example, Mac users might agree that pc users are all boring, dull, and "stiff," and certainly far more boring, dull, and stiff than Mac users. When a Mac user meets a pc user, she categorizes him as a pc user rather than, for example, a Goth or a personal friend called Toby, and assigns the category attributes to him. The ensuing interaction is structured in terms of intergroup relations between the two categories, Mac users and pc users, rather than between two individuals or between a woman and a man.

A central tenet of social identity theory is that the process of depersonalization can apply to oneself—we categorize ourselves in precisely the same way as we categorize others and thus assign to ourselves the prototypical attributes of our group. The implication of this is clear: self-categorization transforms our perceptions, beliefs, attitudes, feelings, and behaviors to conform to the prescriptions of the prototype we have of our group.

Because prototypes define groups, in group contexts people thirst for prototype-relevant information. Because the ingroup prototype defines and evaluates one's own group, and thus through self-categorization one's own self and identity, people are particularly vigilant for information about the ingroup prototype. There are many sources of this information, among which the most immediate and reliable is the behavior of fellow ingroup members who one has already learned are generally highly prototypical group members. To foreshadow the argument I will be presenting, in many group contexts the group leader is viewed by his or her followers to be just such a highly prototypical member.[5]

SOCIAL IDENTITY THEORY OF LEADERSHIP

Social identity theory has a number of implications for the psychology of leadership, which have recently been formalized as the social identity theory of leadership.[6] The key idea is that as group membership becomes increasingly psychologically salient and important to members of the group and members identify more strongly with the group, effective leadership rests increasingly on the leader's being perceived by followers to possess prototypical properties of the group. This is an analysis that quite explicitly assigns followers a significant role in creating the characteristics of its leadership or even creating the leadership itself.

As people identify more strongly with a group, they pay more attention to the group prototype and to what and who is more prototypical—as explained earlier, this is because the prototype defines the group's membership attributes and thus members' self-concept and identity. In these salient group contexts, being perceived to be a highly prototypical leader makes one more influential. There are a number of sound social identity reasons for this.

First, depersonalization means that people conform to the group prototype and thus appear to be influenced by the prototype and thus by those members who are actually more prototypical of the group. Prototypical members appear to have disproportionate influence over the rest of the members of the group. Prototypical leaders appear to be more effective sources of influence.

Second, prototypical group members are liked, as group members, more than less prototypical members. Because there is usually significant agreement on the prototype, the group as a whole likes prototypical members—they are consensually popular in group terms. Such popularity facilitates influence—we are more likely to comply with requests from people we like.[7] Thus prototypical leaders are popular in the eyes of their followers and are readily able to gain compliance with their ideas—they can exercise effective leadership. Furthermore, this popularity instantiates an evaluative status difference between the consensually popular leader and his or her followers.

Third, prototypical members find the group more central and important to self-definition, and therefore identify more strongly with it. They have a greater investment in the group and thus are more likely to behave in group-serving ways. They embody group norms more precisely, and they are more likely to favor the ingroup over outgroups, to treat ingroup members fairly, and to act in ways that promote the ingroup. These behaviors confirm their prototypicality and membership credentials, and encourage group members to trust them to be acting in the best interest of the group even when it may not appear that they are—they are furnished with legitimacy.[8] Thus followers invest their trust in prototypical leaders, which paradoxically allows such leaders to diverge from group norms and be less conformist and more innovative and transformational than non- or less prototypical leaders. Innovation and transformation are, of course, key components of effective leadership.[9]

Finally, because the prototype is so central to group life, information related to the prototype subjectively stands out against the background of other information in the group. Prototypical leaders are probably the most direct source of proto-type information, and therefore are figural against the background of the group. Members pay close attention to their leaders and, as in other areas of social per-ception and inference, attribute their behavior to invariant underlying personality attributes. This inferential bias is called the fundamental attribution error,[10] the correspondence bias,[11] or essentialism.[12] In the context of leadership it causes fol-lowers to construct a charismatic leadership personality for their leader—after all, the behaviors that are being attributed to personality include being the source of influence, being able to gain compliance from others, being popular, having higher status, being innovative, and being trusted. In this way charisma, which plays an important role in transformational leadership,[13] is constructed by group processes rather than being a static personality attribute that is brought to the group.[14] The perception of charisma further facilitates effective and innovative leadership on the part of a prototypical leader.

These leadership processes based on social identity extend to leaders' consider-able power to maintain their leadership position. Because they are trusted, given latitude to be innovative, and invested with status and charisma, they are very effective prototype managers who can define what the group stands for and what the social identity of its members is. They can consolidate an existing prototype, modify it, or dramatically reconstruct it. One of the key attributes of effective leadership is precisely this visionary and transformational activity in which lead-ers are able to change what the group sees itself as being—such leaders can be considered entrepreneurs of identity.[15]

Specifically, prototypical leaders can talk up their own prototypicality and talk down aspects of their own behavior that are nonprototypical. They can identify deviants or marginal members to highlight their own prototypicality or to con-struct a particular prototype for the group that enhances their own prototypical-ity. They can secure their own leadership position by vilifying contenders for leadership and casting the latter as nonprototypical. They can identify as relevant comparison outgroups those that are most favorable to their own prototypicality. They can engage in a discourse that raises or lowers salience—if you are highly prototypical, then raising salience will provide you with the leadership benefits of high prototypicality; if you are not very prototypical, then lowering salience will protect you from the leadership pitfalls of not being very prototypical. Research sug-gests that all these processes are used by leaders to manage their prototypicality.[16]

Generally, leaders who feel they are not, or are no longer, prototypical, strategically engage in a range of group-oriented behaviors to strengthen their membership credentials.[17]

As a final point on the social identity theory of leadership, it is important to bear in mind that social identity leadership processes only, or more strongly, occur in groups with which members identify more strongly. As the group's salience or members' strength of identification with the group weakens, social identity leadership processes also weaken. Leadership becomes less strongly based on group prototypicality and more strongly based on other factors, such as leadership schemas and charismatic personality.

Overall, the social identity theory of leadership, although a relative newcomer to the leadership scene, has already attracted substantial empirical support from laboratory experiments and more naturalistic studies and surveys.[18]

SOCIAL IDENTITY AND FOLLOWERSHIP

The social identity theory of leadership doesn't explicitly theorize about "followership," but it does, as will have become clear from the discussion in this chapter, attribute a very significant role to followers. In salient groups, effective leadership rests on followers' shared perception that the leader is prototypical of the group. This perception generates favorable evaluation of, liking for, and trust in the leader, and perhaps a perception of charisma, which together cause followers to allow the leader to be normatively innovative and transformational. In such groups, leaders who are not considered prototypical by their followers will have a significant uphill struggle. In a very real sense, it is the followers who provide the necessary conditions for effective leadership.

This analysis has a number of important caveats, qualifications, and implications. The key boundary condition is that members identify relatively strongly with the group—the social identity processes that empower prototypicality only come into play when members identify strongly. Clearly if members disagree over the group prototype, then the group will experience a normative schism[19] in which different factions have very different views about who is more prototypical than whom and therefore whom should be trusted, liked, empowered, and so forth as a leader. This is very common in public and political leadership situations, but may also occur in corporate settings. It can often cause the group to split apart into separate groups, or, if one faction is dominant in terms of numbers or power, it can create an unstable leadership situation where the group has a disgruntled minority that actively works to undermine the group and its leadership. It can also cause the group to dissolve, as members dis-identify en masse.

Although normative disagreement in salient groups can create leadership pitfalls, so can excessive normative agreement and homogeneity.[20] Groups where members identify excessively strongly as "true believers" or zealots, and which have an entirely consensual and monolithic normative structure, can endow a prototypical leader with overwhelming power to influence. This is because the social identity leadership processes go to extremes—for example, popularity becomes leader worship, and status differentiation becomes absolute hierarchy. Such groups are often closed, inward looking, and harshly intolerant of normative criticism or dissent; they possess an atmosphere of zealotry, orthodoxy, and extremism and often have all-powerful leaders. In these situations, followers are pretty much prepared to go wherever their leader takes them, and, in the absence of criticism and other reality checks from followers, the leader can simply lose sight of what is right and what is wrong, what is wise and what is foolish. Here, followership sustains a monster.

Because social identity theory is about the relationship between group processes and self-concept, the social identity theory of leadership speaks to the identity dimension of leadership. It is therefore less relevant to leadership contexts where the group's overwhelming function is simply to get a task done than it is to leadership contexts where the group has a more prominent identity-defining function. Although all groups provide people with an identity, this aspect of group life may vary from being quite insignificant (for example, transient decision-making groups) to being critically important (for example, ethnic groups). Although followers may well play a role in leadership in the former, the social identity analysis of the role of followers in leadership is of course more relevant to the latter.

One final point concerns just how much influence followers have over prototypical leaders. It was suggested earlier that social identity processes in salient groups give leaders substantial leeway to be normatively innovative and transformational. Although in extreme groups a leader may have unfettered leeway; under normal circumstances this is unlikely to be the case. Normative innovation needs to occur within the group's parameters of acceptable innovation—parameters that may vary from context to context and from group to group. Leaders who overstep these bounds may be viewed as nonprototypical and a threat to the integrity of the group and its identity, and their leadership would be rejected. For example, Reicher analyzed a riot that occurred in Britain in the early 1980s and found that the rioters took their lead from specific community leadership figures.[21] However, because the riot was a protest against the British government, leaders who encouraged indiscriminate attacks on private property were not influential, whereas leaders who encouraged attacks only on property that represented the government (banks, social security offices, police stations) were influential. Leaders of salient groups have influence over the group, but only within the normative parameters set by their followers. In this respect followers have an enormous influence over their leaders.

Another way in which followers have an active role to play in leadership is through communication. It is difficult to imagine a normal group situation in which followers do not talk to one another; and in salient group contexts they talk to one another a great deal about the group's identity and norms, and about their leaders and their leadership. In this way followers are active players or entrepreneurs in the construction of the identity and normative parameters of their group. Followers proactively provide the normative space and prototype specification within which leaders operate.[22] If leaders step outside these follower-defined parameters, they are unlikely to be effective in leading the group.

CONCLUDING COMMENTS AND A PRESCRIPTION FOR EFFECTIVE FOLLOWERSHIP

From a social identity perspective, followers play an absolutely fundamental role in effective groups—a role that is greatly accentuated in groups that furnish a self-definition and identity and with which people identify relatively strongly. Under these circumstances, followers' evaluations of how well the leader fits the group's identity profile (how prototypical he or she is) significantly affect the leader's ability to influence the group. Followers allow prototypical leaders to be far more effective than nonprototypical leaders—followers follow prototypical leaders more than nonprototypical leaders.

The reason for this is that social cognitive processes associated with group identification render the leader figural against the background of the group, imbue the leader with charisma, generate trust in the leader, and make the leader consensually popular and the perceived source rather than target of influence. In this chapter I described how these relatively automatic social cognitive processes play out.

However, I also noted that prototypicality is ultimately a subjective perception that rests on agreement among followers about what is group normative or not and what attributes define group membership. Although prototypical leaders are given latitude to be innovative, this plays out within parameters set by the group as a whole. In this respect, followers proactively define the group's wider identity and prototype parameters through communication; they talk and make decisions about what it is to be a member of the group, what the group stands for. For example, in the 2004 movie *Sideways*, Miles (Paul Giamatti's character) famously proclaims that Jack (Thomas Haden Church's character), who has a leadership role in the dinner group, can make him do pretty much anything but drink Merlot, Merlot being déclassé to true wine connoisseurs. Miles allows Jack to be innovative, but clearly communicates what he sees as being the identity parameters of the group and thus of Jack's leadership.

In this chapter I also described ways in which social identity leadership processes may be counterproductive or can produce bad leadership. For example, normative disagreement might fragment the group or create a schism in which a majority faction and its leader dominate a minority faction. In contrast, excessive normative homogeneity may sow the seeds for oppressive leadership that loses touch with right and wrong, good and evil.

In keeping with the wider impetus for research on followership, the title of this chapter makes reference to "empowerment of followers." Although the social identity processes I've described have an automatic dimension, they also point to ways in which followers have substantial power to influence leadership. The key empowerment of followers is that in salient groups, leaders are only influential to the extent that they are seen to be prototypical, and it is the followers who largely construct through communication shared representations of their group's identity and associated prototype.

I'd like to close with a speculative prescription for effective social identity–based followership. The aim is to find a balance between insufficient identification or salience and excessive normative heterogeneity on the one hand, where social identity leadership processes do not operate; and excessive identification and normative homogeneity on the other, where zealotry and orthodoxy cause followers to relinquish power to the leader. Two influential factors are uncertainty and communication.

Research framed by *uncertainty-identity theory* has shown that feelings of uncertainty about oneself, one's place in the social world, and things that reflect on one's sense of self, motivate people to identify more strongly with groups, particularly groups that are distinctive and clearly structured to provide an unambiguous and prescriptive identity.[23] However, under conditions of more extreme and more enduring uncertainty, identification and group structure become more extreme—excessive uncertainty may sponsor zealotry and orthodoxy and transform followership into an enabler of autocratic leadership.[24] Thus followership is more adaptive and effective in group contexts where there is only sufficient uncertainty to motivate belonging and identification.

In this kind of environment, free communication among followers about the nature of the group, its identity, and normative attributes is probably essential. This allows followers to construct and modify the prototype and thus to influence leadership. There will also be some disagreement and diversity of opinion within wider parameters of common perspective—this is healthy and serves to limit the power of the leader. Free communication also inhibits pluralistic ignorance, which refers to a situation where people engage in actions or express opinions that they actually disagree with because they erroneously believe, on the basis of lack of accurate information, that such actions or opinions are normative of the group.[25]

Effective followership generally benefits group atmosphere, promotes group functioning and development, and permits innovative, ethical, and healthy leadership. The social identity leadership analysis described in this chapter suggests that effective followership is maximized under conditions of (1) moderate group identification in which (2) members feel relatively secure in their membership, and (3) the group's atmosphere encourages free and open discussion of group norms and the group's identity and (4) celebrates diverse views within shared normative parameters. In contrast, weak identification, low psychological investment in the group, and profound lack of normative consensus create an environment of warring factions that is ripe for exploitation by a powerful autocratic leader—followers have little power. At the opposite extreme, excessive identification, intense uncertainty, orthodoxy, and inhibition of open discussion of identity and group norms create a cultlike environment with few limits on the omnipotent leader's behavior—followers again have little power. Thus caution is warranted at either extreme.

Lead, Follow, *and* Get out of the Way

Involving Employees in the Visioning Process

Melissa K. Carsten and Michelle C. Bligh

O ver the past decade, researchers and practitioners have placed great emphasis on the importance of having an organizational vision. Creating such a vision, however, is often easier said than done. Whereas strategic leaders are responsible for predicting many things about the external market, environment, and customer priorities, vision requires a different type of prediction: one that paints a vivid portrait of the organization's ideal future state. Such corporate leaders as Jack Welch, George Merck, and Bill Gates have all been praised for succeeding in creating and disseminating a vision that effectively charts the direction of their companies.[1] But vision creation is not always a task completed by executive leaders; many companies are beginning to understand the importance of involving followers in the process of vision creation, dissemination, and implementation.

Traditional views of leadership place the process of vision creation in the hands of executive leaders, assuming that they are in the best position to chart the strategic path for a company's future. Further, these traditional views suggest that leaders need merely to articulate a vision to achieve follower buy-in. More recently, however, attention has been shifted to examine followers' perceptions of vision in an effort to determine the difference between effective and ineffective visions. Because followers are integrally involved in moving the organization toward the desired future state, it can be argued that the importance of followers in the creation and realization of vision is equal to, if not greater than, the importance of strategic leaders.

In this chapter, we explore the importance of involving followers in vision creation and implementation. We begin the chapter by defining leaders, followers, and organizational vision. We also introduce the importance of followers' ownership by highlighting the effects that ownership can have on follower and organizational outcomes. Next, we present research findings from two studies that investigate follower participation in vision creation and the subsequent effects on followers' commitment to achieving the vision. Finally, we provide recommendations for involving followers in vision creation, dissemination, and implementation based on the research findings presented in this chapter.

LEADERSHIP, FOLLOWERSHIP, AND ORGANIZATIONAL VISION

It has been noted that without followers there are no leaders.[2] However, researchers and practitioners alike have routinely overlooked the importance of followers in the leadership equation. Leaders are defined as individuals who influence others to adopt certain ideologies and ways of acting upon the world. Followers, in contrast, are those individuals who ascribe to the ideals and directives of others. Defining followers in this way limits our thinking about the potential contribution that they make to an organization's processes and overall effectiveness. Indeed, many researchers have noted that the measure of an organization's success or effectiveness is too often sought by examining influential leaders,[3] frequently ignoring the fact that a leader's success is often dependent on the effectiveness of his or her followers. Thus any examination of leadership behaviors or processes should also include an examination of follower behaviors and processes in an effort to gain a more holistic understanding of this important partnership.

Recent literature on organizational vision has also ascribed to the traditional leader-follower distinction: placing leaders in the active role of creating and articulating the vision and followers in a more passive role of conforming to the visionary direction. Kirkpatrick and Locke defined vision as an idealized goal that the leader wants the organization to achieve in the future.[4] Likewise, other authors have defined vision as a mental image that a leader evokes to portray an idealized future for an organization.[5] These definitions suggest that vision creation and dissemination are largely the responsibility of leaders and say little about how followers can directly contribute to the visioning process. Empirical research on vision has reinforced the dominant focus on leaders by investigating the process of vision creation, articulation, and implementation from the leaders' perspective. Whereas these empirical investigations have created a wealth of knowledge regarding the outcomes of vision articulation, fewer studies have identified the role that followers play in the visioning process. For example, here are some of the important findings on leadership and vision:

- Leaders who espouse a vision that is shared by the entire organization are perceived by followers as being more trustworthy and dynamic, and as having more expertise than those leaders who fail to articulate a vision.[6]

- Leaders who promote an inspiring vision are more strongly revered than those who do not.[7]

- Vision positively affects follower performance by clarifying follower goals and increasing self-efficacy.[8]

- Vision clarifies shared values and identities among followers and promotes unification and drive toward a common goal.[9]

- Vision can have a positive effect on the growth of entrepreneurial firms.[10]

Noticeably absent from this research is an investigation into the role that followers play in creating or disseminating the vision. Yet it is implicitly assumed that follower support is required to advance a vision and move the organization in the desired direction. Whereas many of these studies suggest that positive organizational outcomes can be achieved when a vision is accepted and acted on by followers, there are also accounts of followers who failed to accept their leader's vision. Two relevant examples can be taken from Microsoft and Hewlett-Packard. Bill Gates, CEO of Microsoft, started his company with a simple vision: "A computer on every desktop and in every home." In the late 1970s, this was a revolutionary idea that employees could rally behind, and, as a result, they worked tirelessly to make this dream a reality. In contrast, former CEO of Hewlett-Packard Carly Fiorina articulated a fuzzy vision shortly after being appointed into her new position: "To create an adaptive IT enterprise." Employees of HP struggled to understand the vision and eventually disengaged from the vision altogether. These illustrations highlight the importance of follower acceptance or rejection of a leader's vision and the potential benefits in creating a vision that inspires follower action.

So what is the secret to achieving a successful vision? Although research has yet to identify the silver bullet that will make all visions effective (there likely is no one best approach for all organizations), we believe, and our research suggests, that follower ownership of the vision is one extremely important ingredient.

Ownership is defined as having belonging or possession over something. For organizations, this likely involves organization members feeling that they are invested in and responsible for the outcomes associated with an action or initiative.[11] Researchers have suggested that ownership is created when employees are involved in the design and implementation of a program or initiative. Simply being assigned a project or initiative without knowledge or involvement in its design or alignment with other initiatives is not conducive to the type of ownership that produces increased commitment, conscientiousness, or engagement. With regard to vision, it seems logical that follower ownership should be the goal of any organization that desires movement toward the ideal future state. According to Sashkin, "If the vision remains an idea of the leader—the leader's 'property,' not owned by the organization's members—it cannot succeed."[12]

One step toward promoting follower ownership of the vision is to involve followers in the process of creating and disseminating the vision. The findings of two recent studies suggest that followers who participate in vision creation show stronger internalization of the vision, more goal clarity and empowerment, and less anxiety about organizational change. Conversely, followers who passively receive the vision in a top-down fashion are less knowledgeable about the vision's meaning, perceive weaker alignment between the vision and the organization's purpose, and are less committed to the vision overall.

In the next two sections, we present research findings to communicate the importance of creating follower ownership of the vision. Study 1 qualitatively explores a case of top-down vision creation and dissemination, and reveals the disadvantages of such an approach for the livelihood of the vision. Study 2 presents survey data collected from followers who perceived that their vision was created through a collaborative effort. Taken together, these studies provide some indication that the role of followers in vision creation may be more important than previously thought. These studies provide a baseline for subsequent recommendations that we offer at the end of the chapter.

STUDY 1: A CASE OF VISION MISALIGNMENT

The first study was conducted by interviewing faculty members at a small university regarding a vision that had recently been created and articulated by the university's president. The president did not involve faculty in the creation of the vision, nor did he engage followers in devising methods of communicating or implementing it. Instead, the president single-handedly created a plan to communicate the vision to the university's constituents and a corresponding action plan to be implemented by faculty, staff, and students.

The president's vision was to achieve "transdisciplinarity" within the university setting. According to speeches by the president, transdisciplinarity was defined as a form of scholarship that "forces us to think across, beyond, and through academic disciplines represented at the university to encompass all types of learning and knowledge about an idea, issue, or subject." The vision was designed to take education into the twenty-first century by providing students with a breadth of knowledge, both within and outside their specialty area, which could be applied to such societal issues as poverty, racism, or ethics. The president's hope was to create an environment where university faculty and students worked across the boundaries of their discipline.

Nineteen faculty and staff members participated in interviews concerning their knowledge of the vision, their beliefs about whether the vision would benefit the university, and their perceptions of whether the vision was aligned with the president's action plan for implementation. Interview data were coded to extract major themes regarding employees' understanding of the vision and their feelings about the role the vision would play in their work behaviors. The following lists the frequency with which major themes emerged in the data:

- Across all nineteen interviews, themes regarding the perceived misalignment between the vision and the implementation strategy were mentioned thirty-six times. This finding reveals that followers did not see the utility of the president's action plan and suggests that many followers had not "bought in" to the implementation effort.

- Perceived benefits to the university were mentioned eighteen times, whereas perceived disadvantages of the vision were mentioned thirty-three times. Overall, followers placed greater salience on the disadvantages that the vision would have for the university and its constituents.

- Followers' use of the vision to guide work behaviors and decisions was mentioned eight times. This finding suggests that followers did not place emphasis on how the vision was related to their specific roles or duties within the organization.

- Perception that the vision was a product of or belonged to the leader, rather than the followers, was mentioned twenty-seven times. By and large, followers perceived that the leader had full ownership of the vision.

Overall, many of the interviewees suggested that they did not have a thorough understanding of the vision or the benefits associated with achieving it. One respondent stated, "As a definition, I am not quite sure what it means. I think it means that we are collaborators and that we have a broader vision of problem solving. I don't think that it is well understood. People see transdisciplinarity, and it doesn't just ring a bell for them." Followers also suggested that they could have provided input that would have made the vision more meaningful for the university's constituents. One faculty member offered suggestions for how the vision could have been communicated differently: "In terms of instituting it, sort of doing the top-down approach where you force this on people may not be the right way; it may be better to try and encourage a sort of bottom to top approach where you just create the conditions that allow people to interact more and so on without forcing people into this." Another respondent echoed this sentiment, stating that the communication of the vision as something that the university would undertake at all cost was a bit coercive: "I basically like that the school is making a thrust in that direction, but I think that it should not be coercive—the university should make resources available, and use more of the carrot rather than the stick as the approach."

Throughout the interviews, followers showed a clear lack of ownership, in that many respondents did not agree with the way the vision had been articulated or implemented. When asked about the potential benefits of achieving the vision, one respondent stated, "It seems to me that the question is: Can transdisciplinarity transform [the university] in the way that it intends? And frankly, I am not holding my breath." Another respondent suggested that although she was committed to the vision as a concept and a direction, she did not believe that the vision would be implemented in a useful way. When asked about her commitment to the vision, she stated, "I am very committed to the concept, if you can distinguish between that and the specific way that it is being implemented. I am not very committed at all to the specific way that it is being done."

Overwhelmingly, followers at this university suggested that they did not appreciate the top-down nature with which the vision was being implemented. Many even suggested that there were better ways to achieve the vision than those being proposed by the president. When asked about the strategy for implementing the vision, one respondent stated, "It's not reasonable that there is only one way to do it. There are so many different ways to do it. I really don't like the idea that it's got to be done this way." Many followers even suggested alternative ways that the vision could be enacted to achieve the same results. One respondent offered this suggestion: "Now, of course, nobody is asking me, but it would have seemed to me a little more obvious to require every student to have taken a two-course sequence outside their discipline or something like that to enforce the transdisciplinarity vision as opposed to having one course that everyone is involved in." Suggestions like this occurred quite frequently in the data; however, so did the notion that faculty members' views and opinions were not being acknowledged by the president. One respondent simply put it this way: "Every suggestion that we have come up with that I have personally known about has been dismissed out of hand because they don't even answer. But I think that they're afraid."

The findings of study 1 provide some evidence that followers who receive the vision in a top-down fashion, without extensive knowledge or participation in vision creation or implementation, show more resistance to the vision and less commitment overall. Leaders typically promote a vision because it can serve as a beacon that guides organizational activity and rallies follower energy behind a common goal. However, this case highlights the importance of gaining follower buy-in and promoting ownership of the vision. Leaders who take sole responsibility for creating the vision and the strategy for dissemination run the risk of encountering resistance, misalignment, or, worse, rejection of the vision altogether.

STUDY 2: PROMOTING ALIGNMENT
THROUGH PARTICIPATION

The second study was similarly designed to investigate follower participation in vision creation. We set out to determine (1) whether or not companies were practicing participatory visioning and (2) what, of any, positive outcomes are associated with follower involvement in the visioning process. Survey data were collected from 218 employees at five different companies in the health care, consulting, construction, banking, and technology industries. Respondents consisted of employees at the frontline, supervisory, and middle management levels. All employees stated that they had knowledge of their leader's vision, which in most cases had been in existence for three to seven years. The following are results of this study:

- A total of ninety-eight respondents (46 percent) said that employees were involved in creating their company's vision. This finding suggests that many leaders are actively involving followers in the vision creation effort.

- Of those 46 percent who said that employees were involved in vision creation, 92 percent believed that the vision was aligned with their company's core philosophy. In addition, 85 percent reported that the vision is used to guide the decisions made by their department. This finding suggests that employee involvement in vision creation is associated with departmental decision making that is more closely aligned with the company's vision. In addition to departmental alignment, 62 percent of these respondents said that the vision was shared by all members of the organization, and 78 percent said that the vision helps them understand the purpose of their work. These findings suggest that followers who perceived that vision creation was a collaborative effort were more likely to perceive that their work directly contributed to achieving the organization's vision as well.

- Respondents who reported that employees participated in vision creation felt more empowered, had clearer individual goals, and were less anxious about organizational changes than those who reported that the vision was created entirely by top management.

These findings suggest that followers who perceive that the vision was created through a participatory effort report stronger alignment with the vision and more commitment to making the vision a reality. Nearly half of this sample suggested that their leaders encouraged participation in the visioning process, and it is clear that there are numerous benefits of doing so. For example, employees who perceived vision creation to be a collaborative effort reported more identification with and internalization of the vision. Vision identification, which results from the belief that the vision is aligned with company values, purpose, and philosophy, leads followers to accept and commit to the vision as a desirable organizational state. Identification is also a precursor to vision internalization, which occurs when followers begin to use the vision to guide their individual work. Internalization is similar to ownership in that followers begin to feel that the vision is their own and that they are responsible for and dedicated to making it a reality.

Whereas vision identification and internalization might be dependent on a number of different factors (such as vision content, vision communication, or past history of the vision or organization), these findings suggest that participation in vision creation is an important ingredient in promoting vision acceptance and a sense of vision ownership throughout the organization. Followers in our sample were not only *capable* of offering advice and suggestions on how to make the vision effective; it also appears that they were *motivated* to offer such advice. In the following section, we provide recommendations for how leaders can involve followers in all stages of the vision creation, articulation, and implementation process.

RECOMMENDATIONS FOR PROMOTING PARTICIPATION
Participation in Vision Creation

Despite the increasingly common advice surrounding the importance of having an organizational vision, it is *not* commonly suggested that the process of vision creation is "easy." On the contrary, vision creation, or "visioning," has been equated with attempting to predict the future with far more accuracy than your neighborhood psychic. Involving followers in the vision creation process could take some of the pressure off senior leaders. Followers often have important ideas about what the ideal future state of their company might look like, and provided they have the right outlet to express such ideas, followers are quite capable of tackling leadership challenges and offering fresh new perspectives and opinions.

Leaders who are considering devising a new vision, or even revising an old one, should consider involving followers from the very beginning. As noted in study 2, followers who perceive that the vision was created through a participatory effort reported greater individual and organizational alignment with the vision, and more commitment to making the vision a reality. Furthermore, study 1 revealed that followers who were not involved in creating the vision were less knowledgeable about its meaning to the organization as well as to their individual roles. These followers also failed to recognize the advantages that the vision could offer to the organization. On the basis of this evidence, we recommend that leaders explicitly involve followers in the vision creation process. A good starting point may be to come up with a proposed vision and write it out in five to ten sentences. With this draft vision statement, followers will have a starting point to provide comments, offer suggestions for improvement, or identify weaknesses that the leader may not have detected. The following points can help leaders generate this type of quality participation.

1. **Make it public.** If you are going to create a vision or revise an old one, let the members of your organization know that you will be taking on this endeavor and, more important, that you will be asking for their help. Putting the vision creation process on the organizational "radar" will send a strong message about the vision's importance.

2. **Make it practical.** Don't expect people to knock down your door and flood your e-mail box with suggestions on how to create the new vision. Instead, create a task force of middle and senior managers to hold focus groups with organization members. These focus groups should be composed of five to seven members at a time and held in an environment where open dialogue is encouraged. This strategy will also communicate to organization members that you are serious about collaborating. If additional structure is desired, ask followers specific probing questions about whether they believe the vision is inspiring, believable, and achievable. These vision characteristics have been shown through previous research to be important in determining whether followers will find efficacy in the vision.[13]

3. **Make it comfortable.** Evidence suggests that followers will refrain from speaking up, delivering counterarguments, or offering suggestions when they feel intimidated by those with higher status or more power.[14]

Encourage an open environment where followers can engage in genuine brainstorming (rather than groupthink); otherwise followers have a tendency to tell senior leaders what they *want* to hear rather than what they *should* hear.

4. **Make it count.** Follow through on the suggestions that you are given or provide a clear rationale for why you will not. Defining what the vision is *not* is an important element of this process. Although there is no need to incorporate all suggestions or advice when crafting the final statement, disregarding or leaving out common themes raised in this process may be a warning sign that the vision is not broad enough to incorporate all aspects of what defines the organization and its future.

Participation in Vision Communication

With a newly crafted vision in hand, many leaders will simply post it on a wall, design a placard, or unveil it in the company newsletter without thinking about whether these media will impact followers in the manner they had intended. Leaders should take great care in the methods they use to circulate the vision, as weaker methods may communicate weaker importance. Likewise, leaders should ward off the temptation to simply cascade the vision from the upper to the lower levels of the organization. This was the method employed by the university president in study 1, and followers clearly felt that the vision was being forced on them, leaving them few opportunities to communicate their feedback and feelings about the efficacy of the vision. However, in study 2, followers who perceived avenues for participation suggested that the vision was guiding their own work as well as the decisions of their department or workgroup. Thus leaders should consider processes that involve followers in communicating the vision to all organization members. Creating avenues of communication at many different levels and through various channels of the organization will emphasize the significance of the vision and the value that the organization has put on its utility. Here are some specific suggestions for engaging followers in communicating the vision:

1. **Build a coalition.** Identify those individuals who are behind the vision and enlist their efforts in socializing the vision with other organization members. Encourage conversation around the vision, what it means for the organization, and what it means for the individual.

2. **Do it yourself.** Leaders must also directly communicate the vision to organization members through both formal and informal conversation. The leader must be the first and most dedicated champion of the organization's future state.

3. **Find the holes.** Manage the message as it travels through the different parts of the organization by having followers update you on how the message is being received by organization members. These updates will also help ensure that the message has not been distorted, misdirected, or misinterpreted by employees.

4. **Walk the talk.** Merely communicating the vision is not enough to rally people behind its message. Leaders should embody the vision in everything they do. The vision should come to life through the leader's behaviors and decisions, as well as through all initiatives put forth by the leader. Leaders who demonstrate vision-consistent behaviors will encourage followers at all levels to do the same. To this end, leaders will create an organization that *lives* its vision, rather than one that simply *has* a vision.

Participation in Vision Implementation

There is little consensus in the academic literature on the best way to implement a vision or on the exact leader and follower behaviors that are required to do so. Many times, vision implementation takes the form of a strategic initiative or action plan that is put in place to ensure that the organization is working toward a desired future state.[15] The implementation strategy could be as simple as a plan for vision diffusion or as complex as a plan for people, process, or technology improvement. Gill and Hopper and Potter suggest that regardless of the method of implementation, the leader is responsible for ensuring that followers are behind the implementation effort.[16] However, given that vision implementation can take the form of an organizational change initiative, leaders will likely experience some degree of follower resistance. For example, the vision implementation strategy that was employed in study 1 was met with resistance due to a lack of follower buy-in. Respondents suggested that the plan for implementation was not adequate for achieving the vision, and many offered suggestions for how the action plan should be improved. Indeed, the followers in this study lacked commitment to the implementation strategy, and many displayed frustration over the perceived misalignment between the vision and the president's plan for implementing it.

To avoid such resistance, leaders should consider involving followers in vision implementation. If the leader has already devised a method for implementation, he or she should ensure that followers are integrally involved in evaluating that method prior to rolling it out. This will encourage followers to voice disagreement or suggest alternative methods prior to the strategy's being implemented. In doing so, leaders will increase the chance that their strategy will be met with acceptance rather than resistance. Here are some suggestions for involving followers in creating an implementation strategy:

1. **Use the coalition.** Leaders should utilize the knowledge and understanding of the group that was active in socializing the vision for evaluation of the implementation strategy. This group can aid in the process of ensuring that the strategy is aligned with followers' shared understanding of the vision.

2. **Recruit change agents.** Encourage coalition members and other followers to champion the implementation effort. Change agents can be involved in leading informational sessions, conducting interviews with key stakeholders, or surveying the organization for readiness to receive the implementation.

3. **Build in feedback loops.** Create a forum for change agents to communicate organizational readiness or issues surrounding resistance. Work with followers to address issues that might stifle the implementation effort.

4. **Monitor the results.** Ensure that the implementation effort is achieving desirable results. Talk with followers about whether the strategy has achieved the desired objectives and, if it has not, engage followers in a discussion on how to improve the effectiveness of implementation.

CONCLUSION

Researchers and practitioners agree that vision creation is challenging and time consuming for even the most forward-thinking leaders.[17] Creating an organizational vision requires foresight, creativity, and an ability to envision an unknown future. Given that many leaders exert great amounts of energy while creating their vision statement, it is surprising that some of them fail to ensure that their vision is received and understood in the manner they intended.[18] The findings presented in this chapter offer evidence that the process of vision creation and dissemination requires an ongoing effort by *both* leaders and followers to ensure that the organization can bridge the gap between the current state of affairs and the ideal future. More specifically, leaders and followers can partner in their efforts to promote vision awareness and understanding for all members of the organization. This partnership will not only ensure that followers understand the vision's relevance to their workgroup and role but also may diffuse perceptions that creating, disseminating, and reinforcing the vision are solely the jobs of top management.

Organizations that are engaged in the early stages of vision creation may particularly benefit from understanding the important role that participation plays in follower perceptions of vision. There are clear benefits to involving others in vision creation, thereby helping counter or nullify perceptions that the vision was developed and deployed exclusively by top management. Executive leaders can help publicize their willingness to involve others in vision creation by working with middle managers to create a vision task force or coalition. Middle managers can involve lower-level employees by asking for volunteers or nominating individuals to serve on the coalition. These efforts will assist in promoting follower engagement from the very early stages of the visioning process.

Follower ownership of the vision is an essential element for vision success. However, it also requires that leaders relinquish some of the control that they have over processes and procedures that surround creating and disseminating the vision. To achieve these ends, leaders should understand the important contribution that followers can make, and realize that some processes should be organizational, rather than individual, efforts. The advantages of including followers in all stages of vision creation and implementation are clear: follower involvement is a critical link in the process of transforming the vision from mere corporate rhetoric into a powerful force that both anchors and guides organization members in times of ambiguity and complexity.

chapter TWENTY-ONE

Effective Followership for Creativity and Innovation

A Range of Colors and Dimensions

Kimberly S. Jaussi, Andy Stefanovich,
and Patricia G. Devlin

Effective followers are often undervalued, but they play a pivotal role in organizations that require new ways of doing business. Breakthrough innovations require an infusion of creativity into the thoughts and behaviors of all organization members. Whereas numerous articles and books have pointed to the role of the leader in creating this infusion,[1] practitioners and academics alike have neglected to focus on the roles and responsibilities of followers in this process. To fill that gap, we are calling on our unique academic-practitioner research partnership to ground our thinking and present our thoughts on followership for creativity and innovation in organizations.

STARTING POINTS

We would like first to define creativity in organizations and share some general observations. Creativity at work has been defined as the production of ideas that are both novel and useful.[2] We follow this definition and focus our discussion on followership for this outcome in organizations. Through our partnerships with innovative organizations that constantly search for new forms of being, new ways of working, and new products or services, we have observed several things. First, these organizations fight the ever-lurking threat of stagnancy. They strive constantly to improve themselves and are in continual states of evolution and revolution. Creativity pervades these organizations' values, mission, vision, structures, policies, and metrics. Improvement is often defined and measured in a wide variety of ways, including the number of new patents per year, the degree of diversity in employees, and the advancement of employee engagement through new cultural initiatives.

These creative organizations are extremely people-centric, and they recognize that creativity is an essentially human endeavor.[3] They understand that ideas originate in individuals, and groups of individuals shape, develop, and lead new ideas to fruition. They therefore place a greater degree of concern on honoring both leaders and followers than do more conventional companies. They also facilitate individuals' ability to exercise creativity in their work. Such mechanisms as Google's "free" day, which allows employees to take one day a week to work on pursuing new ideas to grow their business, serve as vehicles for inducing creativity. We should note that these are *effective* vehicles— Google estimates that this mechanism accounts for 50 percent of their new launches.[4]

Our framework is based on several key assumptions. First, all four of the follower types we discuss in this chapter are valuable for organizations to leverage for creative thought and action. There is no assumption of a one best place in our framework. Also, because creativity is based on a number of personality styles and cognitive tendencies, we recognize that individuals come to their organizations with a certain "modus operandi" with respect to creativity. Those tendencies, experiences, and identities should be recognized, acknowledged, and valued. However, everyone can be more effective. Growth and stretch may be necessary depending on the situation or the individual's own desire for new challenges. Our recommendations are focused on helping followers *leverage who they are* as followers for creativity. We also provide suggestions for those followers, if stretch is called for, to *move* in their followership for creativity.

Every member of any firm can be an effective follower for organizational creativity and innovation. Serving themselves, their peers, their leaders, their organization, their families, their communities, and humanity, effective followers for creativity are not bound by hierarchical relationships. Finally, we'd like to clarify that throughout this chapter we are *not* arguing that every follower needs to be creative (creative followership). We *are* talking about effective followership that enhances the creativity and innovation of organizations (followership *for* organizational creativity). With those assumptions on the table, let's first discuss the grounding for our framework, the work of Robert Kelley and Ira Chaleff.[5]

FOUNDATIONS OF FOLLOWERSHIP

Robert Kelley brought the notion of followership to the radar screens of practice and academia in his 1988 *Harvard Business Review* article "In Praise of Followers." Kelley's work in 1988, 1992, and in this volume urges us to value and focus on followers rather than just leaders, and to consider followers with respect to two independent dimensions. One dimension captures thinking style (independent, critical thinking as opposed to dependent, uncritical thinking); the other captures overall activity level (active as opposed to passive). In 1998, Ira Chaleff outlined a variety of things that followers must have the courage to do in order to be effective followers. Chaleff suggested then, and still suggests today (in this volume), that followers have a responsibility to their leaders and their organizations to embrace and activate their courage across the fronts of responsibility, moral action, transformation, challenging, listening, and serving.

To build on the work of these seminal authors, we focus on Kelley's upper-right quadrant: active, independent, critical thinkers whom he calls *effective followers*. Kelley notes that the other quadrants have clear negative implications for the organization, and thus we do not include them in our focus. Chaleff's work underlies our framework in that it takes *courage* to be a follower for organizational creativity and innovation.

DIMENSIONS OF EFFECTIVE FOLLOWERSHIP
FOR CREATIVITY AND INNOVATION

Effective followers for creativity and innovation in organizations can be thought of in terms of two dimensions layered within Kelley's active, independent thinking quadrant (his upper-right quadrant). The first dimension is represented by the colors Red and Blue. The second is represented by 3-D and 1-D at either end.

Red or Blue?

The colors Red and Blue capture the dimension of enthusiasm, energy, and emotions. The energy individuals bring to work can vary depending on outwardly visible enthusiasm, inspiration, and display of emotions. Individuals may display a coolness of ocean blue, a calmness in any setting, the evenness of a cloud-free blue sky on a clear day. Still active in their engagement at work, Blue people are the never-wavering, soothing, calm waters in the creative organization. Red people, by contrast, are hot: high intensity, high emotions, high energy that is sizzling at every chance and boiling over at times, and screaming passion. Red energy is ready to combust—at the extreme, Red is the epitome of active. A Red person can be summarized by the "3 E's": enthusiasm, energy, and emotion.

1-D or 3-D?

The second dimension in our framework is captured by the terms 1-D and 3-D. Independent followers differ in their problem-solving propensities, thinking style, and general preference for structure. 1-Ds are plentiful in business schools and organizations. They like to identify the problem, define the parameters for weighting criteria, generate alternatives, and execute their decisions and plans. They see issues as the issues present themselves—at face value in one dimension. Structure and planning are critical for these followers. They have an extreme distaste for ambiguity, and work independently and diligently at critically reducing uncertainty. Not the least bit *confusion tolerant*,[6] they use clear processes and predefined scripts for defining and solving problems in efforts to reduce confusion to a tolerable level.

3-Ds are at the other end of this spectrum. When faced with a situation, they see not only the objective in the middle, but things that surround that objective which allow it to be completely redefined, reapproached, and re-solved from a

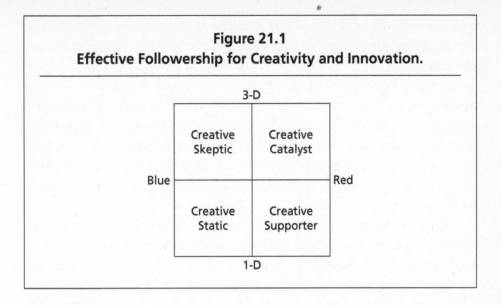

Figure 21.1
Effective Followership for Creativity and Innovation.

```
                        3-D

        Creative            Creative
        Skeptic             Catalyst

Blue  ─────────────────────────────  Red

        Creative            Creative
        Static              Supporter

                        1-D
```

variety of angles. They avoid putting boundaries on the definitions of problems they face, and love a messy situation. 3-Ds thrive on ambiguity, are highly confusion tolerant, and consistently take risks in terms of unconventional thinking and being intellectually irreverent.

Both Reds and Blues play key roles in supporting and enabling creativity, as do 1-Ds and 3-Ds. In the next section, we introduce followers in each quadrant, describe their value to the organization in terms of creativity, and identify what we call the "Plus, Delta"—strategies for harnessing the value added ("Plus") in each cell as well as tactics for growth should the follower be at a place in his or her life or in a particular situation that calls for stretch movement ("Delta").

Figure 21.1 outlines these two dimensions and introduces four types of effective followers for creativity and innovation in organizations.

TYPES OF EFFECTIVE FOLLOWERS FOR CREATIVITY AND INNOVATION IN ORGANIZATIONS
Creative Catalyst
The Creative Catalyst is in the upper-right quadrant of our model; this individual is a Red 3-D.

Creative Catalysts and Their Value Added   The Creative Catalyst is someone who stimulates others to generate ideas, rather than simply having the ideas himself or herself. A Red, the Catalyst is always looking for opportunities to inspire and energize others toward creative thinking. The Catalyst can sense the creative "weather" in a room, and knows how to insert positive energy and inspiration into any situation. As a 3-D, the Catalyst is known for pushing people to challenge their assumptions and to help develop the ideas of others. Catalysts see clear links among seemingly unrelated stimuli, and thrive on bringing those ideas to others as a role model for creativity. As a follower, the Creative Catalyst will be a source of stimulation to his or her leader and peers—as well as to all he or she meets.

The Catalyst serves as one who promotes creativity and innovation through exponential growth. By not only prompting others to be more creative but also teaching them how to be catalysts themselves, the Creative Catalyst has a monumental effect on fostering a climate for creativity. Because the Catalyst spreads so much positive affect and energy (something strongly related to creativity at work)[7] and is such a teacher at heart, always helping others learn to be creative rather than just coming up with answers himself or herself, the Creative Catalyst is a valuable follower to have and be.

Recommendation: Creative Catalyst Plus   While fostering creativity in others, Creative Catalysts can always be sharper and more focused in their abilities to inspire others and stimulate them to new levels of thinking.

- *To remain an effective Catalyst, keep pushing to get more and different stimuli.* At Play, it's called LAMSTAIH™—**L**ook **A**t **M**ore **S**tuff and **T**hink **A**bout **I**t **H**arder.

One Play[8] teammate is a Creative Catalyst who looks deep for new stimuli in a wide range of places, including the Internet, concerts, sporting events, and retail stores. With a smile on his face and perhaps a joke, he shares what he has found with others, framing it in a context that's salient for others and has meaning to them (for example, a project on which they are currently working). He then challenges them to find yet other links and expand the relevance to the current project. Projects end up much richer through this linking and sharing with the rest of the team. Something else also occurs: teammates bring the other links they've found back to the Catalyst, who can then link them to yet other projects.

Catalysts can have others facilitate their efforts at LAMSTAIH, thereby bringing even fresher insights to their teams for further linking. This past year, Play took a Catalyst from a clothing manufacturer and her team to an art museum. In closely looking at a piece of art, they discovered a shocking parallel between a characteristic of an animal in a painting and a new potential design for undergarments. This team is now designing and bringing a revolutionary product to market. The unique stimuli helped cultivate innovative ideas and gave individuals something to then share with others for yet *more* new ideas.

Looking at more stuff must remain a constant pursuit for catalysts. Peers will let the Catalyst stop looking outward, because he or she will be known as the creative person in the group and it will be assumed that the outward focus and sharing is occurring. To avoid the trap of becoming stale, the Creative Catalyst cannot stop exercising LAMSTAIH™.

Recommendation: Creative Catalyst Delta If growth and change are desired, Creative Catalysts could focus on moving further to the upper right than they currently are. The Creative Catalyst can try the following things:

• *Hone time and energy awareness.* The Creative Catalyst in the far upper right knows when it's the right time to push people for ideas or to bring an idea to life. The time and energy around and for an idea is as important as the idea itself. This corner is about a process orientation rather than an outcome orientation about ideas and their intersection with others. Movement toward this corner requires knowledge of how long it will take to introduce an idea and of who and what are the best mechanisms for introducing it, all the while helping others have ideas and share them.

An example to consider while honing this skill is that of one model Creative Catalyst with whom we frequently work. He utilizes the technique of idea dropping for idea prompting. He walks by the desks of carefully selected others (who think they're being singled out randomly), and stops. Seemingly out of the blue to the individuals at their desks, he'll ask a random question, such as, "What would it be like here if we made everyone's salaries public knowledge?" Overall, this technique accomplishes three things. First, it gets the input of others and allows the Catalyst to "gut check." Second, it socializes people to the idea or possibility.

Third, it gives a bit of disturbance, positive energy, and chaos to the recipients of the "idea drop," which forces them to stretch and think about something they haven't thought of yet (and may not be comfortable thinking about).

• *Become a storyteller.* The leadership literature has been plentiful with recommendations regarding leaders' use of language and the need to excel at articulation of goals and visions.[9] Followers, too, have a responsibility for effective articulation, and the Creative Catalyst will be most able to foster creativity in others when his or her storytelling skills are honed. Storytelling can captivate others and paint pictures through metaphors, analogies, and symbols that traditional business language norms simply cannot capture.

For example, even meeting notes can be told as a story—and through the process, become entertaining, captivating, even motivating. Consider this meeting note from Play:

Where's the Remote?

The Emmy's were on last night for most Play teammates. Robert noted how little changes in music and mood could speed up the entire pace of the show; maybe we could use these techniques to keep our engagements on a smooth pace. Robert is using video clips for Client XXX as a way to transition speakers and give them something to comment on before launching into data and numbers.

MTV's Video Music Awards air this Friday and technology is on the list. This is the first year a "Best Ringtone" moon man will be awarded.

With several teammates traveling to NYC over the next few weeks, read this article on the Bohemian Index of New York City. What is a bohemian? *A person with artistic or literary interests who disregards conventional standards of behavior* (American Heritage). So are we business bohemians?

The meeting notes captured the content of the meeting (ideas for a future client engagement) as well as where teammates will be (NYC), but did so in an entertaining and thought-provoking fashion that made employees want to see the next day's notes. Through storytelling, a Creative Catalyst can reach everyone through a positive emotional connection and continue to develop and spread the creative capacity of the organization. Learn to tell stories about everything.

Creative Supporter

The Creative Supporter is in the bottom-right quadrant of our model; this individual is a Red 1-D.

Creative Supporters and Their Value Added   A Creative Supporter has very high energy but is most comfortable thinking in traditional ways and maintaining order. He or she loves to reduce uncertainty and put structure on thinking. Very supportive of people emotionally and a big contributor to the positive energy in an organization, the Creative Supporter has incremental new thoughts that build on existing thoughts and ideas in a small, programmatic fashion.

Because creativity is so inextricably tied to positive emotions and moods, a Creative Supporter is critical to the organization in creating and maintaining that mood and inspiration level. They are the ones bringing pizza or popcorn or Internet research needed for support. They are always scanning the group and are there any time a person needs emotional, logistical, or execution energy and support. This, coupled with their love for process and structure that is necessary for the capturing of the creative product produced, makes the Creative Supporter follower essential for creativity in any organization.

Recommendation: Creative Supporter Plus   The Creative Supporter can be more effective in his or her current location by trying the following suggestions:

• *Articulate preferred processes to let others know how those processes contribute to the larger goal.* In other words, the Creative Supporter should focus on showing others where and how the Supporter's favorite processes and approaches can capture creative efforts and actually bring them to fruition. Sometimes, the best way to convey the value of a process is to demonstrate it right in the creative moment.

Take the example of a recent creative session in an organization. Ideas were presented and sparks were flying. The Creative Supporter of the group, who cannot truly process an idea without first working through the associated costs of implementation, energetically jetted off to get some pricing on the ideas that were being discussed. He came back to the session, and gladly wove them into the discussion. With that direction, the creative effort had another piece of context, the process was more expeditious, and the creative concepts that resulted were grounded in concrete cost structures. He showed others firsthand how his process could be helpful, and the others understood through seeing his process in action.

Recommendation: Creative Supporter Delta   A Supporter's high level of positive energy make him or her a natural to focus on moving upwards in the quadrant toward becoming a Catalyst. By stretching into more complex, unconventional thinking, the Creative Supporter can leverage the bedrock of goodwill created thus far and become more of a conduit for generating ideas. In order to stretch toward that unconventional thinking,

- *Focus on applying the positive energy toward nontraditional thinking by aligning with others who are nontraditional thinkers.*

One Creative Supporter with whom we've worked is passionate, places great emphasis on the emotions, and wants to have an impact on others. She also looks for preestablished rules for a sense of structure, reason, and order in her work. In order to stretch toward unconventional thinking, she has aligned herself with a graphic designer highly focused on the 3-D world. To stretch, the Creative Supporter tries to experience things through the designer's eyes. On a recent trip to a bookstore, the Creative Supporter looked for the essence of a book using its words, while the graphic designer caught the book's meaning through its visual representation. The designer explained how the design is the book's means for driving impression, conversation, and content, which was contrary to the Creative Supporter's usual view that content drives the meaning. Through these kinds of interactions, the Creative Supporter now has a personal reference point of what the designer might think about a certain issue or problem-solving dilemma, and has grown toward more 3-D thinking.

Creative Skeptic

The Creative Skeptic is in the upper-left quadrant of our model; this individual is a Blue 3-D.

Creative Skeptics and Their Value Added   The Creative Skeptic is a Blue follower who will calmly and quietly sit back and then, with very complex thinking and logic, suddenly contradict the group, the perspective, or the ideas being put forth. However, Creative Skeptics always pose these contradictions for the right reasons; they never have a political or alternative agenda and will always be loyal to the cause and the organization. With a style that either jolts or alarms others through bold questions that challenge the line of thinking, the Creative Skeptic revels in his or her role and enjoys mellow time alone for thinking in his or her unconventional way.

The Creative Skeptic keeps people thinking about their assumptions. This questioning can stop dysfunctional groupthink from occurring. However, what makes the Creative Skeptic different from the typical devil's advocate or Kelley's alienated follower is the active but moderate positive energy the Creative Skeptic brings. Because everyone knows that the Skeptic's intentions are pure, followers and leaders alike perk their ears when the Skeptic opens his or her mouth. They know that even though the Skeptic doesn't say much, when he or she does, they're all likely to learn something new from his or her comments.

Recommendations: Creative Skeptic Plus In order to keep teammates understanding that the organization's best interests are at the root of the Creative Skeptic's questioning, we recommend the Skeptic try to remember and use the following suggestions:

• *Concentrate on ensuring that doubts are raised as questions rather than as blanket statements.* Creativity often flourishes within restraints. The Creative Skeptic provides restraints by identifying barriers. His or her questioning can spur new thought about overcoming those barriers. But the Skeptic will have to be sure to keep the questioning going, and not fall into a trap of just making critical statements instead.

For example, instead of saying, "I don't think that will work," a Creative Skeptic could say, "I'm not sure if I see how that will work because of the number of people involved in the program. Is there another way to have the same impact with two hundred people at the same time?"

• *Use additional channels or avenues for clarifying issues behind the initial prompting or questioning.*

One example of this is a recent action by a Creative Skeptic in a marketing meeting. In that meeting, she quietly raised the provocative question of why, if marketing was so important, didn't anyone tend to the company blog, which was live at the time? She sent out a detailed outline of the issue as another channel for communication. The outline addressed why the question was important to consider and why she needed the help of others to accomplish the objective. She raised a difficult question and communicated it in different ways. Her approach strengthened the creative base of the organization in that others are now considering what to add to the blog and how they can integrate things that are currently posted on it into their current client jobs.

• *Use opportunities to articulate positive feelings for and commitment to others and the organization as a whole.*

Because the Creative Skeptic is always raising questions that are seemingly out of nowhere, it is important for the Skeptic to reaffirm at every chance possible that the health of the organization and its members is the primary goal of utmost importance. In doing so, the Skeptic will create a backdrop of goodwill for the questions, which will lessen the potential for feelings that the Skeptic is just out to be critical of others.

Recommendations: Creative Skeptic Delta Should the Creative Skeptic want to stretch into the role of a Creative Catalyst, the change of energy from Blue to Red will be the focus for movement.

• *Make a concerted effort to be more Red while at work.*

Recall that Reds have energy and enthusiasm, and show emotions—and do it in such a way that others can "catch" that positive energy. Although the Skeptic may not be the natural cheerleader that some Creative Supporters are, he or she can try to bring Red energy to the group through purposefully bringing a large smile, some music, or even just an encouraging phrase to the group. Another way to be more Red is to try to have fun at work and involve others in that fun.[10] Call people into the hallway to toss a ball. Drop off a funny comic at someone's desk. Leave a mystery riddle or clue posted to the wall in the hallway. By doing these kinds of playful things at work, the Skeptic will be viewed as more of a Catalyst by others. In fact, our data suggest that having fun at work is a key component of whether or not others in your workplace consider you a Creative Catalyst.[11]

- *Mentor others and teach them to think innovatively.* Because of their quieter nature, Creative Skeptics, in our experience, do best with one-on-one official mentoring relationships to start movement in this area. Through several of these one-on-one relationships, the Skeptic can serve as a Catalyst for many in the organization.

- *Consider personal identity (the way one sees oneself) and think about recrafting it.* Our identities are created through experiences over time, and drive our future behavior.

Recent research based on our data suggests that a creative personal identity, or feeling that one's creativity is an important part of who one is, is a very powerful correlate to one's creativity at work.[12] Our latest work also suggests that this holds for being a Creative Catalyst—if a person feels that helping others be more creative is an important part of who he or she is, that individual actually behaves as a Creative Catalyst.[13] For the Creative Skeptic, this suggests that through such actions as mentoring others for creativity, he or she can create a Creative Catalyst personal identity—which will then lead to more Catalyst behaviors.

Creative Static

The Creative Static is in the bottom-left quadrant of our model; this individual is a Blue 1-D.

Creative Statics and Their Value Added   Like your television set when the cable is out, the Creative Static creates energy without any new content. However, even though the energy that the Creative Static brings is low voltage, the similarities to the cable's being out end there. The Creative Static's cool Blue style, combined with his or her one-dimensional thinking, preference for structure, and need for clear processes, serves to foster creativity in the organization by calming the abundance of emotional and intellectual energy in the creative organization. Like a quiet rock in a stormy sea, this person won't mind completing the details of projects once the discovery-based people are finished with the great idea. The systematic 1-D processing of this person is a valued resource for the creative organization in that through the questions the Static raises in the effort to acquire more context, others are led to more creative thoughts themselves. Those questions, while gathering background information and context for the Static, can help the more integrative thinkers think through their ideas and arrive at more creative solutions.

Recommendation: Creative Static Plus   The Creative Static follower needs to recognize his or her value to the organization and make sure that he or she is leveraging that value for the organization on a day-to-day basis. Our recommendations for effectively leveraging this quiet, cool way of thinking about things in a very structured, one-dimensional fashion involve promoting the value added of the Static's style.

• *Make a conscious effort to ensure that the style isn't a blockade—openly communicate and verbalize to the team how a Creative Static operates and how he or she can add value.*

One Creative Static we know goes out of his way to talk to his team about his style and preferences on a very open and regular basis. He listens, smiles, then reminds people that he's the quiet one and that he needs to go away and think. Just those few words make others understand what is going on with him, appreciate his thinking, and look forward to his input. If he didn't verbalize that, hard feelings and resentment could arise, as others might think that his silence and walking away were indicators of poor collaboration or a bad attitude.

• *Ask for more context and background information when others present problems or questions and expect an answer.* Those questions help not only the Static but also the whole creative process in an organization.

Because of their processing style and preference for taking time in making decisions, Creative Statics need more context in order to feel comfortable responding to questions. Through asking questions that generate greater details about the nature of the problem, Creative Statics can get that context. They should never feel bad about asking so many questions, for that questioning, clarification, and context-seeking process can help others in the organization be more creative by modeling a process for them to use in structuring their own thinking.

Recommendation: Creative Static Delta   Should movement or stretch be desired, the Creative Static has the opportunity to move toward Supporter, toward

Skeptic, or toward a mix of both. Moving either up or over are both very plausible scenarios for the Creative Static. Should the Static want to move toward either direction, we recommend the following:

- *Access passions and transfer them to work.* By considering something one is passionate about outside of work and bringing that passion into work, the Static can move in both directions. Energy levels can heat up when a person is sharing something he or she is passionate about, thereby adding some Red to the Blue of the Static. New, more 3-D ideas can also result from connecting one's passions to work.

For example, the Creative Static discussed previously loves to host parties and social functions. He brings this passion to work by volunteering to host in-house luncheons for clients who are visiting his organization. His energy level is raised for weeks before the event through this sprinkling of his passion into his role at work. He becomes a Creative Supporter for the office by voicing his excitement and enthusiasm. That energy is contagious. He also moves toward Catalyst by sharing his processes for organizing the luncheon and helping others think about how they can use those processes in other projects.

By bringing a passion to work, the Creative Static can also move toward more 3-D thinking. He or she can practice what is called cross-application, which involves taking an aspect of the activity he or she is passionate about and purposefully considering how it can be applied to a work-related problem or situation. Our data suggest that this technique of cross-application is strongly related to creativity at work.[14] The Creative Static, with his or her love for structure and clear processes, should welcome this concrete mechanism for stretching upwards toward more multidimensional thinking.

Figure 21.2 captures our recommendations for all four of these effective followers for creativity in organizations.

EFFECTIVE FOLLOWERSHIP FOR CREATIVITY AND INNOVATION IN ORGANIZATIONS: CONCLUDING THOUGHTS

One primary goal of this chapter is that our detailed descriptions and examples will help followers identify themselves and see how they facilitate creativity in their organization. Another hope is that after reading this chapter they will be

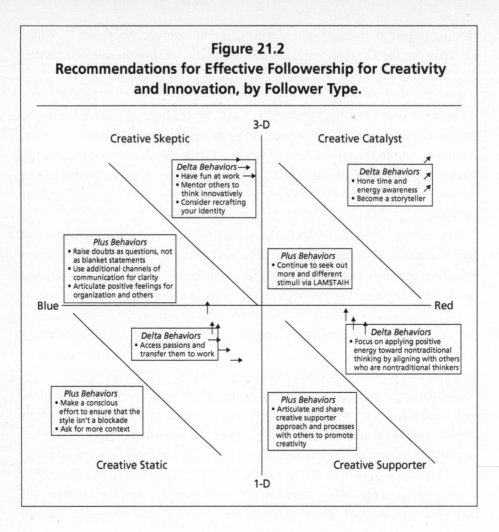

Figure 21.2
Recommendations for Effective Followership for Creativity and Innovation, by Follower Type.

Creative Skeptic | 3-D | Creative Catalyst

Delta Behaviors →
• Have fun at work
• Mentor others to think innovatively
• Consider recrafting your identity

Delta Behaviors
• Hone time and energy awareness
• Become a storyteller

Plus Behaviors
• Raise doubts as questions, not as blanket statements
• Use additional channels of communication for clarity
• Articulate positive feelings for organization and others

Plus Behaviors
• Continue to seek out more and different stimuli via LAMSTAIH

Blue — Red

Delta Behaviors
• Access passions and transfer them to work

Delta Behaviors
• Focus on applying positive energy toward nontraditional thinking by aligning with others who are nontraditional thinkers

Plus Behaviors
• Make a conscious effort to ensure that the style isn't a blockade
• Ask for more context

Plus Behaviors
• Articulate and share creative supporter approach and processes with others to promote creativity

Creative Static | 1-D | Creative Supporter

able to identify the roles of others and celebrate their value added. It takes courage to recognize and celebrate others for their contribution to organizational creativity and innovation. It is yet another responsibility to be added to Ira Chaleff's list of responsibilities followers need to have courage to take.[15] In addition to recognizing others for their value to the creative mission of the organization, our recommendations will, we hope, help give all four types of effective followers the tools and courage to enhance *their* current abilities to facilitate creativity and innovation throughout their organization.

Creativity and innovation in organizations require the recognition and valuing of followership. Our hope is that with this collaborative effort, the world filled with "leader envy" will open its eyes to the beauty of followers and recognize how they, through their marriage with their leaders, each other, and the organization, are truly the driving force for creativity and innovation in organizations.

Conformist, Resistant, and Disguised Selves

A Post-Structuralist Approach to Identity and Workplace Followership

David Collinson

This chapter seeks to contribute to the emerging interest in followership by exploring the construction of follower identities in the workplace from a post-structuralist perspective. Reviewing the literature on followership and identity, the chapter argues that followers are frequently more knowledgeable and oppositional than has often been acknowledged either by the vast majority of studies that focus on leaders or even by the growing number that examine followers. It considers a wider repertoire of follower selves and practices, exploring, in particular, the workplace enactment of conformist, resistant, and disguised identities. The chapter concludes that studies of leadership need to develop deeper understandings of follower and leader identities and of the complex ways that these selves may interact in dialectical ways within asymmetrical organizational processes.

FOLLOWERSHIP AND FOLLOWER IDENTITY

Critiques of leadership romanticism have been particularly influential in developing the growing interest in followership. As early critics of overly heroic views that exaggerate the impact of leaders on organizational performance, Meindl, Ehrlich, and Dukerich suggested that leadership romanticism provides a simplified way of understanding important but causally ambiguous organizational processes.[1] Arguing that leaders' contribution to a collective enterprise is inevitably somewhat constrained and closely tied to external factors outside a leader's control, such as those affecting whole industries, the authors concluded that the continuing "infatuation" with leadership could be used to learn something about followers' motivations. Meindl later developed a "follower-centric" perspective in which he recommended that researchers should no longer be concerned *at all* with leaders.[2] Rather, we should concentrate exclusively on followers' (romanticized) attributions of (charismatic) leaders and their views of themselves as followers, primarily for what they reveal about their own thought systems.[3]

Partly as a result of Meindl's ideas, there is now a growing focus on followership. An increasing number of writers argue that "exemplary," "courageous," and "star" followers are a precondition for high-performing organizations.[4] These writers see effective followership as particularly important in the contemporary context of greater teamworking, "empowered" knowledge workers, and distributed leadership.[5] This reflects the post-heroic view that leadership in organizations can occur at various hierarchical levels and is best understood as a social, collaborative, and interdependent process.

Just as the importance of followership is increasingly being recognized, there is also growing interest in the role of followers' social identity within leadership dynamics. Transformational studies, in particular, suggest that leaders need to identify, satisfy, and even change followers' values and goals.[6] In their self-concept–based theory of charismatic leadership, Shamir, House, and Arthur argue that by engaging followers' identity, charismatic leaders can profoundly transform subordinates' commitment so that they perform above and beyond the call of duty.[7] These authors contend that people are motivated by concerns to express themselves, enhance self-esteem, and retain a sense of self-consistency over time. They suggest that charismatic leaders can "validate" followers' identities by, for example, acting as role models, articulating a vision, and encouraging followers' psychological identification and value internalization.

Similarly, in their follower-centered perspective on leadership, Lord and Brown define leadership as a social process through which leaders can change the way followers envision themselves.[8] They view identities as self-categorizations based on similarities and differences from others (personal identities) and those based on group membership (social identities). For them, the self guides perception and behavior and gives meaning to memory. The authors recommend that leaders influence followers by shifting the salience of different elements of subordinates' identities or by creating new aspects of their self-concept. Leaders should link motivation and reward to followers' identities, "activating" the appropriate self rather than directly stressing specific goals. Such self-relevant linkages will be more powerful motivators because they engage a number of affective, cognitive, and behavioral processes that are not triggered by externally imposed goals.

Both Shamir, House, and Arthur and Lord and Brown highlight the importance of followers' identity for understanding leadership. Yet they seem to take for granted that charismatic leaders can and do shape and manipulate followers' identities and that a close and special relationship exists between leaders and followers. They leave no analytical space for the possibility that followers might be critical of leaders and their frequent distance from followers. These writers also acknowledge that their ideas on follower identity are based on theoretical propositions that have not been tested empirically. As the next section now elaborates, post-structuralist perspectives treat followers as frequently more knowledgeable and oppositional than is typically acknowledged in studies of leadership and followership. The following arguments also draw on empirical research that focuses on the practices and identities of followers who have direct experience of leadership practices within specific organizations.[9]

A POST-STRUCTURALIST APPROACH TO FOLLOWERSHIP

Post-structuralists concentrate on the key interrelated issues of power and identity in organizations. They argue that relations between leaders and followers are typically characterized by asymmetrical power relations and deeply embedded, historically specific control practices. Writers observe that leaders' hierarchical power enables them to define situations in ways that suit their purposes, provide rewards, apply sanctions, gain access to expertise, and secure followers' consent. Accordingly, a post-structuralist interpretation of leadership romanticism would suggest that exaggerated expectations about leaders' impact are evident not only in followers' perceptions but also in the structures of organizational power and in the disproportionate material and symbolic rewards leaders receive. This perspective would view leadership romanticism as a deeply embedded feature of organizational hierarchies.

Influenced by Foucault's ideas, post-structuralists examine the ways that specific "power/knowledge" regimes are inscribed on subjectivities.[10] Foucault explored the "disciplinary power" of surveillance that produces detailed information about individuals, rendering them visible, calculable, and self-disciplining selves. He argued that by shaping identity formation, power is enabling and productive as well as subordinating.[11] One implication of Foucault's post-structuralist ideas is that leaders can exercise power by measuring, evaluating, and rewarding followers' performance. Although identity has often been viewed as a singular, unitary, and coherent entity, post-structuralists emphasize its multiple, fluid, shifting, fragmented, contradictory, and nonrational character.[12] Rather than viewing the self as an objectifiable, cognitive essence, post-structuralists argue that identity processes are fundamentally open, ambiguous, and always in a state of flux and reconstruction.

They also highlight the numerous insecurities that can surround identities, particularly those reinforced by workplace processes. Such insecurities can be primarily material (for example, job loss) or symbolic (for example, career progress), but they will typically embody elements of both. Within many organizations, the concentration of power, the status inequalities, and the disposable nature of employment can intensify followers' material and symbolic insecurities. Historically, and especially in Western societies, there has also been a broad shift in social values from ascription (particularly in feudal societies) to achievement (in meritocratic societies). Although this has facilitated greater freedom and choice ("You can be who you want to be"), it has also led to more precarious, isolated, and insecure identities ("Who am I?"). No longer fixed at birth (by, for example, religion or gender), identity now has to be recursively earned and achieved. Sennett and Cobb describe how meritocratic ideals within a highly unequal society can produce in American manual workers a fundamental "doubt about the self" and a preoccupation with reconstructing a dignified identity in conditions of its continual erosion.[13] Corporate restructuring (such as the recent moves toward more flexible, temporary, and outsourced employment) can further reinforce employee insecurities.

Insecurities about identity can also be exacerbated by the inherent ambiguities of subjectivity itself. Post-structuralists hold that human subjectivity is characterized by a dual experience of self, as both subject (we function as active agents in the world) and object (we reflect back on ourselves and also on the way we believe significant others see us). At the heart of identity construction, therefore, is an inescapable ambiguity of being *both* subject *and* object. Attempts to overcome or deny this subject-object ambiguity by trying to define and secure an entirely coherent and unitary self as either subject (for example, leader) or object (for example, follower) may further reinforce, rather than resolve, the very insecurities that identity strategies are intended to overcome.[14] The search to secure a coherent identity can be especially contradictory given that we rarely, if ever, experience a singular or unitary self. Simultaneously occupying many subjective positions and allegiances, human beings typically construct identities from various diverse aspects of their lives (for example, ethnicity, religion, family, gender, age, occupation, nationality, sexuality, and political beliefs). Although elements of these multiple, coexisting identities may overlap and be mutually reinforcing, in certain circumstances they can also be in tension and even be incompatible.

Building on these post-structuralist ideas about power and identity, the following sections now discuss a number of follower selves that have recurred within my empirical research. In what follows, conformist, resistant, and disguised identities and practices are explored within their asymmetrical organizational conditions and consequences. Although they are by no means exhaustive of possible follower subjectivities, these selves illustrate some of the different follower identities that can be enacted within organizations. Focusing on employees who have direct experience of leadership practices within particular organizations, the following examples also draw on my qualitative empirical research findings over the past thirty years in various U.K. sectors, ranging from manufacturing and financial services to printing, education, and the North Sea oil industry, addressing such topics as leadership, shop-floor culture, gender and masculinity, workplace safety, and managerial careers.

CONFORMIST SELVES

A number of writers have critically examined followers' frequent preference for the apparent comfort and security of conformity (particularly in relation to charismatic leaders). They have described followers' conformist tendencies and their apparent preference to be led by (charismatic) leaders, to whom they attribute exceptional qualities through such processes as transference (see Maccoby in this volume), fantasy,[15] idealization,[16] seduction,[17] and reification.[18] While Milgram's experiments highlighted people's widespread willingness to obey authority,[19] Fromm pointed to "the fear of freedom," whereby individuals try to shelter in the perceived security of being told what to do and what to think, believing that this is a less threatening and more comfortable alternative to the responsibility of making decisions for themselves.[20]

Shamir outlines five main follower motivations, all of which can be viewed as examples of conformist selves.[21] "Position-based" followers respect leaders' formal position in a social institution. "Calculated followers" believe that following will help them achieve their goals. "Safety-based" followers hope that leaders will satisfy their needs for security. "Meaning-based" followers fear chaos and look to leaders to provide order and meaning. Finally, "identity-based" followers seek to enhance their own self-esteem by identifying with leaders they perceive as powerful and attractive. A post-structuralist interpretation would suggest that, far from being separated off as a discrete follower concern, identity-based motivations are implicated in all five of these categories.

Foucault pointed to the way that workplace surveillance systems frequently encourage conformity by producing disciplined selves. Subsequent researchers have highlighted the disciplinary effects of such organizational processes as corporate culture, performance assessment, and new technologies. Central to the production of organizational discipline is the regulation of identity, which is now a key feature of organizational control in "post-bureaucratic" organizations.[22] Post-structuralist perspectives suggest that conforming individuals tend to be preoccupied with securing themselves as valued objects in the eyes of those in authority. This approach illustrates how the behavior of conformist selves can take many different forms, from total deference to calculated careerism, reflecting different degrees of follower commitment to the organization and its leadership.

Equally, post-structuralists argue that when examining the construction of workplace identities, it is important to consider their (unintended) consequences. This is especially the case with regard to the potentially harmful effects of unquestioning conformity. The Nazi extermination of six million Jews, and the explanation from many of those involved that they were just "obeying orders," are chilling reminders of the potential dangers of (follower) conformity. The more recent example of Enron illustrates how leaders in contemporary organizations can suppress dissent and promote conformity, with disastrous consequences for the organization, its employees, and the wider community.[23] As Lipman-Blumen has recently argued, follower conformity can even be a condition and consequence of "toxic" leadership.[24] Desperate to escape existential anxieties (about mortality and meaning) and situational fears (about an uncertain and disorderly world) and to satisfy psychological needs (for security and protection), followers may not only tolerate but also even prefer dysfunctional leaders who engage in destructive and abusive practices, such as coercion, aggression, and narcissism.

Those who aspire to career progress in organizations are especially likely to construct conformist selves. Yet their excessive careerism and intense concern to maintain a positive image of self in the eyes of leaders may have unintended, counterproductive effects, sometimes reinforcing the material and symbolic insecurities they were seeking to overcome through hierarchical advance. Alongside the remuneration, status, and perks of more senior positions, highly ambitious followers can feel compelled to work longer hours, meet tight deadlines, travel extensively, and be geographically mobile at the behest of the company. This in turn may increase stress levels, be incompatible with domestic responsibilities, and even damage personal relationships. Similarly, for the organization, followers' self-promoting strategies can significantly distort communication and undermine the information base on which strategic decisions are made.

By specifying codified blueprints and the "essential" qualities of exemplary followers (for example, integrity, honesty, and credibility), studies of followership sometimes appear to promote and prescribe such conformist follower selves. Clearly, the production of conformist, disciplined selves is one possible and indeed prevalent outcome of contemporary leadership dynamics. Yet is this an inevitable consequence of leadership processes? Post-structuralist writers suggest that other follower identities also often characterize organizational dynamics.

RESISTANT SELVES

Post-structuralist studies highlight the neglected importance of resistant selves in the workplace. Viewing control and resistance as discursive and contested, post-structuralists treat such practices as mutually reinforcing and simultaneously linked, often in contradictory ways. They suggest that particular forms of control often produce oppositional practices, such as strikes, "working to rule," output restriction, whistleblowing, and sabotage.[25] In exceptional cases, subordinates may even (seek to) depose leaders. Even in the disciplinary context of the military, there is a long history of rebellion, mutiny, and spontaneous acts of dissent.[26]

Informed by Foucault's assertion that power invariably produces resistance, especially in the guise of micro acts of local defiance, post-structuralists point to the construction and protection of self as an important motivator for follower resistance.[27] They hold that workplace resistance is not only a primary means through which employees may express discontent but also is a way for followers to construct alternative, more positive identities to those conferred by the organization. Post-structuralists also suggest that followers' resistance can take multiple forms, be shaped by various motives, and be focused on diverse targets. Although employee oppositional selves may be enacted toward customers, those working outside organizations can also express dissent. NGOs like Friends of the Earth and Greenpeace have successfully campaigned to change corporate policies.

Although not all followers' dissent is aimed specifically at leaders, many studies suggest that their resistance does frequently articulate opposition to leaders and the change programs they seek to instigate. This is especially the case when followers perceive leaders to be "out of touch" with organizational realities or when they detect discrepancies between leaders' policies and practices. In such situations, followers can become increasingly cynical. Fleming's research in an Australian call center found that in the face of a corporate culture that treated workers like children, cynicism enabled employees to construct a new, opposing identity.[28] Employees in a U.S. Subaru Isuzu plant detected inconsistencies between the company's teamworking ideal and work intensification. Consequently they refused to participate in corporate rituals, sent highly critical anonymous letters to the company, and used humor to make light of the company's teamworking and continuous improvement philosophies.[29]

In my own research, follower resistance has routinely emerged and has often been aimed specifically at leaders (broadly defined). Although followers have frequently complained about leaders being "distant," their views of leaders have often been quite different from those leaders hold of themselves.[30] Followers have expressed considerable frustration that their voice is ignored, that they have suggestions on how to improve workplace processes but that those in senior positions will not listen to their proposals. In such cases, followers can start to believe that it is impossible to achieve positive change and consequently may psychologically withdraw from the organization.

Research at a U.K. truck manufacturer demonstrated that a corporate culture campaign introduced by the new U.S. senior management team to establish trust with the workforce had precisely the opposite effect.[31] Shop-floor workers dismissed senior management's definition of the company as a team. Fueled by their perceptions of leaders' distance, leaders' disregard for their own views, and their own sense of job insecurity, workers resisted by "distancing" themselves, restricting output and effort, and treating work purely as a means of economic compensation. By psychologically distancing themselves from the organization, followers tended to divide their identity between the "indifferent me at work" and the "real me outside." They built a psychological wall between "public" and "private" selves, privileging the latter and de-emphasizing the former. The company's leaders remained unaware of how their strategies produced contrary effects on the shop floor.

Feminist post-structuralist studies reveal that followers' oppositional selves can also take gendered forms.[32] They demonstrate, for example, how male-dominated shop-floor countercultures are frequently characterized by highly masculine breadwinner identities, aggressive and profane forms of humor, ridicule and sarcasm, and the elevation of "practical," manual work as a confirmation of working-class manhood and opposition to management.[33] Research on female-dominated shop floors and offices suggests that women workers often engage in similarly aggressive, joking, and sexualized cultures of resistance. Women's countercultures are typically shaped by everyday concerns about feminine identity.

Chaleff is one of the few writers on followership to consider the possibility of followers' more oppositional identity. Observing that honest feedback from followers to leaders is frequently absent in organizations, he suggests that close followers need to be more courageous, to voice constructive criticism, particularly if they believe the leader is not acting in the best interests of the company.[34] Chaleff recommends that courageous followers should challenge leaders' views and decisions (while also displaying integrity, responsibility, and service).

Chaleff's focus on courageous followership mirrors Grint's arguments about the potentially positive consequences of "constructive dissent."[35] It also has some similarities with my own examination of "resistance through persistence."[36] Here followers sought to render leaders' decisions more visible through persistent demands for greater information, accountability, and openness. Although this strategy was relatively effective in achieving change, it was also rather uncommon. "Resistance through distance" was much more prevalent. Restricting output, effort, knowledge, and communication, workers constructed countercultural identities in opposition to leaders.

Chaleff draws on Hirschman, who argues that in responding to organizational decline, individuals are likely either to resign from (exit) or to try to change (voice) products or processes they find objectionable.[37] However, a post-structuralist approach would caution against both underestimating the costs and overestimating the possibilities of both voice and exit for employed followers. Although Hirschman assumes that consumer and employee behavior are very similar, it is usually easier to stop buying a product than it is to resign one's job. The growing literature on whistleblowing suggests that followers who express their concerns need to be aware that their actions might damage their careers.[38] Those in senior positions frequently dismiss whistleblowing as disloyalty and as the action of "losers." Accordingly, in many cases followers may prefer to express discontent in ways that protect their continued employment within the organization.

DISGUISED SELVES

For many employees, the possibility of being sanctioned for expressing dissent can reinforce their material (salary) and symbolic (self-respect) insecurities, significantly curbing their willingness to engage in overt resistance. As Heifetz and Laurie observe, "whistleblowers, creative deviants and other such original voices routinely get smashed and silenced in organizational life."[39] Although followers might be highly critical of leaders' practices, they may decide to censor their views and camouflage their actions. Such disguised dissent might be enacted through, for example, absenteeism, foot dragging, disengagement, and irony and satire. Even by doing nothing, followers can undermine leaders' change initiatives.

My research suggests that disguised selves are particularly likely to occur where surveillance has become increasingly pervasive and where hierarchical control is being reconfigured through performance targets. Audit cultures construct identity, providing a quantified measure of a calculable and visible self that can be graded and compared. Under the gaze of authority, individuals are increasingly aware of themselves as visible objects, and, as a consequence of their heightened self-consciousness, they can become increasingly skilled manipulators of self and information. As skilled choreographers, followers learn over time to be more strategic in disguising their response to "the gaze." This dramaturgical notion of self applies Goffman's ideas of impression management to surveillance processes.[40] Goffman argued that interaction is like an information game in which individuals strategically disclose, exaggerate, or deliberately downplay information.

Research on North Sea oil installations found that, despite extensive leadership commitment to safety, many offshore workers either did not report accidents and "near misses" or sought to downplay the seriousness of particular incidents.[41] While company leaders talked proudly about the organization's "learning culture," offshore workers complained about a "blame culture" on the platforms. Believing that disclosure of accident-related information would have a detrimental impact on their appraisal and consequently on their pay and employment security, many offshore workers felt compelled to conceal or downplay information about accidents, injuries, and near misses. Precisely because such practices constituted a firing offense, these workers also disguised their underreporting. When a report based on these findings was presented to the company's senior managers, they expressed considerable surprise. Their reaction illustrates how corporate leaders can become detached from followers and divorced from the realities of production.

Although digital technologies can be used to intensify surveillance, virtual audiences may also provide a new stage for disguised performances. By reconfiguring time and space, technologies like e-mail and cell phones can facilitate dramaturgical claims by leaders and followers about where they are, what they are doing, and even who they are. In addition, online and e-mail protocol raises further questions about the disguised nature of communication. This is not just in relation to the content of messages, but also regards who is being e-mailed, who is copied in, and who is excluded. Equally, users may strategically self-censor their online practices, aware that messages can be monitored, recorded, and stored. Such virtual disguised selves raise important questions for future research on followership (and leadership).

Although the leadership literature tends to assume that it is primarily leaders who use impression management, a post-structuralist approach highlights the importance of followers' disguised selves, especially in the context of intensified material and symbolic insecurities. Such disguised and dramaturgical selves can take primarily conformist (for example, telling leaders what they want to hear[42]) or more oppositional forms (for example, knowledge and output restriction). They may also embody elements of both conformity and resistance, for as Kondo argues, people often "consent, cope, and resist at different levels of consciousness at a single point in time."[43] In turn, this more complicated conception of agency warns against the romanticism of followership.

ROMANTICIZING FOLLOWERSHIP?

This chapter began by discussing critiques of leadership romanticism. Post-structuralists develop this argument by questioning the tendency to romanticize followership and by highlighting some of the unintended and contradictory effects of followers' oppositional selves. Kondo describes how the countercultures of Japanese shop-floor workers that frequently expose managerial inconsistencies can themselves be caught up in contradictions and ironies, simultaneously legitimizing as they challenge dominant organizational and gendered discourses.[44] Although Japanese workers criticized management and questioned the dominant notion of the company as family, they simultaneously took pride in belonging to the organization. Accordingly, Kondo argues that there is no such thing as an entirely "authentic" or "pristine space of resistance" or of a singular identity such as a "true resister" or "class warrior." In her view, people are best understood as multiple selves, whose lives are shot through with contradictions and creative tensions.

Similarly, Meyerson's research on "tempered radicals" shows how senior managers can attempt to effect (gender) change while working within the organization.[45] Tempered radicals are frequently women in senior positions who are committed to their organization, but also to a feminist ideology that is fundamentally at odds with the dominant workplace culture. Seeking to maintain a delicate balance between pursuing change while avoiding marginalization, tempered radicals have to cope with various tensions (such as co-optation, false consciousness, burnout, and ineffectiveness) and contradictions between potentially opposing "personal" and "professional" identities. Seeking to juggle these conflicting loyalties and to achieve piecemeal change, tempered radicals pay a high price, remaining in a heightened state of ambivalence that frequently produces frustration, emotional strain, and self-doubt.

Other feminist studies also highlight the unintended and paradoxical effects of some forms of resistance. They reveal, for example, how male-dominated resistance can reproduce women's subordination. Cockburn examined the exclusionary labor market practices of the National Graphical Association (NGA) and the deep-seated masculine culture of the U.K. printing industry.[46] She demonstrated how the NGA, as a male-dominated craft union, historically sustained its members' "breadwinner wages" by resisting women's entry into printing. Willis describes how working-class "lads" creatively construct a counterculture that celebrates masculinity and the so-called freedom and independence of manual work.[47] Yet this counterculture also facilitated the lads' smooth transition into precisely the kind of shop-floor work that then subordinated them, possibly for the rest of their working lives. Similarly, members of shop-floor countercultures who are highly suspicious and critical of managerial motives and practices can simultaneously express a deep-seated commitment to "management's right to manage."[48] By distancing themselves from organizational decision making, they tend to legitimize and reinforce managerial prerogative and their own subordination.

These studies describe how followers' oppositional selves can symbolically invert dominant values and meanings, but in ways that sometimes cut across emancipatory agendas and unintentionally perpetuate the status quo. Hence, apparently resistant selves may actually reinforce the conditions that sustain followers' subordination. In particular, these studies indicate that when resistance practices are primarily designed to secure a specific notion of self, they often seem to generate unintended outcomes, reproducing the very insecurities—both material (jobs, salaries, wages, and so on) and symbolic (identity, career progress, reputation, and so on)—they were intended to overcome. This is particularly so if certain ("nonrational") emotions, such as anger and aggression, begin to dominate resistance practices. These post-structuralist arguments about followers' identity-seeking strategies highlight the fluid, multiple, and fragmented nature of identity construction as well as its underlying insecurities and narcissistic tendencies. Their focus on the paradoxical, unintended, and potentially contradictory effects of followers' selves caution against any tendency to romanticize followership.

CONCLUSION

This chapter has explored followership and follower identity from a post-structuralist perspective. In particular, it has questioned assumptions that leaders are able effectively to shape followers' identities. The persistence of follower resistance illustrates that leaders cannot always control followers' identities. Various studies reveal that followers' practices might produce outcomes that leaders may not anticipate, be aware of, or indeed even understand. Equally, followers might also disguise their dissent for fear of the sanctions that resistance can produce. Self-censorship should not necessarily be confused with commitment or consent. In certain circumstances, even silence might be an expression of a resistant self.

A post-structuralist approach also warns against replacing the romanticism of leadership with the romanticism of followership. It suggests that rather than being a fixed and objective essence, identity is much more open, negotiable, and ambiguous. Attempts to construct secure and coherent identities may produce contradictory effects, actually reinforcing the very insecurities they are intended to overcome. Illustrating how oppositional discourses might become a means of self-romanticism or heroic self-aggrandizement, post-structuralist studies highlight the potentially disciplinary outcomes of followers' search to secure identities. When employees resist primarily as a means of constructing identity or of aggrandizing self, their oppositional practices may be less effective in generating positive organizational change.

Post-structuralist perspectives emphasize the potential impact of greater follower engagement within organizational processes. They suggest that followers' increased involvement could enhance the productive potential of organizations through, for example, improved communication and the flow of practical solutions to organizational problems. They also suggest that for followers to develop such committed and innovative selves, they would need to feel more recognized and empowered (rather than insecure and undervalued). Equally, if leaders are to cultivate a deeper understanding of followers and their identities, they may need to let go of their own self-preoccupations.[49] As Collins suggests, "level 5 leaders," who are relatively humble and thus less concerned with self, might be more effective.[50] Recent studies suggest that some leaders act in highly narcissistic ways and that current leadership development programs frequently encourage such self-preoccupations.[51]

In sum, post-structuralist perspectives argue that the identities of followers and leaders are frequently a condition and consequence of one another. Whereas Meindl proposed that we should concentrate exclusively on followers, a post-structuralist analysis views the identities and practices of followers and leaders as inextricably linked, mutually reinforcing, and shifting within specific contexts. The current interest in distributed leadership and exemplary followership suggests that the traditional dichotomous identities of leader and follower are increasingly ambiguous and blurred. This challenge to dualistic thinking raises fundamental questions for the future of leadership, both in theory and practice. Exploring how these subjectivities are negotiated in practice within complex organizational power relations is likely to raise a number of currently underexplored issues about what it may mean to be a follower and a leader within contemporary and future organizations.

The Rise of Authentic Followership

Bruce J. Avolio and Rebecca J. Reichard

Leadership is not defined by the exercise of power but by the capacity to increase the sense of power among those led. The most essential work of the leader is to create more leaders.

Mary Parker Follett

Time magazine recently chose an unusual person for Person of the Year. You! On the cover of the magazine, there is a mirror suggesting that "you" are looking at the Person of the Year chosen by *Time.* Why? As we have entered the age of digital democracy, each of "you" is an essential element in how communities, governments, schools, for-profit and not-for-profit organizations function. What implications might this have for the Great Man theory of leadership?

Over the last hundred years, the scientific study of leadership has been heavily influenced by a Western way of thinking or philosophy. As a result, leadership research has emphasized the individual, especially the leader, typically to the exclusion of followers and the context in which leaders and followers interact.[1] Perhaps, as a result, the majority of traditional leadership theories have primarily focused on characteristics of the leader, such as traits, behaviors, and styles, that make the leader more or less effective.[2] The follower has typically been included as an afterthought in most traditional leadership theories. Where the follower has been included, it is usually in terms of what the leader is "doing to" the follower, not the reverse.

When we sat down to write this chapter, we wondered what the field would look like if instead of adopting such a leader-centric emphasis, researchers had focused only on what constituted followers and follower development. For example, if one was implementing a leadership development program, would it be possible to conceive of the focus as being exclusively on followers, such that followers come to be better followers? Would we be able to impact the leader's leadership by totally focusing on the follower? Taking this to the extreme, would we have been better off having focused on developing the most capable followers over the last hundred years of work on leadership theory and practice, as opposed to the most capable leaders?

In recent years and perhaps in response to the complexities associated with globalization, leadership scholars have begun to acknowledge the other side of the leader-follower equation—the role of followers in the leadership dynamic. This focus is in line with suggestions made by Marion and Uhl-Bien, who criticized the field of leadership studies for its tendency to follow a more reductionist strategy, stating, "Leaders are one element of an interactive network that is far bigger than they."[3]

Research on what has been called leader-member exchange and transformational leadership began to emerge in the leadership literature in the mid-1980s with a shift in focus to include the follower in the leadership and follower dynamic. For example, transformational leaders were described by Burns as visionary, intellectually stimulating, highly moral, charismatic, and attentive to the needs of their followers.[4] Yet what made this theory unique was the focus that Burns and later Bass placed on how such leaders worked to transform their followers into leaders.[5]

Indeed, unlike any other prior leadership theory, transformational leadership theory was the first to define the success of leadership as being the development of followers into leaders. The early focus was still on what leaders did to the followers, but in this case, leaders were at least developing followers into leaders.

Work on transformational leadership has increasingly focused on the role of the follower in the leadership dynamic, including how the characteristics of the follower impact how transformational a leader behaves,[6] through to more recent work examining how the effectiveness of transformational leadership varies as a consequence of the orientation of the follower.[7] Attention in the leadership literature in the last few years has shifted even further from what the leader does to the follower, to what has been referred to as "shared" leadership. Here the source of leadership is distributed within the group and not necessarily owned by any one individual.[8]

The most recent shift toward followers is represented in the theory of authentic leadership development (ALD), which explicitly acknowledges leadership development as an interactive process among leaders, followers, and the context in which they find themselves embedded over time.[9] In fact, Gardner and his colleagues stated that "authentic followership is an integral component and consequence of authentic leadership development."[10] Authentic leaders are described as individuals who are acutely self-aware, transparent, ethical, and balanced in the way they gather information and data to make their decisions. In addition to this, authentic followers' focus may be more on "leading up" transparently or ethically.

Authentic followership develops from modeling by the authentic leader and likely vice versa, depending on the qualities and capabilities of the follower, which produces heightened levels of follower and leader self-awareness. This type of developmental engagement also produces higher levels of self-regulation and ultimately positive follower and leader development outcomes, such as heightened levels of trust, engagement, and well-being. Gardner and his colleagues stated the relationships between authentic leaders and followers are characterized by transparency, trust, and openness; guidance toward worthy objectives; and an emphasis on follower development.[11]

This shift in the way in which leadership has been defined from the earliest models of leadership through to ALD has pushed leadership away from being viewed as a compilation of individual traits and behaviors to a dynamic *interaction, activity,* or *process* through which leaders and followers create leadership and ultimately its development. Building on the most recent theory that has attempted to explain authentic or genuine leadership development, the current chapter examines how developing a sense of ownership, trust through vulnerability, and transparency contributes to enhancing follower potential as well as the leader-follower dynamic.

We have chosen to focus on these three core concepts because we feel that they may have the biggest impact on placing followers in an influential leadership role with peers and their leaders. For example, followers who assume ownership for their development would challenge their leader to make their development a priority. To motivate their leaders to do so, followers would have to be willing to make themselves vulnerable by challenging the leader when the leader doesn't live up to the followers' expectations for being developed.

At the same time, followers would need to place themselves in a position of vulnerability, by expressing transparently what they are able and not able to accomplish. Moreover, followers would be more vulnerable to the extent that their leader doesn't value development, but nevertheless followers challenge the leader to invest in their development. We take each of these core concepts and discuss them in more detail in the next sections, including how each contributes to the leadership dynamic.

PSYCHOLOGICAL OWNERSHIP

It was somewhat surprising to us that one does not find much emphasis in the leadership literature on building psychological ownership among leaders, or followers for that matter. You would think that a primary responsibility of leaders is to make those who work with them feel as though they *own* their process, product, and performance. More important, how the follower makes the leader feel a sense of ownership for facilitating the follower's development and performance has generally been ignored in the literature. There is almost no research linking different leadership orientations with building a sense of ownership in leaders or followers.

Previous trends are somewhat ironic in that we are coming to a point when there are many more "owners" needed as most organizations are penetrated at all levels from the outside. Because of the changing nature of how information gets disseminated and received in organizations across the globe, anyone can make a decision that could have a dramatic impact on an organization, and often does in conditions of crisis and dramatic change. For example, a woman working at home for a large insurance provider during her recovery from cancer decided on the day her offices were attacked in the World Trade Center to move all the files to a backup server, which avoided a catastrophic loss of data. This decision was made by a midlevel worker who did not necessarily have the "authority" to do so but who felt a sense of ownership to take action under these extreme conditions. Hence we argue that decisions must be owned at all levels of any dynamic organization, especially by individuals who ultimately want to be perceived as authentic leaders and followers.

We also find that most people coming into organizations today expect the first person they meet to be the "owner" of the solution they are seeking or require. Let us extend that position and suggest it might be better to think of everyone as part owners in the organization than to go down the road of considering "providers" and "internal customers" or, worse yet, "subordinates"! Why? Although customers have become a more vocal entity in organizations, the most active will always be someone who believes he or she is an owner. Yet according to a U.S. poll conducted by the Gallup Leadership Institute at the University of Nebraska in 2004, only 17 percent of followers indicated by agreeing or strongly agreeing that their leader "makes them feel like an owner." So we first explore what it means to be an owner or to take ownership in one's organization.

What Constitutes Psychological Ownership

Followers who endorse statements like "I sense this is my company" and "I feel a very high degree of personal ownership for this organization" are expressing their feelings of psychological ownership.[12] Psychological ownership has been defined as "the state in which individuals feel as though the target of ownership or a piece of that target is theirs."[13] Consequently, a follower may feel responsible for a particular operational target. Such ownership targets may include a large range of physical and nonphysical objects, from homes and cars, to ideas and work-related responsibilities, to customers and organizational units.

Being composed of four positive dimensions (belongingness, self-identity, accountability, and self-efficacy), psychological ownership exists to fulfill the following three basic human needs for both leaders and followers: (1) a need to have a place, (2) a need for self-identity, and (3) a need for efficacy.[14] As each of these capacities, or needs, is more satisfied by a given target, the follower's psychological ownership in that target would be expected to increase.

Developing a Sense of Place   First, the human need for a home or a place to dwell has been described over the years by social psychologists as a fundamental need that exceeds mere physical concerns.[15] The need to have a place is embedded in the belongingness dimensions of psychological ownership. *Belongingness* meets the basic human need for having a place. For example, Ardrey argued that people both take ownership of and also structure their lives around possessions in an attempt to create a sense of place.[16] Through attachment to an object, it becomes a "home" or place for the individual.[17] In the workplace, the need to belong may be fulfilled by one's job, work team, work unit, division, organization, or even industry.

Both leaders and followers can create a sense of belongingness. One way is to show how both are key contributors to the groups they belong to within an organization. A two-hundred-year-old example of how this has been done comes from the U.S. Military Academy at West Point. When cadets first arrive at West Point, they have no leadership responsibility. Their first year, they are developed to be authentic followers who can come to appreciate the importance of leading others and belonging to this venerable institution. Over time, as they learn the values and traditions of the academy, they are given increasing responsibility and ownership over tasks and fellow cadets. The ultimate goal of the academy is to develop leaders of character, who have a sense of belonging, and to do so the follower must come to understand what it means to be a follower and leader of character.

Developing a Sense of Self   The basic human need for creating a self-identity can be met by the psychological ownership dimensions of *self-identity* and *accountability*. First, researchers have noted that groups of people and possessions often act as symbols through which followers identify themselves.[18] In the previous example, cadets over time strongly identify with being part of the select group of individuals who can say they are a West Point graduate.

Targets of ownership can be reinforced by both leaders and followers in becoming part of a follower's personal identity and something that a follower works hard to improve.[19] Specifically, it has been noted that individuals establish, maintain, reproduce, and transform their personal identity through interacting with possessions.[20] Such ownership is highly relevant in organizations where followers need to identify with their work and to see the scope of their responsibilities as being "owned" by them. Such targets become part of the leader's and follower's identity by providing a foundation on which they can each identify their uniqueness relative to others. This is a situation where one would expect the leader to reinforce such ownership.

A group of followers working for the Veterans Administration (VA) hospital described how they serve soldiers who "sacrifice their tomorrows for our todays." These individuals see themselves as serving their nation in a profoundly important way in terms of how they facilitate the health care of veterans. Being owners requires that they provide the safest and most effective care to the nation's veterans, oftentimes challenging their leaders to do so.

Second, the psychological ownership dimension of *accountability* reflects a leader's or follower's need for a sense of self. People who experience higher feelings of psychological ownership expect not only to be able to call others to account for influences on their target of ownership but also to hold themselves accountable. Building on the VA example, health care professionals are increasingly being asked to step up and identify mistakes that are being made, potentially saving tens of thousands of lives. To do so, they have to be willing to make themselves vulnerable by admitting mistakes were made, oftentimes by powerful individuals in hospitals. This requires every follower and leader to embrace transparency in order to convey what he or she observed, a topic we will return to later in this chapter.

Developing a Sense of Efficacy   Finally, psychological ownership meets the basic human need for efficacy or having a sense of confidence. Freedom to control one's actions is a psychological component that results in feelings of efficacy and pleasure and may promote a sense of psychological ownership concerning a particular task, process, and procedure.[21] In practical terms, this efficacy view of psychological ownership is indicated by the following statement: "I need to do this task, *I can do it*, and I therefore own the responsibility for achieving success." An individual who displays such a high level of agency for doing a task will likely feel a greater sense of ownership. In his research, Bandura identified several strategies that leaders and followers can use for building self-efficacy, including experiencing success on increasingly more challenging tasks and observing similar others successfully performing a task.[22]

Benefits of Psychological Ownership

Psychological ownership of both tangible targets (for example, a window office) and intangible targets (for example, organizational reputation) has important emotional, attitudinal, and behavioral implications and effects.[23] When followers feel ownership in an organization, they tend to engage in positive behaviors driven by a sense of responsibility, including the realm of decision making. Because most organizational systems are moving toward higher levels of interdependence on a national and global basis,[24] decisions and processes must be owned at all levels of the organization for it to be optimally effective, adaptive, and sustainable.[25] Being an "owner" enables leaders and followers to make decisions as required, one hopes at the first point of contact. In some instances, every problem has to be owned by everyone who comes in contact with the problem until it is corrected.

When personal identification is integrated with an organizational target, feelings of ownership in that target may drive behaviors that go beyond the prescribed roles in one's job. Leaders and followers with a strong sense of attachment through feelings of psychological ownership would be more likely to be committed to the organization and have lower intentions to leave the organization. In addition, to the extent leaders and followers feel they own a particular task, the more likely they will feel empowered to do something to make sure the task is completed properly. In other words, those who experience feelings of psychological ownership will tend to feel enabled and empowered when it comes to targets of ownership, and, in conjunction with feelings of responsibility for the target, this will likely lead to higher levels of performance. Followers who come to fully identify with their work see their work as an extension of themselves. For example, someone who is in the hospitality industry could see themselves as being totally responsible for the experience that guests have in their facilities. This individual would do everything in his or her power to make sure the experience is exemplary and one that creates positive memories.

TRUST

Given that leadership is based on a *relationship* between a leader and a follower, trust is a key aspect of the leadership dynamic. Trust is a function of the leader's willingness to be viewed as vulnerable by followers. Oftentimes, perceived vulnerability is a result of the willingness of the leader or follower to self-disclose mistakes. Interestingly enough, only 26 percent of followers perceive their leader as being willing to admit when a mistake has been made, according to the 2004 Gallup Leadership Institute poll. We believe there is a need for today's organizational, political, and military leaders to build trust among followers by embracing the vulnerability that accompanies taking accountability for mistakes. What we mean here is that when leaders own their mistakes transparently, they build their followers' trust in their intentions. To the extent that authentic followers model their authentic leader's behavior, actions, and decisions, if leaders own mistakes, so will their followers. Through such a contagion of transparency, a trusting relationship and climate will develop.

Building Trust

The trust literature amply demonstrates that there are a variety of ways that trust can be developed between leaders and followers. Trust evolves in organizations based on positive interpersonal exchanges.[26] Follower trust is characterized by repeated interaction, identification with the group leader or other group members, and perceived interdependence.[27] Trust is a process of uncertainty reduction.[28] For example, leaders can increase follower trust through their initial and consistent behavior in both public and private interactions with the follower or the group to which he or she belongs. In the same vein, followers who step up and take on a challenge without being asked to do so, because they believe it was the right thing to do, would be expected to build trust with the leader. This might be referred to as transactional or condition-based trust.

Trust in the leader may be enhanced or developed when the leader is perceived as forgoing his or her own self-interest to benefit the followers.[29] Self-sacrifice on the part of the leader is a way that a leader signals followers of his or her deep commitments to a course of action, which can build trust in the leader.[30] The same would be true of followers who show the willingness to make sacrifices for the good of the group and organization. Good examples of this are the stories of firefighters who refuse to leave a burning building until all civilians are safely out. Such sacrifice has led to a tremendous level of trust in this profession.

Finally, a mutually trusting relationship can be built when both leader and follower freely self-disclose and express their vulnerability, which should result in a deeper sense of trust that is more relational than conditional. The key to trust building is being comfortable with allowing oneself to be vulnerable, whether one is a follower or leader.

Risk in Vulnerability

We also know that choosing to become vulnerable carries inherent risk for leaders and followers. By admitting mistakes and choosing to be vulnerable, the leader risks being taken advantage of by a follower; the same is true of the follower. Thus it is critical that leaders and followers develop the boundaries within which they will allow themselves to be vulnerable. By clearly specifying the boundaries, they can reduce some of the inherent risk associated with being more vulnerable. It is also important to keep in mind that a healthy, growing relationship is characterized by an expansion of such boundaries as trust deepens between both parties.

In sum, the leader-follower relationship is by its very nature an interdependent one that involves the willingness of the leader and follower to admit mistakes and be vulnerable and the willingness of each not to violate this trust. Having a stronger basis of mutual trust creates the foundation for leaders to provide followers with greater autonomy to make decisions and in turn for those followers to feel a greater sense of efficacy and ownership in outcomes. It also promotes followers' being more transparent with each other, as well as with leaders in unearthing potential problems. Ultimately, trust in the leader creates an expectation by the follower and leader that each will act in a particular manner, which has been referred to as trustee predictability.[31]

Benefits of Trust

We know from prior research that high levels of trust have been associated with high-quality leader and follower relationships.[32] Referring back to our discussion of ownership, we also know that where there are higher levels of trust, people generally feel a sense of responsibility and ownership for stepping up, which results in better performance[33] and extra-role behaviors.[34] If followers take the initiative to create a deep sense of trust with their leaders by being transparent, responsible, and consistent, it is likely that the leaders will in turn reciprocate by sharing more information and trusting followers to take ownership. In this instance, the follower is "leading up" with the leader, just in the same way that the leader may "lead down" with the follower. The outcome of both processes is increased trust and increased engagement between leaders and followers.

TRANSPARENCY

Not only are willingness to appear vulnerable and admit mistakes important for building trust, but they also are likely to be contributing factors to higher leader and follower interactional transparency. Again, the U.S. poll results indicate that leaders are not viewed as very transparent: only 26 percent of followers reported that their leaders say "exactly what they mean." We suspect that followers function the same way with their leaders, given the number of ethical meltdowns over the last five years, in which followers failed to report what they were observing happening in their organizations.

Research from the self-disclosure literature indicates that transparency can be generally defined as a process whereby one individual makes himself or herself known to others by sharing thoughts, values, and feelings.[35] The literature suggests that as individuals interact more often and self-disclose, greater trust will form and more transparency will ensue.[36]

Focusing on the leader and follower relationship, Voglegesang and Crossley defined interactional transparency as "a relationship [climate] free from deceit, where relevant parties have access to understanding decision-making processes, are encouraged to be open regarding feedback and communication, and exhibit actions that are in line with their espoused values."[37] A transparent organization is one whose policies and decision-making processes are open and visible to all members of the workforce.[38] Transparency occurs when leaders and followers say exactly what they mean. And it is through transparency that organizational intelligence blossoms, and in turn so do the processes of followership and leadership.

The establishment of shared values that underlie high trust and transparency provides leaders and followers with a greater assurance that others will act in good faith, guided by the same common goals, thereby leading people to subjugate their own needs for the greater good, as others are doing the same. In a situation like Enron, even though the company's website listed "integrity" as a value, we can assume from what occurred there that this value was not shared by all.

Benefits of Transparency

Transparency fosters a climate where neither alarms nor ideas can be ignored. As information flow is encouraged, the sense of individual and collective efficacy or confidence is likely to increase, which in turn should lead to more reliable and accurate performance as agents take responsibility and ownership for their work. We have also seen that where unexpected negative events occur, managers who are more transparent in their communications with followers have been shown to receive less blame than those who do not share openly.[39] For example, a leader who tells followers that they will know about important events impacting their organization's future as soon as he or she knows is more likely to weather unexpected events that would damage the credibility of leaders who are not as transparent.

Transparency and Psychological Safety

We suggest that there may be linkages between developing higher levels of inter-actional transparency and feelings of psychological safety.[40] When individuals experience a higher level of psychological safety, they are more likely to freely offer their opinions without fear of retaliation from others.[41] For followers to be confident enough to assume ownership over relevant tasks and situations, we expect there would be a need for leaders to create higher levels of psychological safety. In so doing, they will enable the conditions for their followers to step up and lead with a sense of ownership.

Without ownership and transparency, we may continue to have followers who are reluctant to report what they see as being wrong or errors. We know that employees are often reluctant to report their own errors, let alone those of others, out of fear of retaliation, loss of personal image, and other losses, such as their job or financial livelihood.[42]

Edmonson reported that the level of psychological safety felt in work teams influenced team members' intentions to report errors.[43] Where psychological safety was low, team members were more likely to manage an impression that things were okay, and were more unwilling to disclose their errors. A blaming culture, as opposed to an ownership culture, is likely to decrease the reporting of observed problems, mistakes, illegal actions, and unethical behavior.

Creating the conditions for higher levels of psychological safety has been evident recently in the airline industry and in health care organizations where officials have worked very hard to avoid accidents, near misses, and mistakes. By creating an environment where people have felt safe to report incidents without retaliation, the leaders in the airline industry have been able to increase the safety of air travel dramatically in the United States, with health care organizations now following suit.

For example, the airline industry has created something called the two-challenge rule for pilots. With this rule, the copilot can challenge the pilot's actions twice before assuming command of the vessel. The two-challenge rule has been used when the copilot realized that the pilot was not capable of flying the plane and assumed command through the two-challenge rule. Such transactional rules provide copilots with clear boundaries of what they are able and unable to challenge, which is often blurred in such command-and-control systems.

The same is now true in the operating theatre, where nurses are being encouraged to challenge what appears to be an incorrect procedure. Some hospitals are moving toward reporting near misses, such as a pharmacist's putting two bottles of medication whose names begin with the same three letters next to each other on a shelf. By doing so, the pharmacist increases the risk of someone picking up the wrong medication, so it is incumbent on employees to challenge this practice. (The fact that the bottles are next to each other does not mean that a mistake will be made, so identifying it before such mistakes are made would be considered a near miss in that context.)

CONCLUSION

Although leadership has traditionally been defined through an assessment of an individual's specific traits and behaviors, more contemporary leadership theorists have defined leadership as a process grown from the relationship between a leader and follower. The question of whether leadership development programs aimed at the development of *followers* will have a positive impact is still up for debate. However, in this chapter, we discussed three areas of followership that require some attention. First, we discussed the importance of building psychological ownership in followers. Followers with heightened psychological ownership will experience having a sense of place, a sense of self, and a sense of efficacy. Benefits of this extend beyond increased performance and decision making to followers' giving the extra effort required to make the organization a success.

Second, we discussed the importance of building trust in the leader-follower relationship. By building trust through demonstrating vulnerability and self-disclosure in stable situations, the leaders and followers will be able to confidently rely on one another in situations of time pressure and crisis.

Last, we elucidated the importance of building transparency. When a leader or follower says exactly what he or she means, information flow throughout the organization is enhanced, which may not only yield new synergies but also avoid communication blockages that could ultimately result in a crisis for the organization.

NOTES

PART ONE

1. Weber, M. *Max Weber: The Theory of Social and Economic Organization* (A. M. Henderson and Talcott Parsons, trans.). New York: Free Press, 1947.

2. Burns, J. M. *Leadership.* New York: HarperCollins, 1978.

3. Kelley, R. E. "In Praise of Followers." *Harvard Business Review,* 1988, *66*(6), 142–148.

4. Meindl, J. R., Enrlich, S. B., and Dukerich, J. M. "The Romance of Leadership." *Administrative Science Quarterly,* 1985, *30*(1), 78–102.

5. Bass, B. M. *Leadership and Performance Beyond Expectations.* New York: Free Press, 1985.

6. Chaleff, I. *The Courageous Follower.* San Francisco: Berrett-Koehler, 1995.

7. Alford, C. F. *Whistleblowers: Broken Lives and Organizational Power.* Ithaca, N.Y.: Cornell University Press, 2001.

8. Kellerman, B. *Bad Leadership.* Boston: Harvard Business School Press, 2004.

9. Lipman-Blumen, J. *The Allure of Toxic Leaders.* New York: Oxford University Press, 2005.

CHAPTER ONE

1. Ed Hollander was a notable exception in that his work looked at leadership and followership in an interactive way. See Hollander, E. P. *Leadership Dynamics.* New York: Free Press/Macmillan, 1978; Hollander, E. P. "The Essential Interdependence of Leadership and Followership." *Current Directions in Psychological Science,* 1992, *1*(2), 71–75.

2. Kelley, R. E. "In Praise of Followers." *Harvard Business Review,* 1988, *66*(6), 142–148.

3. Kelley, R. E. *The Power of Followership.* New York: Doubleday, 1992; Chaleff, I. *The Courageous Follower.* San Francisco: Berrett-Koehler, 1995.

4. For more on "bad" or toxic leaders, see Kellerman, B. *Bad Leadership.* Boston: Harvard Business School Press, 2004; Lipman-Blumen, J. *The Allure of Toxic Leaders.* New York: Oxford University Press, 2004.

5. Kellerman, 2004; Lipman-Blumen, 2004.

CHAPTER TWO

1. Follett, M. P. *Dynamic Administration: The Collected Papers of Mary Parker Follett.* New York: Routledge, 2003, p. 303.

2. Thomas Aquinas. *De Veritate,* X, 1, "Response."

3. Heidegger, M. *What Is Called Thinking?* (J. G. Gray, trans.) New York: HarperCollins, 1968, p. 15.

CHAPTER THREE

1. Kelley, R. E. "Followership." In G. R. Goethals, G. J. Sorenson, and J. M. Burns (eds.), *Encyclopedia of Leadership* (pp. 504–513). Thousand Oaks, Calif.: Sage, 2004; Rost, J. C. *Leadership for the Twenty-First Century.* Westport, Conn.: Praeger, 1991.

2. Katz, D., and Kahn, R. L. *The Social Psychology of Organizations.* (2nd ed.) New York: Wiley, 1978.

3. Becker, H. J., and Reil, M. M. "Teacher Professionalism and the Emergence of Constructivist-Compatible Pedagogies." Paper presented at the annual meeting of the American Educational Research Association, Montreal, Apr. 1999.

4. Kerr, S. "On the Folly of Rewarding A, While Hoping for B." *Academy of Management Journal,* 1975, *18*(4), 769–783.

5. Heller, T., and Van Til, J. "Leadership and Followership: Some Summary Propositions." *Journal of Applied Behavioral Science,* 1982, *18*(4), 405–414.

6. Howell, J. M., and Shamir, B. "The Role of Followers in the Charismatic Leadership Process: Relationships and Their Consequences." *Academy of Management Review,* 2005, *30*(1), 96–112.

7. Collinson, D. "Rethinking Followership: A Post-Structuralist Analysis of Follower Identities." *Leadership Quarterly,* 2006, *17*(2), 179–189.

8. Kelley, R. E. *The Power of Followership.* New York: Doubleday, 1992.

9. Chaleff, I. *The Courageous Follower: Standing Up to and for Our Leaders.* San Francisco: Berrett-Koehler, 1995.

10. Kelley, 2004.

11. Kelley, 2004.

12. Collinson, 2006.

13. Shamir, B. "Motivation of Followers." In Goethals, Sorenson, and Burns, 2004.

14. Brewer, M. B., and Gardner, W. L. "Who Is This 'We'? Levels of Collective Identity and Self Representations." *Journal of Personality and Social Psychology,* 1996, *50,* 543–549.

15. Lord, R. G., and Brown, D. J. *Leadership Processes and Follower Self-Identity.* Mahwah, N.J.: Erlbaum, 2004.

16. Howell and Shamir, 2005.

17. Eden, D. "Leadership and Expectations: Pygmalion Effects and Other Self-Fulfilling Prophecies in Organizations." *Leadership Quarterly,* 1992, *3*(4), 271–305.

18. Lord and Brown, 2004.

19. Gardner, W. L., and others. "'Can You See the Real Me?' A Self-Based Model of Authentic Leader and Follower Development." *Leadership Quarterly,* 2005, *16,* 343–372.

20. Dionne, S. D., Yammarino, F. J., Howell, J. P., and Villa, J. "Theoretical Letters: Substitutes for Leadership, or Not." *Leadership Quarterly*, 2005, *16*(1), 169–193.

21. Pfeiffer, J. "The Secret of Life at the Limits: Cogs Become Big Wheelers." *Smithsonian*, July 1989, pp. 38–49; Howell, J. P., and others. "Substitutes for Leadership: Effective Alternatives to Ineffective Leadership." *Organizational Dynamics*, 1990, *19*(1), 21–38.

22. Kerr, S., and Jermier, J. M. "Substitutes for Leadership: Their Meaning and Measurement." *Organizational Behavior and Human Performance*, 1978, *22*, 375–403.

23. Howell, J. P., and Dorfman, P. W. "Leadership and Substitutes for Leadership Among Professional Workers." *Journal of Applied Behavioral Science*, 1986, *22*(1), 29–46.

24. Howell, J. P. "'Substitutes for Leadership: Their Meaning and Measurement'— An Historical Assessment." *Leadership Quarterly*, 1997, *8*(2), 113–116; Manz, C. C., and Sims, H. P. "Self-Management as a Substitute for Leadership: A Social Learning Theory Perspective." *Academy of Management Review*, 1980, *5*(3), 361–367.

25. Mossholder, K. W., Niebuhr, R. E., and Norris, D. R. "Effects of Dyadic Duration on the Relationship Between Leader Behavior Perceptions and Follower Outcomes." *Journal of Organizational Behavior*, 1990, *11*, 379–388.

26. Lord and Brown, 2004.

27. Howell, J. P., and Costley, D. L. *Understanding Behaviors for Effective Leadership.* (2nd ed.) Upper Saddle River, N.J.: Prentice Hall, 2006.

28. Whittington, J. L., Goodwin, V. L., and Murray, B. "Transformational Leadership, Goal Difficulty, and Job Design: Independent and Interactive Effects on Employee Outcomes." *Leadership Quarterly*, 2004, *15*, 593–606; Bass, B. M., and Riggio, R. E. *Transformational Leadership.* Mahwah, N.J.: Erlbaum, 2006.

29. Kanter, R. M. "Knowledge Workers." *Executive Excellence*, Jan. 2000, pp. 15–16; Kirkman, B. L., and Rosen, B. "Beyond Self-Management: Antecedents and Consequences of Team Empowerment." *Academy of Management Journal*, 1999, *42*(1), 58–74.

30. O'Toole, J., Galbraith, J., and Lawler, E. E. "The Promise and Pitfalls of Shared Leadership: When Two (or More) Heads Are Better Than One." In C. L. Pearce and J. A. Conger (eds.), *Shared Leadership* (pp. 250–267). Thousand Oaks, Calif.: Sage, 2003.

31. Rost, 1991.

32. Kanter, 2000; Rost, 1991.

33. Burke, C. S., Fiore, S. M., and Salas, E. "The Role of Shared Cognition in Enabling Shared Leadership and Team Adaptability." In Pearce and Conger, 2003, p. 109.

34. Seifter, H. "The Conductor-Less Orchestra." *Leader to Leader.* http://pfdf. org/leaderbooks/121/summer2001/seifter.html. Summer 2001.

35. Burke, Fiore, and Salas, 2003; Barry, D. "Managing the Bossless Team: Lessons in Distributed Leadership." *Organizational Dynamics*, 1991, *20*(1), 31–47; Kelley, 1992; Pearce, C. L., and Sims, H. P. "Vertical Versus Shared Leadership as Predictors of the Effectiveness of Change Management Teams: An Examination of Aversive, Directive, Transactional, Transformational, and Empowering Leader Behaviors." *Group Dynamics: Theory, Research, and Practice*, 2002, 6(2), 172–197.

36. Eisenhardt, K. M., Kahwajy, J. L., and Bourgeois, L. J. "How Management Teams Can Have a Good Fight." *Harvard Business Review*, July 1997, pp. 77–85; Janis, I. L. "Groupthink and Group Dynamics: A Social Psychological Analysis of Defective Policy Decisions." *Policy Studies Journal*, 1973, *2*(1), 19–25.

37. Dimitroff, R. D., Schmidt, L. A., and Bond, T. D. "Organizational Behavior and Disaster: A Study of Conflict at NASA." *Project Management Journal*, June 2005, pp. 28–37.

38. Barry, 1991; Burke, Fiore, and Salas, 2003; Eisenhardt, Kahwajy, and Bourgeois, 1997.

39. LaFasto, F.M.J., and Larson, C. E. *When Teams Work Best.* Thousand Oaks, Calif.: Sage, 2001.

40. Albanese, R., and Van Fleet, D. D. "Rational Behavior in Groups: The Free Riding Tendency." *Academy of Management Review*, 1985, *10*(2), 244–255.

41. Burke, Fiore, and Salas, 2003.

42. Mohammed, S., and Dumville, B. C. "Team Mental Models in a Team Knowledge Framework: Expanding Theory and Measurement Across Disciplinary Boundaries." *Journal of Organizational Behavior,* 2001, *22*(2), 89–106.

43. Pearce, C. L. "The Future of Leadership: Combining Vertical and Shared Leadership to Transform Knowledge Work." *Academy of Management Executive,* 2004, *18*(1), 47–57.

44. Dionne, Yammarino, Howell, and Villa, 2005; Villa, J. R., Howell, J. P., Dorfman, P. W., and Daniel, D. "Problems with Detecting Moderators in Leadership Research Using Moderated Multiple Regression." *Leadership Quarterly*, 2003, *14*(1), 3–23; Whittington, Goodwin, and Murray, 2004.

45. Lord and Brown, 2004; Collinson, 2006, p. 187.

CHAPTER FOUR

1. Although the term *paradigm* was originally applied to systems of theory and research in the physical and natural sciences, a paradigm can also exist in the ways in which people function. An example is the paradigm of modern management, sometimes referred to scientific management. Practitioners are taught and utilize an array of standard techniques for the purpose of organizing, planning, and executing in organizations.

2. I have identified five major categories of leadership contexts: organizations, associations, societies, professions and occupations, and cultural areas. See Stech, E. L. "Toward a Taxonomy of Leadership Contexts." Paper presented at the 6th annual conference of the International Leadership Association, Washington, D.C., Nov. 4–7, 2004.

3. Giuliani, R. W. *Leadership.* New York: Hyperion, 2002.

4. Pearson, C. S. *The Hero Within.* San Francisco: HarperCollins, 1989.

5. Northouse, P. G. *Leadership Theory and Practice.* (3rd ed.) Thousand Oaks, Calif.: Sage, 2004, p. 19.

6. Kirkpatrick, S. A., and Locke, E. A. "Leadership: Do Traits Matter?" *Executive*, 1991, *5*, 48–60.

7. *Roget's 21st Century Thesaurus.* (2nd ed.) New York: Barnes & Noble Books, 1999; *St. Martin's Roget's Thesaurus of English Words and Phrases.* New York: St. Martin's Press, 1965.

8. Northouse, 2004. Of the ten leadership theories or approaches presented by Northouse, six are directly based on or oriented toward work in hierarchical organizations. The classic *Bass & Stogdill's Handbook of Leadership,* 3rd ed. (New York: Free Press, 1990), is subtitled *Theory, Research, and Management Applications,* indicating the general reliance on work done in, about, and for hierarchical organizations.

9. Rost, J. C. *Leadership for the Twenty-First Century.* Westport, Conn.: Praeger, 1993, p. 98.

10. Blake, R. R., and Mouton, J. S. *The Managerial Grid.* Houston, Tex.: Gulf, 1985; Blake, R. R., and Mouton, J. S. *Leadership Dilemmas—Grid Solutions.* Houston, Tex.: Gulf, 1991; Fiedler, F. E. *A Theory of Leadership Effectiveness.* New York: McGraw-Hill, 1967; Blanchard, K. H. *SLII: A Situational Approach to Managing People.* Escondido, Calif.: Blanchard Training and Development, 1985; Kouzes, J. S., and Posner, B. Z. *The Leadership Challenge.* (3rd ed.) San Francisco: Jossey-Bass, 2002.

11. Rost, 1993; Wheatley, M. J. *Leadership and the New Science.* San Francisco: Berrett-Koehler, 1999; Maslow, A. *Maslow on Management.* Hoboken, N.J.: Wiley, 1998, pp. 20–42. Maslow's work is included here because it foreshadowed, in the early 1960s, the notion that workers could take on responsibilities and that they were mature beings who preferred work to idleness, meaningful to meaningless work, and being treated as a whole person rather than as an implement or tool.

12. *Webster's New Collegiate Dictionary.* (11th ed.) Springfield, Mass.: Merriam, 2003.

13. Rost, 1993, p. 105.

14. Rost, 1993, pp. 102–103.

15. Jablin, F. M., and Putnam, L. L. (eds.). *The New Handbook of Organizational Communication.* Thousand Oaks, Calif.: Sage, 2001, pp. 476–479.

16. Maslow, 1998.

17. Wheatley, 1999, p. 165.

18. Chaleff, I. *The Courageous Follower*. (2nd ed.) San Francisco: Berrett-Koehler, 2003.

CHAPTER FIVE

1. Rost, J. C. *Leadership in the Twenty-First Century*. Westport, Conn.: Praeger, 1993.

2. Rost, 1993, p. 102.

3. Chaleff, I. *The Courageous Follower*. (2nd ed.) San Francisco: Berrett-Koehler, 2003; Kelley, R. E. *The Power of Followership*. New York: Currency, 1992.

4. Friedman, T. L. *The World Is Flat*. New York: Farrar, Straus & Giroux, 2005.

CHAPTER SIX

1. Chaleff, I. *The Courageous Follower*. (2nd ed.) San Francisco: Berrett-Koehler, 2003. (Originally published in 1995)

2. Let me acknowledge that some readers will be disconcerted by my using the terms *leader* and *manager* somewhat interchangeably. Most of us would agree on the differences between leadership behaviors and managerial behaviors. In practice, however, the participants with whom I work in organizational settings experience themselves in a hierarchical structure where they must respond to individuals above them in the hierarchy, regardless of the mix of leadership and management skills possessed by those individuals. Therefore, in real-world terms, it is the relationships with those in positions of authority over the workshop participants that are the focus of the developmental examination. I will refer to these as leaders whether or not they display true leadership behaviors.

3. Kelley, R. E. *The Power of Followership*. New York: Doubleday, 1992.

4. Boccialetti, G. *It Takes Two*. San Francisco: Jossey-Bass, 1995.

5. Inquiries for obtaining the self-assessment questionnaires and scoring sheets that I use can be directed to me at www.courageousfollower.com.

6. Maccoby, M. *The Productive Narcissist.* New York: Broadway Books, 2003; Alford, C. F. *Group Psychology and Political Theory.* New Haven, Conn.: Yale University Press, 1994.

7. Culbert, S., and Ullmen, J. *Don't Kill the Bosses.* San Francisco: Berrett-Koehler, 2001.

8. Ryan, K., and Oestreich, D. *Driving Fear out of the Workplace.* San Francisco: Jossey-Bass, 1991.

9. Janis, I. L. *Groupthink.* Boston: Houghton Mifflin, 1982.

CHAPTER EIGHT

1. Columbia Accident Investigation Board Report, Volume 1. www.nasa.gov/columbia/caib/html/VOL1.html. Aug. 2003.

2. Columbia Accident Investigation Board Report, p. 9.

3. Columbia Accident Investigation Board Report, p. 12.

4. *The Implementation of the NASA-Wide Application of the Columbia Accident Investigation Report: Our Renewed Commitment to Excellence,* p. 11. www.nasa.gov/pdf/58676main_Implementation%20033004%20FINAL.pdf. Mar. 30, 2004.

5. *Renewed Commitment to Excellence: An Assessment of the NASA Agency-wide Applicability of the Columbia Accident Investigation Board Report,* p. 10, Jan. 2004.

6. S. Kanu Kogod, Ph.D., Master Certified Coach, Bridges in Organizations, Inc. (www.bridges-in-orgs.com); Scott Coady, Certified Master Somatic Coach, the Institute of Embodied Wisdom (www.somaticwisdom.com).

7. Gladwell, M. *The Tipping Point.* New York: Little, Brown, 2000.

8. Covey, S. *The Seven Habits of Highly Effective People.* New York: Simon & Schuster, 1982.

9. Goldberg, M. C. *The Art of the Question.* Hoboken, N.J.: Wiley, 1998.

10. Columbia Accident Investigation Board Report, pp. 183, 192.

11. Innis, S. H., and Mayfield, A. B. *The Thin Book of Naming Elephants.* Bend, Ore.: Thin Book, 1998, 2004.

12. Pert, C. "Molecules and Choice." *Shift*, Sept.-Nov. 2004.

13. Marquardt, M. J. *Action Learning in Action.* Palo Alto, Calif.: Davies-Black, 1999, p. 4.

14. Other program participants work at NASA headquarters, the U.S. Department of Agriculture, the Department of Justice, and the National Oceanic and Atmospheric Association in the Department of Commerce.

15. Broom, M. F., and Klein, D. C. *Power: The Infinite Game.* Ellicott City, Md.: Sea Otter Press, 1999.

16. Wheatley, M. J. *Turning to One Another.* San Francisco: Berrett-Koehler, 2002.

CHAPTER NINE

1. Wheatley, M. J. *Leadership and the New Science.* San Francisco: Berrett-Koehler, 1999.

2. Cialdini, R. B. *Influence.* New York: Quill, 1984, p. 178.

3. Cialdini, 1984, p. 178.

4. Cialdini, 1984, p. 179.

5. Cialdini, 1984, p. 195.

6. Bies and Tripp argue that perceived violations of formal rules and breaches of social norms and etiquette can produce antisocial behavior in organizations, including acts of revenge. In Bies, R. J., and Tripp, T. M. "Beyond Distrust: 'Getting Even' and the Need for Revenge." In R. M. Kramer and T. Tyler (eds.), *Trust in Organizations.* Thousand Oaks, Calif.: Sage, 1996.

7. Coch, L., and French, J.R.P. Jr. "Overcoming Resistance to Change." *Human Relations,* 1948, *1*, 512–532.

8. Lee, C., and Zemke, R. "The Search for Spirit in the Workplace." In L. C. Spears (ed.), *Reflections on Leadership.* Hoboken, N.J.: Wiley, 1995, p. 110.

9. Wharton, E. "Vesalius in Zante (1564)." *North American Review,* 1902, *175*, 625–631.

CHAPTER ELEVEN

1. Berg, D. N. "Resurrecting the Muse: Followership in Organizations." In E. B. Klein, F. Gabelnick, and P. Herr (eds.), *The Psychodynamics of Leadership*. Madison, Conn.: Psychosocial Press, 1998, p. 1.

2. Rost, J. C. *Leadership for the Twenty-First Century*. Westport, Conn.: Praeger, 1993, p. 102. Rost's most recent definition of leadership is found in this volume, page 57.

3. Rost, J. C. "An Outmoded Concept." Presentation at the Kravis–de Roulet Rethinking Followership Conference, Claremont, California, Feb. 2006.

4. Paraphrase of a statement made by Dr. Rick Bridges, professor of leadership and management, San Diego State University, in a phone conversation, Feb. 2005.

5. Berg, 1998, p. 1.

6. Blackshear, P. B. "The Followership Continuum: A Model for Increasing Organizational Productivity." *Public Manager*, June 2003, p. 10.

7. Lawrence (Lawry) de Bivort, a prominent member of the Organization Development Network (an international organization for organization development professionals and academics), responded to the group's listserv with the post quoted in the chapter. (Subject: Changing Employee Attitudes). May 6, 2003.

8. Pierce, J. L., O'Driscoll, M., and Coglan, A. "Work Environment Structure and Psychological Ownership: The Mediating Effects of Control." *Journal of Social Psychology*, 2004, *144*(5), 507–534.

9. Kelley, R. E. *The Power of Followership*. New York: Doubleday, 1992.

CHAPTER TWELVE

1. Clark, T. B. "The War Ahead." *Government Executive*, 2001, *11*(1). http://www.govexec.com/features/1101/1101edit.htm.

2. Boccialetti, G. *It Takes Two*. San Francisco: Jossey-Bass, 1995, p. 3.

3. Keith, T. "How Do You Like Me Now?" [song lyrics] DreamWorks, Nov. 2, 1999.

4. Rost, J. C. *Leadership for the Twenty-First Century.* Westport, Conn.: Praeger, 1991.

5. MacKenzie, D. "Living Leadership Now." *LiNEZine,* fall 2001. http://line zine.com/6.2/articles/dmlln.htm.

6. Waddell, D. E. "A Situational Leadership Model for Military Leaders." *Aerospace Power Journal,* 1994, *8*(3), 29–42.

7. Waddell, 1994.

8. Wortman, M. S. "Strategic Management and Changing Leader-Follower Roles." *Journal of Applied Behavioral Science,* 1982, *18*(3), 371–383; Treister, N. W., and Schultz, J. H. "The Courageous Follower." *Physician Executive,* 1997, *23*(4), 9–14; Crockett, W. J. "Dynamic Subordinancy." *Training and Development Journal,* May 1981, pp. 155–164; Nolan, J. S., and Harty, H. F. "Followership > Leadership." *Education,* 1984, *104,* 311–312; Kelley, R. E. "In Praise of Followers." *Harvard Business Review,* 1988, *66*(6), 142–148.

9. Chaleff, I. *The Courageous Follower.* (2nd ed.) San Francisco: Berrett-Koehler, 2003.

10. Chaleff, 2003.

11. Chaleff, 2003.

12. Kelley, R. E. *The Power of Followership.* New York: Doubleday, 1992.

13. Chaleff, 2003.

14. Chaleff, 2003.

15. Chaleff, 2003.

16. Chaleff, 2003.

17. Chaleff, 2003.

18. Chaleff, 2003.

19. Senge, P. M. "The Leader's New Role." *Sloan Management Review,* 1990, *32*(1), 7–23.

20. MacKenzie, 2001.

21. MacKenzie, 2001.

22. Rost, 1991.

23. Dixon, E. N. *An Exploration of the Relationship of Organizational Level and Measures of Follower Behaviors.* Unpublished doctoral dissertation, University of Alabama in Huntsville, 2003.

24. Chaleff, 2003.

25. Chaleff, 2003.

26. Chaleff, 2003.

27. Chaleff, 2003.

PART THREE

1. Pelletier, K. L. "Hurts So Good: The Myth of Positive Leadership." Poster session presented at the annual meeting of the American Psychological Association, San Francisco, Aug. 2007; Meindl, J. R. "The Romance of Leadership as a Follower-Centric Theory: A Social Constructionist Approach." *Leadership Quarterly,* 1995, *6*(3), 329–341.

2. Lipman-Blumen, J. *The Allure of Toxic Leaders.* New York: Oxford University Press, 2005.

CHAPTER THIRTEEN

1. Becker, E. *Denial of Death.* New York: Basic Books, 1973.

2. Lipman-Blumen, J. *The Allure of Toxic Leaders.* New York: Oxford University Press, 2005a.

3. See C. Fred Alford's chapter in this volume.

4. Maccoby, M. "Why People Follow the Leader: The Power of Transference." *Harvard Business Review,* Sept. 2004, pp. 1–10.

5. Hankiss, E. *Fear and Symbols.* Budapest: Central European University Press, 2001.

6. Lipman-Blumen, J. *Gender Roles and Power.* Upper Saddle River, N.J.: Prentice Hall, 1984.

7. Becker, E. *Escape from Evil.* New York: Free Press, 1975.

8. www.religioustolerance.org/dc_jones.htm.

9. Kierkegaard, S. *The Concept of Dread.* Princeton, N.J.: Princeton University Press, 1944; Jaspers, K. *Philosophie.* Heidelberg: Springer, 1962; Heidegger, M. *Being and Time.* London: SCM, 1962.

10. Lipman-Blumen, J. "Toxic Leadership: When Grand Illusions Masquerade as Noble Visions." *Leader to Leader,* Spring 2005b, pp. 29–36.

11. Festinger, L., Schacter, S., and Back, K. *Social Pressures in Informal Groups.* Stanford, Calif.: Stanford University Press, 1950.

12. Geertz, C. "Centers, Kings, and Charisma: Reflections on the Symbolics of Power." In *Local Knowledge* (pp. 122–123). New York: Basic Books, 1983.

13. Kuhn, T. *The Structure of Scientific Revolutions.* (2nd ed.) Chicago: University of Chicago Press, 1970.

14. King, M. L., Jr. Vietnam speech, presented at Riverside Church, New York, Apr. 4, 1967.

15. Janis, I. L. *Victims of Groupthink.* Boston: Houghton Mifflin, 1972.

16. Kierkegaard, 1944; Jaspers, 1962; Heidegger, 1962.

17. Pyszczynski, T., Solomon, S., and Greenberg, J. *In the Wake of 9/11.* Washington, D.C.: American Psychological Association, 2003.

18. Lipman-Blumen, 2005a, p. 239.

19. Lipman-Blumen, J., and Leavitt, H. J. *Hot Groups.* New York: Oxford University Press, 1999.

20. Lipman-Blumen, 2005b. The following section draws heavily on this source.

21. Lipman-Blumen, 2005b, p. 32.

22. Quoted from Mitscherlich, A., and Mitscherlich, M. *The Inability to Mourn.* New York: Grove, 1975. In Hankiss, 2001.

CHAPTER FOURTEEN

1. Quotations from letters and most information given without citations are from the Stanley Milgram papers, Yale University Archives, and from interviews conducted by the author.

2. Blass, T. "The Man Who Shocked the World." *Psychology Today,* Apr. 2002, pp. 68–73.

3. Milgram, S. "Behavioral Study of Obedience." *Journal of Abnormal and Social Psychology,* 1963, *67*(4), 371–378.

4. Milgram, S. *Obedience to Authority: An Experimental View.* New York: HarperCollins, 1974a.

5. Abse, D. *The Dogs of Pavlov.* London: Valentine, Mitchell, & Co, 1973.

6. Coughlan, E. *Dying by Degrees: An Emily Goodstriker Mystery.* Winnipeg: Ravenstone, 2000.

7. Arendt, H. *Eichmann in Jerusalem: A Report on the Banality of Evil.* New York: Viking Press, 1963.

8. Blass, T. *The Man Who Shocked the World: The Life and Legacy of Stanley Milgram.* New York: Basic Books, 2004.

9. Milgram, 1974a, experiment 12.

10. Milgram, 1974a.

11. Milgram, 1974a, p. xiii.

12. Milgram, S. "We Are All Obedient." *Listener,* 1974b, pp. 567–568.

13. Milgram, 1974a, p. 188.

14. Milgram, S. "Some Conditions of Obedience and Disobedience to Authority." *Human Relations,* 1965b, *18*(1), 57–76.

15. Milgram, 1974a, p. 205.

16. Milgram, S. "Liberating Effects of Group Pressure." *Journal of Personality and Social Psychology,* 1965a, *1*(2), 127–134.

17. Milgram, 1974a, p. 118.

18. Granberg, D., and Bartels, B. "On Being a Lone Dissenter." *Journal of Applied Social Psychology,* 2005, *35*(9), 1849–1858.

19. Modigliani, A., and Rochat, F. "The Role of Interaction Sequences and the Timing of Resistance in Shaping Obedience and Defiance to Authority." *Journal of Social Issues,* 1995, *51*(3), 107–123.

20. Milgram, S. "The Compulsion to Do Evil." *Patterns of Prejudice,* 1967, *1,* 3–7.

21. Litowitz, D. "Are Corporations Evil?" *University of Miami Law Review*, 2004, *58*, 811–841.

22. Litowitz, 2004, pp. 832–833.

23. Milgram, 1974a, p. 6.

24. Milgram, 1963, p. 371.

25. Pfeiffer, P. D. "An Essay on Authority and Leadership." *Effect*, Fall 2000, pp. 11–14.

CHAPTER FIFTEEN

1. Maccoby, M. "Toward a Science of Social Character." *International Forum of Psychoanalysis*, 2002, *11*, 33–44.

2. Maccoby, M. "Why People Follow the Leader: The Power of Transference." *Harvard Business Review*, Sept. 2004, pp. 76–85.

3. Beck, J. C., and Wade, M. *Got Game*. Boston: Harvard Business School Press, 2004.

4. Henning, M., and Jardim, A. *The Managerial Woman*. New York: Anchor/Doubleday, 1978.

5. Maitland, A. "Employees Want to Hear It 'Straight' from the Boss's Mouth." *Financial Times*, Dec. 1, 2006, p. 9.

CHAPTER SIXTEEN

1. Coloroso, B. *The Bully, the Bullied and the Bystander*. Toronto: HarperCollins, 2002, p. 13.

2. Coloroso, 2002, p. 14.

3. Mullin-Rindler, N. *Relational Aggression and Bullying*. Wellesley, Mass.: Center for Research on Women, 2003.

4. Godfrey, R. *Under the Bridge*. New York: Simon & Schuster, 2005.

5. Mullin-Rindler, 2003; Giannetti, C., and Sagarese, M. *Cliques: Eight Steps to Help Your Child Survive the Social Jungle*. New York: Random House, 2001.

6. Simmons, R. *Odd Girl Speaks Out*. New York: Harcourt Harvest Books, 2004.

7. Li, Q. "Cyberbullying in Schools: Research of Gender Differences." *School Psychology International,* 2006, *27*(2), 1–14.

8. Thorp, D. "Cyberbullies on the Prowl in the Schoolyard." *Australian IT News,* June 29, 2004, http://australianit.news.com.au/articles/0,7204, 99809 00^15322^^nbv^15306,00.html; Willard, N. *An Educator's Guide to Cyberbullying and Cyberthreats.* Center for Safe and Responsible Internet Use, www.csriu.org, 2006.

9. Coloroso, 2002, p. 3.

10. E-mail correspondence with Ira Chaleff, Dec. 24, 2006.

11. Reported on *Global TV News,* Toronto, June 8, 2005.

12. Private conversation with Lori Mignone, June 9, 2005.

13. *Global TV News,* 2005.

14. Lipman-Blumen, J. *The Allure of Toxic Leaders.* New York: Oxford University Press, 2005; Alford, C. F. *Whistleblowers: Broken Lives and Organizational Power.* Ithaca, N.Y.: Cornell University Press, 2001.

15. Pepler, D., and Craig, W. *Making a Difference in Bullying.* Toronto: York University, www.arts.yorku.ca/lamarsh, Report 60, Apr. 2000.

16. Coloroso, 2002.

17. E-mail correspondence with Ira Chaleff, Dec. 24, 2006.

18. Lipman-Blumen, 2005.

19. E-mail correspondence with Ira Chaleff, Dec. 24, 2006.

CHAPTER SEVENTEEN

1. Sennett, R. *The Corrosion of Character.* New York: Norton, 1998.

2. Putnam, R. *Bowling Alone.* New York: Simon & Schuster, 2000.

3. Unless otherwise cited, my empirical claims and quotations are based on the research I did for *Whistleblowers: Broken Lives and Organizational Power.* I interviewed more than two dozen whistleblowers, many for over twenty hours each over the course of two or three years. I also attended their support groups and weekend retreats. Although I did not intend to interview

the "average whistleblower," the whistleblowers I interviewed fit the profile of the average whistleblower remarkably well, insofar as it is possible to know such things. See Miethe's *Whistleblowing at Work,* p. 58. His remains the most empirically extensive published study of whistleblowers and bystanders. See Alford, C. F. *Whistleblowers: Broken Lives and Organizational Power.* Ithaca, N.Y.: Cornell University Press, 2001; Miethe, T. *Whistleblowing at Work.* Boulder, Colo.: Westview Press, 1999.

4. Miethe, 1999, pp. 77–78; Rothschild, J., and Miethe, T. *Keeping Organizations True to Their Purposes.* Washington, D.C.: Aspen Institute, 1996, pp. 15–16; Glazer, M. P., and Glazer, P. M. *The Whistleblowers.* New York: Basic Books, 1989, pp. 206–207. At least one study has found significantly less retaliation: Miceli, M., and Near, J. *Blowing the Whistle.* New York: Lexington Books, 1992, pp. 226–227. As might be expected, most of the difference in degree of retaliation depends on whom and how one counts.

5. Glazer and Glazer, 1989, p. 228.

6. Bauman, Z. *Modernity and the Holocaust.* Ithaca, N.Y.: Cornell University Press, 1989, pp. 213–215. Emphasis mine. Bauman is writing about every modern organization, not just the ones that made the Holocaust. Indeed, that is the thesis of his book.

7. Phillips, D. "FAA Missed Warning on Insulation Burn Test." *Washington Post,* Nov. 8, 1998, p. A1.

8. Johnston, D. D. "On Tax Day, I.R.S. Prepared to Fire Star Whistleblower." *New York Times,* Apr. 17, 1999, p. A1.

9. Glazer and Glazer, 1989, p. 95.

10. Girard, R. *Violence and the Sacred* (P. Gregory, trans.). Baltimore: Johns Hopkins University Press, 1977, pp. 18, 36.

11. Douglas, M. *Purity and Danger.* Harmondsworth, England: Penguin, 1966.

12. Whether a whistleblower works again in his or her profession depends on both age and profession. A doctor or nurse can move to another state and for practical purposes can be considered an independent contractor. A nuclear engineer or a middle-aged auditor for the Navy, in contrast, is dependent on the military-industrial complex, as it used to be called, in

which personal networks dominate and informal blacklisting is readily practiced.

13. Strayer, J. "Feudalism in Western Europe." In R. Coulborn (ed.), *Feudalism in History* (pp. 15–25). Princeton, N.J.: Princeton University Press, 1956, p. 19.

14. Jackall, R. *Moral Mazes.* New York: Oxford University Press, 1988, pp. 109–110.

15. Elias, N. *The Civilizing Process* (E. Jephcott, trans.). Oxford: Blackwell, 1994, p. 450.

16. The only reason it matters is because it suggests that more than one whistleblower must have done some imaginary elaboration in the meantime, describing in full a gun that remained partly concealed by the holster. This is not uncommon with traumatic experience, indeed with all experience.

17. Foucault, M. *Discipline and Punish* (A. Sheridan, trans.). New York: Vintage Books, 1979.

18. Shils, E. "Charisma, Order, and Status." In *Center and Periphery* (pp. 256–275). Chicago: University of Chicago Press, 1975, p. 266.

19. I am taking liberties with Emile Durkheim here, associating the "conscience collective" of *The Division of Labor in Society,* an early work, with Durkheim's developed view of the sacred in *The Elementary Forms of Religious Life* and elsewhere, where he does not use the term. In *The Division of Labor in Society,* Durkheim believes that not much is left of the conscience collective, finding it in "only a very restricted part" of the psychic life of advanced societies (p. 80). This, though, is a little misleading, for by the conscience collective Durkheim refers to a particular mode of social cohesion. That a latent sense of the sacred remains in modern societies, that it is widespread, not confined to the power centers of society, but based on the awe-inspiring distance between individual and society, are central tenets of his. It is in this sense that I am using the term *conscience collective.* See Durkheim, E., and Coser, L. A. *The Division of Labor in Society* (G. Simpson, trans.). New York: Macmillan, 1933; Durkheim, E., and Cladis, M. S. *The Elementary Forms of Religious Life* (J. W. Swain, trans.). New York: Free Press, 1964.

CHAPTER EIGHTEEN

1. Hollander, E. P., and Offermann, L. "Power and Leadership in Organizations: Relationships in Transition." *American Psychologist*, 1990, *45*(2), 179–189.

2. Green, S. G., and Mitchell, T. R. "Attributional Processes of Leaders in Leader-Member Interactions." *Organizational Behavior and Human Performance*, 1979, *23*(3), 429–458; Lowin, A., and Craig, J. R. "The Influence of Level of Performance on Managerial Style: An Experimental Object-Lesson in the Ambiguity of Correlational Data." *Organizational Behavior and Human Performance*, 1968(3), *3*, 440–458.

3. Hollander, E. P. "Conformity, Status, and Idiosyncrasy Credit." *Psychological Review*, 1958, *65*(2), 117–127.

4. Lord, R. G., and Hall, R. J. "Identity, Leadership Categorization, and Leadership Schema." In D. van Knippenberg and M. A. Hogg (eds.), *Leadership and Power* (pp. 48–64). Thousand Oaks, Calif.: Sage, 2003.

5. Meindl, J. R. "The Romance of Leadership as a Follower-Centric Theory: A Social Constructionist Approach." *Leadership Quarterly*, 1995, *6*(3), 329–341.

6. Shamir, B., Pillai, R., Bligh, M. C., and Uhl-Bien, M. *Follower-Centered Perspectives on Leadership*. Greenwich, Conn.: Information Age, 2006.

7. Dienesch, R. M., and Liden, R. C. "Leader-Member Exchange Model of Leadership: A Critique and Further Development." *Academy of Management Review*, 1986, *10*(1), 116–127.

8. Hollander, E. P. "Leadership, Followership, Self, and Others." *Leadership Quarterly*, 1992, *3*(1), 43–54.

9. Manz, C. C., and Sims, H. P. *Superleadership*. Upper Saddle River, N.J.: Prentice Hall, 1989.

10. Ireland, R. D., and Hitt, M. A. "Achieving and Maintaining Strategic Competitiveness in the Twenty-First Century: The Role of Strategic Leadership." *Academy of Management Executive*, 1999, *13*, 43–57.

11. Meindl, 1995; Shamir, Pillai, Bligh, and Uhl-Bien, 2006.

12. Cilliers, P. *Complexity and Postmodernism*. New York: Routledge, 1998.

13. Uhl-Bien, M., and Pillai, R. "The Romance of Leadership and the Social Construction of Followership." In Shamir, Pallai, Bligh, and Uhl-Bien, 2007.

14. Weick, K. E. *Sensemaking in Organizations.* Thousand Oaks, Calif.: Sage, 1995.

15. Weick, K. E. "The Collapse of Sensemaking in Organizations: The Mann Gulch Disaster." *Administrative Science Quarterly,* 1993, *38*(4), 628–652.

16. Fitness, J. "Anger in the Workplace: An Emotion Script Approach to Anger Episodes Between Workers and Their Superiors, Co-Workers and Subordinates." *Journal of Organizational Behavior,* 2000, *21*(2), 147–162.

17. Lord, R. G., and Maher, K. J. *Leadership and Information Processing.* Cambridge, Mass.: Unwin Hyman, 1991; Medvedeff, M. E., and Lord, R. G. "Implicit Leadership Theories as Dynamic Processing Structures." In Shamir, Pallai, Bligh, and Uhl-Bien, 2007.

18. Meindl, J. R., Ehrlich, S. B., and Dukerich, J. M. "The Romance of Leadership." *Administrative Science Quarterly,* 1985, *30*(1), 78–102.

19. Lord, R. G., and Brown, D. J. *Leadership Processes and Follower Self-Identity.* Mahwah, N.J.: LEA, 2004.

20. Carver, C. S., and Scheier, M. F. *On the Self-Regulation of Behavior.* Cambridge: Cambridge University Press, 1998.

21. Johnson, R. E., Chang, C.-H. D., and Lord, R. G. "Moving from Cognition to Behavior: What the Research Says." *Psychological Bulletin,* 2006, *132*, 381–415.

22. Carver, C. S., and Scheier, M. E. "Control Processes and Self-Organization as Complementary Principles Underlying Behavior." *Personality and Social Psychology Review,* 2002, *6*(4), 304–315.

23. Higgins, E. T. "Beyond Pleasure and Pain." *American Psychologist,* 1997, *52*(12), 1280–1300.

24. Markus, H., and Wurf, E. "The Dynamic Self-Concept: A Social Psychological Perspective." *Annual Review of Psychology,* 1987, *38*, 299–337.

25. Lord and Brown, 2004.

26. Collinson, D. "Rethinking Followership: A Post-Structuralist Analysis of Follower Identities." *Leadership Quarterly,* 2006, *17*(2), 179–189.

27. Marion, R. *The Edge of Organization.* Thousand Oaks, Calif.: Sage, 1999; Marion, R., and Uhl-Bien, M. "Leadership in Complex Organizations." *Leadership Quarterly,* 2001, *12*(4), 389–419.

28. Cilliers, 1998.

29. Dragoni, L. "Understanding the Emergence of State Goal Orientation in Organizational Work Groups: The Role of Leadership and Multilevel Climate Perceptions." *Journal of Applied Psychology,* 2005, *90*(6), 1084–1095.

30. Sparrowe, R. T., and Liden, R. C. "Two Routes to Influence: Integrating Leader-Member Exchange and Social Network Perspectives." *Administrative Science Quarterly,* 2005, *50*, 505–535.

31. Cilliers, P. "Boundaries, Hierarchies, and Networks in Complex Systems." *International Journal of Innovation Management,* 2001, *5*, 135–147.

32. Marion and Uhl-Bien, 2001.

33. Ireland and Hitt, 1999.

34. Lord, R. G., and Hall, R. J. "Identity, Deep Structure, and the Development of Leadership Skills." *Leadership Quarterly,* 2005(4), *16*, 591–615.

35. Scott, K. A., and Brown, D. J. "Female First, Leader Second? Gender Bias in the Encoding of Leadership Behavior." *Organizational Behavior and Human Decision Processes,* 2006, *101*, 230–242.

36. Lord and Maher, 1991.

37. Ensari, N., and Murphy, S. E. "Cross-Cultural Variations in Leadership Perceptions and Attribution of Charisma to the Leader." *Organizational Behavior and Human Decision Processes,* 2003, 92(1/2), 52–66.

38. Lord and Hall, 2003.

39. Lord and Brown, 2004.

40. Fitness, 2000; Kohari, N. E., and Lord, R. G. "Consequences of Interactional (In)justice: A Look at Leader Behaviors and Follower Perceptions." In. D. De Cremer (ed.), *Advances in the Psychology of Justice and Affect.* Greenwich, Conn.: Information Age, 2007.

41. Engle, E., and Lord, R. G. "Implicit Theories, Self-Schema, and Leader-Member Exchange." *Academy of Management Journal,* 1997, *40*(4), 988–1010.

42. Cilliers, 1998.

43. Carver and Scheier, 2002.

44. Sparrowe and Liden, 2005.

45. Weick, K. E., and Roberts, K. H. "Collective Mind in Organizations: Heedful Interrelating on Flight Decks." *Administrative Science Quarterly,* 1993, *38*(3), 357–381.

46. Marion and Uhl-Bien, 2001.

47. Kark, R., Shamir, B., and Chen, G. "The Two Faces of Transformational Leadership: Empowerment and Dependency." *Journal of Applied Psychology,* 2003, *88*(2), 246–255.

48. Ritter, B. A. "Leadership Transference: The Generalization of Affective and Motivational Processes." Unpublished doctoral dissertation, University of Akron, 2004.

49. Lord, R. G. "Beyond Transactional and Transformational Leadership: Can Leaders Still Lead When They Don't Know What to Do?" In M. Uhl-Bien, R. Marion, and P. E. Hanges (eds.), *Complexity Theory and Leadership.* Greenwich, Conn.: Information Age, 2007.

50. Barsade, S. G. "The Ripple Effect: Emotional Contagion and Its Influence on Group Behavior." *Administrative Science Quarterly,* 2002, *47*(4), 644–675.

51. George, J. M. "Affect Regulation in Groups and Teams." In R. G. Lord, R. J. Klimoski, and R. Kanfer (eds.), *Emotions in the Workplace* (pp. 183–217). San Francisco: Jossey-Bass, 2002.

52. Marion and Uhl-Bien, 2001.

CHAPTER NINETEEN

1. Chaleff, I. *The Courageous Follower.* (2nd ed.) San Francisco: Berrett-Koehler, 2003; Kelley, R. E. *The Power of Followership.* New York: Doubleday,

1992; Shamir, B., Pillai, R., Bligh, M. C., and Uhl-Bien, M. (eds.), *Follower-Centered Perspectives on Leadership.* Greenwich, Conn.: Information Age, 2006.

2. Chemers, M. M. "Leadership Effectiveness: An Integrative Review." In M. A. Hogg and R. S. Tindale (eds.), *Blackwell Handbook of Social Psychology: Group Processes* (pp. 376–399). Oxford: Blackwell, 2001.

3. Tajfel, H., and Turner, J. C. "An Integrative Theory of Intergroup Conflict." In W. G. Austin and S. Worchel (eds.), *The Social Psychology of Intergroup Relations* (pp. 33–47). Monterey, Calif.: Brooks/Cole, 1979; Turner, J. C., Hogg, M. A., Oakes, P. J., Reicher, S. D., and Wetherell, M. S. *Rediscovering the Social Group.* Oxford: Blackwell, 1987; Hogg, M. A. "Social Identity Theory." In P. J. Burke (ed.), *Contemporary Social Psychological Theories* (pp. 111–136). Stanford, Calif.: Stanford University Press, 2006; Hogg, M. A., and Abrams, D. *Social Identifications.* London: Routledge, 1988.

4. For overviews of social identity theory in the context of organizational science, see the following: Ashforth, B. E., and Mael, F. A. "Social Identity Theory and the Organization." *Academy of Management Review,* 1989, *14*(1), 20–39; Hogg, M. A., and Terry, D. J. "Social Identity and Self-Categorization Processes in Organizational Contexts." *Academy of Management Review,* 2000, *25,* 121–140; Haslam, S. A. *Psychology in Organisations.* (2nd ed.) London: Sage, 2004.

5. There is substantial and wide-ranging empirical support for social identity theory. For recent reviews and overviews, see the following: Abrams, D., Hogg, M. A., Hinkle, S., and Otten, S. "The Social Identity Perspective on Small Groups." In M. S. Poole and A. B. Hollingshead (eds.), *Theories of Small Groups* (pp. 99–137). Thousand Oaks, Calif.: Sage, 2005; Ellemers, N., Spears, R., and Doosje, B. (eds.). *Social Identity.* Oxford: Blackwell, 1999; Hogg, M. A. "Social Identity." In M. R. Leary and J. P. Tangney (eds.), *Handbook of Self and Identity* (pp. 462–479). New York: Guilford, 2003; Hogg, M. A. "The Social Identity Perspective." In S. A. Wheelan (ed.), *The Handbook of Group Research and Practice* (pp. 133–157). Thousand Oaks, Calif.: Sage, 2005b; Hogg, 2006; Hogg, M. A., and Abrams, D. "Intergroup Behavior and Social Identity." In M. A. Hogg and J. Cooper (eds.), *The Sage Handbook of Social Psychology* (pp. 407–431). London: Sage, 2003; Hogg, M. A.,

Abrams, D., Otten, S., and Hinkle, S. "The Social Identity Perspective: Intergroup Relations, Self-Conception, and Small Groups." *Small Group Research*, 2004, *35*(3), 246–276; Postmes, T., and Jetten, J. (eds.). *Individuality and the Group*. London: Sage, 2006.

6. Hogg, M. A. "A Social Identity Theory of Leadership." *Personality and Social Psychology Review*, 2001b, *5*(3), 184–200; Hogg, M. A., and van Knippenberg, D. "Social Identity and Leadership Processes in Groups." In M. P. Zanna (ed.), *Advances in Experimental Social Psychology* (Vol. 35, pp. 1–52). San Diego, Calif.: Academic Press, 2003; van Knippenberg, D., and Hogg, M. A. "A Social Identity Model of Leadership in Organizations." In R. M. Kramer and B. M. Staw (eds.), *Research in Organizational Behavior* (Vol. 25, pp. 243–295). Greenwich, Conn.: JAI Press, 2003.

7. Berscheid, E., and Reis, H. T. "Attraction and Close Relationships." In D. T. Gilbert, S. T. Fiske, and G. Lindzey (eds.), *The Handbook of Social Psychology* (4th ed., Vol. 2, pp. 193–281). New York: McGraw-Hill, 1998.

8. Tyler, T. R. "The Psychology of Legitimacy: A Relational Perspective on Voluntary Deference to Authorities." *Personality and Social Psychology Review*, 1997, *1*(4), 323–345; Tyler, T. R., and Lind, E. A. "A Relational Model of Authority in Groups." In M. P. Zanna (ed.), *Advances in Experimental Social Psychology* (Vol. 25, pp. 115–191). San Diego, Calif.: Academic Press, 1992; Platow, M. J., Reid, S. A., and Andrew, S. "Leadership Endorsement: The Role of Distributive and Procedural Behavior in Interpersonal and Intergroup Contexts." *Group Processes and Intergroup Relations*, 1998, *1*(1), 35–47.

9. Avolio, B. J., and Yammarino, F. J. (eds.). *Transformational and Charismatic Leadership*. New York: Elsevier, 2003.

10. Ross, L. "The Intuitive Psychologist and His Shortcomings." In L. Berkowitz (ed.), *Advances in Experimental Social Psychology* (Vol. 10, pp. 174–220). San Diego, Calif.: Academic Press, 1977.

11. Gilbert, D. T., and Malone, P. S. "The Correspondence Bias." *Psychological Bulletin*, 1995, *117*, 21–38.

12. Haslam, N., Rothschild, L., and Ernst, D. "Essentialist Beliefs About Social Categories." *British Journal of Social Psychology*, 2000, *39*(1), 113–127.

13. Avolio and Yammarino, 2003.

14. Haslam, S. A., and Platow, M. J. "Your Wish Is Our Command: The Role of Shared Social Identity in Translating a Leader's Vision into Followers' Action." In M. A. Hogg and D. J. Terry (eds.), *Social Identity Processes in Organizational Contexts* (pp. 213–228). Philadelphia: Psychology Press, 2001.

15. Reicher, S., and Hopkins, N. "On the Science of the Art of Leadership." In D. van Knippenberg and M. A. Hogg (eds.), *Leadership and Power* (pp. 197–209). London: Sage, 2003.

16. Reicher and Hopkins, 2003; Reicher, S. D., and Hopkins, N. "Self-Category Constructions in Political Rhetoric: An Analysis of Thatcher's and Kinnock's Speeches Concerning the British Miners' Strike (1984–5)." *European Journal of Social Psychology,* 1996, *26*(3), 353–371.

17. Platow, M. J., and van Knippenberg, D. "A Social Identity Analysis of Leadership Endorsement: The Effects of Leader Ingroup Prototypicality and Distributive Intergroup Fairness." *Personality and Social Psychology Bulletin,* 2001, *27*(11), 1508–1519.

18. For summaries of empirical work, see the following: Ellemers, N., de Gilder, D., and Haslam, S. A. "Motivating Individuals and Groups at Work: A Social Identity Perspective on Leadership and Group Performance." *Academy of Management Review,* 2004, *29*(3), 459–478; Hogg, 2001b; Hogg and van Knippenberg, 2003; van Knippenberg and Hogg, 2003; van Knippenberg, D., van Knippenberg, B., De Cremer, D., and Hogg, M. A. "Leadership, Self, and Identity: A Review and Research Agenda." *Leadership Quarterly,* 2004(6), *15,* 825–856.

19. See, for example, Sani, F., and Reicher, S. D. "Contested Identities and Schisms in Groups: Opposing the Ordination of Women as Priests in the Church of England." *British Journal of Social Psychology,* 2000, *39*(1), 95–112.

20. Hogg, M. A. "From Prototypicality to Power: A Social Identity Analysis of Leadership." In S. R. Thye, E. J. Lawler, M. W. Macy, and H. A. Walker (eds.), *Advances in Group Processes* (Vol. 18, pp. 1–30). Oxford: Elsevier, 2001a;

Hogg, M. A. "Social Identity and Misuse of Power: The Dark Side of Leadership." *Brooklyn Law Review,* 2005a, *70,* 1239–1257; Hogg, M. A. "Uncertainty-Identity Theory." In M. P. Zanna (ed.), *Advances in Experimental Social Psychology* (Vol. 39, pp. 69–126). San Diego, Calif.: Academic Press, 2007; Hogg, M. A. "Organizational Orthodoxy and Corporate Autocrats: Some Nasty Consequences of Organizational Identification in Uncertain Times." In C. A. Bartel, S. Blader, and A. Wrzesniewski (eds.), *Identity and the Modern Organization* (pp. 35–59). Mahwah, N.J.: Erlbaum, forthcoming.

21. Reicher, S. D. "The St Pauls' Riot: An Explanation of the Limits of Crowd Action in Terms of a Social Identity Model." *European Journal of Social Psychology,* 1984, *14*(1), 1–21.

22. Hogg, M. A., and Reid, S. A. "Social Identity, Self-Categorization, and the Communication of Group Norms." *Communication Theory,* 2006, *16*(1), 7–30; Reicher and Hopkins, 2003.

23. Hogg, 2007.

24. Hogg, 2001a; Hogg, 2005a; Hogg, forthcoming.

25. Prentice, D. A., and Miller, D. T. "Pluralistic Ignorance and the Perpetuation of Social Norms by Unwitting Actors." In M. P. Zanna (ed.), *Advances in Experimental Social Psychology* (Vol. 28, pp. 161–209). San Diego, Calif.: Academic Press, 1996.

CHAPTER TWENTY

1. Collins, J. C., and Porras, J. I. "Organizational Vision and Visionary Organizations." *California Management Review,* 1991, *34*(1), 30.

2. Goffee, R., and Jones, G. "Followership—It's Personal, Too." *Harvard Business Review,* 2001, *79*(11).

3. Meindl, J. R. "The Romance of Leadership as a Follower-Centric Theory: A Social Constructionist Approach." *Leadership Quarterly,* 1995, *6*(3), 329–341.

4. Kirkpatrick, S. A., and Locke, E. A. "Direct and Indirect Effects of Three Core Charismatic Leadership Components on Performance and Attitudes." *Journal of Applied Psychology,* 1996, *81*(1), 36–51.

5. Conger, J. A. *The Charismatic Leader*. San Francisco: Jossey-Bass, 1989.

6. Posner, B. Z., and Kouzes, J. M. "Rating Leadership and Credibility." *Psychological Reports*, 1988, *63*, 527–530.

7. Conger, J. A., Kanungo, R. N., and Menon, S. T. "Charismatic Leadership and Follower Effects." *Journal of Organizational Behavior*, 2000, *21*(7), 747.

8. Kirkpatrick and Locke, 1996.

9. Shamir, B., House, R. J, and Arthur, M. B. "The Motivational Effects of Charismatic Leadership: A Self-Concept Based Theory." *Organization Science*, 1993, *4*(4), 577–594.

10. Baum, J. R., Locke, E. A., and Kirkpatrick, S. A. "A Longitudinal Study of the Relation of Vision and Vision Communication to Venture Growth in Entrepreneurial Firms." *Journal of Applied Psychology*, 1998, *83*(1), 43–54.

11. Pierce, J. L., Kostova, T., and Dirks, K. T. "Toward a Theory of Psychological Ownership in Organizations." *Academy of Management Review*, 2001, *26*(2), 298–310.

12. Sashkin, M. "True Vision in Leadership." *Training and Development Journal*, 1986, *40*(5), 60.

13. Levin, I. M. "Vision Revisited: Telling the Story of the Future." *Journal of Applied Behavioral Science*, 2000, *36*(1), 91–107.

14. Dansereau, F., and Markham, S. E. "Superior-Subordinate Communication: Multiple Levels of Analysis." In F. M. Jablin, L. L. Putnam, K. H. Roberts, and L. W. Porter (eds.), *Handbook of Organizational Communication*. Thousand Oaks, Calif.: Sage, 1987; Vanderslice, V. J. "Separating Leadership from Leaders: An Assessment of the Effect of Leadership and Follower Role in Organizations." *Human Relations*, 1988, *41*(9), 677–696.

15. Hopper, A., and Potter, J. *Intelligent Leadership*. London: Random House, 2000; Kotter, J. P. *Leading Change*. Boston: Harvard Business School Press, 1996; Zaccaro, S. J. *The Nature of Executive Leadership*. Washington, D.C.: American Psychological Association, 2001.

16. Gill, R. "Change Management—or Change Leadership?" *Journal of Change Management*, 2003, *3*(4), 307–407; Hopper and Potter, 2000.

17. Collins and Porras, 1991; Levin, 2000.

18. Larwood, L., Falbe, C. M., Krieger, M. P., and Miesing, P. "Structure and Meaning of Organizational Vision." *Academy of Management Journal,* 1995, *38*(3), 740–769.

CHAPTER TWENTY-ONE

1. For more reading on the role of leadership in creativity, see Jaussi, K. S., and Dionne, S. D. "Leading for Creativity: The Role of Unconventional Behavior." *Leadership Quarterly,* 2003, *14*(4–5), 475–498; Mumford, M. D., Scott, G. M., Gaddis, B., and Strange, J. M. "Leading Creative People: Orchestrating Expertise and Relationships." *Leadership Quarterly,* 2002, *13*(6), 705–750; Woodman, R., Sawyer, J., and Griffin R. "Toward a Theory of Organizational Creativity." *Academy of Management Review,* 1993, *18*(2), 293–321; Tierney, P., Farmer, S. M., and Graen, G. B. "An Examination of Leadership and Employee Creativity: The Relevance of Traits and Relationships." *Personnel Psychology,* 1999, *52*(3), 591–620; Oldham, G. R., and Cummings, A. "Employee Creativity: Personal and Contextual Factors at Work." *Academy of Management Journal,* 1996, *39*(3), 527–556.

2. Amabile, T. M. "A Model of Creativity and Innovation in Organizations." *Research in Organizational Behavior,* 1988, *10*, 123–167.

3. Perry-Smith, J. E., and Shalley, C. E. "The Social Side of Creativity: A Static and Dynamic Social Network Perspective." *Academy of Management Review,* 2003, *28*(1), 89–106; Thompson, L. "Improving the Creativity of Organizational Work Groups." *Academy of Management Executive,* 2003, *17*(1), 96–109; Ford, C. M. "A Theory of Individual Creative Action in Multiple Social Domains." *Academy of Management Review,* 1996, *21*(4), 1112–1142.

4. Conlin, M. "Champions of Innovation." *BusinessWeek,* June 19, 2006, pp. 18–21.

5. Kelley, R. E. *The Power of Followership.* New York: Doubleday, 1992; Chaleff, I. *The Courageous Follower.* (2nd ed.) San Francisco: Berrett-Koehler, 2003.

6. To learn more about confusion tolerance, refer to "Clearly Blurry," a Red paper by Play, available at www.lookatmorestuff.com/clearly-blurry.pdf. 2004.

7. Amabile, T. M., Barsade, S. G., Mueller, J. S., and Staw, B. M. "Affect and Creativity at Work." *Administrative Science Quarterly,* 2005, *50*(3), 367–403.

8. Play is a creativity and innovation consultancy located in Richmond, Virginia. Known for its irreverent style and breakthrough thinking, Play has led numerous Fortune 500 organizations through change efforts focused on increasing innovation. As an organic, unique, team-based organization, Play's internal processes and physical office space are used as exemplars for organizations seeking to foster creativity and innovation.

9. Conger, J. A., and Kanungo, R. N. *Charismatic Leadership in Organizations.* Thousand Oaks, Calif.: Sage, 1998; Conger, J. A. *The Charismatic Leader.* San Francisco: Jossey-Bass, 1989.

10. Jaussi, K., and Aldag, R. *Fun and Followership.* Presented at the Kravis–de Roulet Rethinking Followership Conference as part of the panel "Follower Strategies for the Management of Distance from One's Leader," Claremont, California, Feb. 2006; see also Aldag, R. J., and Sherony, K. M. *Fun at Work: Measurement and Correlates.* Paper presented at the national meeting of the American Psychological Society, Chicago, June 2004.

11. Jaussi, K. S., Carroll, E., and Dionne, S. D. *The Real Deal Rubs Off on Others: Authentic Leadership and the Importance of Fun.* Paper presented at the Gallup Leadership Summit, Omaha, Nebraska, June 11, 2004.

12. Jaussi, K. S., Randel, A. E., and Dionne, S. D. (2007). "I Am, I Think I Can, and I Do: The Role of Personal Identity, Self-Efficacy, and Cross-Application of Experiences in Creativity at Work." *Creativity Research Journal,* 2007, *19*(1), 1–12.

13. Jaussi, K. S., Devlin, P., and Randel, A. E. *Developing Those Who Will Lead Others Towards Creativity at Work: The Role of a Leader's Creative Catalyst Personal Identity, Fun at Work, and Follower's Leader-Inspired Creative Role Identity.* Paper presented at the Gallup Leadership Summit, Oct. 2006.

14. Jaussi, Randel, and Dionne, forthcoming.

15. Chaleff, 2003, pp. 35–56.

CHAPTER TWENTY-TWO

1. Meindl, J., Ehrlich, S. B., and Dukerich, J. M. "The Romance of Leadership." *Administrative Science Quarterly,* 1985, *30*(1), 78–102.

2. Meindl, J. "The Romance of Leadership as a Follower-Centric Theory: A Social Constructionist Approach." *Leadership Quarterly,* 1995, *6*(3), 329–341.

3. Yet, by eschewing any consideration of leaders in favor of an exclusive focus on followers, Meindl tends to invert and reproduce a dichotomy between followers and leaders. Reacting against the one, dominant side of the polarity (leaders), he shifts to the other (followers). Rather than replace a "leader-centric" approach with a "follower-centric" analysis, this chapter argues for a more dialectical understanding of the complex, interactional relationships between leaders and followers.

4. Kelley, R. E. "Followership." In G. R. Goethals, G. J. Sorenson, and J. M. Burns (eds.), *Encyclopedia of Leadership.* Thousand Oaks, Calif.: Sage, 2004.

5. Raelin, J. *Creating Leaderful Organizations.* San Francisco: Berrett-Koehler, 2003.

6. Burns, J. M. *Leadership.* New York: HarperCollins, 1978.

7. Shamir, B., House, R. J., and Arthur, M. B. "The Motivational Effects of Charismatic Leadership: A Self-Concept Based Theory." *Organization Science,* 1993, 4(4), 577–594.

8. Lord, R. G., and Brown, D. J. *Leadership Processes and Follower Self-Identity.* Mahwah, N.J.: Erlbaum, 2004.

9. Meindl, Ehrlich, and Dukerich's research methods drew on archival (the popular press, business periodicals, and student dissertation topics) and experimental studies (attributions by undergraduate business school students in relation to fictitious cases). A post-structuralist analysis would hypothesize that undergraduate students and the media will be more likely to romanticize (distant) leaders than will (proximate) followers employed in organizations who have more direct experience of being led.

10. Foucault, M. *Discipline and Punish.* London: Allen & Unwin, 1977; Foucault, M. *The History of Sexuality.* London: Allen & Unwin, 1979.

11. Foucault's emphasis on the way that identity can be incorporated into disciplinary processes clearly has some resonance with Lord and Brown's focus on the "self-regulating" nature of identity. However, Lord and Brown's recommendation that leaders should try to influence followers' identity illustrates the very disciplinary processes post-structuralists seek to critique. Lord and Brown also argue that identity consists of a confederation of selves that vary across time and context and that the "working self-concept" acts as a self-regulating mechanism that simplifies processing. A post-structuralist approach would suggest that this rather mechanistic and functionalist model underestimates the ambiguities and tensions that may characterize multiple identities in the workplace.

12. A considerable number of different intellectual traditions have examined self, identity, and subjectivity. These include the philosophical approaches of existentialism and phenomenology; the sociological theories of symbolic interactionism, interpretative sociology, and social anthropology; and the more cognitive perspectives of social psychology and psychoanalysis. Recently there has been a resurgence of interest in identity issues within social theory and in management and organization studies. In the area of leadership, most studies of identity concentrate on leaders. Social psychologists have developed the social identity theory of leadership, which asserts that people strive for a positive self-concept and that social identity is implicated in all forms of leadership. It suggests that leadership is contingent on the degree to which leaders are perceived as "prototypical" of the group's identity and predicts that followers will endorse leaders they see as quintessentially embodying the values of groups with which they strongly identify.

13. Sennett, R., and Cobb, J. *The Hidden Injuries of Class.* Cambridge: Cambridge University Press, 1977.

14. Collinson, D. L. "Identities and Insecurities: Selves at Work." *Organization,* 2003, *10*(3), 527–547.

15. Gabriel, Y. "Meeting God: When Organizational Members Come Face to Face with the Supreme Leader." *Human Relations,* 1997, *50*(4), 315–342.

16. Shamir, B. "Taming Charisma for Better Understanding and Greater Usefulness: A Response to Beyer." *Leadership Quarterly,* 1999, *10*(4), 555–562.

17. Calas, M. B., and Smiricich, L. "Voicing Seduction to Silence Leadership." *Organization Studies,* 1991, *12*(4), 567–602.

18. Gemmill, G., and Oakley, J. "Leadership: An Alienating Social Myth." *Human Relations,* 1992, *45*(2), 113–129.

19. Milgram, S. "Behavioral Study of Obedience." *Journal of Abnormal and Social Psychology,* 1963, *69*(2), 137–143; see also Blass in this volume.

20. Fromm, E. *The Fear of Freedom.* London: Routledge, 1977.

21. Shamir, B. "Motivation of Followers." In Goethals, Sorenson, and Burns, 2004.

22. Alvesson, M., and Willmott, H. "Identity Regulation as Organizational Control: Producing the Appropriate Individual." *Journal of Management Studies,* 2002, *39*(5), 619–644.

23. Tourish, D., and Vatcha, N. "Charismatic Leadership and Corporate Cultism at Enron: The Elimination of Dissent, the Promotion of Conformity and Organizational Collapse." *Leadership,* 2005, *1*(4), 455–480.

24. Lipman-Blumen, J. *The Allure of Toxic Leaders.* New York: Oxford University Press, 2005.

25. Other forms of follower agency could be characterized as more Machiavellian or unprincipled, including "misbehavior," lying, deceit and subterfuge, aggression and violence, retaliation and revenge.

26. Prince, L. "The Neglected Rules: On Leadership and Dissent." In A. Coulson (ed.), *Trust and Contracts.* Cambridge: Polity Press, 1998.

27. Foucault, 1977; Jermier, J. M., Knights, D., and Nord, W. R. (eds.). *Resistance and Power in Organizations.* London: Routledge, 1994.

28. Fleming, P. "Metaphors of Resistance." *Management Communication Quarterly,* 2005, *19*(1), 45–66.

29. Graham, L. *On the Line at Subaru-Isuzu.* Ithaca, N.Y.: ILR Press, 1995.

30. Collinson, D. L. "Questions of Distance." *Leadership,* 2005, *1*(2), 235–250.

31. Collinson, D. L. "Strategies of Resistance: Power, Knowledge and Subjectivity in the Workplace." In K. Grint (ed.), *Work and Society*. Cambridge: Polity Press, 2000; Collinson, D. L. "Dialectics of Leadership." *Human Relations*, 2005, *58*(11), 1419–1442.

32. Ashcraft, K. L., and Mumby, D. K. *Reworking Gender*. London: Sage, 2004.

33. Willis, P. *Learning to Labor*. London: Saxon House, 1977.

34. Chaleff, I. *The Courageous Follower*. San Francisco: Berrett-Koehler, 1995; see also Chaleff this volume.

35. Grint, K. *Leadership: Limits and Possibilities*. New York: Palgrave Macmillan, 2005.

36. Collinson, 2000.

37. Hirschman, A. D. *Exit, Voice and Loyalty*. Cambridge, Mass: Harvard University Press, 1990.

38. Miceli, M. P., and Near, J. P. "What Makes Whistleblowers Effective? Three Field Studies." *Human Relations*, 2002, *55*(4), 155–167; see also Alford this volume.

39. Heifetz, R. A., and Laurie, D. L. "The Work of Leadership." *Harvard Business Review*, Jan.-Feb. 1997, pp. 124–134.

40. Goffman, E. *The Presentation of Self in Everyday Life*. Harmondsworth: Penguin, 1959.

41. Collinson, D. L. "Surviving the Rigs: Safety and Surveillance on North Sea Oil Installations." *Organization Studies*, 1999, *20*(4), 579–600.

42. In such cases, effective leaders need to retain a critical awareness that followers may, for example, seek to construct (overly) positive impressions of themselves and that such self-promoting strategies could significantly distort organizational communication.

43. Kondo, D. K. *Crafting Selves*. Chicago: University of Chicago Press, 1990, p. 224.

44. Kondo, 1990.

45. Meyerson, D. E. *Tempered Radicals*. Boston: Harvard Business School Press, 2001.

46. Cockburn, C. *Brothers*. London: Pluto, 1983.

47. Willis, 1977.

48. Collinson, D. L. *Managing the Shopfloor.* Berlin: Walter de Gruyter, 1992.

49. Sinclair, A. *Leadership for the Disillusioned.* Crows Nest, Australia: Allen & Unwin, 2007.

50. Collins, J. *Good to Great.* London: Random House, 2001.

51. Kodish, S. "The Paradoxes of Leadership: The Contribution of Aristotle." *Leadership,* 2006, *2*(4), 451–468; Jones, A. "Developing What? An Anthropological Look at the Leadership Development Process Across Cultures." *Leadership,* 2006, *2*(4), 481–498.

CHAPTER TWENTY-THREE

1. Dorfman, P. W., and House, R. J. "Cultural Influences on Organizational Leadership: Literature Review, Theoretical Rationale, and GLOBE Project Goals." In R. J. House, P. J. Hanges, M. Javidan, P. W. Dorfman, and V. Gupta (eds.), *Culture, Leadership, and Organizations* (pp. 51–73). London: Sage, 2004; Avolio, B. J. "Promoting More Integrative Strategies for Leadership Theory Building." *American Psychologist,* 2007, *62,* 25–33. Hofstede, G. "Cultural Constraints in Management Theories." *Academy of Management Executive,* 1993, *7*(1), 81–94.

2. Graen, G. B., and Uhl-Bien, M. "Relationship-Based Approach to Leadership: Development of Leader-Member Exchange (LMX) Theory of Leadership over Twenty-Five Years: Applying a Multi-Level, Multi-Domain Perspective." *Leadership Quarterly,* 1995, *6*(2), 219–247.

3. Marion, R., and Uhl-Bein, M. "Leadership in Complex Organizations." *Leadership Quarterly,* 2001, *12*(4), 414.

4. Burns, J. M. *Leadership.* New York: HarperCollins, 1978.

5. Burns, 1978; Bass, B. M. "Leadership: Good, Better, Best." *Organizational Dynamics,* 1985, *13*(3), 26–40.

6. Dvir, T., and Shamir, B. "Follower Developmental Characteristics as Predictors of Transformational Leadership: A Longitudinal Field Study." *Leadership Quarterly,* 2003, *14*(3), 327–344.

7. Benjamin, L., and Flynn, F. J. "Leadership Style and Regulatory Mode: Value from Fit?" *Organizational Behavior and Human Decision Processes,* 2006, *100*(2), 216–230.

8. Sivasubramaniam, N., Murry, W. D., Avolio, B. J., and Jung, D. I. "A Longitudinal Model of the Effects of Team Leadership and Group Potency on Group Performance." *Group and Organization Management,* 2002, *27*(1), 66–96.

9. Luthans, F., and Avolio, B. J. "Authentic Leadership: A Positive Developmental Approach." In K. S. Cameron, J. E. Dutton, and R. E. Quinn (eds.), *Positive Organizational Scholarship* (pp. 241–261). San Francisco: Berrett-Koehler, 2003.

10. Gardner, W. L., Avolio, B. J., Luthans, F., May, D. R., and Walumbwa, F. O. "Can You See the Real Me? A Self-Based Model of Authentic Leader and Follower Development." *Leadership Quarterly,* 2005, *16*(3), 346.

11. Gardner, Avolio, Luthans, May, and Walumbwa, 2005.

12. Pierce, J. L., O'Driscoll, M. P., and Coghlan, A. M. "Work Environment Structure and Psychological Ownership: The Mediating Effects of Control." *Journal of Social Psychology,* 2004, *144*(5), 507–534.

13. Pierce, J. L., Kostova, T., and Dirks, K. T. "Toward a Theory of Psychological Ownership in Organizations." *Academy of Management Review,* 2003, *26*(2), 298–310.

14. Pierce, Kostova, and Dirks, 2003.

15. Ardrey, R. *The Territorial Imperative.* New York: Dell, 1966; Duncan, N. G. "Home Ownership and Social Theory." In J. S. Duncan (ed.), *Housing and Identity* (pp. 98–134). London: Croom Helm, 1981.

16. Ardrey, 1966.

17. Pierce, Kostova, and Dirks, 2003.

18. Abrams, D., and Hogg, M. A. "Metatheory: Lessons from Social Identity Research." *Personality and Social Psychology Review,* 2004, *8*(2), 98–106; Belk, R. W. "Possessions and the Extended Self." *Journal of Consumer Research,* 1988, *15*, 139–168; Rousseau, D. M. "Why Workers Still Identify with Organizations." *Journal of Organizational Behavior,* 1998, *19*(3), 217–233.

19. Brown, G., Lawrence, T. B., and Robinson, S. L. "Territoriality in Organizations." *Academy of Management Review,* 2005, *30*(3), 577–594.

20. Dittmar, H. *The Social Psychology of Material Possessions.* New York: St. Martin's Press, 1992.

21. Bandura, A. *Self-Efficacy: The Exercise of Control.* New York: Freeman, 1997.

22. Bandura, 1997.

23 Pierce, Kostova, and Dirks, 2003.

24. Friedman, T. L. *The World Is Flat.* New York: Farrar, Straus & Giroux, 2006.

25. Roberts, K. H., and Bea, R. "Must Accidents Happen? Lessons from High-Reliability Organizations." *Academy of Management Executive,* 2001, *15*(3), 70–78.

26. Jones, G. R., and George, J. M. "The Experience and Evolution of Trust: Implications for Cooperation and Teamwork." *Academy of Management Review,* 1998, *23*(3), 531–546.

27. Meyerson, D., Weick, K., and Kramer, R. "Swift Trust and Temporary Groups." In R. Kramer and T. Tyler (eds.), *Trust in Organizations* (pp. 166–195). Thousand Oaks, Calif.: Sage, 1996.

28. Holmes, J. G., and Rempel, J. K. "Trust in Close Relationships." In C. Hendrick (ed.), *Close Relationships* (pp. 187–220). Thousand Oaks, Calif.: Sage, 1989.

29. Avolio, B. J. *Leadership Development in Balance: Made/Born.* Mahwah, N.J.: Erlbaum, 2005.

30. Avolio, 2005.

31. Rempel, J. K., Holmes, J. G., and Zanna, M. P. "Trust in Close Relationships." *Journal of Personality and Social Psychology,* 1985, *49*(1), 95–112.

32. Dirks, K. T. "The Effects of Interpersonal Trust on Work Group Performance." *Journal of Applied Psychology,* 1999, *84*(3), 445–455; Dirks, K. T. "Trust in Leadership and Team Performance: Evidence from NCAA Basketball." *Journal of Applied Psychology,* 2000, *85*(6), 1004–1012.

33. Dirks, 1999; Dirks, 2000; Klimoski, R. J., and Karol, B. L. "The Impact of Trust on Creative Problem Solving Groups." *Journal of Applied Psychology,*

1976, *61*, 630–633; McAllister, D. J. "Affect- and Cognition-Based Trust as Foundations for Interpersonal Cooperation in Organizations." *Academy of Management Journal,* 1995, *38*(1), 24–59.

34. Wat, D., and Shaffer, M. A. "Equity and Relationship Quality Influences on Organizational Citizenship Behaviors: The Mediating Role of Trust in the Supervisor and Empowerment." *Personnel Review,* 2005, *34*(4), 406–422; Podsakoff, P., MacKenzie, S., Moorman, R., and Fetter, R. "Transformational Leader Behaviors and Their Effects on Followers' Trust in Leader, Satisfaction, and Organizational Citizenship Behaviors." *Leadership Quarterly,* 1990, *1*(1), 107–142.

35. Jourard, S. M. *Self-Disclosure: An Experimental Analysis of the Transparent Self.* Oxford: Wiley, 1971.

36. Gibbons, D. E. "Friendship and Advice Networks in the Context of Changing Professional Values." *Administrative Science Quarterly,* 2004, *49*(2), 238–362.

37. Voglegesang, G. R., and Crossley, C. D. *"Toward an Understanding of Relational and Climatic Transparency."* Paper presented at the Gallup Leadership Institute Summit, Washington, D.C., Oct. 2006.

38. Lundgren, J., and Moore, P. "When Organizations Are Transparent, the Light Shines Through." *Oncology Nursing Society News,* 2004, *19*(6), 3.

39. Korsgaard, M. A., Whitener, E. M., and Brodt, S. E. "Trust in the Face of Conflict: The Role of Managerial Trustworthy Behavior and Organizational Context." *Journal of Applied Psychology,* 2002, *87*(2), 312–319.

40. Voglegesang and Crossley, 2006.

41. Katz, D., and Kahn, R. *The Social Psychology of Organizations.* New York: Wiley, 1978.

42. Tucker, A. L., and Edmonson, A. "Why Hospitals Don't Learn from Failures: Organizational and Psychological Dynamics That Inhibit System Change." *California Management Review,* 2003, *45*(2), 55–72; Zhao, B., and Olivera, F. "Error Reporting in Organizations." *Academy of Management Review,* 2006, *31*(4), 1012–1030.

43. Edmonson, A. C. "Psychological Safety and Learning Behavior in Work Teams." *Administrative Science Quarterly,* 1999, *44*(2), 350–383.

INDEX

A

Abse, D., 198

Accountability: and commitment, 120; and excellence and quality, 120–121; and psychological ownership, 331

Adair, R., 75, 137

Adelphia Communications, 81

Agentic shift, 203

Aggression, and Milgram's obedience experiments, 200–201

Alford, C. F., 76, 237

Alienated, as followership style, 7, 13

Allport, G., 196

The Answer Is Horse, 199

Anxiety, existential, 184, 192

Ardrey, R., 330

"Are Corporations Evil?" (Litowitz), 206

Arendt, H., 199

Aristotle, 21

Arthur, M. B., 310, 311

Asch, S., 207

Authentic leadership development (ALD), 327–328

Authority: changing attitude toward, 213; and courageous followers, 72, 78–79, 164, 166–167, 170–171; in leadership-followership state paradigm, 49, 50, 51, 52; in organizational position para-digm, 45, 46; standing up to, 78, 79, 171; ways of relating to, 76. *See also* Obedience experiments, Milgram's

Authority Relations Inventory, 75

Avolio, B. J., 325

B

Bandura, A., 331

Bartels, B., 204

Bass, B. M., 2, 326

Bauman, Z., 239, 251

Beam, J., 164–165

Beck, J. C., 214

Becker, E., 181

Beedle, P., 86

Bellak, G., 198

Berg, D. N., 175

Bies, R. J., 348n6

Bin Laden, O., 29

Blake, R. R., 46

Blanchard, K. H., 46

Blass, T., 195

Bligh, M. C., 277

Blind obedience, 201–202

Blumen, L. S., 219

Boccialetti, G., 75, 156

Bonaparte, N., 181

Brewer, M. B., 29

Brown, D. J., 38, 311, 370n11

Bullying, children's, 219–236; actions to stop, 231–232, 234–235; as adult problem, 226–227; adults as enabling, 227–229; bystanders to, 220–221, 225–226, 227–230; components of system of, 225–226; creating norm to prevent, 232–233; defined, 222–223; reasons for persistence of, 221–222; types of, 223–225

Bureaucratic social character, 213, 214, 215, 216

Burke, C. S., 35

Burns, J. M., 2, 326

Buxton, C., 195

Bystanders to bullying: adults as, 227–229; impact of bullying on, 229; innocence of, 220–221; intervention by, 231–232; lack of focus on, 221; reasons for nonintervention by, 230; role of, 225–226; teaching children skills as, 234–235

C

Campbell, J., 95

Carsten, M. K., 277

Catholic Church, and followers, 60

CEOs: confronting, 82–83; follower behaviors of, 174

Chaleff, I., 3, 6, 52, 60, 111, 113, 119, 121, 124, 128, 161, 162, 164, 174, 175, 293, 306, 317–318

Challenger space shuttle disaster, 36

Character. *See* Social character

Charismatic leadership, 12, 183, 271, 310, 311

Cialdini, R., 116, 117, 119

Claremont McKenna College, leadership overemphasis at, 89–93

Clark, W., 141

Coady, S., 98, 100

Cobb, J., 312

Cockburn, C., 321

Coercion, 48, 49, 201, 248

Collaborative leadership, 57, 61, 63, 171–172, 215–217

Collaborators, 57, 58, 60, 63

Collective self-concept, 36–37

Colleges, leadership emphasis in admissions process of, 89–93

Collins, J., 322

Collinson, D., 29, 38, 309

Coloroso, B., 222

Columbia space shuttle disaster, 36, 96–97

Commitment: and accountability, 120; barriers to, 117–118; and courageous followership, 118–120; shared, connecting leaders and followers, 115–117

Communication: leaders influenced by, of followers, 274, 276; in leadership-followership state paradigm, 51; and role orientation, 26, 28, 35; of vision, 287–288

Complexity theory, 260–262

Conflict, constructive, 36

Conflict resolution, and bullying, 22

Conformity: and groupthink, 35–36; identity characterized by, 313–315, 320; of "natural followers," 44

Confusion tolerance, 294

Conscience, courageous, 14–15

Conscience collective, 250–251, 357n19

Conservative movement, follower role advocated by, 60

Contexts: and follower role orientations, 30–31, 34, 37; for leadership, 42, 344n2

Coughlan, E., 199

Counter-anthropomorphism, 205

Courageous conscience, 14–15

The Courageous Follower (Chaleff), 6, 67, 70, 71, 72, 74, 85, 111, 113, 124, 128

Courageous followers: challenging authority, 72, 78–79, 166–167, 170–171; and fear, 80, 119; and followership styles matrix, 74–75;

giving support to leaders, 72, 73–75, 86, 165–166; and leadership-followership state paradigm, 52; learning skills of, 82–84; and media accounts of leadership failures, 81–82; paradox of, 82; participating in transformation, 72, 167–169; responsibility assumed by, 72, 164–165; sources of values of, 79; taking moral action, 73, 84–86, 169–170

Courageous followership: and commitment, 118–120; course on, at Georgetown University, 112–114, 115; creating culture of, 128–136; implementing, in contemporary organizations, 121, 176; model of attitudes and behaviors of, 72–73; organizational level of people exhibiting behaviors of, 173–174; as way to transform organizational culture, 110–112, 124–125

Covey, S., 21, 102

Creative Catalysts, 295–299

Creative Skeptics, 300–303

Creative Statics, 303–305

Creative Supporters, 299–300

Creativity, 292. *See also* Followers for creativity

Crossley, C. D., 335

Culbert, S., 76

Culture: changed American, 211; contemporary, and large organizations, 70; and followership, 10–11; valuing human dignity, 69, 86–87. *See also* Organizational culture

Cyberbullying, 225

D

De Bivort, L., 142, 349n7

Democracy: in digital age, 325; and whistleblowers, 237–238

Department of Defense, whistleblower at, 244–246

Depersonalization: applied to self, 269; defined, 268–269; and leadership, 270

Devlin, P. G., 291

Disguised identity, 318–320, 371n25, 372n42

Dixon, G., 155

The Dogs of Pavlov (Abse), 198

Douglas, M., 244

Dragoni, L., 261

Drucker, P., 21

Dukerich, J. M., 310, 369n9

Durkheim, E., 250–251, 357n19

"Dying by Degrees" (Coughlan), 199

Dylan, B., 112

E

Eden, D., 30

Edmonson, A. C., 336

Education: enabling independent followers, 32; Jesuit, at Georgetown University, 114–115, 124–125

Ehrlich, S. B., 310, 369n9

Elias, N., 248

Ellard, K., 224

Elms, A., 206

Employee, self-management programs for, 32

Employees: as barrier to culture of courageous followership, 133; 4-D Followership Model of, 144–148; increasing engagement and effectiveness of, 129–130; not considered in change initiatives, 142–143; self-perceptions of, as followers, 140–141

Enron, 30, 81, 190, 315, 335

Error reporting, 336–337

Ethics, of followership, 20–24

Exhilaration, 191, 192–194

Expectations: leader, 30, 34; team, 37

Experience, enabling independent followers, 32

F

FAA, airline insulation standards, 239–240

Fastow, A., 190

Fear: and courage, 80–81, 119; situational, 184, 192

Feedback, 18, 83, 160, 289

Feminist studies, and resistant selves, 317, 320–321

Fiedler, F. E., 46

Fiore, S. M., 35

Fiorina, C., 280

Fleming, P., 316

Follett, M. P., 17, 325

Follow, defined, 64

Follower role orientations, 25–39; antecedents and outcome of, 27; defined, 26; future research on, 37–39; independent, 31–34, 38; interactive, 27–31, 37–38; shifting, 34–37, 38, 51–52; value of, 25–26

Followers: as collaborators, 57, 58, 60, 63; constraints on leaders, 263–264, 273–274; defined, 54, 278; disempowered, 76–77; employees' perceptions of themselves as, 140–141; future research on, 62–63; as independent agents in organizations, 256–257; leaders' influence on, 264–266; negative connotation of term, 14, 72, 158–159; as outmoded concept, 63–64; ownership of vision by, 280, 290; paradoxes of, 161–163; participation of, in vision, 285–289, 290; psychological ownership among, 328–332, 337; redefining, 56–61; resistance by, 216, 315–318, 320–321; roles and responsibilities of, 13, 14–15, 72, 162–163; self-regulation by, 259–260; sensemaking by, 257–259; as serving common purpose with leaders, 71; situations requiring behavior of, 61–62; toxic, 220,

225–226. *See also* Courageous followers; Employees; Followers for creativity; Leader-follower relationship

Followers for creativity, 291–307; assumptions underlying research on, 292–293; courage needed by, 293, 306; dimensions of, 294–295; model of, 295; and previous work on followership, 293; recommendations on, 306; types of, 295–305

Followership: areas for research on, 9–15; contemporary focus on, 6, 310, 326–328; defined, 48–49, 54–55, 139; ethics of, 20–24; and follower identity, 310–311; 4-D model of, 144–148; implications of Milgram's obedience experiments for, 200–206; lack of attention given, 1–3, 5, 143–144, 160, 253, 291; leadership literature on, 255–256; need to teach skills of, 12–13, 220, 233; as outmoded concept, 54–56; post-structuralist approach to, 311–313, 369n9; relationship between leadership and, 93, 97–98, 138–139; researching leadership from vantage point of, 11–12; romanticizing, 320–321, 322; as shifting role, 34–37, 51–52, 174–176; and social identity theory, 272–274, 275–276, 310; terminology used for, 14, 54–56, 139; and vision, 279–280. *See also* Courageous followership

Followership styles: Chaleff's model of, 74–75; hypothetical exercises to explore, 77–78; model of, 7–9; preferred by leaders, 13, 170; self-assessment of, 75–77, 346n5

Foucault, M., 249, 312, 314, 316, 370n11

4-D Followership Model, 144–153; application of, 149–153; overview of, 144–148

Freud, S., 187, 196, 215

J

Jackall, R., 247–248
Janis, I. L., 80
Jaussi, K. S., 291
Jesus, 125
Jones, J., 29, 186
Jung, C., 141

K

Kellerman, B., 6, 12, 67
Kelley, R. E., 2, 5, 6, 28, 60, 67, 68, 69, 75,
   111, 143, 164, 293, 294
Kennedy, J. F., 192
King, M. L. Jr., 190–191
Kirkpatrick, S. A., 43, 279
Kleiner, K., 89
Knowledge economy, leadership in,
   211–212, 256
Kogod, S. K., 98, 108
Kondo, D. K., 320
Kouzes, J. S., 46
Kuhn, T., 189

L

LaFasto, F.M.J., 36
Larson, C. E., 36
Laurie, D. L., 318
Leader-follower paradigm, 42–44
Leader-follower relationship: collaborative, and courage, 171–172; as continuum, 219; as dichotomy, 55–56;
   and follower structures, 257–263; in
   leader-follower organization, 174–176;
   leadership literature on, 255–256;
   new model of, 71; as partnership in
   reciprocal following, 17–24;
   transparency in, 334–337; trust in,
   332–334, 337
Leaders: challenging, 72, 78–79, 166–167,
   170–171; contemporary need for,
   210–212; courage to support, 72, 73–75,
86, 165–166; creation of courageous
   followers by, 121; defined, 209–210,
   278; in disguise, star followers as, 8;
   failures of, and courageous followership, 81–82; followers' constraints on,
   263–264, 273–274; followership styles
   preferred by, 13, 170; influence on
   followers, 264–266; overemphasis on
   value of, 158–159; reasons for following, 215; servant, 86, 121, 123, 125; as
   serving common purpose with
   followers, 71; as teachers and learners,
   163; teaching skills for confronting,
   82–84. See also Toxic leaders
Leadership: as barrier to courageous
   followership culture, 132; charismatic,
   12, 183, 271, 310, 311; collaborative,
   57, 61, 63, 171–172, 215–217; contexts
   for, 42, 344n2; defined, 48, 56, 61, 139,
   311; follower substitutes for, 31–32;
   follower-based neutralizers of, 33;
   followers not considered in study of,
   1–2, 5; inalienable truths of, 159–161;
   and management, 45, 56, 156–158,
   346n2(ch.6); overemphasized in
   college admissions process, 89–93;
   relationship between followership and,
   93, 97–98, 138–139; researching,
   from followership vantage point,
   11–12; as shifting role, 34–37, 51–52,
   174–176; social identity theory of,
   269–272, 274–275, 370n12; stereotypi-
   cal, 155–156; terminology used for,
   14; transformational, 110, 256,
   265, 271, 326–327; and vision,
   277, 279
Leadership Alchemy program: changes
   resulting from, 106–108; employment
   after participation in, 107, 348n14;
   followership role of graduates of,
   101–104; leadership themes, 97; new
   future created by graduates of,

Oestreich, D., 80
O'Keefe, S., 97
Organizational culture: creating, of courageous followership, 128–136; designing initiative to change, 134–135; of NASA, 96–97; not ready for participative management, 122–124; transforming, with courageous followership, 110–112, 124–125
Organizational position paradigm, 45–47
Organizational vision. *See* Vision, organizational
Organizations: all-leader, 158–159; change initiatives of, and employees, 142–143; creative, 292; followers as independent agents in, 256–257; hierarchical, 45, 76, 122–124, 345n8; individual morality in, 197, 202–206; informal structures of, 260–263; leader and follower, 161; leader-follower, 173, 174–176; sacredness of, 249–251; social, and disruptive moral behavior, 239, 243–244, 356n6; sources of power of, 247–249; surveillance in, and employee identity, 318–320, 371n25
Orpheus Chamber Orchestra, 35
Ownership: psychological, among followers, 328–332, 337; of vision, 280, 290

P

Paradigms: defined, 41–42, 344n1; leader-follower, 42–44; leadership-followership organizational position, 45–47; leadership-followership state, 47–52
Park, S., 112, 113
Participation: bystander, 232; follower, in vision creation, 285–289, 290; student, 91–92; in transformations, 72, 167–169
Pearson, C. S., 43
Peer pressure, 12–13, 204, 230
Pfeiffer, P., 207–208
Physical bullying, 223–224

Pillai, R., 257
Play, 296–297, 368n8
Political gamesmen, 28–29
Posner, B. Z., 46
Post-structuralist approach: to followership, 311–313, 369n9; to identity, 312–313, 322–323, 370n11; and romanticizing followership, 320–321, 322; and workplace identities, 313–320
Potter, J., 288
Power: of follower role, 77; and social identification, 276; sources of, of organizations, 247–249; and whistleblowers, 251
The Power of Followership (Kelley), 6, 12, 111
Pragmatics, as followership style, 7–8, 13
Prototypes: defined, 268; and followership, 272–274; and leadership, 270–272, 274–275
Pryor, D., 245

R

Recruitment, and courageous followership culture, 130
Reichard, R. J., 325
Reicher, S. D., 274
Relational bullying, 224–225
Relational self-concept, 29–30
Resistance: by followers, 216, 320–321; identity characterized by, 315–318, 320; leadership's approach to, 216. *See also* Whistleblowers
Retention, and courageous followership culture, 129
Rethinking Followership Conference, 3
Reward systems, 30–31
Riggio, R., 6
Risk: and courage, 78–79; and courageous followership culture, 130–131
Rochat, F., 205
Rost, J. C., 35, 45, 47, 48, 53, 54, 139, 158, 173

Roth, W., 241
Rowley, C., 183
Ryan, K., 80

S

Salas, E., 35
Sarbanes-Oxley Act, 157
Sartre, J.-P., 243
Sashkin, M., 280
Self-concepts: collective, 36–37; further research on, 38–39; individualized, 33–34; relational, 29–30; working (WSC), 260, 262. *See also* Identity; Social identity theory
Self-regulation, by followers, 259–260
Senge, P. M., 171
Sennett, R., 237, 312
Sensemaking, by followers, 257–259
Servant-leaders, 86, 121, 123, 125
Service economy, leadership in, 211–212
Shamir, B., 28, 29, 310, 311, 314
Sheep, as followership style, 7, 28
Shifting follower role orientation, 34–37, 38, 51–52
Shils, E., 250
-*Ship* (suffix), defined, 47–48, 54
Skilling, J., 190
Skills: for bystanders to bullying, 234–235; courageous followership, 82–84; followership, 12–13, 220, 233
Social character: and collaborative leadership, 215–217; defined, 212; and reasons for following leaders, 215; and resistance to leadership, 216; shift from bureaucratic to interactive, 212–214
Social identity theory: and followership, 272–274, 275–276, 310; of leadership, 269–272, 274–275, 370n12; overview of, 268–269. *See also* Identity; Self-concepts
Social loafers, 36
Star followers, as followership style, 8, 13

Stech, E. L., 41
Stefanovich, A., 291
Students, classroom participation of, 91–92
Suicide bombers, 9–10
Supervisors, follower behaviors of, 174
Support: by courageous followers, 72, 73–75, 86, 165–166; by students, 93

T

Taylor, F., 156
Teaching: courageous followership skills, 82–84; followership skills, 12–13, 220, 233; as responsibility of leaders and followers, 163; skills as bystanders to bullying, 234–235
The Tenth Level (Bellak), 198
Terminology, for followership/leadership, 14, 54–56, 139
Thomas Aquinas, 19
Toxic followers, bystanders to bullying as, 220, 225–226
Toxic leaders, 181–194; costs of being close to, 190–191; courageous followership culture as antidote to, 131; defined, 182–183; follower responsibility to stand up to, 14–15; as followership issue, 12; human needs contributing to following, 183–185; illusions offered by, 185–189, 192, 193; reasons for following, 183
Training: enabling independent followers, 31–32; and hesitancy to change, 109–110; limited results of, 110; and Milgram's obedience experiments, 199
Transference, 215
Transformational leadership, 110, 256, 265, 271, 326–327
Transformations, participation in, 72, 167–169
Transparency, in leader-follower relationship, 334–337
Tripp, T. M., 348n6